ROUTLEDGE LIBRARY EDITIONS:
INTERNATIONAL TRADE POLICY

Volume 15

# A MODEL FOR THE STUDY OF INTERNATIONAL TRADE POLITICS

# A MODEL FOR THE STUDY OF INTERNATIONAL TRADE POLITICS

The United States Business Community and
Soviet–American Relations
1975–1976

WILLIAM F. KOLARIK, JR

Routledge
Taylor & Francis Group
LONDON AND NEW YORK

First published in 1987 by Garland Publishing, Inc.

This edition first published in 2018
by Routledge
2 Park Square, Milton Park, Abingdon, Oxon OX14 4RN

and by Routledge
711 Third Avenue, New York, NY 10017

*Routledge is an imprint of the Taylor & Francis Group, an informa business*

© 1987 William F. Kolarik

*British Library Cataloguing in Publication Data*
A catalogue record for this book is available from the British Library

ISBN: 978-1-138-06323-5 (Set)
ISBN: 978-1-315-14339-2 (Set) (ebk)
ISBN: 978-1-138-30618-9 (Volume 15) (hbk)
ISBN: 978-1-315-14169-5 (Volume 15) (ebk)

**Publisher's Note**
The publisher has gone to great lengths to ensure the quality of this reprint but points out that some imperfections in the original copies may be apparent.

**Disclaimer**
The publisher has made every effort to trace copyright holders and would welcome correspondence from those they have been unable to trace.

# A Model for the Study of International Trade Politics:

## The United States Business Community and Soviet–American Relations
### 1975–1976

WILLIAM F. KOLARIK, JR.

GARLAND PUBLISHING, INC.
NEW YORK & LONDON • 1987

For a complete list of the titles in this series,
see the final pages of this volume.

Library of Congress Cataloging-in-Publication Data

Kolarik, William F.
   A model for the study of international trade
politics.

   (Foreign economic policy of the United States)
   Originally presented as the author's thesis (Ph.D.)--
Kent State University, 1981.
   Bibliography: p.
   1. United States--Commerce--Soviet Union--
Mathematical models.  2. Soviet Union--Commerce--
United States--Mathematical models.  3. United States--
Foreign relations--Soviet Union.  4. Soviet Union--
Foreign relations--United States.  5. Businessmen--
United States--Attitudes.  I. Title  II. Series.
HF3105.K64  1987    382'.0947'0730724       87-23788

ISBN 0-8240-8086-6

All volumes in this series are printed on acid-free,
250-year-life paper.

Printed in the United States of America

## ACKNOWLEDGEMENTS

This research effort was made possible by a 1976 Summer Dissertation Fellowship granted by the International Studies Association and funded by the Ford Foundation. The author would also like to express his appreciation to all those individuals--in academia, government, and the business community--who contributed in one way or another to the completion of this project. In particular, I would like to thank Robert W. Clawson of Kent State University for stimulating my interest in Soviet-American politics and trade, for providing logistical support through KSU's International Programs Center, and for furnishing continuous intellectual guidance throughout my graduate study. Additionally, I am grateful to numerous other KSU faculty members for their direct and indirect contributions: to Boleslaw A. Boczek for his assistance in crystallizing the concept of the "Soviet Area Executive" and for constantly reinforcing scholarly discipline, to Richard W. Taylor for his invaluable support in securing university financial assistance throughout my graduate career, to John K. Ryans for his advice on questionnaire construction and survey interpretation, to Steven R. Brown for his guidance on factor analytic techniques and for his thorough

methodological critique, to Thomas Hensley for his
comprehensive criticism of the initial dissertation
proposal, and to Jerry Lewis for his assistance in my
research into the literature on "elites."

Thanks also go to James Savory of KSU Computer
Services for his invaluable aid in developing computer
programs for this project, to Leo Parent of George Mason
University for his advice on statistical methods, to Karen
Taylor and Robert Teal of the U.S. Department of Commerce
for their help in developing the bibliography and for
providing statistical data on U.S.-Soviet trade, to Jimmy
Moyer of the Department of Commerce and Allen Lenz of the
National Security Council Staff for their continuous moral
support and advice, and to the Commerce Department's Emily
Gooding for furnishing after-hours typing and logistical
support which was critical to the preparation of the
initial manuscript.  Of course, this study would not have
been possible without the participation of the hundreds of
senior U.S. business executives who took time out of their
busy schedules to complete survey questionnaires or
participate in personal interviews.

Last but certainly not least, I want to express my
deep gratitude to my wife, Denise, for her tremendous
patience and support throughout the six years during which
this manuscript was prepared; as well as for her vital role

as a sounding-board and intellectual catylyst. Her talent
for breaking conceptual logjams contributed in no small way
to the development of the International Trade Politics
Model.

TABLE OF CONTENTS

ILLUSTRATIONS

TABLES

CHAPTER I

COMMERCIAL ISSUES IN SUPERPOWER RELATIONS

## Political Dimensions of
## Soviet-American Trade
## 1972-1981

Together with efforts to control the arms race,
commercial issues have been a central feature of relations
between the United States and the Soviet Union since the
early 1970s.  Indeed, during the uneasy U.S.-U.S.S.R.
"detente" which spanned the 1972-1979 period, outstanding
bilateral trade questions more often than not were the
prime focus of attention of both Washington and Moscow.
Clear and formal recognition of the key importance of trade
and economic issues to overall political relations was
initially provided by both superpowers in the "Principles
of Relations Between the USA and the USSR" signed at the
Nixon-Brezhnev summit meeting in Moscow in May of 1972.[1]
Subsequently, the importance of trade issues was further
underlined in a series of commercial agreements between the
two governments concluded from 1972 to 1974.[2]

It has been widely recognized that, from a Soviet
perspective, a prime motive for embarking on a policy of

1

detente and for concluding numerous commercial, scientific
and technical agreements with Western countries has been
the desire to obtain for the Soviet economy a massive and
long-term infusion of Western technological knowhow and
capital equipment in the hope of reviving the badly stagnating Soviet economy. Alternatively, an immediate objective of U.S. foreign policy in 1971-1972 was to capitalize
on the Soviet preference for certain kinds of U.S. products
and technology by quietly linking prospects for Soviet-
American trade to progress on major international issues
such as Berlin, the Vietnam war and arms control.[3]

It also appears that the Nixon-Kissinger strategy of
the early 1970s incorporated a longer-term objective:  An
underlying premise of the 1972-1974 U.S.-Soviet commercial
agreements was that, in a relationship which has been
primarily competitive, the area of trade offered
significant possibilities for enlarging the sphere of
cooperation. Similarly, it was hypothesized that
cooperation on economic matters would eventually have a
"spill-over" or "ripple" effect which could moderate
competitive aspects of U.S.-Soviet relations. Expansion of
trade, it was argued, is a key for gradually building a web
of cooperative interrelationships which would provide both
the United States and the Soviet Union with a vested
interest in mutual restraint on divisive issues.[4]

Subsequently, however, it has been demonstrated that although trade may have a beneficial impact on U.S.-U.S.S.R. relations, the conduct of Soviet-American trade, like world trade in general, is extremely sensitive to political and economic influences emanating from both domestic and international arenas. Since early to mid-1974 political developments substantively unrelated to trade matters have been a major limiting factor on the conduct of Soviet-American commerce. The "spill-over" or "ripple" effect has operated in both directions, with the commercial arena providing a convenient battleground for U.S.-Soviet differences on a whole host of foreign policy problems and for fundamental U.S.-Soviet disagreements on issues of "human rights."

By way of background, following an initial wave of popular enthusiasm for detente in 1972, the U.S. political climate for Soviet-American commerce slowly but steadily deteriorated. U.S. public and government goodwill toward the U.S.S.R. progressively evaporated in response to a series of events which stimulated growing concerns about Soviet trustworthiness and intentions. The most important factors that exercised a negative influence on U.S. perceptions of the U.S.S.R. during 1972-1978 include the following: the Soviet Union's material support of Arab nations in their October 1973 war with Israel, similar

Soviet support of Vietnamese communists preceding the collapse of Saigon in 1975, indications of Soviet "adventurism" in Africa and elsewhere throughout the latter half of the 1970s, media reports of Soviet subversion in connection with the successes of various West European communist parties during 1975-1976, and continuing U.S. discomfiture over Soviet "human rights" violations, including restrictions on the ability of Soviet citizens to emigrate to foreign countries. Finally, there is no discounting the effects on U.S. opinion of highly publicized, vociferous attacks throughout the 1970s by Nobel laureate and Soviet exile Alexander Solzhenitsyn on U.S. policies toward his homeland.[5]

As a direct result of these and other developments, beginning in late 1974 the U.S. Government initiated a series of concrete measures which sought to force modifications in Soviet behavior on human rights and foreign policy issues through the application of U.S. economic "leverage." Whereas the declared aim of the 1971-1974 Nixon-Kissinger foreign policy was to encourage moderation in Soviet internal and foreign policies through private bargaining that quietly linked trade prospects to Soviet behavior, U.S. policy from 1975 onward increasingly gravitated toward overt, widely publicized attempts to pressure the Soviets using U.S. trade legislation and other economic sanctions. In terms of its impact on U.S.-Soviet relations, one of the most significant U.S. Government actions was the passage of the Jackson-Vanik Amendment to the Trade Reform Act of 1975. Intended primarily as a means to ease the way for Jews wishing to leave the U.S.S.R., the Jackson-Vanik Amendment made the granting of Most-Favored-Nation (MFN) tariff status to the U.S.S.R. and Soviet eligibility for U.S. Government export credit programs conditional upon the free emigration of Soviet citizens from the U.S.S.R. The implementation of the Trade Reform Act in late 1974 provoked a rapid and vehement reaction by the Soviet Government, which publicly repudiated the conditions of the Jackson-Vanik Amendment and refused to put into effect the 1973 U.S.-Soviet trade pact as well as several related economic and commercial agreements (including a settlement on the U.S.S.R.'s lend-lease debt from World War II).[6]

Apart from Jackson-Vanik, from 1974 onward the U.S. implemented a number of other economic measures intended primarily to influence Soviet behavior. Notable examples include the Stevenson and Church Amendments to the 1975 Export-Import Bank Authorization Bill, which further tightened restrictions on Soviet eligibility for official U.S. Government export credits. Subsequently, the initiative to use trade as a "lever" on the U.S.S.R. passed from Congress to the Executive branch, best exemplified by President Jimmy Carter's re-imposition in July 1978 of U.S. export controls on sales of oil industry equipment to the Soviet Union. (Controls on such "non-strategic" U.S. equipment and technologies had been lifted in 1971.) President Carter's action was motivated by the U.S.S.R.'s persecution of Soviet human rights activist Anatoly Sharansky, as well as other Soviet political dissidents.[7]

Finally, the general deterioration of U.S.-U.S.S.R. relations during the latter half of the 1970s culminated in the Soviet Union's massive invasion of Afghanistan in December 1979. Indeed, this event is often regarded as formally marking the demise of the Soviet-American detente initiated during the Nixon era. Once again, the principal U.S. response to the Soviets' actions predictably was economic in nature. In an effort to demonstrate the costs of aggressive international behavior to the U.S.S.R., the Carter Administration implemented new restrictions on exports of U.S. equipment and technology to the Soviets and, most importantly, sharply curtailed large-scale agricultural sales to the U.S.S.R. through a partial grain embargo.

Hence, in the aftermath of the Soviet invasion of Afghanistan and the resulting U.S. economic retaliation, the outlook for U.S.-Soviet commercial and political relations is currently more dismal than at any time since the years of the Cold War. Nonetheless, despite the likelihood of a new U.S.-Soviet arms race and the presence of a newly-elected and strongly anti-Soviet Reagan Administration in Washington, Soviet-American commercial issues remain at the center of controversy. As it seeks to develop a coherent foreign policy approach towards the U.S.S.R., the new Administration is having to grapple with most of the same vexing economic issues which complicated U.S.-Soviet relations during the 1970s. Once again, U.S. policy-makers must weigh whether trade can or should be used as either a "carrot" or "stick" to encourage modifications in Soviet domestic policies or international behavior. Likewise, apart from its role as an instrument of U.S. foreign policy, Soviet-American trade will once again be debated in terms of its intrinsic merits; i.e., what are the potential risks, costs, and benefits of U.S.-Soviet trade and which side stands to gain or lose the most? As in the past, deliberations on the preceding questions will not be confined to the halls of government. Rather, as the Administration searches for a comprehensive economic and political strategy vis-a-vis the Soviet Union, the efficacy of various policy alternatives and policy actions will be debated on a national level.

In sum, from the early 1970s to the present Soviet-American trade and economic issues have continuously exhibited high political content of compelling interest to the political scientist. Furthermore, commercial questions are likely to remain central to the future evolution of superpower relations. Thus, comprehensive research into the past political dynamics of U.S.-Soviet trade is not only warranted, but is imperative. Such historical inquiry can furnish a more complete theoretical understanding of U.S.-Soviet political processes, and also yield new substantive insights into controversial Soviet-American trade issues. In this way, then, on-going U.S. policy debates can be placed on a more sound informational foundation.

Therefore, it is the purpose of the present study to conduct an investigation along the historical lines suggested above, specifically focusing on U.S. business opinion about Soviet-American commercial and political issues during 1975-1976. Because U.S. companies have played a key role in U.S.-Soviet economic relations since 1972, the politically relevant views of senior U.S. businessmen constitute a necessary subject for thorough political analysis. Likewise, the years 1975 and 1976 constitute a critical period following the passage of the Jackson-Vanik Amendment, and a time for which hard empirical information on business opinion is available in the form of survey and interview data. The following sections provide further elaboration of the underlying rationale for this research effort.

## The Political Role of the U.S. Company

As noted, since 1972 U.S. companies have played a key role in U.S.-Soviet economic relations. For this reason, and because commercial issues have been a central element in U.S.-Soviet political relations since the early 1970s, the activities of these U.S. "trade actor" companies are a matter of necessary concern for the political scientist wishing to gain a more complete understanding of the recent evolution of superpower relationships. Since international trade policy is a vital component of overall foreign policy, those companies which have made serious efforts to explore business prospects with the U.S.S.R. demand scholarly attention as an important constituency relative to U.S. Government policies toward the Soviet Union. These companies also warrant study for a slightly different reason: concerns related to international trade (e.g., recession or prosperity, profit and loss) may induce corporate actions which are not intended to be political, but which nonetheless can have important international political ramifications. For example, if large numbers of U.S. firms evaluate their companies' business experiences

in the Soviet market negatively, it is logical to expect
that trade levels between the U.S. and U.S.S.R. would
suffer. Clearly then, from a post-behavioral standpoint
and strictly on policy grounds, a major political inquiry
into trade actor companies is imperative. Such a study can
not only have practical worth, but theoretical value as
well.

### The Role of the Soviet Area Executive

In using the terms "company," "corporation," or
"firm," it is all too easy to lose sight of the fact that
these entities are not monolithic personalities, but
complex organizations composed of people with individual
needs, objectives, and values. While the literature known
as "organization theory" is vast and often conflicting,
several prominent authors have consistently emphasized
aspects of organizational behavior which appear to be
relevant here. Specifically, Victor A. Thompson and
Herbert Simon, among others, have pointed to what they
perceive as the vital role of the expert specialist in
organizations.[8] According to their research, the
specialist often exercises decisive influence over
organizational policy affecting his area of competence by
virtue of superior access to information and deference of
colleagues to expertise. This state of affairs is seen as
especially characteristic of highly differentiated

structures where the division of labor within the organization is most pronounced. Chester I. Barnard and Wroe Alderson both agree that a prime function of senior executive talent in business organizations is to decide matters of high policy and general purpose.[9] Many writers, including Alderson, have also recognized what E. Wight Bakke termed the "fusion process": where the executive seeks to impose his personality (as expressed in attitudes, beliefs, and values) on the organization, while the organization, conversely, ". . . will attempt to impress its pattern upon the individual and make of him an agent of its organizational purposes." The former tendency Bakke termed the "personalizing process" while the latter he labeled the "socializing process."[10]

This classic literature of organization theory supports the results of contemporary academic, business, and government research which has investigated U.S. corporate strategy in Soviet-American trade. These studies strongly suggest that at any one time in a given company, prime responsibility for devising and/or executing Soviet business efforts is usually assumed by a high ranking company officer. Among this senior executive's overall duties, then, it is possible to discern a role as a country specialist--a role as his firm's "U.S.S.R. man" which allows him to wield major influence over the company's general policy toward business with the Soviet Union.[11] Consequently, when dealing with the U.S. Government, the U.S. news media, relevant interest groups, or Soviet officialdom, this senior executive generally acts as his company's principal spokesman on those U.S.-Soviet economic and political issues of concern to the firm. Because the U.S.S.R. is usually only one of the concerns with which this executive must cope, and since there is an absence of standardization of titles in American business, for convenience this company officer will be referred to as his firm's Soviet Area Executive (SAE).

If one accepts Bakke's thesis on the organizational fusion process, and if it is assumed--on the basis of available evidence--that in most cases a link exists between a person's views on the one hand, and subsequent individual behavior on the other, then the views of SAEs on Soviet-American issues are important for their probable impact on SAE actions and company behavior toward the U.S.S.R. as well as the U.S. Government.[12] Therefore, because they are a key element in an important chain of national-international linkages, careful research into the politically relevant opinions, attitudes and expectations of SAEs is imperative. In particular, as suggested earlier, historical inquiry into SAEs' perspectives can contribute to a more complete theoretical and substantive understanding of the dynamics of Soviet-American political processes. This, in turn, can help to place on-going U.S. policy debates concerning U.S.-U.S.S.R. economic and political issues on a more solid informational basis.

Hence, as a first step in the appropriate direction, this study is designed to present a comprehensive analysis of the views and perceptions held by Soviet Area Executives of U.S. "trade actor" companies in the critical years 1975-1976, the period immediately following Congressional passage of the Jackson-Vanik Amendment to the omnibus Trade Reform Act in December 1974. U.S.-U.S.S.R. relations have never recovered from that initiative. Indeed, it can be argued that the implementation of the Amendment marked the beginning of the end of Soviet-American detente. An analysis of SAEs' viewpoints during 1975-1976 will be greatly facilitated by the availability of hard empirical data for this time interval. Inclusive survey and interview information on the opinions of relevant executives was gathered during June 1975 and during July-September 1976. More will be said below concerning methodological questions; suffice it to say that the ensuing analysis will center on the presentation of the 1975-1976 survey and interview findings.

In accord with the objectives of this study, the following text will focus on key issues of overall

U.S.-Soviet relations which from 1972 to the present have consistently formed the environment for commercial relations between the superpowers. This environment has been characterized by continuous and intense controversy over a wide range of difficult questions. However, four primary issue-areas can be delineated and will provide the focus for the ensuing discussion of executive viewpoints during the 1975-1976 period:

1. Moral questions of U.S.-U.S.S.R. economic relations (linkage of the U.S. Government's Soviet trade policies to Soviet performance in the area of human rights and Jewish emigration).

2. Foreign policy questions posed by U.S.-Soviet trade (linkage of the U.S. Government's Soviet trade policies to Soviet foreign policy behavior around the world).

3. National security questions posed by U.S.-Soviet trade (issues of technology transfer, questions of Soviet energy development and resource interdependence, and implications of trade for Soviet military capabilities).

4. Economic questions (the material costs and benefits) of U.S.-Soviet commercial relations and their political implications.

While the originality of this project is perhaps readily apparent, it requires further emphasis. A review of political science literature demonstrates that the discipline has virtually ignored the part that corporate actors have played in superpower interrelationships over the past ten years. While this subject has been examined by a number of authors, for the most part these writers have not been political scientists, but rather historians, economists, or businessmen. Almost without exception their work has been of a purely descriptive nature and has given only secondary attention to the political dimension of corporate interaction with the U.S.S.R.[13] The present study is therefore distinguished by its attention to a neglected but vitally important area of political research, its theoretical as well as substantive emphasis, and its heavy reliance on the research tools of the social scientist. Fundamentally, then, this research effort not only has post-behavioral justification in terms of its social utility, but is also consistent with the goal of all political scientists to help build cumulative scientific knowledge of political phenomena.

FOOTNOTES

[1]"Basic Principles of Relations between the United States and the Union of Soviet Socialist Republics," signed in Moscow, May 29, 1972. Reprinted in U.S.-Soviet Commercial Relations: The Interplay of Economics, Technology Transfer, and Diplomacy, by John P. Hardt and George D. Holliday, 93d Cong., 1st sess., 1973, pp. 81-83.

[2]Agreements signed from 1972-1975 include a comprehensive trade agreement, several agricultural agreements (including a long-term grain purchase agreement), a maritime agreement, a tax convention, a fishing agreement, and a communique establishing a Joint U.S.-U.S.S.R. Commercial Commission. For the texts of these agreements, see the following sources: U.S. Congress, House, Committee on Foreign Affairs, U.S.-Soviet Commercial Relations: The Interplay of Economics, Technology Transfer, and Diplomacy, by John P. Hardt and George D. Holliday, 93d Cong., 1st sess., 1973, pp. 84-96; U.S. Department of Commerce, Bureau of East-West Trade, U.S.S.R. Affairs Division, U.S.-Soviet Commercial Agreements 1972, Washington, D.C. 1978.

[3]This objective is perhaps best evidenced in the following statement by former Secretary of State Henry Kissinger before the Senate Finance Committee in 1974: "The argument was made to the Soviet Union that we could not expand trade until their foreign policy actions were consistent with a more normal economic relationship; and we put forward a number of issues that had to be settled . . ." See U.S. Congress, Senate, Committee on Finance, The Trade Reform Act of 1973. Hearings before the Committee on Finance on H.R. 10710, 93d Cong., 2d sess., 1974, p. 468. Also see the statements by Arthur A. Hartman, Assistant Secretary of State for European Affairs in U.S. Congress, Senate, Committee on Foreign Affairs, Detente: Hearings before the Subcommittee on Europe, 93d Cong., 2d sess., 1974, pp. 45-65.

[4]For a more detailed look at this approach to Soviet-American relations see Marshall D. Shulman, "On Learning to Live with Authoritarian Regimes," Foreign Affairs 55 (January 1977): 326-338; Marshall D. Shulman, "Toward a Western Philosophy of Coexistence," Foreign Affairs 51 (October 1973): 221-236; Daniel H. Yergin, "Politics and Soviet-American Trade: The Three Questions," Foreign Affairs 55 (April 1977): 517-538; Daniel H. Yergin, "Strategies of Linkage in Soviet-American

Relations," paper presented at the Annual Meeting of the
American Political Science Association, Chicago, September
1976. (Mimeographed.); Philip S. Gillette, "The
Interaction of Trade and Political Detente in Soviet-
American Relations," paper presented at the Central Slavic
Conference, St. Louis, November 1974. (Mimeographed.);
U.S. Department of State, Department of State Bulletin 71
(October 14, 1974), "Detente with the Soviet Union: The
Reality of Competition and the Imperative of Cooperation,"
statement by Secretary Kissinger, pp. 505-519. Also see
the statements by Helmut Sonnenfeldt, senior adviser on
Soviet affairs to former Secretary of State Kissinger in
U.S. Department of Commerce, Bureau of East-West Trade,
Office of East-West Policy and Planning, Advisory Committee
on East-West Trade, "Summary Minutes and Transcript of
Proceedings, June 6, 1978," pp. 35-46. Also see Helmut
Sonnenfeldt, "Russia, America, and Detente," Foreign
Affairs 56 (January 1978): 275-294.

[5]For an overview of the gradual undermining of the
detente process during the 1970s, see the following: Karl
E. Birnbaum, "Human Rights and East-West Relations,"
Foreign Affairs 55 (July 1977): 783-799; Seyom Brown, "A
Cooling-Off Period for U.S.-Soviet Relations," Foreign
Policy, Fall 1977, pp. 3-21; John C. Campbell,
"Soviet-American Relations: Detente and Dispute," Current
History 69 (October 1975): 113-116, 146-147; Adam B. Ulam,
"Detente Under Soviet Eyes," Foreign Policy, Fall 1976, pp.
145-159; Marshall D. Shulman, "Toward a Western Philosophy
of Coexistence," Foreign Affairs 51 (October 1973):
221-236; Daniel H. Yergin, "Politics and Soviet-American
Trade: The Three Questions," Foreign Affairs 55 (April
1977): 517-538; U.S. Department of Commerce, Bureau of
East-West Trade, Office of East-West Policy and Planning,
"Major East-West Trade Issues," Washington, D.C. 1978.
(Mimeographed.)

[6]For an exhaustive treatment of the politics of the
Jackson-Vanik Amendment see Paula Stern, Water's Edge:
Domestic Politics and the Making of American Foreign Policy
(Westport, Conn.: Greenwood Press, 1979).

[7]For discussion of economic "leverage" and "linkage"
in Soviet-American relations see the testimony contained in
U.S. Congress, Senate, Committee on Foreign Relations,
Detente: Hearings before the Subcommittee on Europe, 93d
Cong., 2d sess., 1974; U.S. Congress, Senate, Committee on
Finance, The Trade Act of 1973. Hearings before the
Committee on Finance on H.R. 10710, 93d Cong., 2d sess.,
1974; Daniel H. Yergin, "Strategies of Linkage in

Soviet-American Relations," paper presented at the Annual Meeting of the American Political Science Association, Chicago, September 1976. (Mimeographed.) Also see the interesting exchange of views on "Human Rights Considerations and the Future of East-West Trade" between Helmut Sonnenfeldt, former senior advisor to the Secretary of State on Soviet Affairs, and Jerry Goodman, Executive Director of the National Conference on Soviet Jewry, in U.S. Department of Commerce, Bureau of East-West Trade, Office of East-West Policy and Planning, Advisory Committee on East-West Trade, "Summary Minutes and Transcript of Proceedings, June 6, 1978," pp. 18-63.

[8]Victor A. Thompson, Modern Organization (New York: Knopf, 1961), pp. 25-57; Herbert A. Simon, Administrative Behavior, 2nd ed. (New York: Macmillan, 1957), pp. 8-11, 134-135.

[9]Chester I. Barnard, The Functions of the Executive (Cambridge, Mass.: Harvard University Press, 1962), pp. 231-234; and Wroe Alderson, Marketing Behavior and Executive Action: A Functionalist Approach to Marketing Theory (Homewood, Ill.: Richard D. Irwin, 1957), pp. 364-384.

[10]E. Wight Bakke, The Fusion Process (New Haven: Yale University, Labor and Management Center, 1953), p. 17. Also see Alderson, Marketing Behavior and Executive Action, p. 366.

[11]For example, a 1977 study by Business International Corp. concluded that: "Although (the company's) top authority is always the chief executive and board of directors, in many instances for all practical purposes decisions are taken by one director or senior vice president to whom the East European unit reports. Other board members are involved where problems cross divisional boundaries, where approval is needed for nontraditional types of business . . . , for large investments and high level PR work, protocol agreements, major buy-back deals and policy changes." See Business International S.A., Corporate Strategy, Planning, Organization and Personnel Practices for Eastern Europe (Geneva: Business International, 1977), p. 27. In support of Business International's findings, James H. Giffen has noted that: "While decentralized line and staff functions might be advantageous in operating in some markets, it is not recommended for planned economies. . . . Planning and operations should . . . either rest with a single individual or group which has the authority to cut across

corporate lines in order to plan and consummate those
transactions which are in the overall best interests of the
company." James H. Giffen, "Developing a Market Program
for the U.S.S.R.," Columbia Journal of World Business 8
(December 1973): 63-64. Also see the following: James R.
Basche, Jr., Evolving Corporate Policy and Organization for
East-West Trade (New York: Conference Board, 1974); Thomas
A. Wolf, "Industry Problems in East-West Trade," Columbus:
Ohio State University, Department of Economics, 1975, p.
31. (Mimeographed.); John W. DePauw, "Soviet-American
Trade: A Case Study of U.S.-Soviet Commercial
Negotiations," paper presented at the Annual Meeting of the
Southern Conference on Slavic Studies, Birmingham, Ala.,
October 1977. (Mimeographed.)

[12]Although there is certainly no deterministic
relationship between an individual's attitudes and beliefs
on the one hand, and behavior on the other, there is
impressive evidence that under appropriate circumstances
attitudes can condition and predispose a person toward
particular courses of action. Specifically, numerous
studies strongly suggest that the relationship between
attitudes and action is greatly dependent upon
"situational" variables such as reference groups,
organizational roles, norms and similar factors. In this
regard, it would appear that attitude-behavior consistency
is greatly encouraged when attitudes have direct relevance
to an individual's organizational role, where the
individual has wide freedom of action, and when numerous
behavior options exist. Hence, the situational context of
Soviet Area Executives would appear to be particularly
conducive to attitude-behavior consistency on U.S.-U.S.S.R.
issues relevant to the firm. For discussions of the
general conditions under which attitude-behavior
consistency is most likely, see the following: Alan G.
Weinstein, "Predicting Behavior from Attitudes," Public
Opinion Quarterly 36 (Fall 1972): 355-360; Allen E. Liska,
"Emergent Issues in the Attitude-Behavior Consistency
Controversy," American Sociological Review 39 (April
1974): 261-272; Steven J. Gross and C. Michael Niman,
"Attitude-Behavior Consistency: A Review," Public Opinion
Quarterly 39 (Fall 1975): 358-368; Alan C. Acock and
Melvin L. DeFleur, "A Configurational Approach to
Contingent Consistency in the Attitude-Behavior
Relationship," American Sociological Review 37 (December
1972): 714-726; Irving Crespi, "What Kinds of Attitude
Measures Are Predictive of Behavior?" Public Opinion
Quarterly 35 (Fall 1971): 327-354; Lyle G. Warner and
Melvin L. DeFleur, "Attitude as an Interactional Concept:
Social Constraint and Social Distance as Intervening

Variables between Attitudes and Action," <u>American Sociological Review</u> 34 (April 1969): 153-169; Howard Schuman, "Attitudes vs. Actions <u>Versus</u> Attitudes vs. Attitudes," <u>Public Opinion Quarterly</u> 36 (Fall 1972): 347-354; Robert Brannon et al., "Attitude and Action: A Field Experiment Joined to a General Population Survey," <u>American Sociological Review</u> 38 (October 1973): 625-636.

[13]For example, see Franklyn D. Holzman and Robert Legvold, "The Economics and Politics of East-West Relations," in <u>World Politics and International Economics</u>, ed. C. Fred Bergsten and Laurence B. Krause (Washington, D.C.: Brookings Institution, 1975); Zygmunt Nagorski, Jr., <u>The Psychology of East-West Trade: Illusions and Opportunities</u> (New York: Mason and Lipscomb, 1974); James H. Giffen, <u>The Legal and Practical Aspects of Trade with the Soviet Union</u> (New York: Praeger, 1971); Marshall I. Goldman, <u>Detente and Dollars</u> (New York: Basic Books, 1975); and Samuel Pisar, <u>Coexistence and Commerce: Guidelines for Transactions between East and West</u> (New York: McGraw-Hill, 1970).

# CHAPTER II

## ALTERNATIVE PARADIGMS

In order to meet theoretical objectives and to avoid a self-contained, discrete approach to the problem at hand, one must pose the question of whether there is any single paradigm into which the proposed research can be integrated. If there is a suitable paradigm, it must be determined how the selected approach will contribute in a meaningful way to the building of cumulative theoretical knowledge of political phenomena.

Unfortunately, a thorough survey of the literature of political science suggests only limited applicability of existing, ready-made paradigms to the subject at hand. Throughout the literature of political science, the importance of politically relevant attitudes, beliefs and perceptions of nongovernmental personalities who are prominent in political processes is implicitly and explicitly recognized. However, this recognition apparently has not been accompanied by the development of a systematic and flexible framework for the study of these political phenomena. This is reflective, perhaps, of the fact that most major empirical studies of politically

21

relevant attitudes and beliefs have either been ambitious
efforts to assess the political culture of entire nations,
or similarly broad-based attempts to measure public opinion
on a variety of issues.[1] Little empirical research on
the politically relevant views of businessmen has been
conducted and, as discussed below, available studies
generally do not display a strong paradigmatic foundation.

## The "Interest Group" Approach

A major problem in locating a workable paradigm for
the present study is that many frameworks which are
appealing at first glance treat politically relevant
attitudes, beliefs, and perceptions as secondary to other
components of the approach which are deemed more
important. Such is the case with the "interest group"
concept, which has been the most frequently used approach
in political studies of U.S. business. In the interest
group approach, orientations of key individual group
members are recognized as being significant, but they are
also regarded as ancillary to other considerations.
Studies of interest groups, rather than focussing on the
orientations of key individual group members, have for the
most part strived to identify group "interests" and
"influence" and to establish clear-cut causal relationships
between these concepts and the political decisions of
governments. As noted by Russett and Hanson, these efforts

have encountered difficult methodological problems which
have often led to inconclusive results. This is certainly
true of most studies of American business which have
explicitly or implicitly relied upon the interest group
approach. As Salamon and Siegfried have observed:
"Depending on which examples one chooses, . . . it is
possible to conclude that American corporations are either
politically impotent or politically omnipotent."[2]

There is a further difficulty in applying the interest
group framework to the subject at hand. The focus of the
present study is not a business interest "group" in the
classical sense of a chamber of commerce or manufacturer's
association, but rather a collection of individual
executives whose attitudes and actions can affect interest
group stances on the domestic political scene. Although
many Soviet Area Executives of U.S. companies are members
of organizations which from time to time have been active
in U.S.-Soviet economic and political affairs, these
organizations in themselves are not the principal object of
study. Consequently, the usefulness of the literature on
U.S. business interest groups to the present study appears
limited, although these studies do demonstrate scholarly
recognition of the importance of activities of U.S.
business in domestic policy processes.

## The "Elite" Approach

Writings concerned with political "elites," to the extent that they center around the idea of a ruling elite or power elite, appear inappropriate to the present topic. The "elite" approach would seem to require one to make the highly controversial assumption that the U.S. business community comprises a ruling elite or power elite as conceptualized by Domhoff, Marx, and others.[3] In addition, the approach makes no direct conceptual provision for an investigation of attitudes and opinions. Lastly, because of its preoccupation with power and power relationships, the approach suffers from serious methodological problems. Noting these problems, Russett and Hanson conclude that:

> Probably no aspect of political science has been analyzed so thoroughly as has the problem of power, with such indeterminate empirical results. Efforts to establish convincingly the existence and scope of a power elite, for example, have generally failed to be convincing by the standard criteria of empirical social science.[4]

Nonetheless, as suggested in Chapter I and in following discussions, the present study does in a limited sense recognize Soviet Area Executives of U.S. corporations as an "elite." This is because these individuals play a prominent role in their companies' decision-making processes and are their firms' spokesmen on Soviet-American economic and political issues. Such an interpretation of

the term "elite", however, makes no sweeping assumptions
and is much more limited than the theses of Mills,
Domhoff, and others.

### The "Multinational Corporation" Approach

Numerous political studies of multinational corporations (MNCs) have appeared in recent years. However, this
voluminous literature would appear to be of little help in
dealing with the present topic. Most studies in this area
tend to focus on relationships between MNCs and developing
nations with specific attention to the political, social,
and cultural impact of company behavior on host countries.
In addition, the MNC is usually conceptualized by most
analysts as an "actor" in the international political arena
having a considerable degree of autonomy from any given
governmental authority. Although it is significant that
studies of MNCs generally recognize the important role
which private companies play in international politics, it
would be problematic to adopt without qualification the
corporation-as-actor approach to the present study of
business attitudes and opinions. This is because
individual executives, and not corporations per se, are the
focus of the analysis. Furthermore, the current topic is
less concerned with the autonomous operations of large
"stateless" companies in developing areas than with the
activities of United States companies of all sizes within

the U.S. political system and in U.S.-Soviet bilateral relations. As noted earlier, the discipline of political science has largely ignored the role of corporate actors in superpower relations and in relations between other industrial countries.[5]

## The "Decision-Making" Approach
### Political Decision Models

The literature on political decision-making would seem to suggest another possible framework for the present study.[6] After all, although high-level business executives have considerable organizational influence and responsibility, they are still part of a larger decisional unit--the company--and act on behalf of the company. As discussed earlier (p. 9), it is the importance of U.S. companies to Soviet-American relations which provides the justification for a study of Soviet Area Executives. However, while political decision-making approaches do have a certain relevance to the broader conceptualization of the present study, the most frequently used political decision models leave something to be desired as central frameworks for the analysis of executive viewpoints.

A major difficulty posed by political decision approaches is that for the most part they have been designed specifically for the analysis of governmental foreign policy processes. This macro-analytic perspective

is not readily adaptable to a corporate context. Apart
from this problem, however, there are additional
difficulties. Like the interest group approach, the
decision-making paradigm makes conceptual allowances for
the attitudes and perceptions of key personalities. But
despite the fact that most decision-making studies
recognize perceptions as important decisional "input and
conversion variables," the prime focus of the approach is
the "decision situation" (a specific problem) and the act
of choosing among policy alternatives (i.e., the decision)
that may bring about a solution.[7] In contrast, the topic
at hand does not center on a specific company decision or
decision situation per se. Instead the object of study is
the attitudinal orientations of key executives as these
viewpoints may contribute to corporate behavior that can
affect national-international linkage patterns involving a
wide range of political and economic issues.

Corporate Decision Models

While not part of the literature of political science,
models of corporate decision-making developed by
specialists in business administration would appear to be
more applicable to the current topic than political
decision models tailored specifically to the analysis of
the foreign policy behavior of governments. However,
although they have a micro-analytic perspective, corporate

decision-making models share with political decision models the methodological limitations noted above.

Nonetheless, studies of corporate decision-making and related writings on the "strategic planning" of corporate policy are important in that they corroborate the findings of organization theorists such as Alderson, Barnard, and Thompson that senior executives in business enterprises generally play a pivotal role in company policy decisions that affect their areas of expertise and speciali-zation.[8] Recent studies of corporate planning and decision-making go even somewhat farther than the classic organization theorists in that they place greater emphasis on the role that executive attitudes and beliefs play as important conditioning factors that impinge on executive behavior and ultimately on company decisions. Not only is the connection between executive attitudes and the formulation of company policies made explicit, but analysts such as Aguilar, Keegan, Collings, Klein, and Stevenson document and underline the importance of executive perceptions of the "business environment" as a major formative influence on attitudes. By "scanning" the business environment, an executive picks up informational signals that are incorporated into views on company matters and issues. Environmental stimuli may have either political or economic dimensions and may originate in either the domestic business environment, the international business environment, or even within the company itself.[9]

Unfortunately, even more so than political decision models, corporate decision-making models appear to be case-specific, at least as far as political phenomena are concerned. This is because the corporate decision process is rarely depicted as giving careful consideration to political implications of company decisions solely as they affect the company's political environment. Possible political consequences of alternative decisions are generally weighed only to the degree that they may have a feedback effect on the firm. Similarly, political factors in the environment are usually considered important only to the extent that they may affect company fortunes. Thus, because corporate decision-making approaches fail to give sufficient attention to the broader political dimensions of the corporate environment, it would appear especially difficult to employ such a framework successfully in an effort to make a theoretical contribution to the discipline of political science.[10]

## The Russett-Hanson Approach

Perhaps the best testimony to the discipline's failure to develop an appropriate framework for the topic at hand can be found in Russett and Hanson's landmark 1975 study of the foreign policy beliefs of American businessmen and military officers.[11]  Based on survey research,

interviews, content analysis, and events analysis, the work

of Russett and Hanson represents the most comprehensive

investigation of the politically relevant views of U.S.

businessmen since the wide-ranging study conducted by

Bauer, Dexter and Pool in 1963.[12]  Nonetheless, although

they make an important contribution to this area of

political research, Russett and Hanson are frustrated in

their efforts to adapt the most often used paradigms of

political science to a phenomenon which they feel is

extremely important on theoretical as well as policy

grounds.  Nevertheless, Russett and Hanson succeed in

developing a series of arguments demonstrating the

importance of business executives to U.S. policy processes

and the theoretical potential of research into the

perceptions of "politically influential figures about the

structure and behavior of world politics."[13]  In making

their case for an investigation of the foreign policy

beliefs of American businessmen, Russett and Hanson

corroborate and lend further support to the justification

for the present analysis:

> We think it is important to look carefully at
> whatever evidence is available about elites'
> preferences and perceptions about international
> politics. . . . We mean first those people who
> participate at high levels in the political
> process, such as party politicians and officials,
> senior civil servants, leaders in the mass media,
> and leaders of interest groups involved in

political activities. Along with them <u>we include</u>
<u>high-level executives of major corporations</u> and
labor unions, and more generally the kind of
professional and upper-status people who we know
are especially likely to vote, to take an interest
in international affairs, to make campaign
contributions, and to lobby. We thus are
identifying the sorts of people especially
relevant to political decision making, . . .
(Italics mine).

. . . . . . . . . . . . . . . . . . . . . . . . . .
   Although they do not hold official positions
in the policymaking arena, such people have an
importance, actual or potential, in forming the
climate of opinion within which policy-
makers must operate. It is well known that
political interest and activity are closely
correlated--though certainly in no one-to-one
correspondence--with high socioeconomic status.
Such people are, on the average, more likely to be
informed about politics (especially international
politics), and to take part in political
activities. In doing so, they help to define the
limits of action available to policy-makers. . . .
. . . . . . . . . . . . . . . . . . . . . . . . . .
   . . . the perceptions of most persons
concerned with world politics have changed at a
faster rate, and at more-nearly discontinuous
jumps, than has the behavior of governments. With
those changes in perceptions have come equally
significant changes in preferences.
. . . . . . . . . . . . . . . . . . . . . . . . . .
   . . . on purely theoretical grounds it is hard
to find another country where we would expect the
perceptions and policy preferences of its
public--at least that portion attentive to and
informed about foreign policy--to matter more.
Moreover, insofar as power relationships and
nations' behavior have changed importantly in
recent years, it seems reasonable to expect
intranational influences to matter more in such
periods than during times of long-term continuity
in nations' foreign policies. . . .
. . . . . . . . . . . . . . . . . . . . . . . . . .
   Moreover, businessmen of high status who are
interested in politics inevitably form the
reservoir from which new policy makers will be
recruited. . . . For all these reasons the study
of elite perspectives becomes important, and in

looking closely at those of businessmen we need
not assume that top business executives are
especially important--only that they form a part
of the wider elite that cannot help but matter in
politics.[14]

At this point, it must be stressed that Russett and

Hanson, in accepting as useful the concept of "elite

perspectives," at the same time reject the usual

assumptions made in most major analyses of elites:

> Use of the word "elite" in this context does
> not imply acceptance of any "power elite" theories
> or of any ideas about interlocking interests or
> even conspiracies that direct the government. We
> simply use the word to mean "leaders" or prominent
> individuals.[15]

Through the above rationale, Russett and Hanson lay

some of the necessary groundwork for their study of

American businessmen--as well as for possible future

studies of "elite perspectives." But the question remains

as to what theoretical content such an approach can have.

A partial answer to this critical question is evident from

the fact that Russett and Hanson do not try to relate

businessmen's viewpoints to causal factors such as

sociological (age, education, etc.) or social-

psychological (i.e., personality) variables. Since the

authors do not try to trace the origins of businessmen's

foreign policy beliefs, their theoretical objectives must

lie in another direction. In this regard, a careful

reading of Russett and Hanson suggests a dual theoretical

goal. First, a primary goal expressed by the authors is to

conduct an extensive examination of several major economic
and ideological "theories" of foreign policy choice (e.g.,
Marxism, Imperialism, Anticommunism) via the measurement of
attitudes and beliefs as a hypothesis testing procedure:

> We do not for a moment imagine that beliefs,
> preferences and attitudes about politics are to be
> equated with political acts, attempts to
> influence, or the successful exercise of political
> power. . . .
> Instead, we have moved to a logically prior
> step of inquiry. By asking about the beliefs,
> preferences and attitudes of corporate executives
> we are trying to discover whether those attitudes
> are consistent with what various theorists about
> economic or other motivations would have us
> expect. A question we ask prior to that about
> their behavior is simply, are their attitudes what
> would be predicted? . . .
> . . . it is an inquiry that could in principle
> serve almost as a "critical experiment" to
> determine the direction of future investigation
> into questions about economic influence. If
> attitudes are such as would be predicted by
> economic influence theories, then there is good
> reason to redouble efforts to trace the exercise
> of power and influence. If, on the contrary, the
> attitudes do not bear much resemblance to those
> predicted, then it may be time to move on to
> other, more promising kinds of inquiries.[16]

The arguments of Russett and Hanson, it would appear,
pose a strong case for the validity of their approach as a
theoretical objective that can contribute to the building
of cumulative political knowledge. However, in addition to
the testing of existing theories and hypotheses, a second
theoretical consideration seems implicit in the authors'
logic. That goal is the attainment of at least a minimal
predictive capability vis-a-vis "elite" viewpoints on key

foreign policy issues and the implications of these
viewpoints as they help define the limits of action
available to U.S. Government policy-makers.  Because the
ability to predict political phenomena presupposes its
explanation and since explanation is the goal of theory, to
the extent that the Russett-Hanson approach can improve the
forecasting of events it is a valid theoretical basis for
an empirical political study.  As noted by Russett and
Hanson:

> Whatever the facts, prescriptions for avoiding
> a repetition of past tragedies will depend
> centrally on the diagnosis of why past ones
> occurred. We cannot comprehend the future until we
> understand how people view their past and present.
> (Italics mine).[17]

Efforts to predict, which are clearly evident in Chapter 8
of the Russett-Hanson study, can be characterized as
hypothesis generation--which is generally accepted as a
legitimate theoretical objective of political science.[18]

What implications does the Russett-Hanson study have
for the subject at hand?  The Russett and Hanson study
appears to rest on a sound theoretical foundation despite
its repudiation of the more familiar frameworks for
political analysis.  Their approach also furnishes an
attractive rationale for investigating the attitudes and
beliefs of American businessmen and therefore appears to
have considerable relevance to the present topic.
Nonetheless, it can be argued that as a framework for the

present study the Russett-Hanson approach is deficient in
several respects. Specifically, the present study requires
a more flexible and better detailed conceptual framework
which allows for possible linkages between executive
attitudes, executive actions, and company behavior; as well
as between company behavior on one hand, and U.S. as well
as Soviet governmental activity on the other. Russett and
Hanson describe only in the most general terms the link
between executive viewpoints and possible corporate action
aimed at the U.S. Government, and do not address directly
the possibility of cross-national corporate behavior that
could affect foreign governments. Since the principal
focus of the Russett-Hanson research (i.e., the
relationship between economic interests and political
ideology) is considerably different from that of the
present study, it is completely understandable that their
approach gives only marginal attention to the executive's
corporate environment and the series of national-
international linkages which has been alluded to throughout
this study. Both the Russett-Hanson study and the present
analysis investigate businessmen's viewpoints because of
their implications from a policy standpoint. However, each
study differs substantially from the other in its
perspective on the subject.

## The "Linkage Politics" Approach

What remaining approaches appear applicable to a study
of U.S. business attitudes and perceptions? As stated in
Chapter I, Soviet Area Executives of U.S. corporations are
a significant component of a chain of national-international
linkages which can affect U.S.-Soviet relations. Thus,
upon first examination Rosenau's "linkage politics" framework would appear to be highly appropriate to the topic.[19]
As Rosenau has contended: "Inquiries into the politics of
foreign trade . . . are . . . rich with findings and
insights bearing on linkage phenomena." However, Rosenau
also argues that ". . . national-international linkages
have never been subjected to systematic, sustained and
comparative inquiry."[20] Traditional subdivisions of
political science, Rosenau alleges, have failed to generate
research paradigms relevant to the political realities of a
shrinking and increasingly interdependent world. He claims
that interchanges between individual polities and the
international environment have not been given sufficient
attention by specialists in comparative and international
politics. Compartmentalization of the discipline into
these sub-fields, Rosenau argues, has hindered the
development of "linkage theory":

> Students of comparative politics tend to take
> the international environment for granted, as if
> national systems were immune to external
> influences and had full control over their own

destinies. Similarly, students of international
politics tend to make a series of simplifying
assumptions about the international behavior of
national systems, as if all such systems reacted
in the same way to the same stimuli.

To be sure, it has long been recognized that
national political systems, like all organized
human groups, exist in, are conditioned by, and
respond to a larger environment. Nor is it denied
that international political systems, like all
interdependent groups, are shaped by and are
responsive to developments that occur within the
units of which they are comprised. (Italics
mine).[21]

However, as Rosenau points out: "To acknowledge the

interdependence of national and international systems is

not necessarily to make conceptual allowance for it."[22]

Consequently, in an attempt to fulfill a perceived need,

Rosenau articulates a tentative framework for the analysis

of linkage politics.

### Linkage Politics Defined

Precisely what is a national-international "linkage"?

Rosenau defines the concept as any recurrent sequence of

behavior that originates in one system and is reacted to in

another. Dissecting the concept, he distinguishes between

outputs (the initial stage of a linkage) and inputs (the

terminal stage of a linkage). Outputs and inputs, in turn,

are then classified according to whether they occur in a

polity or in the international system:

Polity Outputs: Those sequences of behavior that
originate within a polity and that either culminate in
or are sustained by their environment.

Environmental Outputs: Those sequences of behavior
that start in the external environment of a polity and
that are either sustained or terminated within the
polity.

Polity Inputs: Those behavioral sequences within a
polity to which environmental outputs give rise.

Environmental Inputs: Those behavioral sequences in
the external environment to which the polity outputs
give rise.[23]

Next, Rosenau distinguishes between inputs and outputs
according to their purposefulness. Direct polity outputs
and direct environmental outputs are intended to generate a
response in other systems. In contrast, indirect polity
and indirect environmental outputs are defined as patterns
of behavior which are not intentionally designed to produce
boundary-crossing responses but do so anyway by means of
certain linkage processes. Environmental and polity inputs
are likewise categorized as either direct or indirect,
yielding a total of eight types of possible inputs and
outputs.[24] Elaborating further on his framework, Rosenau
notes that connections between the various kinds of inputs
and outputs are made possible by a series of linkage
processes, of which there are three basic types:

Penetrative Processes: Occur when members of one
polity serve as participants in the political
processes of another; i.e., they share with those in
the penetrated polity the authority to allocate its
values (a military occupation, foreign aid missions,
etc.).

Reactive Processes: Are brought into being by
recurrent and similar boundary-crossing reactions
rather than by the sharing of authority. Actors who

initiate the output do not participate in the
allocative activities of those who experience the
input, but the behavior of the latter is nevertheless
a response to behavior undertaken by the former (e.g.,
the effects of the Arab-Israeli conflict on national
elections in the U.S.).

Emulative Processes:  A special form of the reactive
linkage process which is established when the input is
not only a response to the output but takes
essentially the same form as the output.  It
corresponds to the so-called "diffusion" or
"demonstration" effect whereby political activities in
one country are perceived and emulated in another
(aspirations to industrialize, the spread of
nationalism, etc.).[25]

These linkage processes, Rosenau states, occur where

environmental and polity inputs and outputs converge as

depicted in Figure 1:

FIGURE 1. THE ROLE OF LINKAGES IN POLITICAL SCIENCE

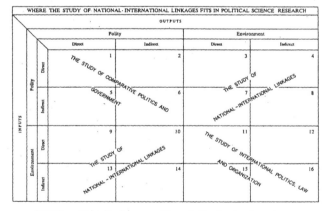

SOURCE: James N. Rosenau, "Toward the Study of National-
International Linkages," in Linkage Politics, ed. James N. Rosenau
(New York: Free Press, 1969), p. 50.

Therefore, national-international linkages are of
eight basic kinds (cells 3, 4, 7, 8, 9, 10, 13, 14).
Proceeding from this point, Rosenau finally assembles his
framework for the analysis of linkage politics in the
matrix reproduced in Figure 2.  This matrix lists
twenty-four items characteristic of polities and six
sub-environments of the international system that are
capable of interacting in linkage processes.  As noted by
Rosenau, these two groups of variables together provide a
minimum of 144 areas in which national-international
linkages can occur.[26]

### Linkage Politics:  A Critique

Although it appears that Rosenau has succeeded in
developing a conceptual approach for the study of linkages,
it is difficult to categorize his framework as a "model" or
"theoretical framework" in the strictest sense of these
terms.  The framework is plagued by some serious
methodological defects, as Rosenau himself admits.[27]
Most importantly, the various categories which he outlines
in his linkage matrix are fuzzy and overlapping, and some
key concepts would seem difficult to operationalize
empirically.  Furthermore, we are left to guess how linkage
processes affect individual polities--i.e., a polity is
simply conceptualized as a "black box."[28]  In reality,
then, Rosenau's linkage framework is really a conceptual

# FIGURE 2. ROSENAU'S LINKAGE POLITICS MATRIX

A PROPOSED LINKAGE FRAMEWORK

| ENVIRONMENTAL →<br><br>POLITY — Outputs and Inputs | The<br>Contiguous<br>Environment | The<br>Regional<br>Environment | The<br>Cold War<br>Environment | The<br>Racial<br>Environment | The<br>Resource<br>Environment | The<br>Organizational<br>Environment |
|---|---|---|---|---|---|---|
| **Actors** | | | | | | |
| 1. Executive Officials | | | | | | |
| 2. Legislative Officials | | | | | | |
| 3. Civilian Bureaucrats | | | | | | |
| 4. Military Bureaucrats | | | | | | |
| 5. Political Parties | | | | | | |
| 6. Interest Groups | | | | | | |
| 7. Elite Groups | | | | | | |
| **Attitudes** | | | | | | |
| 8. Ideology | | | | | | |
| 9. Political Culture | | | | | | |
| 10. Public Opinion | | | | | | |
| **Institutions** | | | | | | |
| 11. Executive | | | | | | |
| 12. Legislatures | | | | | | |
| 13. Bureaucracies | | | | | | |
| 14. Military Establishments | | | | | | |
| 15. Elections | | | | | | |
| 16. Party Systems | | | | | | |
| 17. Communications Systems | | | | | | |
| 18. Social-Institutions | | | | | | |
| **Processes** | | | | | | |
| 19. Socialization and Recruitment | | | | | | |
| 20. Interest Articulation | | | | | | |
| 21. Interest Aggregation | | | | | | |
| 22. Policy-Making | | | | | | |
| 23. Policy-Administration | | | | | | |
| 24. Integrative-Disintegrative | | | | | | |

SOURCE: James N. Rosenau, "Toward the Study of National-International Linkages," in Linkage Politics, ed. James N. Rosenau (New York: Free Press, 1969), p. 52.

checklist for examining linkage phenomena--an inventory of things to be aware of and look for when conducting research in comparative or international politics. While the framework has theoretical potential, this potential is limited to a great degree by conceptual imprecision.

Apart from already noted deficiencies, Rosenau's framework has a number of further problems which constrain its application to the present topic. Despite the fact that corporate behavior in the domestic and international arenas can easily be placed in a linkage perspective, there is no place in Rosenau's macro-analytical approach for internal corporate dynamics and the role of key executives in motivating company behavior. In effect, intra-corporate linkages are ignored and there is little conceptual justification for focussing on the attitudes, beliefs, and perceptions of U.S. business executives. Although Rosenau stresses the significance of attitudes as important determinants of the behavior of political actors, his framework gives recognition only to broad attitudinal orientations like "ideology," "political culture," and "public opinion" as they refer to the predispositions of entire national populations. The importance of attitudes at lower levels of analysis goes unrecognized. This is not surprising, however.

A careful reading suggests that Rosenau encountered
considerable difficulty in building attitudinal factors
into his framework. Rosenau's conceptual problems appear
to stem from the centrality to his formulation of the
definition of a linkage as a "recurrent sequence of
behavior." As noted by Russett and Hanson, attitudes are
not synonomous with behavior but occur prior to behavior
and may condition the behavior of political actors.
Throughout his analysis Rosenau is intuitively aware of
this distinction and gropes for an acceptable way to
integrate attitudinal factors into his behavior-based
framework. To draw an analogy, Rosenau attempts the
equivalent of fitting a square peg to a round hole. The
linkage framework, based as it is on "recurrent sequences
of behavior," does not yield to his efforts.

### Linkage Politics: Conclusion

In concluding this discussion it must be stressed that
despite the previously noted defects of Rosenau's work, an
observation made earlier holds true: Rosenau's approach
does have conceptual flexibility which enables activities
of U.S. corporations to be viewed as a component of a chain
of national-international linkages which can affect
Soviet-American relations. Rosenau makes it clear that
U.S. corporate behavior can and should be subsumed into a
broader framework that takes account of overt corporate

political action on domestic and international fronts as
well as indirect political consequences stemming from
trading concerns (e.g., profit or loss, recession or
prosperity).  Furthermore, Rosenau's analysis demonstrates
vividly that domestic political actors, including
corporations, do not exist in a vacuum but are affected by
political as well as economic forces originating in the
international environment.  In this sense, Rosenau's
formulation complements the studies on corporate strategic
planning and environmental scanning that were discussed
earlier.

### A Framework for the Analysis
### of International Trade
### Politics

From the preceding survey, it has been shown that each
of the paradigms which appears most relevant to the topic
at hand suffers from some theoretical and/or practical
deficiency which would seem to preclude the use of that
particular approach.  While it is undeniably desirable to
integrate the present study into an existing research
framework that is flexible, comprehensive, and airtight by
the standards of science, the fact must be acknowledged
that the discipline of political science (as well as
business administration) has as yet failed to develop such
a framework.  Therefore, in the absence of the best of all
possible worlds, one must make do with what is available

and build upon past work to the extent possible.

Consequently, the construction of a new paradigm which

incorporates the best features of existing approaches while

avoiding many of their pitfalls would appear to be the

optimal course of action. The diagram shown in Figure 3

represents such an attempt, drawing principally on the most

attractive aspects of the corporate decision-making,

Russett-Hanson, and linkage politics approaches. The pri-

mary components of this innovative framework--labelled the

"International Trade Politics Model"--are described below.

## Elements of the Model

Trade Actor Companies: American firms which, from 1972 to
the present, have made significant efforts to explore
prospects for direct commercial relations with the
Soviets. Under this definition, "significant efforts" to
develop business refer to past or on-going negotiations
and/or existing contracts as well as protocol agreements
for commodity and/or scientific-technical exchanges. The
term "commodity" in this usage encompasses both goods and
services. A "company" or "firm" is defined as a privately
owned commercial entity capable of making major business
decisions on an independent basis. An "American" company
is one which is both headquartered and incorporated in the
United States. Consistent with the reference to "direct
commercial relations," the definition excludes U.S.
companies which have had only indirect contacts with the
U.S.S.R. through an intermediary (e.g., via agents or
business subcontracted by another U.S. firm) or that have
worked exclusively through foreign subsidiaries.[29]

Corporate Decision Structures: All trade actor companies
have a decision structure which has the final say on
company policy vis-a-vis U.S.-Soviet economic and political
matters. The decision structure, which in most
corporations is comprised of a board of directors,
formulates general policy on the basis of inputs from the
Soviet Area Executive, various intra-corporate influences

**FIGURE 3. INTERNATIONAL TRADE POLITICS MODEL** *

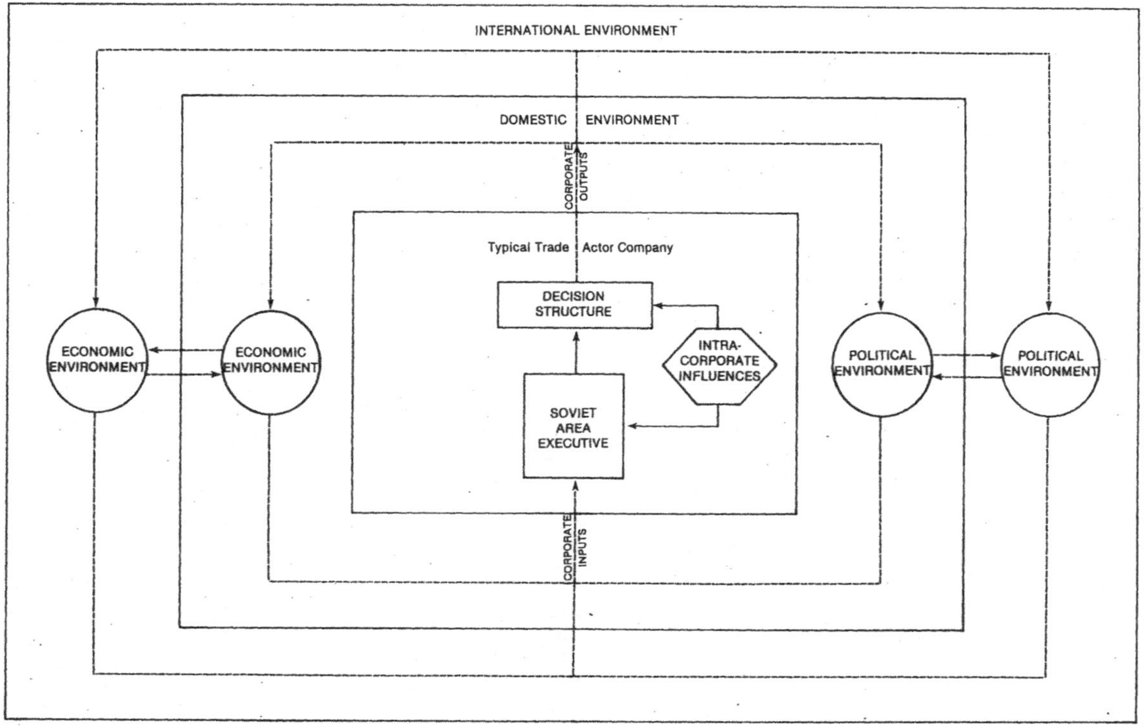

INTERNATIONAL ENVIRONMENT

DOMESTIC ENVIRONMENT

POLITICAL ENVIRONMENT

POLITICAL ENVIRONMENT

ECONOMIC ENVIRONMENT

ECONOMIC ENVIRONMENT

Typical Trade Actor Company

INTRA-CORPORATE INFLUENCES

DECISION STRUCTURE

SOVIET AREA EXECUTIVE

CORPORATE OUTPUTS

CORPORATE INPUTS

* Dashed lines indicate linkage processes.

(e.g., the nature of the firm's business) and influences
from the corporate environment.

Soviet Area Executives (SAEs):  Senior company executives,
stationed in the U.S., who have exercised prime
responsibility over existing or prospective business
relations between trade actor companies and the Soviet
Union.  Foreign-based employees of U.S. companies are
excluded from the definition.[30]

Domestic Political Environment:  All political factors
external to trade actor companies but within the boundaries
of the United States that are capable of interacting with
these companies (public opinion, the U.S. Government, etc.).

International Political Environment:  All political factors
external to trade actor companies and the boundaries of the
United States, but which nonetheless are capable of
interacting with the U.S. political system, the U.S.
economic system, and trade actor companies.

Domestic Economic Environment:  All economic and financial
factors external to trade actor companies but within the
boundaries of the United States that are capable of
interacting with these companies.

International Economic Environment:  All economic and
financial factors external to trade actor companies and the
boundaries of the United States, but which nonetheless are
capable of interacting with the U.S. economic system, the
U.S. political system, and trade actor companies.

Information Transfer:  The communication of data between
output and input loci.

National-International Linkages (Macro-Linkages):  Any
recurrent sequence of behavior that originates in one
political and/or economic system and as a result of
information transfer is reacted to in another political
and/or economic system.  As noted by Rosenau, national-
international linkages may be reactive, emulative, or
penetrative.  (As suggested below, however, in the case of
Soviet-American relations macro-linkage processes appear to
be primarily of the reactive type.)  National-international
linkages consist of the following four types of elements:

   Polity Outputs:  Those sequences of behavior that
   originate within a polity and as a result of
   information transfer either culminate in or are
   sustained by the polity's environment.

Environmental Outputs:  Those sequences of behavior
that start in the external environment of a polity and
that as a result of information transfer are either
sustained or terminated within the polity.

Polity Inputs:  Those behavioral sequences within a
polity to which environmental outputs give rise as a
result of information transfer.

Environmental Inputs:  Those behavioral sequences in
the external environment to which polity outputs give
rise as a result of information transfer.

These outputs and inputs can be classified as either
direct or indirect according to the following criteria:

Direct Environmental/Polity Outputs:  Behavior within
a polity or the external environment purposefully
designed by its originators to generate boundary
crossing responses confined to certain political
and/or economic structures.

Indirect Environmental/Polity Outputs:  Behavior
within a polity or the external environment not
purposefully designed by its originators to generate
boundary crossing responses, but which nonetheless do
so.

Direct Environmental/Polity Inputs:  Behavior within a
polity or the external environment which is generated
in the political and/or economic structures
purposefully targeted by direct outputs.  Actual
effects on the specified structures may or may not be
those that were intended.

Indirect Environmental/Polity Inputs:  Behavior within
a polity or the external environment which is
stimulated by indirect outputs, or is generated in
political and/or economic structures not purposefully
targeted by direct outputs.  Such effects are ipso
facto unintended.

Domestic Linkages (Micro-Linkages):  Any recurrent
sequence of behavior that originates within one political
and/or economic structure of a given polity and as a
result of information transfer is reacted to in another
structure within that same polity, and which
simultaneously is associated with the initial or terminal
stages of a macro-linkage.  Domestic linkages consist of
the following elements:

Internal Outputs:  Behavior that originates within one political and/or economic structure of a given polity and as a result of information transfer is reacted to in another structure within that same polity.

Internal Inputs:  Behavior within the structures of a given polity to which internal outputs give rise.

Internal outputs and inputs can be classified as either direct or indirect according to the following criteria:

Direct Internal Outputs:  Internal outputs purposefully designed by their originators to generate a response confined to certain domestic political and/or economic structures.

Indirect Internal Outputs:  Internal outputs not purposefully designed by their originators to generate a response within domestic political and/or economic structures, but which nonetheless do so.

Direct Internal Inputs:  Internal inputs which are generated in the political and/or economic structures purposefully targeted by direct internal outputs. Actual effects on the specified structures may or may not be those that were intended.

Indirect Internal Inputs:  Internal inputs which are stimulated by indirect internal outputs, or are generated in political and/or economic structures not purposefully targeted by direct internal outputs.  Such effects are _ipso facto_ unintended.

Corporate Outputs:  A specialized form of internal or polity outputs which involves behavior by one or more trade actor companies which is directed toward the corporate environment.  Corporate outputs may or may not be the result of corporate inputs.

Corporate Inputs:  A specialized form of internal, environmental, or polity inputs which yields behavior within one or more trade actor companies.  Corporate inputs may or may not result in corporate outputs.

Conversion Variables:  Attitudes, beliefs and perceptions of Soviet Area Executives on questions and issues relevant to U.S.-U.S.S.R. economic and political relations.  Such viewpoints at a minimum predispose an SAE to favor or oppose certain courses of action in the formulation of

company policies which affect his area of responsibility
(see Assumptions 3-5).

## Premises and Assumptions

Premise 1:  Private companies are entities which can be
differentiated from their environment.

Premise 2:  The model does not exhibit full system
characteristics in that no assumptions are made which
require system equilibrium or, conversely, the
specification of a stress point where system breakdown will
occur.  In other words, although the model may give rise to
so-called "feedback" processes, such processes are not
necessary for system maintenance.

Assumption 1:  The behavior of trade actor companies can
affect Soviet-American economic and/or political matters
in the domestic as well as the international political and
economic environments.  This assumption refers to the
collective behavior of numerous trade actor companies, as
well as the activities of a few prominent firms (or, in
some instances, the behavior of just one important
company).  The assumption does not require that behavior of
trade actor companies always exercises an impact on
Soviet-American economic and political issues, only that
this occur with some frequency.  Note that no inference is
drawn regarding "group" activity.  Trade actor companies
may or may not act together with a conscious appreciation
of common interests.  The assumption requires only that the
summation of individual corporate behavior have the
capacity for affecting Soviet-American political and
economic matters.

Assumption 2:  Soviet Area Executives exercise considerable
formative influence over their companies' policies on
Soviet-American trade and political matters.  This
influence often has a decisive impact on the character of
corporate decisions, but at a minimum SAE activities help
to define the limits of action available to corporate
decision structures and contribute to the corporate climate
in which decision structures must operate.  (Other
influences on a given decision structure may include the
personality characteristics of its members, a variety of
intra-corporate variables, and information received from
the corporate environment.)  Most SAEs likely have a great
deal of autonomy on many matters within their sphere of
responsibilities and generally submit only basic issues to
corporate decision structures.  Thus, for all intents and

purposes, an SAE can actually be his company's decision
structure on many Soviet-American political issues.

Assumption 3:  Soviet Area Executives as well as other
participants in corporate decision structures continuously
scan the corporate environment for political and economic
information relevant to past, present, or possible future
company commercial relations with the U.S.S.R.  The
corporate "environment" is assumed to include a firm's
domestic as well as international political and economic
environments.

Assumption 4:  Relevant information gleaned from the
corporate environment exercises a considerable formative
influence on SAE attitudes, beliefs and perceptions
concerning Soviet-American economic and political matters.
This formative influence often has a decisive impact on the
character of SAE orientations, but at a minimum
environmental information helps to limit the range of
individual viewpoints.  Other influences on the attitudes
of a given SAE may include the personality characteristics
of the individual and a variety of intra-corporate factors
such as the nature of the firm's business, the extent of
its international operations, etc.  Whereas personality
characteristics are assumed to have minimal influence on
executive attitudes, intra-corporate variables are
acknowledged as a meaningful conditioning factor which can
affect how executives interpret environmental information.

## Linkage Scenarios

Employing the preceding elements of the model, a

series of linkage scenarios can be hypothesized.  While

many different combinations of linkage processes can be

postulated using the International Trade Politics

framework, background research suggests some likely

patterns which will serve to illustrate the numerous

possibilities.

## Linkage Scenario 1

Attitudes and perceptions of Soviet Area Executives in a host of companies motivate SAE behavior which, combined with other influences, contributes to decisions in numerous firms to take overt domestic political action aimed at certain domestic institutions (e.g., lobbying the U.S. Government) on Soviet-American economic and/or political issues (e.g., technology transfer policy). The aggregate activities of these trade actor companies are then combined with other influences and contribute to the formulation of U.S. Government policy decisions vis-a-vis the U.S.S.R. (e.g., approval of export licenses). These policy decisions are perceived and interpreted by the Soviet leadership and thereby affect the U.S.S.R.'s political and economic decision processes.

In sum, this sequence of events can be characterized as a reactive national-international linkage process initiated in the U.S. whereby direct corporate outputs (which are internal outputs) stimulate direct internal inputs in the U.S. Government. These in turn contribute to direct polity outputs which generate environmental inputs in designated Soviet decision structures:

**Scenario 1**

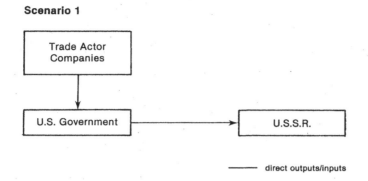

Note that the Soviet Union is conceptualized as being part of the international environment of the U.S. since in this instance the national-international linkage process is triggered on the U.S. side.

Linkage Scenario 2

Soviet authorities make decisions on U.S.-U.S.S.R. political and/or economic issues and take actions designed to influence the U.S. political system through trade actor companies (e.g., diversion of Soviet purchases of equipment and technology to non-U.S. sources avowedly because of elaborate U.S. export control procedures). Soviet Area Executives collectively perceive the Soviet actions as having a potential or actual impact on their firms (e.g., a reduction in company sales to the U.S.S.R.). Based on their perceptions, Soviet Area Executives recommend to their respective boards of directors that their companies take appropriate overt political action aimed at certain

domestic institutions (e.g., lobbying the U.S. Government
for a streamlining of export control procedures). As in
the case of Linkage Scenario 1, aggregate activities of
trade actor companies are merged with other influences and
contribute to the formulation of U.S. Government policy
decisions on U.S.-Soviet trade and political issues.

Once again, a reactive national-international linkage
has occurred, although in this example the process has been
initiated by means of a direct polity output by the
U.S.S.R. resulting in direct corporate inputs (which are in
this instance environmental inputs). Corporate inputs in
turn stimulate direct corporate outputs which generate
direct internal inputs in designated U.S. political
structures:

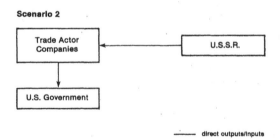

**Scenario 2**

Trade Actor Companies ← U.S.S.R.

U.S. Government

——— direct outputs/inputs

Note that the U.S. is conceptualized as being part of the
international environment of the U.S.S.R. since in this

case the national-international linkage process is triggered on the Soviet side.

## Linkage Scenario 3

Soviet authorities make political decisions and take actions not directly aimed at trade actor companies or the U.S. political system (e.g., support of Third World revolutionary movements) but which nonetheless influence U.S. Government and public perceptions of the Soviet Union. Soviet actions similarly have an unanticipated impact on perceptions of the U.S.S.R. held by Soviet Area Executives. Soviet Area Executives collectively perceive Soviet actions as constituting a renewed international communist threat. Also, SAEs see Soviet activities as having a deleterious impact on the domestic and inter-governmental political climates for U.S.-Soviet trade. As a result, Soviet Area Executives recommend to their directors changes in the level of company involvement in commercial relations with the U.S.S.R.

Again, a reactive national-international linkage is involved, but in this instance it would seem to result from direct polity outputs by the U.S.S.R. which give rise to indirect environmental inputs in the United States. These environmental inputs involve behavioral reactions within the U.S. Government, U.S. public opinion, and trade actor companies (i.e., corporate inputs) as a result of

perceptions of the international environment. In addition,
environmental inputs to U.S. public opinion trigger
indirect internal outputs which in turn generate indirect
corporate inputs in trade actor companies:

**Scenario 3**

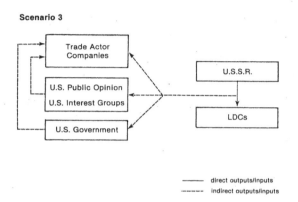

——— direct outputs/inputs
------- indirect outputs/inputs

## Linkage Scenario 4

Soviet authorities make political decisions and
implement domestic measures not intended to influence the
U.S. political system nor trade actor companies (e.g.,
suppression of Soviet political dissent). Nevertheless,
the actions have an impact on U.S. Government perceptions
of the Soviet Union. At the same time, Soviet actions have
an unanticipated impact on other U.S. political
structures. In particular, Soviet Area Executives
collectively perceive Soviet measures as having either a
positive or negative effect on the domestic and

inter-governmental political climates for U.S.-Soviet trade
and therefore advocate to their directors appropriate
adjustments in the level of company involvement with the
Soviet Union.

In this case, the reactive linkage is comprised of
indirect polity outputs by the U.S.S.R. which generate
indirect environmental inputs in the United States,
including corporate inputs via SAEs' perceptions of their
firms' domestic and international environments:

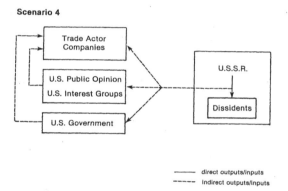

**Scenario 4**

Linkage Scenario 5

U.S. Government authorities make political decisions
and implement measures designed to influence the Soviet
political system (e.g., protests over the U.S.S.R.'s
suppression of political dissent and Soviet emigration
policies). As expected, the actions have an impact on

Soviet Government perceptions of the United States
(although the actual effects may not be those intended).
However, U.S. actions simultaneously influence U.S.
political structures and Soviet Area Executives. This
impact may or may not be the result of purposeful design.
To the extent the impact is motivated by purpose, the
effects may or may not be those actually desired (e.g.,
U.S. actions may stimulate desired perceptions by the
public that the U.S. is "getting tough with the Russians";
at the same time U.S. Government behavior unintentionally
generates public and SAE perceptions that U.S. policy no
longer supports Soviet-American trade). Evaluating these
signals from the corporate environment, SAEs recommend to
their directors appropriate adjustments in the level of
company involvement with the Soviet Union.

In this scenario direct polity outputs from the U.S.
yield direct environmental inputs in the U.S.S.R. At the
same time, these polity outputs by the U.S. Government
yield direct and indirect internal outputs in the U.S.
which ultimately result in direct and indirect internal
inputs, including corporate inputs:

**Scenario 5**

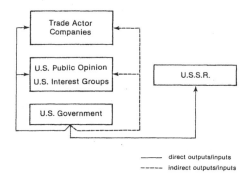

```
                                    ———— direct outputs/inputs
                                    – – – – indirect outputs/inputs
```

Linkage Scenario 6

Factors in the domestic or international economic environments influence SAE attitudes and perceptions regarding the desirability of conducting business with the U.S.S.R. In periods of recession, Soviet Area Executives may perceive the U.S.S.R. as an attractive growth market. However, in periods of prosperity the U.S.S.R. may be perceived as a less desirable commercial partner depending to some extent on the relative profitability of Soviet business. Based on these considerations, SAEs recommend appropriate measures to their boards of directors.

Note that in this instance the reactive linkage process occurs when indirect environmental outputs from the international economic system result in indirect polity inputs in the U.S. in the form of corporate inputs. Similar signals are received by Soviet Area Executives from the domestic economic environment (i.e., indirect internal

outputs) which also lead to corporate inputs (i.e.,
indirect internal inputs):

**Scenario 6**

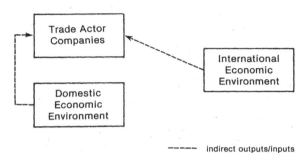

----- indirect outputs/inputs

Linkage Scenario 7

Observe that the preceding linkage scenarios can
easily complement and reinforce one another. All national-
international linkage patterns noted above can in turn
trigger new macro-linkages. For example, scenarios 3, 4,
5, and 6 terminate in corporate inputs where SAEs recommend
to their directors changes in the level of company
involvement with the U.S.S.R. It is conceivable, then,
that direct corporate outputs would follow (e.g., decisions
to reduce activity in the U.S.S.R.) intended to influence
certain Soviet economic structures (e.g., direct
environmental inputs to Soviet foreign trade organizations).
Such developments could produce a change in overall levels
of U.S.-Soviet trade. Because of the centrality of trade
matters to U.S.-U.S.S.R. political relations, the

previously described corporate outputs could also have an unanticipated but substantial impact on Soviet political processes (e.g., indirect environmental inputs into the Politburo). This could in turn result in direct polity outputs aimed at the U.S. Government as well as trade actor companies:

**Scenario 7**

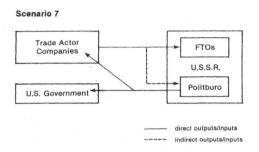

—————— direct outputs/inputs
- - - - - indirect outputs/inputs

These national-international linkages which in essence form a reciprocal or synergistic relationship are labelled "fused linkages" by Rosenau. He defines a fused linkage as:

> . . . one in which the patterned sequence of behavior does not terminate with the input. Stated in positive terms a fused linkage is conceived to be a sequence in which an output fosters an input that in turn fosters an output.[31]

The concept of a fused linkage appears to be a useful one and hence will be retained and employed in the analyses that follow.

How the Model Can Contribute to Theory

Perhaps more so than in Chapter I of this study, the
above scenarios graphically illustrate the potential and
actual importance of SAE attitudes, beliefs and perceptions to U.S. political processes and Soviet-American
economic and political relations. Executive viewpoints
play a pivotal role in the Trade Politics Model as key
conversion variables in a complex series of behavioral
sequences. SAE attitudes contribute to as well as result
from linkage processes. Consequently, the actual
measurement of these viewpoints, either from a contemporary
or an historical standpoint, can contribute not only to our
substantive knowledge of superpower relations, but also to
the building of cumulative theoretical knowledge of
political phenomena. To be specific, the measurement of
these attitudes and perceptions can help to substantiate
the existence of the linkage scenarios hypothesized above.
Each of the behavioral sequences which have been described
embodies a series of empirically testable propositions
whose viability hinges on the presence of certain types of
executive orientations. Thus, the confirmation of
viewpoints logically compatible or incompatible with a
given scenario is a valuable partial test of the scenario's
elemental propositions.[32] Attitudinal measurement,
therefore, is a meaningful first step or "critical

experiment" which enables the analyst to screen hypothetical linkage scenarios and, focussing on those scenarios which "survive," can lead to the derivation and exhaustive testing of specific propositions.[33] In addition, attitude measurement can be suggestive of new linkage scenarios which merit further investigation.

In summary, then, an inventory and analysis of relevant attitudes, beliefs, and perceptions of U.S. executives within the context of the Trade Politics Model can contribute to hypothesis testing as well as hypothesis generation vis-a-vis the dynamics of Soviet-American relations. By identifying with greater precision possible linkage processes at both the national and international levels, political scientists will enhance their capabilities for predicting likely developments in Soviet-American relations (including related occurrences in the U.S. political arena). To the extent that the ability to predict these political phenomena is improved, there is a resulting contribution to the twin goals of explanation and theoretical understanding. Furthermore, it is necessary to emphasize that findings of the present study, while they are based on the Soviet-American case, should not be viewed as case-specific. The corporate linkage processes which are indicated in the following text may have wide application to various bilateral country relationships where both economic and political issues are prominent and where private companies in either nation comprise a significant autonomous force. Because the Soviet-American experience may be indicative of more generalized behavior, the present analysis should therefore be viewed as an initial effort aimed at the development of narrow and medium-gauge theories which cut across the sub-fields of comparative and international politics.

Future research in the directions that have been suggested will hopefully be aided by the flexibility of the Trade Politics Model. This framework synthesizes macro and microanalytic approaches and in essence builds a bridge from the level of the individual business executive to the broad reaches of the international political and economic systems. Although the framework has been developed to study the Soviet-American case, there appears to be no conceptual barrier which would preclude slight adaptations to allow its application to a variety of political contexts (e.g., French-Swiss relations). In fact, the model would appear to be a useful tool for the investigation of corporate linkages involving lesser developed countries, including political studies of the operations of multinational corporations in these nations. Thus, the Trade Politics Model may be capable of providing a more solid conceptual foundation for such studies than has been the case thus far.

The Trade Politics Model owes its flexibility to a combination of elements from the Russett-Hanson, corporate decision-making, and linkage politics approaches. First, the model implicitly recognizes the validity of the efforts of Russett and Hanson to justify their study through the argument that private businessmen as a rule comprise a politically prominent population in industrial democracies like the United States.[34] In addition, the Trade Politics Model incorporates and renders more explicit the Russett-Hanson study's inductive logic whereby attitudinal measurement is used as an instrument for hypothesis testing, hypothesis generation, and, hence, theory building. At the same time, however, the model builds upon Russett and Hanson's work by placing executives in a corporate context. The corporate setting is then embellished in considerable detail by drawing on the writings of organization theorists and specialists in business administration. Specifically, the model recognizes the significance of "environmental scanning," accepts as valid Bakke's "fusion process," notes the importance of expert specialists in organizations, and acknowledges the impact which senior executives can have on corporate decision processes. Finally, the model is completed by coupling it to Rosenau's linkage politics approach. This is necessitated because, as noted earlier, neither the Russett-Hanson nor corporate decision-making approaches gives due consideration to the political implications of corporate behavior and the broad political dimensions of the corporate environment. However, major adjustments have been made to Rosenau's approach to mitigate its defects and upgrade its theoretical potential. Measures taken include the rejection of Rosenau's linkage matrix with its fuzzy classification scheme, recognition of the importance of information transfer in linkage processes, and elaboration of the paradigm to take into account linkage dynamics within as well as between polities.

This blend of three theoretical approaches yields an isomorphic and formalized model that is a valuable instrument for political research. By focussing on executive viewpoints as key conversion variables and through the use of inductive generalization, the Trade Politics Model capitalizes on the strengths of each of its three component parts while simultaneously minimizing their individual weaknesses. This is not to say that the Trade Politics Model is without shortcomings, but only that these flaws do not hopelessly cripple the model's theoretical potential. All models used in political research are defective to some degree, particularly as regards the resistance of many concepts to operationalization. In the Trade Politics Model, for example, the notion of "direct" (intentional) and "indirect" (unintentional) outputs/inputs is conceptually useful but virtually impossible to measure empirically. However, in order to make a theoretical contribution the Trade Politics Model does not necessarily require the analyst to measure slippery concepts like "intent." Nor is it necessary to operationalize and quantify concepts like "interest," "interest group," "influence," or "political power." All that is required is the identification of attitudes, beliefs, and perceptions, which are phenomena readily measurable by survey and interview techniques.[35] Finally, it should be noted that because the Trade Politics Model incorporates no assumptions about "system maintenance" and "system breakdown," it avoids the methodological problems associated with the systems approach.[36] Likewise, the model is designed to avoid preoccupation with a discrete "decision situation"--a major criticism of both the political and corporate decision-making approaches.[37]

## Existing Political Science Propositions: A Partial Test

Apart from the theoretical potential of the Trade Politics Model, the collection and analysis of data on business views in the U.S.-Soviet case can be intrinsically useful in another respect. Note once again the inductive theoretical reasoning of Russett and Hanson:

> . . . By asking about the beliefs, preferences and attitudes of corporate executives we are trying to discover whether those attitudes are consistent with what various theorists about economic or other motivations would have us expect. A question we ask prior to that about their behavior is simply, are their attitudes what would be predicted? . . .
> . . . it is an inquiry that could in principle serve almost as a "critical experiment" to determine the direction of future investigation into questions about economic influence. If attitudes are such as would be predicted by economic influence theories, then there is a good reason to redouble efforts to trace the exercise of power and influence. If, on the contrary, the attitudes do not bear much resemblance to those predicted, then it may be time to move on to other, more promising kinds of inquiries.[38]

Therefore, it follows that this research effort can make a further theoretical contribution to political science by specifying whether survey and interview data obtained in this exercise appear consistent or inconsistent with other analysts' findings and hypotheses concerning the political views and behavior of U.S. business. Such a partial test is conducted at appropriate points in the following text, and is based on a comprehensive survey of relevant literature.

Additionally, it merits emphasis that, to the extent that collected attitudinal data on SAEs corroborate other studies of American business, the findings of the present

research effort will be placed on a firmer empirical
foundation.  Once again, this will also contribute to the
building of cumulative scientific knowledge of political
phenomena.

FOOTNOTES

[1]For example, see the following: Gabriel A. Almond and Sidney Verba, The Civic Culture: Political Attitudes and Democracy in Five Nations (Princeton: Princeton University Press, 1963).

[2]Lester M. Salamon and John J. Siegfried, "Economic Power and Political Influence: The Impact of Industry Structure on Public Policy," American Political Science Review 71 (September 1977): 1026-1043. For studies of U.S. business which implicitly or explicitly utilize the interest group approach, see the following: Edwin M. Epstein, The Corporation in American Politics (Englewood Cliffs, N.J.: Prentice-Hall, 1969); Raymond Bauer, Ithiel DeSola Pool, and Lewis Dexter, American Business and Public Policy, 2nd ed. (Chicago: Aldine-Atherton, 1972). For studies which apply some elements of the interest group approach specifically to U.S. companies in East-West trade see Jeffrey M. Brookstone, The Multinational Businessman and Foreign Policy: Entrepreneurial Politics in East-West Trade and Investment (New York: Praeger, 1976); also see Connie M. Friesen, The Political Economy of East-West Trade (New York: Praeger, 1976).

[3]For studies of U.S. business which are based primarily on the elite approach, see the following: David Horowitz, ed., Corporations and the Cold War (New York: Monthly Review Press, 1969); G. William Domhoff, Who Rules America? (Englewood Cliffs, N.J.: Prentice-Hall, 1967); David S. McLellan and Charles E. Woodhouse, "The Business Elite and Foreign Policy," Western Political Quarterly 13 (March 1960): 172-190. Also see C. Wright Mills, The Power Elite (New York: Oxford University Press, 1956); Robert Presthus, Elites in the Policy Process (New York: Cambridge University Press, 1974); Dankwart A. Rustow, "The Study of Elites: Who's Who, When and How," World Politics 18 (July 1966): 690-717; Lester G. Seligman, "Political Elites Reconsidered: Process, Consequences and Values," Comparative Politics 6 (January 1974): 299-314; Jack L. Walker, "A Critique of the Elitist Theory of Democracy," American Political Science Review 60 (June 1966): 285-295.

[4]Bruce M. Russett and Elizabeth C. Hanson, Interest and Ideology: The Foreign Policy Beliefs of American Businessmen (San Francisco: W. H. Freeman, 1975), p. 23.

[5]If one accepts the standard definition of a multinational corporation as a business enterprise which owns and operates production facilities in one or more foreign countries, then many companies involved in U.S.-U.S.S.R. trade (and East-West trade in general) are not multinationals. In this regard, Jeffrey M. Brookstone's political study of U.S. corporations in East-West trade can be criticized because it tends to overlook this crucial distinction. See Jeffrey M. Brookstone, The Multinational Businessman and Foreign Policy: Entrepreneurial Politics in East-West Trade and Investment (New York: Praeger, 1976). For a review of political studies of the multinational corporation see Neil H. Jacoby, "The Multinational Corporation," Center 3 (May-June 1970): 37-55. Also see Joseph S. Nye, Jr., "Multinational Corporations in World Politics," Foreign Affairs 53 (October 1974): 153-175; Peter F. Drucker, "Multinationals and Developing Countries: Myths and Realities," Foreign Affairs 53 (October 1974): 121-134; and Robert O. Keohane, "Not 'Innocents Abroad': American Multinational Corporations and the United States Government," Comparative Politics 8 (January 1976): 307-320.

[6]See the review of decision-making approaches contained in Patrick M. Morgan, Theories and Approaches to International Politics: What Are We to Think? (San Ramon, Ca.: Consensus Publishers, 1972), pp. 141-159. Also see James E. Dougherty and Robert L. Pfaltzgraff, Jr. eds. Contending Theories of International Relations (Philadelphia: Lippincott, 1971), pp. 312-344.

[7]See Morgan, Theories and Approaches, pp. 142-144.

[8]Norman Berg, "Strategic Planning in Conglomerate Companies," Harvard Business Review 43 (May-June 1965): 79-92; Charles Hofer, "Research on Strategic Planning: A Survey of Past Studies and Suggestions for Future Efforts," Journal of Economics and Business 28 (Spring-Summer 1976): 261-286.

[9]F. J. Aguilar, "Formulating Company Strategy: Scanning the Business Environment," doctoral dissertation, Harvard Business School, June 1975; W. J. Keegan, "Scanning the International Business Environment: A Study of the Information Acquisition Process," doctoral dissertation, Harvard Business School, June 1967; R. L. Collings, "Scanning the Environment for Strategic Information," doctoral dissertation, Harvard Business School, June 1968; H. E. Klein, "Incorporating Environmental Examination into

the Corporate Strategic Planning Process," doctoral
dissertation, Columbia University, 1973; H. H. Stevenson,
"Defining Corporate Strengths and Weaknesses: An
Exploratory Study," doctoral dissertation, Harvard Business
School, March 1969. See these and similar studies
discussed in Charles W. Hofer, "Research on Strategic
Planning: A Survey of Past Studies and Suggestions for
Future Efforts," Journal of Economics and Business 28
(Spring-Summer 1976): 264-266.

[10]It should be noted that appreciation for the
importance of political factors in the corporate
environment is most highly developed in the business
literature on foreign investment risks. For example, see
the following: Stefan H. Robock, "Political Risk:
Identification and Assessment," Columbia Journal of World
Business 6 (July-August 1971): 6-20; Jean Boddewyn and
Etienne F. Gracco, "The Political Game in World Business,"
Columbia Journal of World Business 7 (January-February
1972): 45-56. Also see the political risk categories used
in Haner's business environment risk index in F. T. Haner,
"Balancing International Risk and Profit," Planning Review
6 (March 1978): 9-12.

[11]Bruce M. Russett and Elizabeth C. Hanson, Interest
and Ideology: The Foreign Policy Beliefs of American
Businessmen (San Francisco: W. H. Freeman, 1975).

[12]Raymond A. Bauer, Ithiel DeSola Pool, and Lewis
Dexter, American Business and Public Policy, 2nd ed.
(Chicago: Aldine-Atherton, 1972).

[13]Russett and Hanson, Interest and Ideology, p. 1.

[14]Ibid., pp. 2, 5-6, 24.

[15]Ibid., pp 24-25.

[16]Ibid., pp. 23-25.

[17]Ibid., p. 25.

[18]Ibid., pp. 245-270.

[19]James N. Rosenau, "Toward the Study of National-
International Linkages," in Linkage Politics, ed. James N.
Rosenau (New York: Free Press, 1969), pp. 44-63.

[20]James N. Rosenau, "Political Science in a
Shrinking World," in Linkage Politics, p. 4.

[21]Ibid., p. 2.

[22]Ibid., p. 4.

[23]Definitions reproduced from James N. Rosenau, "Toward the Study of National-International Linkages," in Linkage Politics, pp. 45-46.

[24]Ibid.

[25]Ibid., p. 46.

[26]Ibid., pp. 49, 52.

[27]For example, ". . . it must be admitted that the various categories are imprecise, incomplete, impressionistic, and overlapping. Our purpose at this stage is to be suggestive, not exhaustive." See James N. Rosenau, "Toward the Study of National-International Linkages," in Linkage Politics, p. 51.

[28]This, of course, is a criticism similar to those made about Easton's early "systems" formulation for political analysis. See David Easton's landmark article, "An Approach to the Analysis of Political Systems," World Politics 9 (April 1957): 383-400.

[29]The exclusion from the definition of U.S. companies which have had only indirect contacts with the U.S.S.R. reflects the fact that these firms are likely to have a more transitory and incidental relationship with Soviet business organizations than companies which deal directly in the hopes of establishing continuous business contacts. (Subcontractors, for example, generally take part in U.S.-Soviet trade only as a result of initiatives taken by other firms.) Such an indirect relationship is likely to have an insular effect vis-a-vis company concern with U.S.-U.S.S.R. political and economic issues. Thus, the firm is less apt to play a significant role in the dynamics of the Soviet-American relationship.

[30]On many issues, important differences in viewpoints have been found between home office personnel in the U.S. and their foreign-based marketing staffs. See Thomas A. Wolf, "Industry Problems in East-West Trade," unpublished manuscript, Department of Economics, Ohio State University, February 1975. This divergence in outlook apparently reflects the relative insulation of foreign-based personnel from company decision-making as well as the U.S. political-economic context. For a number

of reasons, it appears that most U.S. companies base their
senior executive for Eastern Europe in the United States,
usually at company headquarters. See Business
International S.A., Corporate Strategy, Planning,
Organization and Personnel Practices for Eastern Europe
(Geneva: Business International, 1977). Thus,
geographical location would seem to be a logical criterion
for drawing the line between executives who are part of the
U.S. political context and those who are not.

[31]Rosenau, "Toward the Study of National-International Linkages," in Linkage Politics, p. 46.

[32]This procedure, whereby attitudinal measurement is
used as an indicator of linkage processes, is based on
inductive inference. That is, patterns of behavior
(generalizations) are postulated on the basis of specific
observations. The patterns logically account for the
observed phenomena, but do not necessarily follow from the
phenomena. See Lawrence Mayer, Comparative Political
Inquiry: A Methodological Survey (Homewood, Ill.: Dorsey
Press, 1972), pp. 287-288.

[33]For supporting arguments, see Russett and Hanson,
Interest and Ideology, p. 25, as quoted above, p. 33.

[34]Russett and Hanson, Interest and Ideology, as
quoted above pp. 30-32.

[35]Note that in order to make a theoretical
contribution, it is not even mandatory to test attitudes
against sociological variables. Indeed, if the assumptions
of the model regarding the significance of environmental
stimuli are correct, then we would expect only a weak
association between these variables and SAE attitudes.

[36]See Lawrence Mayer, Comparative Political Inquiry,
pp. 125-142.

[37]For an examination of foreign policy decision-
making processes, see James E. Dougherty and Robert L.
Pfaltzgraff, Jr., eds. Contending Theories of International
Relations (Philadelphia: Lippincott, 1971), pp. 312-344.

[38]Russett and Hanson, Interest and Ideology, pp.
23-25.

CHAPTER III

RESEARCH PROCEDURE

Alternative Research Strategies

As stated earlier, the purpose of this research effort
is to investigate comprehensively the views and perceptions
held by Soviet Area Executives in American trade actor
companies during the years 1975-1976.  This goal embodies
two objectives.  A major aim is to provide scholars and
U.S. Government policy-makers with substantive information
relevant to U.S. business' role in key issues of the
domestic and international politics of U.S.-Soviet
relations.  At the same time, it is hoped that application
of the International Trade Politics Model to the Soviet-
American case will result in a significant contribution to
our theoretical understanding of political phenomena.

To meet these twin research goals the ensuing analysis
will rely principally on results obtained from surveys and
personal interviews of Soviet Area Executives conducted by
the author during 1975-1976, when the present project and
the International Trade Politics Model were first being
conceptualized.  At that time, the decision to collect
these data reflected a number of considerations, one of

75

which was the availability of sufficient funding to execute
an exhaustive survey/interview effort. More importantly,
however, comprehensive background research during 1974-1975
had indicated that U.S.-Soviet relations were evolving
through a period of considerable historical significance.
Likewise, background study had clearly shown that survey
and interview techniques offered the only feasible route
for accurately measuring businessmen's attitudes and
opinions. All alternative data-gathering procedures
embodied crippling weaknesses.

To be specific, as was true then as well as now, the
utility of a library research approach to the topic at hand
appears limited. As has been noted repeatedly, from the
inception of detente to the present few social scientists
have conducted scholarly studies examining the role of
corporate actors in superpower relations. Additionally,
however, available scholarly studies and other publicly
available material (e.g., newspaper and magazine articles,
government documents) present some significant analytical
problems. Specifically, it is often difficult when using
these sources to sample the SAE population with any
precision, to differentiate SAE views from views held by
the business community at large, and to achieve a
sufficient level of detail on SAE attitudes. Consequently,
even the application of quantitative content analysis

techniques to newspapers and similar sources from the 1975-1976 period would likely yield disappointing results.

In contrast to the library research and content analysis approaches, survey and interview techniques, despite well-known methodological limitations, are capable of detailed and direct measurement of attitudinal phenomena. Indeed, these techniques are widely recognized as powerful tools for opinion research. Survey research, in particular, can furnish ordinal and interval data amenable to statistical analysis.

All this is not to say that library and other public sources are without value, but only that they are by themselves insufficient for projects of the kind contemplated here. To the extent that scholarly studies, government documents and other publicly available information can supplement "harder" data obtained from the surveys and interviews conducted during 1975-1976, they should be incorporated into the present study. In particular, these data sources can help to corroborate survey and interview findings, document alternative points of view on various U.S.-Soviet issues, and direct interested readers to additional substantive information on such issues. Fundamentally, then, library and other public sources can place survey and interview results on a more solid empirical foundation and can give additional perspective to these data. Hence, such materials can make an important contribution to the theoretical and practical goals of this project.

In sum, then, although relying principally on 1975-1976 survey and interview findings, this study of Soviet Area Executives nevertheless reflects a broad-based research effort. This should be self-evident from the following summary of data sources.

## Data Sources

### 1975 Survey of Soviet Area Executives (Survey 1)

Utilizing a broad set of SAE attitudes indicated by an earlier background study, a survey questionnaire was devised in the summer of 1975 to obtain a more accurate attitude profile of the entire population of Soviet Area Executives. The questionnaire, containing 44 questions on the most basic U.S.-U.S.S.R. economic and political issues, was mailed in June to all relevant American corporations and yielded a highly satisfactory response of 48.4%. (Because of the key importance of these data to the present analysis, complete details on the methodology employed are provided in a separate section below.)

### 1976 Survey of Soviet Area Executives (Survey 2)

Conducted during the summer of 1976, this survey of Soviet Area Executives was executed in order to achieve an

attitude profile with better detail than that obtained by
Survey 1, to clear up new questions generated by the first
survey, and to gain a longitudinal perspective on certain
SAE viewpoints. (The last objective was deemed
particularly important in view of the rapid deterioration
in the domestic and international climate for U.S.-U.S.S.R.
trade between 1975 and 1976.) Hence, the second survey
employed a questionnaire considerably longer than that used
for the first, incorporating 84 items. The questionnaire
was mailed to an enlarged population of 386 trade actor
companies, and resulted in a response rate of 52.6%.
(Again, because of the importance of these survey data to
the current research effort, additional details on survey
methods are furnished in the following text.)

Personal Interviews

During August and September 1976, 28 personal
interviews were conducted nationwide with a sample of
those Soviet Area Executives who had responded to the 1976
survey. This group was not intended to be a
scientifically selected random sample. Rather, the
primary purpose of the interviews was to acquire added
insight into the more structured data accumulated from
previous surveys and background research. (Further
elaboration of interview techniques is furnished below.)

## Library Research

An extensive effort has been made to locate all scholarly studies as well as other publicly available information (newspaper and magazine articles, etc.) that have substantive, theoretical, and methodological relevance to the topic at hand. Hence, the bibliography to this study represents an exhaustive survey of the literature of political science (scholarly journals, books, unpublished research papers, etc.) as well as a review of pertinent studies conducted by specialists in business administration. Where appropriate, reference to relevant materials is made throughout this analysis.

## Internal Unclassified U.S. Government Documents

Although some useful federal documents were obtained through library research, numerous other pertinent U.S. Government materials were obtained directly through the auspices of the Bureau of East-West Trade, U.S. Department of Commerce. Documents collected (see bibliography) include relevant research papers, internal memos, official correspondence, transcripts of government hearings and advisory committee meetings, etc. These data, like material obtained via library research, are referred to at various appropriate points in the following text.

## Survey and Interview Methodology

As mentioned above, the author executed two separate mail surveys of Soviet Area Executives in June of 1975 (Survey 1) and July of 1976 (Survey 2), followed by a series of personal interviews with selected executives in August and September of 1976. Because of the centrality of resulting data to this project it is necessary to document precisely the research procedures that were employed. In addition, because of difficult methodological problems of studying businessmen and their companies, future investigations of U.S. business by other analysts should benefit considerably from a detailed description of the experience gained in this research effort.

### Survey Sampling of Trade Actor Companies

As mandated by the International Trade Politics Model, a primary procedural goal of both Survey 1 and Survey 2 was to obtain representative samples of American trade actor companies which, from 1972 up to the time of each survey, had explored business possibilities with the Soviets (see definition of "trade actor," above p. 45). To achieve this goal, efforts were made to survey all relevant firms-- i.e., to locate and study an entire population or universe of companies. The author was aided toward this end by comprehensive lists of pertinent firms assembled from public and private information sources by Washington Forum,

Inc. Washington Forum, a business information firm which serves institutional investors, regularly compiles for its clients lists of U.S. companies "which have entered negotiations or signed agreements with Soviet trade organizations." Prior to each survey, the author requested and obtained from the Forum its most recent list of U.S. companies seeking ties with the U.S.S.R. The first list, dated April 1974, contained 270 companies and was the core of the 1975 survey population. A revised inventory, issued in September 1975, listed 550 firms and was the basis of the 1976 survey. At the time of each survey the respective lists were updated as well as subjected to an intensive review to verify the Forum's work. This was accomplished through careful examination of publicly available information (Wall Street Journal, New York Times, Commerce Department trade fair lists, etc.) as far back as 1972. This procedure confirmed the basic comprehensiveness of both Washington Forum lists, although some additional trade actor firms were discovered and included in the respective survey populations.

An especially thorough check of the September 1975 Forum list was made possible by increased funding support for Survey 2. Public relations (PR) officers of all 550 companies on the 1975 Forum list were telephoned during June 1976 to determine the accuracy of the Forum's information. Consequently, it was necessary to delete a few companies which erroneously had been placed on the list. Telephone canvassing also enabled the author to pinpoint within corporate conglomerates the specific subsidiaries which had explored the Soviet market. Where it was apparent that the central headquarters of the corporate parent was allowing subsidiaries to operate in the Soviet market with virtually a free hand, each subsidiary was considered a separate company for survey purposes. (This was consistent with the definition of a "company" as a business entity capable of making major marketing decisions on an independent basis.) Conversely, when it was evident that Soviet business activity throughout the conglomerate had been closely controlled and coordinated by the central headquarters staff, the parent company was retained in the survey population while affiliates were crossed off the list. Where the parent company and a subsidiary had explored Soviet business—but independently of one another—both were retained in the survey population.

Financial support for the 1976 survey also enabled a follow-up inquiry to be sent to all executives who failed to respond to the two successive waves of survey questionnaires mailed out during the summer of 1976. The purpose of this inquiry was to determine reasons for the

failure to respond (see below, p. 100). This exercise
yielded a total of 25 firms the executives of which
reported only limited or insignificant contacts with the
Soviets, or said that all company contacts were being
handled through an intermediary (e.g., a trading company,
an agent, or via subcontracted business) or through foreign
subsidiaries. Clearly, these firms should not have been
included in the survey population in the first place.

Finally, a number of additional ex post facto checks
were employed to enhance further the accuracy of both
survey populations. First, incoming questionnaires from
Survey 1 and Survey 2 were screened according to responses
on four questions designed to verify that the company had
indeed explored or been involved in business with the
U.S.S.R. Companies that clearly had had no significant
Soviet contacts were eliminated from the respective survey
population and their returned questionnaires were
discarded. Similarly, if in response to a query on "your
company's main office location" the respondent entered a
foreign main office location (e.g., in the case of a U.S.
subsidiary of a foreign-based multinational corporation)
then that company also was excluded from the relevant trade
actor population. This was to insure that both lists of
companies surveyed would consist exclusively of "American"
companies as defined earlier (see p. 45).

Utilizing the above procedures, additions and subtractions from the Forum lists yielded a final population of 225 trade actor companies for the 1975 survey and 386 companies for the 1976 survey. The exhaustive efforts just described render it likely that both groups of companies surveyed closely approximated a universe of trade actor companies at their respective points in time. This is especially probable of Survey 2, where increased funding permitted special measures to target the trade actor population with great precision. In any event, both surveys included virtually all major U.S. companies responsible for the bulk of U.S.-Soviet trade in 1975-1976. While it is conceivable that a few small trade actor firms were inadvertently excluded, it is unlikely that this could have had a meaningful impact on the validity of the surveys.

Lastly, it should be noted that in February 1978 the Washington Forum released its most recent update of U.S. companies that have sought commercial ties with the U.S.S.R. Interestingly, this list shows only marginal variation from the Forum's September 1975 inventory. This suggests that most U.S. firms inclined to do business with the Soviets had already approached the market by the time of Survey 2. If the trade actor population indeed has remained basically unchanged since 1976, then the findings

of Survey 2 and associated linkage processes have special
relevance to present and future U.S.-Soviet relations.
Linkages, it must be remembered, are not discrete events
but rather are patterns of behavior which can reoccur.

Survey Sampling of Soviet Area Executives

A Soviet Area Executive, it will be recalled, has been
defined as a senior company executive, stationed in the U.S.,
who has exercised prime responsibility for his firm's existing
or prospective business relations with the Soviet Union.
Consistent with the International Trade Politics Model, it was
necessary in both surveys to pinpoint the correct executive in
each trade actor company in the respective survey
populations.  This difficult task was rendered even more
formidable by the fact that most companies employ more than
one executive on their U.S.S.R. business staffs, thereby
requiring the outside analyst to identify Soviet Area
Executives from among their subordinates.

Survey 1

Several complementary procedures were used in Survey 1
to locate Soviet Area Executives in trade actor companies.
First, a thorough search of publicly available information
was conducted to find the names and titles of candidates
for the survey population.  Next, these candidates were
appraised using the SAE categorization system described

below (see p. 89). Questionnaires were then mailed to
those individuals who appeared to qualify as Soviet Area
Executives. Where specific names could not readily be
ascertained, each trade actor company was mailed three
questionnaires, addressed to the firm's President, Chairman
of the Board, and Vice President International. By blan-
keting each firm in this manner, it was anticipated that
each company's information filtering processes would route
at least one of the questionnaires to the senior company
official responsible for Soviet business. Returned
questionnaires were scrutinized carefully to eliminate
possible multiple responses from those companies that
received three questionnaires. This was achieved through
painstaking evaluation of a series of questions on personal
and company variables such as the respondent's age, place
of birth, the number of people employed by the firm, the
company's main office location, net sales volume, etc.
This review confirmed that most companies that received
three questionnaires only responded with one, a fact which
indicates that corporate information routing practices are
more efficient than had been supposed. Apparently, all
three questionnaires usually ended up on the desk of the
company's current Soviet Area Executive, who almost
invariably provided the firm's sole response. In

retrospect, therefore, it probably would have been sufficient to send only one questionnaire to each company.

## Survey 2

As noted above, additional funding support for Survey 2 permitted telephone canvassing of all firms in the 1976 trade actor population. This provided the analyst with a unique opportunity to pinpoint the Soviet Area Executive in each company. Thus, during telephone conversations with each firm's public relations officer, inquiries were made to find out the name and mailing address of "the senior executive in your company who is currently handling your firm's business relations with the U.S.S.R." A questionnaire was then addressed specifically to that individual. Only 5 companies categorically refused to provide the name of their Soviet Area Executive. In those cases, the questionnaire was simply mailed to the Vice President International (or an equivalent) of the firm, whose name was secured from the Standard & Poor's Directory or a similar source. (Drawing on the lessons of Survey 1, it was expected that the questionnaire would eventually be routed to the correct executive, if other than the addressee.) Public relations officials in 16 other companies said that it would "take some time" for them to locate their Soviet Area Executive. In these instances, the questionnaire was mailed to the PR executive for referral.

Targeting of Soviet Area Executives via telephone
canvassing undoubtedly reduced the influence of corporate
information routing practices on the sampling process. The
procedure was especially helpful in minimizing the number
of questionnaires filled out by junior executives or those
with little functional responsibility for Soviet business.
Finally, it also enabled questionnaire cover letters and
envelopes to be addressed individually using the
executive's name and correct title; a widely accepted
technique for increasing the response rate of mail
surveys. Consequently, although both samples are
undoubtedly highly representative, the sample obtained from
Survey 2 is likely to be somewhat more accurate than that
which resulted from Survey 1.

## Screening Procedures

In order to distinguish SAEs from lower level
executives, an executive classification scheme was
developed and applied in both surveys. Specifically, to
qualify as a Soviet Area Executive a corporate official had
to fall into one of four occupational roles:

1. Principal Senior Executive. This designation
typically describes either the President or Chairman of
the Board. In some cases, this classification also may
include the "division manager" (in General Motors, for
example). It designates a top decision-making rank.
Also included within this category are positions such
as General Manager and Executive Vice President.

2. <u>Senior International Executive</u>. This category designates a top company officer who is charged with devising or managing international programs. Most often, such executives hold a title such as Vice President International; though occasionally with large firms "U.S.S.R. Vice President" or something similar is used. These executives often have a strong "sales" orientation.

3. <u>Senior All-Purpose Executive</u>. This category is usually marked by the title of Executive Vice President or Senior Vice President, but also includes vice presidents "without portfolio." These individuals are usually generalists who may be charged with looking into the possibilities for entry into new international markets along with a score of other duties. Also, they may oversee the development of such new programs.

4. <u>Senior Operations Specialist</u>. In many firms, the operational end of Soviet or other "exotic" marketing is handed over to a Project Manager, Sales Manager, Group Vice President, or someone with a similar title indicating that he is either a product specialist or responsible for coming up with new ideas and developing concepts. In any case, this category describes executives who are charged by nature of their <u>other</u> specialty with getting into the international market.

These categories were based on functional criteria because of the bewildering proliferation of unique titles within American business. They were, for research purposes, both exclusive and exhaustive. Using the above classification scheme, all returned questionnaires in both surveys were screened to verify that they had been filled out by relevant company executives. This was accomplished in part by evaluating responses to a question on "your company position." Another important aspect of the screening process in both surveys was an examination of replies to a question asking whether the respondent had "ever been involved in a decision relative to a business deal with the Soviet Union." Where it was evident that the returned questionnaire had been completed by a junior executive and/or a person not involved in Soviet business, that questionnaire was omitted from the respective survey's final sample. Elimination of these questionnaires from the samples had the effect of slightly reducing survey response rates, since the pertinent trade actor companies were still counted as part of the survey populations.

## Questionnaire Development

### Survey 1

Selection of questions for Survey 1 was guided primarily by the findings of background research conducted throughout 1974 and early 1975. This research suggested some likely, although extremely general, SAE viewpoints on key U.S.-U.S.S.R. economic and political issues. Survey 1, therefore, was undertaken mainly to identify these viewpoints with greater precision and to verify scientifically their presence among SAEs in the entire trade actor population.

Translating findings from background research into items for the questionnaire required great care in order to avoid prejudicing survey results. Construction of questions and questionnaire format was influenced considerably by advice from specialists in market analysis

familiar with problems of surveying business executives.
In addition, the questionnaire was submitted to the
scrutiny of a number of high-level business executives who
were not part of the survey population. As a result of
these steps, numerous qualifiers and intensifying terms
were inserted in the questionnaire and certain phrases
changed or deleted to increase clarity and eliminate bias.
Also, it was deemed advisable to adopt a highly structured
questionnaire format consisting primarily of questions
which could be answered by entering a check ($\checkmark$) on
agree-disagree/yes-no scales. By designing the
questionnaire to be easy to complete in a minimum of time
and by giving it a neat, crisp appearance, it was hoped to
enhance the response rate and overcome the business
community's general resistance to survey analysis.
Response rates on questionnaires sent to businesses are
typically extremely low, largely because companies are
routinely inundated with survey requests (from government,
marketing/consulting organizations, research institutes,
etc.) which can add significantly to a firm's operating
costs.

The final survey instrument consisted of 44 questions,
equally divided between subjective attitudinal items and
objective inquiries (e.g., age, religion, corporate
income). The latter were included to obtain a profile of

Soviet Area Executives and their companies as well as to test possible causal relationships between executive viewpoints and conventional political and sociological research variables. An ordinal scoring system was applied to all the attitudinal items and, where appropriate, to some of the objective questions as well. All items were given a variable name or number.

Lastly, it should be pointed out that a scale labelled the "Detente Index" was constructed arithmetically from several attitudinal items on the questionnaire. The Detente Index was designed to measure the respondent's overall attitude toward continuance of detente--without specifically featuring that term. It consisted of four questions, each of which focussed on one of the major conceptual components of U.S.-Soviet detente: trade, scientific cooperation, cultural exchange, and diplomatic (i.e., political) relations. Each component question was phrased to elicit an opinion concerning the continued desirability of expanded Soviet-American contacts in each of the aforementioned areas. Scoring of the Detente Index was accomplished through summation of weighted responses to each question.

## Survey 2

Selection of questions for the 1976 survey was determined primarily by findings of Survey 1. Results of the first exercise led to considerably more ambitious goals for the second survey. These goals, as mentioned earlier, were to acquire additional detail on executive attitudes, to resolve new questions raised by the initial survey, and to trace the evolution of some key variables during the important period following the passage of the Jackson-Vanik Amendment. Consequently, it is not surprising that the resulting questionnaire for Survey 2 was almost twice as long as that used for Survey 1.

Because of the length of Survey 2 and for reasons described above, it was decided to employ the highly structured questionnaire format used previously. Following the procedure employed in Survey 1, framing of questions again was guided by the advice of business survey research specialists. Likewise, the questionnaire was pre-tested on several senior business executives. As was true in the 1975 effort, these precautions substantially enhanced the precision and objectivity of the survey instrument.

Eighty-four questions comprised the final questionnaire, consisting of 64 attitudinal inquiries and 20 objective items. Since the format was similar to that of Survey 1, the same ordinal scoring procedures were used for most items. Again, all questions were assigned a variable name or number.

Unlike Survey 1, Survey 2 did not incorporate a comprehensive Detente Index due to space limitations on the questionnaire. Instead, only one of the component questions from the Index was retained, that being the question seeking the respondent's attitude toward the continued desirability of expanded trade with the Soviet Union. It was assumed, based on the findings of Survey 1, that this single query would be an accurate and sufficient indicator of any major shift in executive opinion on the concept of detente.

Finally, unlike Survey 1, all questionnaires mailed in Survey 2 were inconspicuously coded by number to allow the analyst to identify responding companies. This was done to permit follow-up questionnaires to be sent to non-respondents, to simplify the subsequent screening of incoming questionnaires, and to facilitate the selection of a sample of executives for personal interviews.

### Questionnaire Transmittal

#### Survey 1

To maximize the response rate to Survey 1, an instructional cover letter was included with each questionnaire describing the survey as an independent academic research project "to determine accurately, for the first time, attitudes of the American business community on issues related to U.S.-Soviet trade and detente."

Consistent with the methodology described above, most
letters were addressed by corporate title to either the
"President," "Chairman of the Board," or "Vice President
International," although some were addressed individually
by name. Recipients were informed that they were part of a
"select group of prominent U.S. international businessmen"
and that their participation in the survey was therefore
important to the success of the project. In return for
their cooperation, respondents were offered a summary of
research results upon separate request. To ease fears that
individual responses might be identified publicly, the
executives were assured that "all data analysis will be
made at the aggregate level. We will be dealing only with
anonymous totals." In closing, the recipient was asked to
return the questionnaire in an enclosed postpaid envelope
by June 30, 1975. All questionnaires were mailed from June
15-23, giving recipients an ample 1-2 week period to
respond.

## Survey 2

The transmittal procedure used for Survey 2 was
similar to that of Survey 1, but involved several important
differences intended to boost the response rate. First,
the telephone canvassing described earlier enabled all
cover letters to be addressed individually by name and
corporate title. In addition, having just received funding

support for this study, an effort was made to lend additional legitimacy and prestige to the survey by describing it as part of a project "being sponsored by the Ford Foundation through the International Studies Association." Most importantly, whereas Survey 1 was based on a single mass mailing, additional funding for Survey 2 permitted two successive waves of questionnaires.

The first group of questionnaires was mailed from July 15-20, 1976, with recipients being asked to complete and return the questionnaire by August 6. Subsequently, in the hope of enhancing the response rate, a second set of questionnaires was sent between September 8-9 to those executives who failed to respond (i.e., non-respondents) to the July request. Questionnaires and cover letters used in this second wave were identical to those employed in July, except that it was necessary to cite a new deadline return date of September 21.

### Summary of Rejection Criteria

Consistent with the above sampling procedures and in keeping with the definitions of a "trade actor" and "Soviet Area Executive," incoming questionnaires from Survey 1 and Survey 2 were screened and rejected if the respondent: (1) said that his company had never explored or been involved in business with the U.S.S.R., (2) entered a foreign main office location (e.g., in the case of a U.S. subsidiary of

a foreign-based multinational company), (3) clearly
indicated that he was not a senior level company executive,
or (4) said that he personally had never been involved in a
business decision concerning the U.S.S.R. Furthermore, as
noted earlier, returned questionnaires from Survey 1 were
screened to preclude more than one questionnaire from any
given company from being incorporated into the survey
sample. Where more than one questionnaire was returned
from a particular company, the response received from that
company's Soviet Area Executive was retained in the sample
while all others were deleted. In rare instances where it
was difficult to determine which response had come from the
current SAE, the questionnaire first received was selected
for the sample.

The possibility of multiple responses was minimized in
Survey 2 because all companies initially were provided with
only one questionnaire apiece. Nonetheless, there was some
danger of double counting after September 8, 1976, when the
second wave of questionnaires was sent to non-respondents.
After that date all incoming questionnaires were screened
accordingly using the company identification system
previously noted. When it was clear that two questionnaires had come from the same firm, the aforementioned
elimination procedure employed in Survey 1 was utilized
(see p. 87).

## Response Rates

Survey 1 yielded a total of 123 responses. As a result of the rigorous screening process detailed above, it was necessary to reject 14 of the returned questionnaires from the sample, leaving 109 valid cases. These 109 questionnaires translate into a 48.4% response rate for a final population of 225 trade actor companies.

For Survey 2, a total of 178 responses were received from the first group of questionnaires mailed in July. The second wave of questionnaires yielded another 40 questionnaires, bringing the total to 218. Fifteen of these questionnaires were subsequently rejected from the sample, resulting in 203 valid cases. Given 386 companies in the final survey population, this meant a response rate of 52.6% for Survey 2.

By accepted standards of survey research, both the 1975 and 1976 surveys achieved extremely high rates of return given the limitations of mail questionnaires. Background research has revealed only one other comparable mail survey that has attained a superior response. Nonetheless, as outlined below, a final effort was made to dispel any remaining doubts about the representativeness of the samples.

Bias Test

Despite highly satisfactory rates of return, the analyst was aware that both surveys might be heavily biased due to self-selection factors which can affect any mail survey's response patterns.  In particular, attitide/ opinion distributions indicated by both surveys suggested the possibility that most responses had come from those executives and companies that had been <u>successful</u> in business dealings with the Soviets.  Conversely, it was hypothesized that those who had had unfavorable experiences might be disinclined to complete the two questionnaires. If this occurred to any substantial degree, then both surveys would be invalidated.

Funding support for Survey 2 permitted the analyst to test for this possibility.  To determine reasons for non-response, a follow-up inquiry was mailed to those executives who had failed to respond to the two successive waves of survey questionnaires that were sent out during July-September 1976.  It was assumed that any substantial bias found in the 1976 survey would be a sufficient indicator of similar bias in the 1975 survey.  To maximize the return rate, the follow-up questionnaire was kept extremely short, consisting of a one page "check list" which briefly enumerated potential reasons for non-response.  The addressee was informed that the purpose

of the inquiry was "to determine the general reaction of
American companies to their experiences in the Soviet
market." The recipient was also told that the inquiry was
"a continuation of a study funded by the Ford Foundation
through the International Studies Association." However,
no mention was made of the two previous questionnaires that
had been sent to the addressee. Lastly, recipients were
instructed to "check below one or more of the answers which
seem most appropriate."

The follow-up inquiry was mailed to 193 non-
respondents and resulted in 71 replies, yielding a 36.8%
rate of return. Considering that this group had already
demonstrated stiff resistance to survey analysis, the
response rate was surprisingly good. Results are shown in
Table 1. Of the 71 executives who replied, only 21%
indicated some degree of negativism vis-a-vis their
U.S.S.R. business experiences. In contrast, almost 34%
said that they had had productive contacts with the Soviets
and expressed optimism about the future. An additional 35%
(25 executives) reported that their firms had had only
limited or insignificant contacts with the U.S.S.R., or
indicated that all company contacts were being handled
through foreign subsidiaries or intermediaries (e.g., a
trading company, an agent, or via subcontracted business).
These 25 firms should not have been surveyed in the first

TABLE 1

PROFILE OF NON-RESPONDENTS, 1976 SURVEY

| | Percent | F |
|---|---|---|
| Our company has not had <u>any</u> significant contacts with the Soviets in recent years. | 21.1 | 15 |
| In recent years, all significant contacts we have had with Soviet trade organizations have been <u>indirect</u> contacts through an intermediary (e.g., a trading company, an agent, or via subcontracted business) or through our foreign subsidiaries. | 8.5 | 6 |
| We have had only extremely limited and incidental contacts with the Soviets, and do not view the U.S.S.R. as an important growth market for our company. | 5.6 | 4 |
| In recent years our company has had significant contacts with the U.S.S.R., but we are not as interested in this market as we once were <u>because more attractive international markets have opened up.</u> | 4.2 | 3 |
| In recent years our company has had significant contacts with the Soviets, but we are not as interested in this market as we once were <u>because our domestic business has been on the upswing.</u> | 2.8 | 2 |
| Our company has had significant contacts with the Soviets over the past few years, but so far no significant business has materialized. Therefore, because of the time and expenses involved, we have abandoned active efforts to penetrate this market. | 7.0 | 5 |
| In recent years our company has done significant business with the U.S.S.R., but we do not feel it has been worthwhile. Therefore, we are no longer really interested in actively pursuing the Soviet market at this time. | 1.4 | 1 |
| Our company has had productive contacts with the Soviets in recent years, and we are optimistic for the future. | 33.8 | 24 |
| In recent years our company has had productive contacts with the Soviets, but we are pessimistic about the future of this market because of the difficulties in financing. | 5.6 | 4 |
| Our company has a standing policy of not responding to inquiries of this type. | 5.6 | 4 |
| Other. | 4.2 | 3 |

N=71

place because they did not meet criteria specified in the
Trade Politics Model. Six percent said that their company
has a standing policy of not responding to questionnaires,
and about 4% provided miscellaneous other responses.

If these results are representative of the remaining
non-respondents, then it is evident that the propensity to
respond to Survey 2--and by implication Survey 1--was not
significantly dependent on favorable or unfavorable company
business experiences with the U.S.S.R. Thus, this
variable does not appear to have introduced meaningful bias
into the findings of both surveys. Instead, failure to
respond to the surveys appears principally due to a
combination of other factors: inadvertent inclusion in the
surveys of firms having only marginal Soviet contacts, the
desire of many companies to keep confidential their views
on U.S.-Soviet economic and political issues, the busy
schedule of many executives which often does not allow time
to complete questionnaires, and standing corporate policies
against participation in surveys of all kinds.

## Interview Techniques

In addition to the comprehensive 1975-1976 surveys,
supplementary funding permitted a series of personal
interviews with SAEs to be conducted throughout the United
States from August 9-September 3, 1976. The primary
purpose of these interviews was to acquire added insight

into the more structured data accumulated from surveys and background research. Thus, during each interview the analyst pursued three interrelated objectives: (1) to stimulate the participant to elaborate freely on his views, thus supplying illuminating details, (2) to clear up evident paradoxes in data already collected, and (3) to obtain new data through verbal replies to open-ended oral questions. Such data is vital and could not be secured in any other way. Finally, during interviews an effort was also made to acquire various important psychological intangibles, which are impossible to glean by other methods.

To achieve the aforementioned goals, 28 executives were chosen for interviews from among the respondents to Survey 2. In view of financial constraints and the analyst's limited objective of supplementing data already collected, a scientifically determined interview sample was not a primary nor a necessary objective. Rather, the following criteria were employed to select executives for interviews:

Geographical Accessibility: As a result of economic necessity, executives of companies located in the Midwest dominated the interview sample, accounting for 62% of the firms visited. The Chicago-Detroit-Cleveland-Pittsburgh corridor provided the best opportunity for cost-effective travel.

Level of Company Technology: Given the centrality of technology transfer issues to national security debates on U.S.-Soviet trade, a concerted effort was made to interview a sub-sample of executives representing companies possessing so-called "high technology." Approximately 48% of the entire interview sample consisted of such companies. Of this 48%, half were interviews with West Coast companies dealing in "frontier" technologies (e.g., state-of-the-art electronics, scientific instrumentation, optical/electro-optical, and photographic equipment)

Involvement in a "Scientific-Technical" Cooperation Agreement: Again, in view of the consistent controversy surrounding U.S.-Soviet technology transfer issues, it was deemed advisable to include in the interview sample a number of U.S. firms which had signed scientific and technical (S&T) exchange agreements with the U.S.S.R. Executives of 8 of these companies were visited, representing about 16% of the approximately 50 U.S. firms which had concluded such S&T agreements as of September 1976.

Discussion of other salient characteristics of the interview sample is provided in the following chapters, and is deferred for the time being in order to facilitate more effective comparison with overall patterns in the 1976 survey data.

Executives who agreed to personal interviews were assured in advance that all statements made would be reported in anonymous form only. Hence, all interview data in the following text are presented in such a way so as to render individual executives and companies unidentifiable. The interviews themselves were generally relaxed and frank question and answer sessions that lasted an average of 1 hour and 45 minutes each. However, although relatively unstructured, interviews were not freestyle conversations. During each session, the analyst was guided by a prepared question and answer sheet which insured that key matters

would be brought up in a methodical manner. Subject matter
for the interview questionnaire included items which could
not be accommodated by the highly structured format used
for both surveys, points raised by contradictions in survey
findings, and new issues which occasionally surfaced during
the course of interview discussions. As a result of the
latter, the questionnaire was revised continuously in order
to extract as much useful information as possible from
remaining interviews. The final version of the interview
questionnaire consisted of 19 questions.

## Survey Data Processing

Attitudinal data obtained from the 1975 and 1976
surveys were subjected to intensive statistical analysis to
ascertain theoretically relevant patterns in the data.
Toward this objective, computer programs of the Statistical
Package for the Social Sciences (SPSS) were utilized
throughout. The SPSS is the most widely used and
comprehensive set of computer programs specifically
tailored to the manipulation of social science data.[1]
All SPSS programs were executed using the Burroughs 6812
computer at Kent State University.

To achieve a clear picture of executive viewpoints,
the first step in the data analysis procedure was to
produce simple frequency distributions for all variables in
each survey. Next, to identify and clarify underlying

attitude dimensions which might contribute to linkage
processes, attitudinal data were subjected to intensive
R-factor analyses and crosstabulations. Finally, Q-factor
analyses were conducted on both sets of data in order to
construct typologies of like-minded executives whose shared
viewpoints could predispose them toward behavior having
important implications for U.S.-Soviet relations. To
facilitate future work by other analysts, additional
details on the R and Q-factor procedures employed in this
study are provided below.[2]

Data Analysis Mechanics:  R-Factor Analysis

To obtain initial (i.e., unrotated) R-factor matrices
from each set of survey data, attitudinal variables from
each survey were factor analyzed employing principal
component analysis. For this purpose, the SPSS PA1 program
was utilized. The principal component method was chosen
because, unlike alternative inferential factoring
techniques, it alone incorporates no prior assumptions
about the underlying structure of the data.[3] After
obtaining initial factor matrices from each set of data,
the analyst experimented with various methods of rotation
to obtain the most meaningful terminal solutions. After
careful evaluation of results, the widely-used Varimax
method was selected over other orthogonal techniques and
was preferred to oblique rotation. Among orthogonal

methods, Varimax rotation, which in essence maximizes the variance of squared factor loadings in each column, characteristically produced the most clearly defined factors. At the same time, Varimax offered the advantage of a relatively simple output format, where a single rotated factor matrix represents both factor pattern and factor structure matrices. Oblique rotation, on the other hand, lacked this feature although it did produce slightly better defined factors. This small gain in empirical precision, however, was deemed not sufficiently meaningful to justify the introduction of additional mathematical complexity to the analysis.[4]

Preliminary R-factor analyses of each survey incorporated all attitudinal variables in an effort to detect the possible presence of even the most diffuse attitude dimensions. Next, having identified a number of meaningful attitude complexes in each survey, further factor analyses were conducted to obtain more precise definition of these theoretically important dimensions. Hence, attitudinal variables which loaded only on uninterpretable factors and those having only weak correlations with meaningful dimensions were gradually eliminated from successive factor analyses.[5] This procedure resulted in a highly parsimonious solution for the 1975 survey data, yielding a final total of 3 factors

extracted from 12 attitudinal variables (Table 35). The
solution for the 1976 survey, however, was considerably
more complex, consisting of 7 factors derived from 23
variables (Table 38).

Consistent with the principle of parsimony, an effort
was subsequently made to simplify further the 1976 data,
employing higher-order factor analysis for this purpose.
Thus, drawing once again on the SPSS factor program, factor
scores were generated for all 203 cases in the 1976 survey
on each of the 7 first-order factors, thereby producing a
203 x 7 factor score matrix. In this way, then, the 7
first-order factors were in effect transformed into 7
composite variables corresponding to the respective columns
of the aforementioned matrix. Put differently, 7 "new"
variables were created from 7 factors themselves made up of
variables. Next, the 7 composite factor score variables
were subjected to factor analysis--i.e., the first-order
factors were themselves factored in an attempt to identify
second-order factors representing broad attitude complexes
present in the data.[6] The end result of this procedure
was a highly parsimonious solution for the 1976 survey
consisting of three theoretically meaningful second-order
factors (Table 39).

Data Analysis Mechanics: Q-Factor Analysis

In the early stages of this project, all survey data were initially coded and arranged following the standard procedure whereby each computer data record represents a specific entity (case) and the record's columns register the entity's scores on various characteristics (variables). Data from the 1975 survey were therefore ordered in a 109 x 44 matrix with cases in the rows and variables in the columns. Similarly, 1976 survey data were arranged in a 203 x 84 matrix, again with cases down the left side and variables across the top (Figure 4a). Since computers normally manipulate data read in columns, this matrix format was essential to produce the frequency distributions, crosstabulations, and R-factor analyses necessary for this study. These statistical procedures, like most methods of aggregate data analysis in political science, focus on the collective characteristics of numerous cases (whether these cases are individuals, interest groups, or nations) and the relationships between these characteristics.

Q-factor analysis stands in marked contrast to the aforementioned techniques. To construct typologies, Q-analysis correlates entities--not their characteristics. Therefore, an entirely different type of data array is required, one where the usual matrix positions of entities

# FIGURE 4. COMPARISON OF R AND Q DATA MATRICES

a. Matrix format for R-analysis.

|  | Variables | | | | | | |
|---|---|---|---|---|---|---|---|
| Cases | $V_1$ | $V_2$ | $V_3$ | . | . | . | $V_N$ |
| $C_1$ | $C_1V_1$ | $C_1V_2$ | $C_1V_3$ | . | . | . | $C_1V_N$ |
| $C_2$ | $C_2V_1$ | $C_2V_2$ | $C_2V_3$ | . | . | . | $C_2V_N$ |
| $C_3$ | $C_3V_1$ | $C_3V_2$ | $C_3V_3$ | . | . | . | $C_3V_N$ |
| . | . | . | . | . | | | . |
| . | . | . | . | . | | | . |
| . | . | . | . | . | | | . |
| $C_N$ | $C_NV_1$ | $C_NV_2$ | $C_NV_3$ | . | . | . | $C_NV_N$ |

b. Matrix format for Q-analysis.

|  | Cases | | | | | | |
|---|---|---|---|---|---|---|---|
| Variables | $C_1$ | $C_2$ | $C_3$ | . | . | . | $C_N$ |
| $V_1$ | $V_1C_1$ | $V_1C_2$ | $V_1C_3$ | . | . | . | $V_1C_N$ |
| $V_2$ | $V_2C_1$ | $V_2C_2$ | $V_2C_3$ | . | . | . | $V_2C_N$ |
| $V_3$ | $V_3C_1$ | $V_3C_2$ | $V_3C_3$ | . | . | . | $V_3C_N$ |
| . | . | . | . | . | | | . |
| . | . | . | . | . | | | . |
| . | . | . | . | . | | | . |
| $V_N$ | $V_NC_1$ | $V_NC_2$ | $V_NC_3$ | . | . | . | $V_NC_N$ |

and their characteristics are transposed. In other words,
variables become cases and cases become variables. After
this reversal of positions, each computer record then
represents a specific variable and the record's 80 columns
register the scores of numerous cases on that variable
(Figure 4b).[7]

A simple FORTRAN computer program was therefore
developed to transpose each data matrix. However, rather
than transposing all variables in each set of data, the
analyst transposed only those variables which had been
retained in each survey's final R-factor analysis (Figures
5a and 5b). This procedure, it was believed, would yield
the most clearly defined, meaningful typologies; a
conclusion based on the well-founded assumption that
earlier frequency distributions, crosstabulations, and
successive R-factor analyses had identified those variables
with the greatest theoretical potential. Consequently,
transposed 1975 survey data yielded a matrix with 12
variables down the left hand side and 109 cases across the
top. Similarly, a 23 x 203 transposed matrix was generated
for the 1976 survey.[8]

Next, efforts were directed at initiating the
factoring process. This step was hampered, however, by a
serious limitation of the SPSS factor analysis
program--i.e., its inability to process more than 100 items

**FIGURE 5. TRANSPOSING SELECTED VARIABLES FROM R TO Q FORMAT**

a. Before transposing to Q format.

$$
\begin{array}{c}
 \\ C_1 \\ C_2 \\ C_3 \\ \cdot \\ \cdot \\ \cdot \\ C_N
\end{array}
\begin{array}{c}
\begin{array}{ccccccc} V_1 & V_2 & V_3 & \cdot & \cdot & \cdot & V_N \end{array} \\
\begin{bmatrix}
C_1V_1 & C_1V_2 & C_1V_3 & \cdot & \cdot & \cdot & C_1V_N \\
C_2V_1 & C_2V_2 & C_2V_3 & \cdot & \cdot & \cdot & C_2V_N \\
C_3V_1 & C_3V_2 & C_3V_3 & \cdot & \cdot & \cdot & C_3V_N \\
\cdot & \cdot & \cdot & \cdot & \cdot & \cdot & \cdot \\
\cdot & \cdot & \cdot & \cdot & \cdot & \cdot & \cdot \\
\cdot & \cdot & \cdot & \cdot & \cdot & \cdot & \cdot \\
C_NV_1 & C_NV_2 & C_NV_3 & \cdot & \cdot & \cdot & C_NV_N
\end{bmatrix}
\end{array}
$$

b. After transposing to Q format, with variable 2 excluded.

$$
\begin{array}{c}
 \\ V_1 \\ \\ V_3 \\ \cdot \\ \cdot \\ \cdot \\ V_N
\end{array}
\begin{array}{c}
\begin{array}{ccccccc} C_1 & C_2 & C_3 & \cdot & \cdot & \cdot & C_N \end{array} \\
\begin{bmatrix}
V_1C_1 & V_1C_2 & V_1C_3 & \cdot & \cdot & \cdot & V_1C_N \\
 & & & & & & \\
V_3C_1 & V_3C_2 & V_3C_3 & \cdot & \cdot & \cdot & V_3C_N \\
\cdot & \cdot & \cdot & \cdot & \cdot & \cdot & \cdot \\
\cdot & \cdot & \cdot & \cdot & \cdot & \cdot & \cdot \\
\cdot & \cdot & \cdot & \cdot & \cdot & \cdot & \cdot \\
V_NC_1 & V_NC_2 & V_NC_3 & \cdot & \cdot & \cdot & V_NC_N
\end{bmatrix}
\end{array}
$$

in a single run. Put differently, the SPSS factor package
can manipulate a correlation matrix whose maximum
dimensions are no larger than 100 x 100.[9] This problem
was overcome for the 1975 data by simply eliminating the
last 9 out of the 109 total cases in the survey. Because
all cases in the data matrix were ordered randomly and
since only 8.2% of all cases were affected, this solution
presented only minimal possibilities for distortion of
findings. Subsequently, the remaining 100 cases were
Q-factor analyzed, again using the PA1 Varimax technique
discussed above.[10] This factoring process resulted in
ten factors, three of which were well-defined, meaningful
categories of executives that are discussed in the text
below (Table 37). Identification of these important
typologies from among error factors and the usual
uninterpretable factor "noise" was facilitated by
computer-generated factor scores for each of the 12
variables on each factor produced (Table 36). These scores
enabled the analyst to delineate a distinctive attitude
profile characteristic of executives falling into a given
category. Finally, as a further aid to interpretation,
frequency distributions for attitudinal variables were
computed for those cases having high loadings on
theoretically important factors. Thus, for example,
frequency tables summarizing responses on attitudinal

variables were generated for those 36 executives who correlated highly on Factor 1.

Q-factor analysis of the 1976 survey data proved considerably more difficult than for the 1975 study. Meeting the 100 item limitation of the SPSS factor program would have required deletion of 103 out of a total of 203 cases, representing 50.7% of all collected data. Such a solution would have risked substantial distortion of research findings and therefore clearly was not acceptable. As a result, it was necessary to devise an alternative, more complex factoring strategy.

First, while wholesale deletion of data was not permissible, it was necessary and acceptable to eliminate from further analysis the last 3 out of the survey's 203 total cases. (Again, only a tiny 0.8% of the randomly ordered data were affected, thus minimizing chances for introducing bias to the study.) Next, the remaining 200 cases in the data matrix were divided into two sub-groups, labeled A and B, consisting of the first hundred and the second hundred cases, respectively. These two sub-groups were then factored separately from one another, resulting in 18 factors (i.e., typologies) for Group A and 19 for Group B. Factor scores were also calculated for factors in each sub-group, yielding a 23 x 18 factor score matrix for A and a 23 x 19 matrix for B. These factor scores allowed

the analyst to ascertain some interesting, distinctive
typologies within each subgroup of executives. However,
while this provided some solid clues to likely overall
patterns in the data, composite typologies incorporating
all 200 cases were necessary to obtain a complete, accurate
categorization of executives.

To achieve this objective, the analyst employed a
variate of the technique previously utilized to arrive at a
second-order R-factor solution for the 1976 data.
Recalling that factor scores for a given factor allow the
treatment of that factor as a composite variable, the two
separate sets of factor scores generated for each sub-group
of executives were combined into a single data matrix.
These composite factor score variables were then themselves
factored to produce higher-order factors representing
comprehensive typologies of executives. Put differently,
this meant factoring the original factors in an effort to
identify correlations between factors extracted from Group
A and those derived from B.[11]

Before the second-order factoring could be executed,
however, substantial manipulation of the data was necessary
to merge the factor score matrices of the two sub-groups
and arrange the resulting combined matrix in the format
required for Q-analysis. First, the two factor score
matrices were entered in separate data files on Kent State

University's Burroughs 6812 computer (Figures 6a and 6b).
The matrix in each file was then transposed employing an
elementary FORTRAN program devised for this purpose. This
yielded an 18 x 23 matrix for Group A and a 19 x 23 matrix
for Group B, with variables in both matrices now listed
across the top rather than down the side (Figures 6c and
6d). Having thus arranged the data so that the variables
in each column were in one-to-one correspondence, it was a
straightforward matter to merge both files via a simple
computer command, thereby producing a single 37 x 23 matrix
(Figure 7a). Next, this combined matrix was itself
transposed, resulting in the 23 constituent variables being
returned to their prior position down the matrix's
left-hand side. Note, however, that 37 columns were now
situated across the top of the matrix; each column
representing one of the composite factor score variables
originally derived from separate factor analyses of the two
executive sub-groups. Thus, factor scores for the 18
factors extracted from Group A were now listed in the
matrix's first 18 columns, whereas scores for Group B's 19
factors were now positioned in columns 19-37 (Figure 7b).

Having manipulated the factor score data into the
necessary consolidated format, it was now possible to run
the PA1/Varimax factor program. The end result was 18
second-order factors, three of which are meaningful

FIGURE 6. INITIAL TRANSPOSE PROCEDURE FOR FACTOR SCORE MATRICES, EXECUTIVE SUBGROUPS A AND B

a. Original factor score matrix, Group A.

b. Original factor score matrix, Group B.

c. Transposed factor score matrix, Group A.

d. Transposed factor score matrix, Group B.

**FIGURE 7. COMBINING AND TRANSPOSING FACTOR SCORE MATRICES, EXECUTIVE SUB-GROUPS A AND B**

a. Combined factor score matrix, Groups A and B.

|  | $V_1$ | $V_2$ | $V_3$ | $V_4$ | . | . | . | $V_{23}$ |
|---|---|---|---|---|---|---|---|---|
| $fs_{1a}$ | $fs_{1a}V_1$ | $fs_{1a}V_2$ | $fs_{1a}V_3$ | $fs_{1a}V_4$ | . | . | . | $fs_{1a}V_{23}$ |
| $fs_{2a}$ | $fs_{2a}V_1$ | $fs_{2a}V_2$ | $fs_{2a}V_3$ | $fs_{2a}V_4$ | . | . | . | $fs_{2a}V_{23}$ |
| $fs_{3a}$ | $fs_{3a}V_1$ | $fs_{3a}V_2$ | $fs_{3a}V_3$ | $fs_{3a}V_4$ | . | . | . | $fs_{3a}V_{23}$ |
| . | . | . | . | . | . | . | . | . |
| . | . | . | . | . | . | . | . | . |
| . | . | . | . | . | . | . | . | . |
| $fs_{18a}$ | $fs_{18a}V_1$ | $fs_{18a}V_2$ | $fs_{18a}V_3$ | $fs_{18a}V_4$ | . | . | . | $fs_{18a}V_{23}$ |
| $fs_{1b}$ | $fs_{1b}V_1$ | $fs_{1b}V_2$ | $fs_{1b}V_3$ | $fs_{1b}V_4$ | . | . | . | $fs_{1b}V_{23}$ |
| $fs_{2b}$ | $fs_{2b}V_1$ | $fs_{2b}V_2$ | $fs_{2b}V_3$ | $fs_{2b}V_4$ | . | . | . | $fs_{2b}V_{23}$ |
| $fs_{3b}$ | $fs_{3b}V_1$ | $fs_{3b}V_2$ | $fs_{3b}V_3$ | $fs_{3b}V_4$ | . | . | . | $fs_{3b}V_{23}$ |
| . | . | . | . | . | . | . | . | . |
| . | . | . | . | . | . | . | . | . |
| . | . | . | . | . | . | . | . | . |
| $fs_{19b}$ | $fs_{19b}V_1$ | $fs_{19b}V_2$ | $fs_{19b}V_3$ | $fs_{19b}V_4$ | . | . | . | $fs_{19b}V_{23}$ |

b. Combined factor score matrix, Groups A and B, transposed to Q-analysis format.

|  | $fs_{1a}$ | . | $fs_{18a}$ | $fs_{1b}$ | . | . | $fs_{19b}$ |
|---|---|---|---|---|---|---|---|
| $V_1$ | $V_1fs_{1a}$ | . | $V_1fs_{18a}$ | $V_1fs_{1b}$ | . | . | $V_1fs_{19b}$ |
| $V_2$ | $V_2fs_{1a}$ | . | $V_2fs_{18a}$ | $V_2fs_{1b}$ | . | . | $V_2fs_{19b}$ |
| $V_3$ | $V_3fs_{1a}$ | . | $V_3fs_{18a}$ | $V_3fs_{1b}$ | . | . | $V_3fs_{19b}$ |
| $V_4$ | $V_4fs_{1a}$ | . | $V_4fs_{18a}$ | $V_4fs_{1b}$ | . | . | $V_4fs_{19b}$ |
| . | . | . | . | . | . | . | . |
| . | . | . | . | . | . | . | . |
| . | . | . | . | . | . | . | . |
| $V_{23}$ | $V_{23}fs_{1a}$ | . | $V_{23}fs_{18a}$ | $V_{23}fs_{1b}$ | . | . | $V_{23}fs_{19b}$ |

typologies into which falls a substantial proportion of all cases in the 1976 survey (Table 40). Again, as in the case of the 1975 Q-analysis, identification of important typologies was facilitated by computer-generated factor scores (although in this instance for second-order factors rather than for first-order factors) (Table 41). Similarly, frequency distributions were also computed for those cases falling into the most theoretically important categories. For example, for second-order Factor 5, consisting of Factor 1, Group A, and Factor 1, Group B, frequency tables summarizing responses on attitudinal variables were produced for those cases having high loadings on either of the two first-order factors.

FOOTNOTES

[1]Norman H. Nie et al. SPSS:   Statistical Package for
the Social Sciences, 2nd ed. (New York:  McGraw-Hill,
1975); C. Hadlai Hull and Norman H. Nie, eds., SPSS Update:
New Procedures and Facilities for Releases 7 and 8 (New
York:  McGraw-Hill, 1979).

[2]A complete explanation of the mathematical and
conceptual complexities of factor analysis is beyond the
scope of this study.  Suffice it to say that the term
"factor analysis" refers to a host of alternative
techniques for the detection of underlying patterns among a
larger number of measures.  Factor analysis assumes that a
correlation matrix is permeated with the shared variance of
inter-correlated variables and that the variance within the
matrix can be described in terms of a smaller number of
common factors that account for the major part of that
variance.  [Benjamin Fruchter, Introduction to Factor
Analysis (Princeton, N.J.:  Van Nostrand, 1954), p. 44.]  A
factor is thus a hypothetical construct or dimension which
delineates a cluster of variables in a given set of data.
It follows that factor analysis has immense capabilities
for simplifying phenomena, and thereby can help the human
mind overcome inherent limitations for discerning
regularity among large numbers of variables.  When this
data-reduction technique is used to delineate similarities
among individuals, nations or other entities, the analysis
is termed Q-factor analysis.  This procedure, which has had
wide application in taxonomic studies, requires a data
matrix in which variables (columns) refer to entities and
cases (rows) are their characteristics.  Alternatively,
factor analysis employed to discern patterns among the
characteristics of entities is known as R-factor analysis.
This technique, which is the most frequently used factor
procedure in political science, involves factor-analyzing a
data matrix where variables (columns) refer to the
characteristics of entities and cases (rows) refer to the
entities themselves.  For further explanation of factoring
methods see Fruchter, Introduction to Factor Analysis, as
cited above; Frederick N. Kerlinger, Foundations of
Behavioral Research (New York:   Holt, Rinehart, and
Winston, 1964), pp. 659-660; R. J. Rummel, Applied Factor
Analysis (Evanston, Ill.:  Northwestern University Press,
1970), pp. 192-197; R. J. Rummel, "Understanding Factor
Analysis," Journal of Conflict Resolution 11 (December
1967):  444-479.  Also see the excellent non-technical
explanation of the fundamentals of factor analysis in John
H. Daily, "Underlying Patterns of Legislative Voting

Behavior: The Case of the 105th Ohio House of Representatives," (Master's thesis, Kent State University, 1968), pp. 18-36.

[3]Unlike other factor analytic techniques, principal component analysis makes no assumptions about the data having common or unique parts. There is thus no need to make communality estimates, thereby removing a major source of indeterminacy from the factoring process. As Nie explains, the principal component method simply takes the data as given and computes the best linear combination of variables--best in the sense that the particular combination of variables accounts for more variance in the data as a whole than any other linear combination of variables. Successive factors are extracted in this manner, with any given factor representing that linear combination that accounts for the most residual variance after the effect of the previous component is removed from the data. See Nie et al., SPSS, pp. 470-471, 479-480. For further information on alternative methods for the extraction of initial factor matrices see Rummel, Applied Factor Analysis, pp. 112-113, 338-345; Benjamin Fruchter and Earl Jennings, "Factor Analysis," in Computer Applications in the Behavioral Sciences, ed. Harold Borko (Englewood Cliffs, N.J.: Prentice-Hall, 1966), pp. 243-249; and Harry H. Harman, Modern Factor Analysis (Chicago: University of Chicago Press, 1967), pp. 136-146. In an effort to conserve cases, all PA1 programs for the R-factor analyses were executed using Option 2, pairwise deletion of missing data. See Nie, SPSS, pp. 504. A major uncertainty in all factor models concerns the question of when to stop extracting factors. Thorough application of the principal component technique, for example, almost always yields a total number of factors equal to the total number of variables. Clearly this is not a parsimonious reduction of the data. It is therefore desirable to select some criterion which enables one to exclude unimportant factors before rotating the initial factor matrix to a terminal solution. Unfortunately, however, no agreement exists as to the best method for identifying and eliminating trivial or substantively meaningless factors. As Rummel notes, this poses a formidable methodological problem: ". . . in rotation the inclusion or exclusion of one small factor may change the rotated factor structure. In other words, the loading and interpretation of all rotated factors may differ for the same data, preliminary solution, and rotation criterion by virtue of the different number of factors rotated." (Rummel, Applied Factor Analysis, p. 35.)

Although there appears to be no perfect answer to the
number of factors problem, a careful study of relevant
literature led to the decision to employ the widely used
eigenvalue-one criterion for all factor analyses in this
study. This method, which extracts for rotation all those
factors having eigenvalues greater than or equal to one,
treats as significant only those components that account
for at least the total variance of a single variable.
While this procedure, like competing mathematical
approaches, can be criticized on a number of grounds, a
range of studies strongly supports the use of eigenvalue-
one as a stopping point for factor analysis. See, for
example, Henry F. Kaiser, "The Application of Electronic
Computers to Factor Analysis," Educational and
Psychological Measurement 20 (Spring 1960):  141-151; Henry
F. Kaiser, "Image Analysis," in Problems in Measuring
Change, ed. C. W. Harris (Madison:  University of Wisconsin
Press, 1963), pp. 156-166; Louis Guttman, "Some Necessary
Conditions for Common Factor Analysis," Psychometrika 19
(June 1954): 154-155; and Rummel, Applied Factor Analysis,
pp. 359, 362-364. For a comprehensive review of the number
of factors problem and alternative solutions see Rummel,
Applied Factor Analysis, pp. 349-367; Fruchter,
Introduction to Factor Analysis, pp. 77-81; Raymond B.
Cattell, "Extracting the Correct Number of Factors in
Factor Analysis," Educational and Psychological Measurement
18 (Winter 1958):  791-838; Lloyd G. Humphreys and Daniel
R. Ilgen, "Note on a Criterion for the Number of Common
Factors," Educational and Psychological Measurement 29
(Autumn 1969):  571-578; and Lloyd G. Humphreys, "Number of
Cases and Number of Factors:  An Example Where N is Very
Large," Educational and Psychological Measurement 24 (Fall
1964):  457-466.

[4]Factor rotation is a technique whereby reference
vectors (i.e., the factors) extracted from an initial
factor solution (in this instance principal component
analysis) are relocated in an effort to identify clusters
of interrelated variables with greater precision. Rotation
is usually necessary because, more often than not, initial
factors are not easily interpreted. Most rotational
solutions therefore attempt to render results more
meaningful by simplifying the factor matrix, in most
instances through the application of Thurstone's simple
structure concept. Basically, this means relocating the
reference vectors so that each variable loads on as few
factors as possible, and as many zeroes as possible appear
in the resulting rotated factor matrix. Besides obtaining
factors which are easier to interpret, a second major
benefit of rotation is that it produces factors which are

relatively stable. Compared to initial factors, factor
loadings of rotated factors are much less sensitive to the
inclusion or exclusion of a given variable or variables.
It follows, then, that these factors tend to vary less from
one analysis to the next, which greatly facilitates
scientific explanation.

Among the many available rotational techniques, the
major choice for the analyst was whether to select an
orthogonal method or an oblique method. (In orthogonal
rotation, the reference vectors are rotated as a rigid
frame, with each factor joining every other factor at a
right angle. Thus orthogonal factors are in principal
uncorrelated. Oblique methods, on the other hand, permit
each reference axis to rotate freely and individually,
enabling a better fit to each cluster of variables as well
as providing information about the amount of actual
correlation between the factors.) For reasons cited in the
text, the orthogonal Varimax method was preferred to
oblique solutions. According to Harman, the Varimax
solution ". . . seems to be the 'best' parsimonious
analytical solution in the sense that it correlates best
with the intuitive concept of that term. . . ." (Harman,
Modern Factor Analysis, p. 311.) For a thorough treatment
of the computational intricacies of the Varimax method see
Harman, Modern Factor Analysis, pp. 304-309. For
additional details on the concept of simple structure see
Louis L. Thurstone, Multiple-Factor Analysis (Chicago:
University of Chicago Press, 1947), p. 335. Rotational
problems and procedures are discussed in Rummel,
"Understanding Factor Analysis," pp. 473-477; Rummel,
Applied Factor Analysis, pp. 369-394; Fruchter,
Introduction to Factor Analysis, pp. 106-131, 194-196;
Fruchter and Jennings, "Factor Analysis," pp. 249-256;
Kerlinger, Foundations of Behavioral Research, pp. 671-674;
and Nie et al., SPSS, pp. 472-473, 482-486.

[5]Rotated factor solutions frequently contain error
and incidental factors. Depending on the context of the
analysis, the investigator is normally free to display
these factors without interpretation or, alternatively, to
conduct successive factor analyses in an attempt to refine
the data and minimize statistical noise. The latter
course, as the text indicates, necessitates the gradual
removal of superfluous variables from the original
correlation matrix. Unfortunately, statistical criteria
have limited utility in accomplishing this objective.
While error and incidental factors can often be identified
by low factor loadings, they sometimes have high factor
loadings as well. In any event, there exists no clear-cut,
preferred test for determining the statistical significance

of a given factor loading or of the average loading on a
factor. It follows that human judgment based on a
familiarity with the data must play a key role in arriving
at a final factor solution. Statistical tests are
primarily useful as supplementary decision criteria in
instances of uncertainty. In the case of the present
study, the Guilford-Lacey criterion was employed when it
was unclear whether to retain or exclude a given variable
from the respective factor analyses. Using this test, a
loading that exceeds $2.58 \times \frac{1}{\sqrt{n}}$ is significantly different
from 0 at the .01 level. See U.S. Department of Defense,
Army Air Forces Aviation Psychology Program, Printed
Classification Tests, by J. P. Guilford and J. I. Lacey,
Research Report No. 5 (Washington, D.C.: Government
Printing Office, 1947), p. 889. The major literature on
the application of tests of significance to factor loadings
includes the following: M. S. Bartlett, "Tests of
Significance in Factor Analysis," British Journal of
Psychology, Statistical Section 3 (June 1950): 77-85; M.
S. Bartlett, "A Further Note on Tests of Significance in
Factor Analysis," British Journal of Psychology,
Statistical Section 4 (March 1951): 1-2; C. Radhakrishna
Rao, "Estimation and Tests of Significance in Factor
Analysis," Psychometrika 20 (June 1955): 93-111; and Sten
Henrysson, "The Significance of Factor Loadings: Lawley's
Test Examined by Artificial Samples," British Journal of
Psychology, Statistical Section 3 (November 1950):
159-165. For a discussion of the types of experimental and
statistical error often encountered in factor analysis see
Cattell, "Extracting the Correct Number of Factors," pp.
795-799. Problems of interpretation in factor analysis are
reviewed in Rummel, Applied Factor Analysis, pp. 477-479,
and Fruchter, Introduction to Factor Analysis, pp. 149-154.

[6]The SPSS program calculates factor scores for a
case using the formula: $f_i = fsc_{1i}z_1 + fsc_{2i}z_2 + fsc_{3i}z_3 + \ldots + fsc_{ni}z_n$, where $fsc_{ji}$ is the
factor-score coefficient for variable j and factor i, and
$z_j$ is the case's standardized value on variable j. (Nie
et al., SPSS, p. 489.) Like all other formulas for
generating factor scores, the SPSS procedure produces a
score for each case on each factor pattern. In calculating
a factor score for a given case on a given factor, each
variable is first assigned a weight proportional to its
contribution to that factor. Next, the pattern weight of
each variable is multiplied by the case's data on that
variable. The products for all the variables are then
summed to yield the case's factor score on the factor in
question. Thus, a case's high or low factor scores will
necessarily reflect its high or low values on a factor's

constituent variables. It follows that factor scores
permit factors to be treated as composite variables for
research purposes, e.g., as variables in higher-order
factor analysis. (See Rummel, "Understanding Factor
Analysis," pp. 469-470.) Viewed another way, factor scores
enable the reduction of the number of variables in a study
without deleting the contributions of the individual
tests. (Fruchter and Jennings, "Factor Analysis," p.
262.) Factor scores can also be used to compare cases on
factor patterns. This can be especially helpful in
interpreting typologies resulting from Q-factor analysis.
Whereas factor scores derived from a R-factor analysis
measure the involvement of an entity with sets of
intercorrelated characteristics, factor scores generated
from a Q-analysis indicate the prominence of a
characteristic in different groups of intercorrelated
entities. This is because in Q-factor analysis the normal
matrix positions of entities and their characteristics are
reversed (see p. 110; also note 2 p. 121 above.

Factor scores cannot usually be calculated for a case
having missing values on one or more variables in the
factor analysis. Despite the fact that only 4.7% of all
data in the 1976 R-factor study was missing, a sizeable
number of cases did take missing values on at least one
variable. Hence, obtaining a sufficient number of factor
scores to conduct the second-order factoring was
problematic. This difficulty was solved, however, by using
a SPSS program feature which replaces the missing values of
a variable with the mean of that variable. In this
instance, missing observations were replaced by the mean
for any case in which up to one-half of the variables had
missing values. See Nie et al., SPSS, pp. 489-490, 496.
Several studies using factor scores for second-order
analyses are Steven R. Brown, "Perspective,
Transfiguration, and Equivalence in Communication Theory:
Review and Commentary," in Communication Yearbook 3, ed.
Dan Nimmo (New Brunswick, N.J.: Transaction Books, 1979),
pp. 51-64; Robert L. Savage, "Policy Traditions in the
American States," paper presented at the 1979 meeting of
the Southwestern Political Science Association, Fort Worth,
Texas, 28-31 March 1979; and Daily, "Underlying Patterns of
Legislative Voting Behavior." Perhaps the best overall
treatment of higher-order factor analysis is contained in
Thurstone, Multiple-Factor Analysis, pp. 411-439. Also see
Kerlinger, Foundations of Behavioral Research, pp. 674-676,
and Raymond B. Cattell, "Higher Order Factor Structures and
Reticular-vs-Hierarchical Formulae for Their Interpreta-
tion," in Studies in Psychology, ed. Charlotte Banks and
P. L. Broadhurst (New York: Barnes and Noble, 1966),
pp. 223-265.

[7]For an additional explanation of the difference between Q and R-analysis see note 2, above p. 121.

[8]Just as in the case of the 1976 first-order R-factor analysis, derivation of factor scores for both the 1975 and 1976 Q-analyses required replacement of missing data by the means of the respective characteristic variables (see note 6, above pp. 125-126). This time, however, it was necessary to replace missing data with the means of data read in rows rather than columns. This was required because, as stated in the text, the normal matrix positions of entities and their characteristics were now reversed. Since SPSS can only perform missing data replacement for information read in columns, it was therefore necessary to edit manually each transposed matrix. Again, in the case of the 1976 survey, only 4.7% of all data were missing. The comparable figure for the 1975 survey was only 2.7%. For a fuller discussion of the computation and uses of factor scores see note 6, pp. 125-126.

[9]Despite this limitation, it must be emphasized that at the time of the analysis SPSS was the best set of programs available. This was particularly true with regard to its great flexibility in handling missing values.

[10]For a discussion of the advantages of the PA1/Varimax combination see pp. 107-108.

[11]Perhaps the best example of a prior application of this methodology in Q-analysis is Daily, "Underlying Patterns of Legislative Voting Behavior," pp. 38-39. Also see Brown, "Perspective, Transfiguration, and Equivalence," pp. 58-64, and Savage, "Policy Traditions in American States."

CHAPTER IV

VIEWPOINTS OF AMERICAN EXECUTIVES ON BASIC ISSUES
OF SOVIET-AMERICAN COMMERCIAL RELATIONS

In the preceding chapters the importance of trade
issues to superpower relations has been documented, the
political significance of Soviet Area Executives in trade
actor companies has been demonstrated, and an innovative
theoretical model in which executive attitudes play a key
political role has been developed. Methods of data
acquisition and analysis for the 1975-1976 period have also
been described in exhaustive detail. It follows, then,
that the next step in this study is the presentation of
survey and interview findings and the evaluation of these
findings from a theoretical perspective.

Sample Profiles: Soviet Area Executives

Survey responses for 1975 (i.e., Survey 1) show that
at that time the typical Soviet Area Executive was
Protestant, Republican, with a Bachelor's Degree, and was
born in the Midwestern U.S. (Table 2). The age
distribution of the sample closely approximates a normal
curve, with the mean and median ages both equal to 51
years. A substantial majority of the respondents had

TABLE 2

PROFILE OF SOVIET AREA EXECUTIVES OF U.S. CORPORATIONS, 1975

|  | Percent | F* |
|---|---|---|
| Occupation** |  |  |
| Principal Senior Executive | 30.3 | 33 |
| Senior International Executive | 24.8 | 27 |
| Senior All-Purpose Executive | 22.0 | 24 |
| Senior Operations Executive | 22.9 | 25 |
|  |  | N=109 |
|  |  |  |
| Education |  |  |
| High School | 4.7 | 5 |
| Bachelor's Degree | 47.7 | 51 |
| Master's Degree | 27.1 | 29 |
| Ph.D. | 7.5 | 8 |
| Law | 13.1 | 14 |
|  |  | N=107 |
|  |  |  |
| Religion |  |  |
| Protestant | 62.5 | 64 |
| Roman Catholic | 13.5 | 14 |
| Jewish | 2.9 | 3 |
| Other | 3.8 | 4 |
| No Preference | 17.3 | 18 |
|  |  | N=103 |
|  |  |  |
| Political Party Preference |  |  |
| Democrat | 10.5 | 11 |
| Republican | 59.0 | 62 |
| Independent | 22.9 | 24 |
| No Preference | 7.6 | 8 |
|  |  | N=105 |
|  |  |  |
| Age |  |  |
| 20-29 | 0 | 0 |
| 30-39 | 11.0 | 12 |
| 40-49 | 35.8 | 39 |
| 50-59 | 33.0 | 36 |
| 60 and Above | 20.2 | 22 |
|  |  | N=109 |

TABLE 2 (continued)

PROFILE OF SOVIET AREA EXECUTIVES OF U.S. CORPORATIONS, 1975

|  | Percent | F* |
|---|---|---|
| Birthplace*** | | |
| East | 31.8 | 34 |
| Midwest | 46.7 | 50 |
| South | 10.3 | 11 |
| West | 4.7 | 5 |
| Foreign Born | 6.5 | 7 |
| | | N=107 |
| | | |
| Tenure at Present Post (Yrs.) | | |
| 1-5 | 64.2 | 70 |
| 6-10 | 19.3 | 21 |
| 11-15 | 8.3 | 9 |
| 16 and Above | 8.3 | 9 |
| | | N=109 |

*Variations in the number of cases (N) are attributable to "no answers" which are excluded from all calculations. The total N for the 1975 survey is 109 executives.

**Categories constructed employing the criteria specified above, p. 89.

***Categories constructed from classifications developed by the University of Michigan's Survey Research Center.

held their corporate posts for only a relatively short time: some 64.2% had occupied their positions for five years or less, although the mean was about seven years. This is not unusual in view of the high turnover characteristic of top level U.S. corporate positions. A surprising number of responses (30.3% of the total) came from Principal Senior Executives, with the balance of responses almost evenly distributed among remaining categories of executives. Because Senior International Executives are usually responsible for their firms' overseas business, it was anticipated originally that questionnaires returned by these executives would prevail by a wide margin.

Indeed, survey responses for 1976 (i.e., Survey 2) conform to this expectation (Table 3), with 36.9% of returned questionnaires coming from Senior International Executives and only 18.2% from Principal Senior Executives. (One factor which may be responsible for these different response patterns is the "de-glamorization" of U.S.-Soviet trade during 1975-1976, which likely resulted in more routine handling of Soviet business by company international departments rather than by corporate chief executives.) In other respects, such as age and tenure at company post, the composition of the 1976 sample of executives does not differ substantially from that obtained

TABLE 3

PROFILE OF SOVIET AREA EXECUTIVES OF U.S. CORPORATIONS, 1976

|  | Percent | F* |
|---|---|---|
| Age | | |
| 20-29 | 2.0 | 4 |
| 30-39 | 13.3 | 26 |
| 40-49 | 31.6 | 62 |
| 50-59 | 37.8 | 74 |
| 60 and Above | 15.3 | 30 |
|  |  | N=196 |
| | | |
| Occupation** | | |
| Principal Senior Executive | 18.2 | 37 |
| Senior International Executive | 36.9 | 75 |
| Senior All-Purpose Executive | 10.7 | 40 |
| Senior Operations Executive | 25.1 | 51 |
|  |  | N=203 |
| | | |
| Tenure at Present Post (Yrs.) | | |
| 1-5 | 59.8 | 119 |
| 6-10 | 24.6 | 49 |
| 11-15 | 7.0 | 14 |
| 16 and Above | 8.5 | 17 |
|  |  | N=199 |

*Variations in the number of cases (N) are attributable to "no answers" which are excluded from all calculations. The total N for the 1976 survey is 203 executives.

**Categories constructed employing the criteria specified above, p. 89.

in the 1975 exercise. The mean and median ages of
executives in the 1976 survey were 49 and 50 years,
respectively. Also, 59.8% of the respondents had held
their posts for five years or less, with a mean of about
seven years (the same mean as the previous year).

### Sample Profiles: Trade Actor Companies

As is evident from Tables 4 and 5, there is great
similarity in the composition of the 1975 and 1976 survey
samples despite the fact that the latter is nearly twice
the size of the former. These survey data show that the
vast majority of American companies pursuing Soviet
business in 1975-1976 had annual sales of less than one
billion dollars and employed fewer than 20,000 people.
Most were also multinational companies with equity in
foreign manufacturing facilities, and most were engaged in
some line of manufacturing--especially the fabrication of
capital equipment. Given the predominance of manufacturing
companies, it is not surprising that both surveys point to
intense Soviet business activity during 1975-1976 in the
industrial Midwest and East.

The data also suggest that the American firms that
were doing business with the U.S.S.R. in 1975-1976 were not
newcomers to world markets, but on the contrary were
seasoned veterans of international business. More than half
the companies in each survey derived one-third or more of

TABLE 4

CHARACTERISTICS OF TRADE ACTOR COMPANIES, 1975-1976

| | 1975 | | 1976 | |
|---|---|---|---|---|
| | Percent | F* | Percent | F* |
| Major Line of Business** | | | | |
| Agriculture | 3.7 | 4 | 0 | 0 |
| Mining | 1.9 | 2 | 2.0 | 4 |
| Construction | 0.9 | 1 | 1.0 | 2 |
| Manufacturing | 62.6 | 67 | 71.6 | 141 |
| Transport, Communications, Etc. | 3.7 | 4 | 2.5 | 5 |
| Wholesale and Retail Trade | 6.5 | 7 | 8.6 | 17 |
| Services | 14.0 | 15 | 10.1 | 20 |
| Nonclassifiable | 6.5 | 7 | 4.1 | 8 |
| | | N=107 | | N=197 |
| | | | | |
| Corporate Headquarters*** | | | | |
| East | 36.3 | 37 | 39.6 | 78 |
| Midwest | 38.2 | 39 | 30.5 | 60 |
| South | 8.8 | 9 | 15.7 | 31 |
| West | 16.7 | 17 | 14.2 | 28 |
| | | N=102 | | N=197 |
| | | | | |
| Consolidated Net Sales | | | | |
| Less than $1 Billion | 60.6 | 60 | 65.2 | 107 |
| $1 Billion - $2 Billion | 19.2 | 19 | 14.0 | 23 |
| More than $2 Billion | 20.2 | 20 | 20.7 | 34 |
| | | N= 99 | | N=164 |
| | | | | |
| Number of Employees | | | | |
| Less than 20,000 | 59.2 | 61 | 66.7 | 118 |
| 20,000 - 40,000 | 12.6 | 13 | 13.0 | 23 |
| Greater than 40,000 | 28.2 | 29 | 20.3 | 36 |
| | | N=103 | | N=177 |

TABLE 4 (continued)

CHARACTERISTICS OF TRADE ACTOR COMPANIES, 1975-1976

| | 1975 | | 1976 | |
|---|---|---|---|---|
| | Percent | F* | Percent | F* |
| Percent Business Volume from International Operations | | | | |
| 0-32% | 47.6 | 49 | 47.1 | 89 |
| 33-66% | 47.6 | 49 | 43.4 | 82 |
| 67-100% | 4.9 | 5 | 9.5 | 18 |
| | | N=103 | | N=179 |

*Variations in the number of cases (N) are attributable to "no answers" which are excluded from all calculations. Survey results reported for 1975 are based on a total N of 109 companies. Results for the 1976 survey reflect a total N of 203 companies.

**The categories employed are those of the Standard Industrial Classification System developed by the Technical Committee on Industrial Classification of the U.S. Office of Management and Budget. Vague responses as well as conglomerate companies were considered nonclassifiable. Where a respondent entered two major lines of business, the first was given priority for purposes of classification.

***Categories constructed from classifications developed by the University of Michigan's Survey Research Center.

TABLE 5

BUSINESS PROFILE OF TRADE ACTOR COMPANIES, 1975-1976
(Percentaged Horizontally)

|  | Yes | No | Don't Know | (N)* |
|---|---|---|---|---|
| **Is your company currently fulfilling a contract with a Soviet foreign trade organization?** | | | | |
| 1975 | 61.1% | 38.0% | 0.9% | (108) |
| 1976 | 60.5 | 38.5 | 1.0 | (200) |
| **Is a "protocol" or "letter of intent" currently in operation between your company and a Soviet foreign trade organization?** | | | | |
| 1975 | 47.2 | 46.2 | 6.6 | (106) |
| 1976 | 37.7 | 58.3 | 4.0 | (199) |
| **Has your company recently negotiated or is it now in contact with Soviet foreign trade representatives?** | | | | |
| 1975 | 96.3 | 3.7 | 0 | (109) |
| 1976 | 88.2 | 10.8 | 1.0 | (203) |
| **Did your company conduct any business with Soviet foreign trade organizations during the 1950-1965 period?** | | | | |
| 1975 | 26.9 | 63.9 | 9.3 | (108) |
| 1976 | 21.3 | 73.8 | 5.0 | (202) |
| **Did your company conduct any trade with the U.S.S.R. before WWII?** | | | | |
| 1975 | 35.2 | 47.2 | 17.6 | (108) |
| 1976 | 21.4 | 67.2 | 11.4 | (201) |

TABLE 5 (continued)

BUSINESS PROFILE OF TRADE ACTOR COMPANIES, 1975-1976
(Percentaged Horizontally)

| | Yes | No | Don't Know | (N)* |
|---|---|---|---|---|
| Does your company deal in high-technology product lines (such as electronic computers and data processing, programmed machine tools, state-of-the-art electronics, advanced optical or photographic technology, etc.)? | | | | |
| 1975 | 55.0 | 43.1 | 1.8 | (109) |
| 1976 | 48.5 | 51.0 | 0.5 | (200) |
| | | | | |
| Does your company hold equity in foreign production facilities? | | | | |
| 1975 | 82.1 | 17.9 | 0 | (106) |
| 1976 | 75.4 | 24.6 | 0 | (195) |

*Variations in the number of cases (N) are attributable to "no answers" which are excluded from all calculations. Survey results reported for 1975 are based on a total N of 109 companies. Results for the 1976 survey reflect a total N of 203 companies.

their total business volume from international operations, as evidenced by a mean of 35% in 1975 and 38% in 1976 (Table 4). In contrast, as of the mid-1970s, Soviet business evidently comprised only a tiny share of the business volume of most American companies involved in U.S.-U.S.S.R. commerce. Ninety-eight percent of the companies in the 1976 survey derived less than one-third of their total business volume from Soviet-American trade, the mean being 4.3% and the median 1.2%. (Comparable figures for the 1975 survey are not available.)

Results from both surveys document the rapid pace of U.S.-Soviet business in 1975-1976. A total of about 60% of the companies in each sample were fulfilling contracts with the Soviet Union at the time of the respective surveys (Table 5). Similarly, 88% (1976) and 96% (1975) of the executives reported recent or on-going negotiations with Soviet foreign trade organizations (FTOs). In addition, 38% (1976) and 47% (1975) of the companies were, as of the survey dates, in the lengthy pre-contract "letter of intent" stage of concluding a transaction with a Soviet foreign trade organization.

Survey data further confirm that during 1975-1976 Soviet FTOs tended to favor U.S. companies with which they had had pre-detente experience (i.e., prior to 1972). Some 21.4% of the 1976 sample and 35.2% of the 1975 sample

indicated that their companies had had pre-World War II
trade contacts with the U.S.S.R., whereas 21.3% (1976) and
26.9% (1975) reported that their firms had conducted
business with the Soviets during the 1950-1965 "Cold War"
period (Table 5). Also, 28.8% of the 1976 sample and 25%
of the 1975 sample said that their companies had
successfully concluded their first Soviet contract some
time between 1966 and 1971; a period of considerable
U.S.-Soviet tension over Vietnam, the U.S.S.R.'s invasion
of Czechoslovakia, and other issues.

Both surveys tend to substantiate the well publicized
point that the Soviets have sought out as their business
partners a large number of U.S. companies possessing
sophisticated technologies. From 48.5% (1976) to 55.0%
(1975) of survey respondents reported that their firms
dealt in sensitive high-technology product lines such as
computers, state-of-the-art electronics, programmed machine
tools, optical or photographic equipment, etc. Executives
of 47 companies in the 1976 survey (about 23% of the
sample) further indicated that their firms had entered into
"scientific-technical cooperation" (S & T) agreements with
the U.S.S.R.'s State Committee for Science and Technology.
Since about 50 U.S. firms are known to have concluded such
agreements as of end-1976, it is noteworthy that an

overwhelming 94% majority of these companies responded to
the second survey.

Interestingly, although a much higher than average
level of corporate technology might be expected for firms
with S & T pacts, this did not turn out to be the case.
According to responding executives, 55% of companies having
S & T agreements also possessed sophisticated technologies.
This compares with 45% for the 153 firms not having such
agreements, and is not markedly higher than the 49% noted
above for the overall sample of 203 firms.  In terms of
other company characteristics, firms having S & T
agreements closely resembled other companies active in the
Soviet market in the mid-seventies.  Several divergences
deserve mention, however:   First, executives of firms
having both S & T agreements and then-current contracts
with Soviet FTOs indicated that Soviet business contributed
a smaller share to their firms' total annual corporate
income (mean of 3.4%) than was the case for executives of
firms which did not have scientific-technical pacts (mean
of 4.9%).  Additionally, comparing firms having S & T
agreements with those not having such agreements, a 17%
greater proportion of executives from the former said that
their companies had been either a pre-World War II or Cold
War trade partner of the U.S.S.R.

## Sample Profile:    Personal Interviews

As noted in Chapter III, primary criteria for the
interview selection process were geographical
accessibility, level of company technology, and whether or
not a company had an existing S & T agreement with the
U.S.S.R.  Despite constraints imposed by these criteria,
the final interview sample differed only marginally from
the overall 1976 survey sample in terms of response
patterns on attitudinal variables, personal attributes, and
company characteristics.

Regarding attitudinal variables, mean attitude scores
of the interview group on the 1976 survey were carefully
compared with scores for the 175 executives not belonging
to this sub-sample.  This examination revealed meaningful
differences on only 3 of 64 attitudinal variables.
Likewise, a comparison of corporate and personal attributes
for the interview sub-sample shown in Tables 6-8 with
characteristics of the overall sample displayed in Tables
3-5 shows a high degree of similarity in most categories.
Principal differences include the following:  (1) most
executives interviewed were slightly older than those in
the overall survey sample and their tenure at their company
posts was somewhat longer, and (2) relatively speaking,
companies visited were somewhat more concentrated in the
Midwest, had a slightly greater propensity to have been a

TABLE 6

PROFILE OF SOVIET AREA EXECUTIVES IN 1976 INTERVIEW SAMPLE

|  | Percent | F* |
|---|---|---|
| Age |  |  |
| 30-39 | 3.7 | 1 |
| 40-49 | 29.6 | 8 |
| 50-59 | 48.1 | 13 |
| 60 and Above | 18.5 | 5 |
|  |  | N= 27 |
| Occupation** |  |  |
| Principal Senior Executive | 21.4 | 6 |
| Senior International Executive | 39.3 | 11 |
| Senior All-Purpose Executive | 14.3 | 4 |
| Senior Operations Executive | 25.0 | 7 |
|  |  | N= 28 |
| Tenure at Present Post (Yrs.) |  |  |
| 1-5 | 55.6 | 15 |
| 6-10 | 22.2 | 6 |
| 11-15 | 3.7 | 1 |
| 16 and Above | 18.5 | 5 |
|  |  | N= 27 |

*Variations in the number of cases (N) are attributable to "no answers" which are excluded from all calculations. The total N for the 1976 interview sample is 28 executives.

**Categories constructed employing the criteria specified above, p. 89.

TABLE 7

CHARACTERISTICS OF TRADE ACTOR COMPANIES IN 1976 INTERVIEW SAMPLE

|  | Percent | F* |
|---|---|---|
| Major Line of Business** | | |
| Manufacturing | 67.9 | 19 |
| Wholesale and Retail Trade | 17.9 | 5 |
| Services | 7.1 | 2 |
| Nonclassifiable | 7.1 | 2 |
|  | | N= 28 |
| Corporate Headquarters*** | | |
| East | 17.9 | 5 |
| Midwest | 57.1 | 16 |
| South | 0 | 0 |
| West | 25.0 | 7 |
|  | | N= 28 |
| Consolidated Net Sales | | |
| Less than $1 Billion | 57.9 | 11 |
| $1 Billion - $2 Billion | 15.8 | 3 |
| More than $2 Billion | 26.3 | 5 |
|  | | N= 19 |
| Number of Employees | | |
| Less than 20,000 | 70.8 | 17 |
| 20,000 - 40,000 | 8.3 | 2 |
| Greater than 40,000 | 20.8 | 5 |
|  | | N= 24 |

TABLE 7 (continued)

CHARACTERISTICS OF TRADE ACTOR COMPANIES IN 1976 INTERVIEW SAMPLE

|  | Percent | F* |
|---|---|---|
| Percent Business Volume from International Operations | | |
| 0-32% | 53.8 | 14 |
| 33-66% | 42.3 | 11 |
| 67-100% | 3.8 | 1 |
|  |  | N= 26 |

*Variations in the number of cases (N) are attributable to "no answers" which are excluded from all calculations. The total N for the 1976 interview sample is 28 companies.

**The categories employed are those of the Standard Industrial Classification System developed by the Technical Committee on Industrial Classification of the U.S. Office of Management and Budget. Vague responses as well as conglomerate companies were considered nonclassifiable. Where a respondent entered two major lines of business, the first was given priority for purposes of classification.

***Categories constructed from classifications developed by the University of Michigan's Survey Research Center.

TABLE 8

BUSINESS PROFILE OF TRADE ACTOR COMPANIES IN 1976 INTERVIEW SAMPLE
(Percentaged Horizontally)

| | Yes | No | Don't Know | (N)* |
|---|---|---|---|---|
| Is your company currently fulfilling a contract with a Soviet foreign trade organization? | 67.9% | 32.1% | 0% | (28) |
| Is a "protocol" or "letter of intent" currently in operation between your company and a Soviet foreign trade organization? | 39.3 | 53.6 | 7.1 | (28) |
| Has your company recently negotiated or is it now in contact with Soviet foreign trade representatives? | 85.7 | 14.3 | 0 | (28) |
| Did your company conduct any business with Soviet foreign trade organizations during the 1950-1965 period? | 25.0 | 75.0 | 0 | (28) |
| Did your company conduct any trade with the U.S.S.R. before WWII? | 39.3 | 53.6 | 7.1 | (28) |
| Does your company deal in high technology product lines (such as electronic computers and data processing, programmed machine tools, state-of-the-art electronics, advanced optical or photographic technology, etc.)? | 48.1 | 51.9 | 0 | (27) |
| Does your company hold equity in foreign production facilities? | 70.4 | 29.6 | 0 | (27) |

*Variations in the number of cases (N) are attributable to "no answers" which are excluded from all calculations. Survey results reported are based on a total N of 28 executives from 28 companies that were selected for the 1976 interview sample.

pre-World War II trade partner of the U.S.S.R., derived
somewhat less of their total business from international
operations, and were slightly more inclined to specify some
form of wholesale or retail trade as their major line of
business.

Most of the differences indicated above are of minor
importance. It follows, then, that a case can be made that
the interview sample is highly representative of the
overall 1976 survey sample, even though a representative
interview sample was not a prime nor a necessary objective
given the analyst's limited purpose of illustrating and
supplementing data collected from other sources.

### General Attitudes of Executives Toward U.S.-Soviet Trade and Detente: 1975

An in-depth historical discussion of the attitudes of
U.S. businessmen on questions of Soviet-American
commercial and political relations first requires an
accurate evaluation of executives' fundamental
orientations toward the concepts of U.S.-U.S.S.R. trade and
detente. In other words, during the 1975-1976 period how
did these capitalist businessmen react to the very idea of
doing business and pursuing other forms of accommodation
with the United States' principal ideological, political,
and military adversary?

Survey data for 1975 indicate that in that year SAEs,
like most Americans, ardently supported the general thaw in
U.S.-Soviet relations which had begun in the early 1970s.
Evidence of this is provided in Table 9, which summarizes
executives' scores on the Detente Index. (This scale, it
will be recalled, was designed to measure executives' views
on the desirability of detente without specifically
mentioning that term.)[1] According to responses on this
index, 96.2% of all executives in the 1975 survey favored
to some degree the pursuit of detente with the Soviet
Union. Particularly remarkable is the intensity of
executives' support: Some 72.4% of the businessmen
indicated that they strongly favored the continuance of
detente, whereas a much smaller 23.8% fell into the "favor,
but not strongly" category. Also noteworthy is that not a
single respondent strongly opposed detente, while a mere 3%
indicated only mild opposition to the idea.

Given SAEs' strong support in 1975 for the general
concept of detente, which aspects of detente did they see
as being most desirable? This question can be answered by
breaking down the Detente Index into its four constituent
variables to provide a more detailed perspective on
respondents' attitudes. In this connection, an examination
of Table 10 reveals a somewhat surprising pattern: Among
the four key elements of detente--commercial relations,

TABLE 9

ATTITUDES OF SOVIET AREA EXECUTIVES TOWARD DETENTE, 1975*

|  | Percent | F* |
|---|---|---|
| Favor Detente Strongly | 72.4 | 76 |
| Favor Detente, But Not Strongly | 23.8 | 25 |
| Not Sure; It Depends | 1.0 | 1 |
| Oppose Detente, But Not Strongly | 2.9 | 3 |
| Oppose Detente Strongly | 0 | 0 |
|  |  | N=105 |

*Table employs the Detente Index to measure indirectly this attitude dimension. See above, p. 93, for an explanation of the Detente Index. Calculations exclude those respondents who failed to answer one or more of the index's component questions. Total number of cases (N) for the 1975 survey is 109 executives.

TABLE 10

ORIENTATION OF SOVIET AREA EXECUTIVES TOWARD
COMPONENTS OF DETENTE, 1975

| | With the U.S.S.R. We Should Continue to Improve: | | | |
|---|---|---|---|---|
| | Trade | Scientific Cooperation | Cultural Exchange | Diplomatic Relations |
| Agree Strongly | 70.4% | 28.4% | 56.5% | 66.4% |
| Agree, But Not Strongly | 23.1 | 41.3 | 35.2 | 28.0 |
| Not Sure; It Depends | 3.7 | 25.7 | 5.6 | 3.7 |
| Disagree, But Not Strongly | 2.8 | 1.8 | 1.9 | 0.9 |
| Disagree Strongly | 0 | 2.8 | 0.9 | 0.9 |
| (N)* | (108) | (109) | (108) | (107) |

*Variations in the number of cases (N) between columns are attributable to "no answers" which are excluded from all calculations. The total N for the 1975 survey is 109 executives.

scientific cooperation, cultural exchange, and diplomatic
relations--executives voiced the greatest support in almost
equal measure for continued expansion of Soviet-American
trade and further efforts to improve diplomatic (i.e.,
political) relations with the U.S.S.R.  Although some
readers might anticipate that international businessmen
would view trade as being of singular importance, this
simply was not the case.  In fact, respondents assigned
marginally greater weight to the desirability of political
detente, with 94.4% favoring sustained efforts to improve
diplomatic relations compared to 93.5% for those who
supported increased trade.  Opinions on trade, however,
were held somewhat more intensely.  Some 70.4% "strongly"
supported improved commercial ties, whereas the comparable
figure for diplomatic relations was slightly lower at
66.4%.  Interestingly, scientific cooperation with the
Soviet Union was the least favored component of detente.
Despite the fact that a substantial 70% majority felt that
such cooperation is desirable, only 28% indicated strong
support, and nearly 26% were "not sure" about the idea.

    The prominence of political factors in executives'
thinking in 1975 is further illustrated by the fact that
81% of the survey respondents said that developing stronger
trade ties with the U.S.S.R. will contribute significantly

to world peace (Table 11). Thus, the positive contribution
of trade to detente was embraced as an important
justification for pursuing business with the Soviet Union.
This, of course, is indicative of widespread adherence by
SAEs to the so-called "spill-over" hypothesis that was
discussed earlier, which was one of the basic precepts of
the original Nixon-Kissinger strategy of detente.

Likewise, it will be recalled that Administration
policy in the first half of the 1970s strongly opposed overt
Congressional efforts to use trade as a lever to force
changes in the U.S.S.R.'s internal policies. Reflecting
this stance, a substantial 86% majority of 1975 survey
respondents opposed the highly-publicized and controversial
Jackson-Vanik Amendment to the 1975 Trade Reform Act, which
made a relaxation of restrictive Soviet emigration policies
a pre-condition for the granting of U.S. Most-Favored-
Nation tariff status to the U.S.S.R. However, whereas the
Administration's objections to Jackson-Vanik were based on
the belief that the measure would be ineffective and
threaten detente's international political objectives, an
added dimension is evident in executives' opposition to
this legislation: Instead of high-publicity tactics aimed
at achieving immediate moderation of Soviet domestic
policies, some businessmen advocated the steady growth of
U.S.-Soviet economic relations as an alternative, more

TABLE 11

ATTITUDES OF SOVIET AREA EXECUTIVES ON GENERAL
U.S.-U.S.S.R. POLITICAL ISSUES, 1975
(Percentaged Horizontally)

| | Agree Strongly | Agree But Not Strongly | Not Sure, Depends | Disagree But Not Strongly | Disagree Strongly | (N)* |
|---|---|---|---|---|---|---|
| Developing stronger trade ties with the U.S.S.R. will contribute significantly to world peace. | 50.5% | 30.3% | 11.0% | 3.7% | 4.6% | (109) |
| The U.S. should continue to withhold Most-Favored-Nation status from the U.S.S.R. under provisions of the Jackson Amendment until the Soviet Government relaxes its restrictive emigration policies. | 4.6 | 6.4 | 2.8 | 18.3 | 67.9 | (109) |
| The U.S. can help eliminate the worst features of the Soviet political system through closer trade ties, because continuous trade will help the Soviet system evolve in a slow but steadily positive manner. | 27.5 | 25.7 | 22.9 | 13.8 | 10.1 | (109) |

*Total number of cases (N) for the 1975 survey is 109 executives.

subtle and longer-term means for accomplishing this goal.
Specifically, a 54% majority of 1975 survey respondents
said that closer U.S.-Soviet trade ties can help eliminate
the worst features of the Soviet political system, because
continuous trade will help the Soviet system to evolve in
a slow but steadily positive manner.[2]

## Attitudinal Relationships

It follows from the preceding opinion distribution
that a series of statistically significant correlations are
to be expected between the above attitudes.  As is evident
from Table 12, values of Pearson's r derived from
crosstabulations of respective pairs of variables indeed
document the presence of a number of meaningful
relationships which serve to illustrate further the
importance of political factors in executive orientations
in 1975.  In particular, Table 12 clearly confirms that the
tendency to view U.S.-Soviet trade favorably was strongly
and directly correlated with:  (1) support for improved
diplomatic relations with the U.S.S.R. ($r = .70$), (2)
adherence to the view that U.S.-Soviet trade will have a
beneficial impact on world peace ($r = .68$), and (3) the
expectation that trade can contribute to a positive evolution of the Soviet political system ($r = .35$).  Consistent with these relationships, Table 12 also verifies that
executives who supported increased U.S.-Soviet trade had a

TABLE 12

CORRELATES OF ATTITUDES TOWARD SOVIET-AMERICAN COMMERCE, 1975*
(Percentaged Horizontally)

| | We Should Continue to Improve Trade Relations with U.S.S.R. | | | |
|---|---|---|---|---|
| | Agree | Not Sure, Depends | Disagree | Pearson's r** or (N) |
| Entire Sample | 93.5% | 3.7% | 2.8% | (108) |
| U.S. should continue improving diplomatic relations with U.S.S.R. | | | | .70 |
|   Agree | 97.0 | 1.0 | 2.0 | (100) |
|   Not sure, depends | 25.0 | 75.0 | 0 | (4) |
|   Disagree | 50.0 | 0 | 50.0 | (2) |
| Stronger trade ties with U.S.S.R. will contribute significantly to world peace. | | | | .68 |
|   Agree | 98.9 | 0 | 1.1 | (88) |
|   Not sure, depends | 91.7 | 8.3 | 0 | (12) |
|   Disagree | 37.5 | 37.5 | 25.0 | (8) |
| Closer U.S. trade ties with U.S.S.R. will help the Soviet political system to evolve in a slow but steadily positive manner. | | | | .35 |
|   Agree | 96.6 | 0 | 3.4 | (58) |
|   Not sure, depends | 92.0 | 8.0 | 0 | (25) |
|   Disagree | 88.0 | 8.0 | 4.0 | (25) |
| U.S. should withhold MFN from U.S.S.R. pending relaxation of Soviet emigration restrictions. | | | | -.39 |
|   Agree | 75.0 | 8.3 | 16.7 | (12) |
|   Not sure, depends | 10.0 | 0 | 0 | ( 3) |
|   Disagree | 95.7 | 3.2 | 1.1 | (93) |

*Cases are omitted from the respective crosstabulations where the respondent failed to answer one or both of the variables being compared.
**All Pearson's correlations are significant at the p = .01 level.

moderate negative propensity toward the Jackson-Vanik
Amendment (r = -.39). Turning to Table 13 reveals, not
surprisingly, a similar although slightly stronger
correlation between opposition to Jackson-Vanik and the
idea that trade will be helpful to peace (r = -.43).
Finally, taking a closer look at the trade-peace or
"spill-over" concept, it is further evident from Table 13
that businessmen who had faith in this idea also had a
moderate tendency to see trade as a liberalizing influence
on Soviet domestic politics (r = .50).

General Attitudes Toward Trade and Detente: 1976

Consistent with 1975 survey data, survey results for
1976 provide evidence for continued strong advocacy by SAEs
for U.S.-Soviet trade and detente. However, the data also
point to some reduction in enthusiasm during the 13 month
period between the two surveys.

Most importantly, respondents' overall support for
increased trade with the Soviet Union dropped to 81%, down
from 93.5% a year earlier (Table 14). In addition, 1976
data show diminished intensity of support for U.S.-Soviet
commercial relations. Whereas 70.4% of executives favored
trade "strongly" in 1975, a much smaller majority of 52%
felt this way in 1976. On the other hand, the category of
executives who were "not sure" about the desirability of

TABLE 13

CORRELATES OF ATTITUDES TOWARD THE TRADE-PEACE HYPOTHESIS, 1975*
(Percentaged Horizontally)

| | Stronger Trade Ties With U.S.S.R Will Contribute to World Peace. | | | |
| | Agree | Not Sure, Depends | Disagree | Pearson's r** or (N) |
|---|---|---|---|---|
| Entire Sample | 80.8% | 11.0% | 8.3% | (109) |
| U.S. should withhold MFN from U.S.S.R. pending relaxation of Soviet emigration restrictions. | | | | -.43 |
| Agree | 41.7 | 25.0 | 33.3 | (12) |
| Not sure, depends | 100.0 | 0 | 0 | (3) |
| Disagree | 85.1 | 9.6 | 5.3 | (94) |
| Closer U.S. trade ties with U.S.S.R. will help the Soviet political system to evolve in a slow but steadily positive manner. | | | | .50 |
| Agree | 94.8 | 3.4 | 1.7 | (58) |
| Not sure, depends | 80.8 | 16.0 | 4.0 | (25) |
| Disagree | 50.0 | 23.1 | 26.9 | (26) |

*Cases are omitted from the respective crosstabulations where the repondent failed to answer one or both of the variables being compared.

**All Pearson's correlations are significant at the p = .01 level.

TABLE 14

ATTITUDES OF SOVIET AREA EXECUTIVES ON GENERAL
U.S.-U.S.S.R. ISSUES, 1976
(Percentaged Horizontally)

| | Agree Strongly | Agree But Not Strongly | Not Sure, Depends | Disagree But Not Strongly | Disagree Strongly | (N)* |
|---|---|---|---|---|---|---|
| At this time, the U.S. Government should try to improve trade relations with the U.S.S.R. | 52.3% | 29.1% | 13.1% | 2.5% | 3.0% | (199) |
| Developing stronger trade ties with the U.S.S.R. will contribute significantly to world peace. | 41.6 | 30.7 | 15.8 | 8.9 | 3.0 | (202) |
| Trade is a normal condition which should exist between two nations having diplomatic relations, and should not be conditional upon negotiable differences on world issues nor on either country's domestic political policies. | 41.4 | 29.3 | 11.6 | 11.1 | 6.6 | (198) |

*Variations in the number of cases (N) are attributable to "no answers" which are excluded from all calculations. Total N for the 1976 survey is 203 executives.

improved Soviet trade ties grew in 1976 to 14%, increasing
from a mere 3.7% in 1975. Likewise, though the percentage
of respondents opposing the expansion of trade contacts
remained small at 6%, this was up from a tiny 2.8% in 1975.

This evolution of views toward trade during 1975-1976
was paralleled by the emergence of an analogous attitudinal
pattern on relevant political variables. It is worth
noting, for example, that while confidence in the "spill-
over" hypothesis discussed earlier remained high in 1976,
this concept was nonetheless slightly less popular than in
the previous year. As opposed to the 81% figure cited for
1975, 73% of executives in the 1976 survey indicated a
belief that stronger U.S.-Soviet trade ties will contribute
significantly to world peace. Virtually all of this change
is attributable to a reduction from 51% to 42% in the
category of executives who felt "strongly" about the
trade-peace connection, coupled with a rise in the
proportion of executives who were either "not sure" or
rejected the proposition.[3]

Another moderate shift of opinion is indicated on the
highly-publicized and hotly-debated issue of whether the
U.S. Government should link prospects for the expansion of
Soviet-American trade to the U.S.S.R.'s performance on
human rights matters or to Soviet positions on outstanding
international political questions. Recalling that 86% of

those in Survey 1 explicitly rejected the Jackson-Vanik
Amendment to the Trade Reform Act of 1975, a comparatively
smaller proportion of executives implicitly rejected the
Amendment in the 1976 survey.  Specifically, 71% of respondents to Survey 2 said that trade is a normal condition
which should exist between nations having diplomatic relations, and should not be made conditional upon negotiable
differences on world issues nor on either country's domestic political policies.  Especially noteworthy is that
while 68% of the 1975 sample "strongly" opposed Jackson-
Vanik, only 42% of 1976 respondents felt strongly about the
overall linkage question.  Although these variations might
be attributable to differences in the framing of the two
survey questions being compared, if one views the responses
in the context of the broad range of aforementioned attitude
changes, this suggests instead a gradual trend of weakening
resistance to the idea of employing U.S. trade policy as a
lever for achieving U.S. political objectives toward the
U.S.S.R.

Attitudinal Relationships

Crosstabulations and Pearson's correlations of items
from the 1976 survey, when contrasted with the previous
analysis of relationships among variables in the 1975
survey, further corroborate above indications of a moderate
dampening of business support for trade/detente during

1975-1976. Most importantly, although Table 15 shows that in 1976 executive support for U.S.-Soviet trade remained highly correlated with the concept that trade will contribute to peace (r = .55), an important reduction in the strength of this relationship is evident from 1975 (r = .68).

In comparison with those executives who in 1976 remained committed to U.S. Government efforts to upgrade U.S.-Soviet commercial relations, much greater skepticism toward the trade-peace hypothesis is evident in the enlarged category of 1976 respondents who said they were "not sure" about the desirability of closer trade ties. Whereas 53.9% of the latter were either uncertain about or rejected the trade-peace concept, this was true of only 19.8% of those who supported trade expansion. It should be noted, however, that in 1975 doubts about the trade-peace connection were voiced by only 13.9% of those favoring expanded trade, suggesting that even among those most supportive of trade some deterioration in the credibility of the trade-peace hypothesis took place between the two surveys.

In a similar vein, there is further evidence that between Survey 1 and Survey 2 SAEs gradually adopted a somewhat less strident posture on the leverage/linkage issue. Although the strength of the relationship between trade attitudes and the linkage question remained unchanged

TABLE 15

CORRELATES OF ATTITUDES TOWARD SOVIET-AMERICAN COMMERCE, 1976*
(Percentaged Vertically)

| | We Should Continue to Improve Trade Relations with U.S.S.R. | | |
| --- | --- | --- | --- |
| | Agree | Not Sure, Depends | Disagree |
| Stronger trade ties with the U.S.S.R. will contribute significantly to world peace. | | | |
| Agree | 80.2% | 46.2% | 27.3% |
| Not sure, depends | 13.0 | 38.5 | 9.1 |
| Disagree | 6.8 | 15.4 | 63.6 |
| (N) | (162) | (26) | (11) |
| [r = .55] | | | |
| Trade with U.S.S.R should not be conditioned upon negotiable differences on world issues nor on Soviet domestic policies. | | | |
| Agree | 77.1 | 61.5 | 27.3 |
| Not sure, depends | 12.1 | 7.7 | 18.2 |
| Disagree | 10.8 | 30.8 | 54.5 |
| (N) | (157) | (26) | (11) |
| [r = .39] | | | |

*Cases are omitted from the respective crosstabulations where the respondent failed to answer one or both of the variables being compared. All Pearson's correlations are significant at the p = .01 level.

from 1975 to 1976 (r = .39 for both years), one must again
call attention to the fact that a substantially higher
proportion of respondents to the last survey said they were
"not sure" about the desirability of closer U.S.-Soviet
trade ties. Consistent with the above-noted uncertainty
with which this category regarded the trade-peace
hypothesis, these executives likewise displayed less
opposition to linkage than their counterparts who
maintained a favorable disposition towards trade. Some
61.5% of those "not sure" about the utility of trade
expansion also opposed linkage of U.S. Government
commercial policies to Soviet foreign policies or human
rights practices, 8% were uncertain about the wisdom of
this, and 30.8% were positively inclined toward such
action. In contrast, a substantially higher 77.1% of those
who supported U.S.-Soviet trade expansion likewise rejected
the use of trade policy as a lever on the U.S.S.R., whereas
12.1% were "not sure," and only 10.8% leaned toward the use
of economic leverage. It is notable that, consistent with
the previously-cited evolution of opinion on the
trade-peace hypothesis, the 77.1% figure for the pro-trade
group--although still a strong majority--indicates less
vigorous opposition to linkage/leverage from this category
than was the case in 1975, when an overwhelming 88.1% of

this group of executives repudiated the Jackson-Vanik
Amendment.

### Businessmen's Reactions to
### International Political
### Events

How can the above changes on trade/detente variables
and the relationships among them be accounted for?  Survey
data for 1976 suggest that a principal reason for the shift
in attitudes was the emergence during the 1975-1976 period
of a growing executive perception of a renewed
international communist threat.  Unquestionably, the
origins of this phenomena are rooted in intense publicity
of two distinct political developments during the period
under investigation.  Of foremost importance is the fact
that 20% of 1976 survey respondents indicated that
then-recent Soviet foreign policy activities, particularly
the U.S.S.R.'s widely publicized military intervention in
Angola via Cuban proxy forces, had adversely affected their
outlook on doing business with the U.S.S.R. (Table 16).[4]
Although 62% said that Soviet international behavior had
had no impact on their inclination to take part in Soviet
trade, it is perhaps more meaningful that another 19% were
"not sure" in this regard, suggesting that they too had
been unsettled by recent events.  Hence, fully 40% of the
sample indicated at least some degree of anxiety over
Soviet foreign policy trends.

TABLE 16

EXECUTIVES' REACTIONS TO WORLD POLITICAL DEVELOPMENTS, 1976

(Percentaged Horizontally)

| | Agree Strongly | Agree But Not Strongly | Not Sure, Depends | Disagree, But Not Strongly | Disagree Strongly | (N)* |
|---|---|---|---|---|---|---|
| In general, recent Soviet foreign policy (e.g., Angola) has adversely affected the outlook of the U.S. business community toward trade with the U.S.S.R. | 12.2% | 44.7% | 18.8% | 21.8% | 2.5% | (197) |
| Specifically, recent Soviet foreign policy activities (e.g., Angola) have adversely affected your company's outlook on doing business with the U.S.S.R. | 5.2 | 15.1 | 18.8 | 36.5 | 24.5 | (192) |
| In general, the increased strength of communist parties in W. Europe has adversely affected the outlook of the U.S. business community toward trade with the U.S.S.R. | 5.3 | 20.1 | 22.8 | 42.3 | 9.5 | (189) |
| The increased strength of communist parties in W. Europe has adversely affected your company's outlook toward trade with the Soviets. | 5.2 | 8.4 | 14.1 | 48.7 | 23.6 | (191) |

*Variations in the number of cases (N) are attributable to "no answers" which are excluded from all calculations. Total N for the 1976 survey is 203 executives.

Interestingly, when asked to evaluate the effect of Angola and other reports of Soviet "adventurism" on the disposition of U.S. business in general (as opposed to the impact on their own firms) a strong 57% majority replied that these activities had caused a decrease in the general desire of the U.S. business community to conduct trade with the U.S.S.R. In comparing this response with the previous one, it would thus seem at first glance that the actual impact of Soviet foreign policy actions on U.S. business opinion was much less pronounced than SAE's perception of that impact. Indeed, personal interviews confirmed that executives tended to believe that other businessmen pursuing trade with the Soviets had been affected more by reports of Soviet adventurism than they themselves had. At the same time, however, interviews also revealed that SAEs were of the opinion that Angola and similar Soviet activities had had the most telling influence on businessmen in non-trade actor companies--i.e., on executives of firms which had as of that point in time devoted only marginal attention to the trade possibilities opened up by U.S.-Soviet detente. These executives, it was contended, inherently possessed a relatively uninformed and more cautious view of the thaw in U.S.-Soviet relations. Given this wariness, and the fact that their companies had no existing stake in the Soviet market, such executives were therefore seen as especially sensitive to negative developments in the climate for detente.  In sum, then, SAEs viewed then-recent Soviet international behavior as having had the greatest deterrent effect on executives of new-to-market companies and not on those already having a vested interest in Soviet-American commerce.

Apart from uneasiness over Angola, 1976 survey data document the influence of a second and somewhat less important factor on the evolution of SAEs' thinking during 1975-1976.  Specifically, 13% of survey respondents stated that their willingness to do business with the Soviets had been negatively affected by perceptions of the growing power of West European communist parties (Table 16). Again, another 14% were "not sure" of their feelings on the matter.  Thus, following intense media coverage during 1975-1976 of advances by the so-called "Eurocommunist" movement, more than one-fourth of all executives in the 1976 survey alluded that they had developed doubts and questions about the wisdom of trading with the U.S.S.R.[5]

Once more, as in the case of the impact of Soviet foreign policy behavior, respondents viewed the U.S. business community in general as having been troubled more by the rise of Eurocommunism than they themselves had.  In this regard, fully 25% categorically said that the increased strength of West European communists had adversely

affected the overall outlook of U.S. business on
Soviet-American trade. In view of the fact that this
figure is far below respondents' comparable assessment of
the impact of 1975-1976 Soviet foreign policy activities,
it follows that of the two factors, the U.S.S.R.'s
international behavior was regarded by SAEs as being by far
the dominant opinion-forming influence on businessmen in
non-trade actor companies.

Under questioning during interviews, several SAEs
argued that executives in trade actor and non-trade actor
firms alike were far more likely to perceive a direct
causal link between Moscow and events in Angola than to
hold the U.S.S.R. accountable for the increasing political
clout of Eurocommunist parties. Likewise, it was also
thought that most U.S. businessmen would regard the Angola
affair as having a much higher probability of evoking a
U.S. Government policy response adversely affecting the
commercial sphere.

Added insight into the implications of the preceding
set of survey opinions can be gained by looking at several
meaningful relationships between these key variables. In
this regard, 1976 survey data reveal that those executives
who indicated that perceptions of Soviet adventurism had
negatively affected their outlook on U.S.-Soviet trade had
a like tendency to say that the growing political influence

of the Eurocommunists had had the same effect (r = .56)
(Table 17). Hence, 41% of those who said that the
U.S.S.R.'s recent international behavior had had an adverse
impact on their desire to do business with the Soviets
reported an identical reaction to the increasing political
power of the Eurocommunists. (Conversely, 61.5% of those
who were perturbed by the Eurocommunists were similarly
unsettled by trends in Soviet foreign policy.) Viewed from
another perspective, a small but meaningful 8.5% of the
total 1976 survey sample evidently discerned the emergence
of a renewed, coordinated effort by the U.S.S.R. to subvert
Western nations and Third World countries alike.

Although widespread U.S. media coverage of the
U.S.S.R.'s activities in Angola, the Horn of Africa,
Vietnam, etc. during 1975-1976 renders it clear why many
SAEs would perceive expansionist Soviet behavior in these
areas, it is perhaps less obvious why some respondents
simultaneously saw the U.S.S.R. as being responsible for
the growing prominence of West European communist parties
during this time period. A likely explanation for this
connection was indicated in personal interviews conducted
with several of those executives who perceived a Soviet
hand in the Eurocommunist movement. In the course of these
discussions, it became apparent that persistent reports of
Soviet attempts to capitalize on the highly unstable

TABLE 17

REACTIONS TO THE "EUROCOMMUNIST" MOVEMENT BY REACTIONS
TO SOVIET FOREIGN POLICY, 1976*
(Percentaged Vertically)

Recent Soviet Foreign Policy Activities
(e.g., Angola) have Adversely Affected
Your Company's Outlook on Doing Business
with the U.S.S.R.

|  | Agree | Not Sure, Depends | Disagree |
|---|---|---|---|
| The increased strength of Communist Parties in West Europe has adversely affected your company's outlook toward trade with the Soviets. | | | |
| Agree | 41.0% | 14.7% | 4.3% |
| Not sure, depends | 15.4 | 38.2 | 6.9 |
| Disagree | 43.6 | 47.1 | 88.8 |
| (N) | (39) | (34) | (116) |
| **[r = .56] | | | |

*Cases are omitted from the crosstabulation where the respondent
failed to answer one or both of the variables being compared.

**Significant at the p = .01 level.

political situation then prevailing in Portugal had

suggested, to at least a few executives, the probability

that the Soviets were also somehow to blame for the growing

influence of the Italian and French communist parties. In

this regard, media accounts of substantial Soviet financial

assistance to Alvaro Cunhal's Portuguese Communist Party

evidently were particularly damaging to the Soviet Union's

image among some SAEs.[6]

Survey data for 1976 point to a number of additional,

statistically significant relationships involving, on the

one hand, the above orientations toward the rise of

Eurocommunism and Soviet foreign policy activities, and,

secondly, other survey measures of executive attitudes

toward U.S.-Soviet trade and detente (Table 18).

Specifically, those executives who in 1976 were inclined to

say that they had adopted a more negative view on trading

with the Soviets as a result of recent Soviet international

behavior, or who had been similarly affected by the growing

political influence of West European communists, also

displayed corresponding tendencies to:

(1) Question to a moderately greater degree the
desirability, in principle, of continued U.S.
Government efforts to improve U.S. trade ties with
the U.S.S.R. ($r = -.34$; $r = -.36$).

(2) Be slightly less opposed to linkage of U.S.
trade policies vis-a-vis the U.S.S.R. to Soviet
performance on human rights matters and Soviet
international behavior ($r = -.15$; $r = .20$).

TABLE 18

CORRELATES OF ATTITUDES TOWARD WORLD POLITICAL DEVELOPMENTS, 1976*

(Percentaged Vertically)

| | Recent Soviet Foreign Policy Activities (e.g., Angola) Have Affected Your Company's Outlook on Doing Business with the U.S.S.R. | | | The Increased Strength of Communist Parties in W. Europe Has Adversely Affected Your Company's Outlook Toward Trade with the Soviets. | | |
|---|---|---|---|---|---|---|
| | Agree | Not Sure, Depends | Disagree | Agree | Not Sure, Depends | Disagree |
| **At this time, the U.S. Government should try to improve trade relations with the U.S.S.R.** | | | | | | |
| Agree | 63.2% | 85.3% | 87.2% | 61.5% | 70.4% | 87.4% |
| Not sure, depends | 21.1 | 14.7 | 10.3 | 15.4 | 29.6 | 9.6 |
| Disagree | 15.8 | 0 | 2.6 | 23.1 | 0 | 3.0 |
| (N) | (38) | (34) | (117) | (26) | (27) | (135) |
| | | | $[r=-.34]$ | | | $[r=-.36]$ |
| **Trade with the U.S.S.R should not be conditional upon negotiable differences on world issues nor on Soviet domestic policies.** | | | | | | |
| Agree | 71.1 | 69.4 | 72.4 | 57.7 | 77.8 | 72.8 |
| Not sure, depends | 7.9 | 16.7 | 11.2 | 19.2 | 14.8 | 9.6 |
| Disagree | 21.1 | 13.9 | 16.4 | 23.1 | 7.4 | 17.6 |
| (N) | (38) | (36) | (116) | (26) | (27) | (136) |
| | | | $[r=-.15]$** | | | $[r=-.20]$ |
| **Stronger trade ties with the U.S.S.R. will contribute significantly to world peace.** | | | | | | |
| Agree | 59.0 | 63.9 | 77.8 | 61.5 | 66.7 | 74.6 |
| Not sure, depends | 15.4 | 27.8 | 13.7 | 15.4 | 22.2 | 14.5 |
| Disagree | 25.6 | 8.3 | 8.5 | 23.1 | 11.1 | 10.9 |
| (N) | (39) | (36) | (117) | (26) | (27) | (138) |
| | | | $[r=-.25]$ | | | $[r=-.20]$ |

*Cases omitted from the respective crosstabulations where the respondent failed to answer one or both of the variables being compared. Unless noted otherwise, Pearson's correlations are significant at the $p = .01$ level.

**Significant at the $p = .05$ level. As shown, the relationship between these two variables is somewhat obscured, because of the necessity to collapse five response categories into three for purposes of tabular presentation.

(3) View with slightly greater skepticism the idea
that U.S.-Soviet trade will contribute
significantly to world peace (r = -.25; r = -.20).

It will be recalled that both surveys provide

substantial evidence that many U.S. businessmen justified

their pursuit of Soviet business in terms of its likely

contribution to "world peace." In this connection, 1975

and 1976 survey results document a strong positive

relationship between adherence to the trade-peace

hypothesis and support for U.S. Government efforts to

improve U.S.-Soviet trade ties. Both these variables, in

turn, seemingly are linked to businessmen's perceptions of

Soviet aggressiveness during 1975-1976, as indicated by

relationships (1) and (3) above. It follows that these

intercorrelations raise a central question concerning the

likely sequence of events among the aforementioned

variables: Did perceptions of a growing Soviet threat

undermine the credibility of the trade-peace hypothesis,

leading to reduced willingness to do business with the

U.S.S.R. and less support for U.S. Government efforts to

improve U.S.-Soviet trade relations? Alternatively, did

growing doubts about the trade-peace connection generate

similar doubts about the wisdom of U.S. Government efforts

to improve trade relations with the U.S.S.R., as well as

contribute to increased sensitivity to events like Angola?

First of all, Table 19 displays a three-way crosstabulation with attitudes toward the trade-peace hypothesis as the dependent variable, executives' reactions to recent Soviet foreign policy behavior as the independent variable and attitudes toward U.S. Government efforts to strengthen trade ties with the U.S.S.R. as the control variable. A cursory examination of this table immediately reveals a striking fact: As a result of the application of the control, the relationship between the Soviet foreign policy variable and the world peace variable virtually disappears. This is evidenced by a partial correlation between the independent and dependent variables of only -.04, compared to the previously noted total correlation between these variables of -.25. On the basis of this outcome, and assuming that the result is not due to exogenous factors, one is led to conclude that executives' reactions to Soviet foreign policy behavior during 1975-1976 had no direct causal influence on adherence to the trade-peace hypothesis. Conversely, whether or not an executive embraced the trade-peace hypothesis appears to have had little direct bearing on his response to Soviet activities in Africa, etc. In other words, the evidence suggests that the apparent direct connection between these variables is in fact spurious. A better understanding of

TABLE 19

ATTITUDES TOWARD THE TRADE-PEACE HYPOTHESIS BY REACTIONS TO SOVIET
FOREIGN POLICY, CONTROLLING FOR ATTITUDES TOWARD TRADE, 1976*
(Percentaged Vertically)

| | We Should Continue to Improve Trade Relations with U.S.S.R. | | | | | | | | | |
| Stronger Trade Ties with the U.S.S.R. will Contribute Significantly to World Peace. | Agree | | | Not Sure | | | Disagree | | | |
| | Business Outlook Adversely Affected by Recent Soviet Foreign Policy. | | | Business Outlook Adversely Affected by Recent Soviet Foreign Policy. | | | Business Outlook Adversely Affected by Recent Soviet Foreign Policy. | | | |
| | Agree | Not Sure | Disagree | Agree | Not Sure | Disagree | Agree | Not Sure | Disagree | (N) |
|---|---|---|---|---|---|---|---|---|---|---|
| Agree | 79.2% | 62.1% | 84.3% | 37.5% | 80.0% | 33.3% | 16.7% | 0% | 33.3% | 33.3% |
| (N) | (19) | (18) | (86) | (3) | (4) | (4) | (1) | (0) | (1) | (1) (136) |
| Not Sure | 12.5 | 31.0 | 8.8 | 37.5 | 20.0 | 50.0 | 0 | 0 | 0 | 33.3 |
| (N) | (3) | (9) | (9) | (3) | (1) | (6) | (0) | (0) | (0) | (1) (32) |
| Disagree | 8.3 | 6.9 | 6.9 | 25.0 | 0 | 16.7 | 83.3 | 0 | 0 | 33.3 |
| (N) | (2) | (2) | (7) | (2) | (0) | (2) | (5) | (0) | (0) | (1) (21) |
| Total | 100% | 100% | 100% | 100% | 100% | 100% | 100% | 0% | 100% | 100% |
| (N) | (24) | (29) | (102) | (8) | (5) | (12) | (6) | (0) | (6) | (3) (189) |

*Cases are omitted from the crosstabulation where the respondent failed to answer one or more of the three variables under consideration. Partial correlation of the independent and dependent variables is $r = -.04$, which is not statistically significant.

this finding can be gained by carefully evaluating the data displayed in Table 19 in the context of supplementary information obtained in personal interviews.

As is clearly evident from Table 19, a sizeable plurality of 86 executives (42% of all executives in the 1976 survey sample) said that their willingness to do business with the U.S.S.R. had not been affected by recent Soviet foreign policy activities, while at the same time they remained committed to the trade-peace hypothesis and supported continued U.S. Government efforts to strengthen Soviet-American trade ties. Of course, the question which comes immediately to mind is why events in Africa (and elsewhere) failed to have any discernible impact on this group's assessment of the political desirability of Soviet-American trade. Discussions with 16 businessmen who fell into this category suggest an explanation for this phenomena. To the analyst's surprise, personal interviews revealed that these businessmen perceived Soviet involvement in Africa, the Eurocommunist movement, etc. during 1975-1976 as further evidence of the need for an expanded and stable U.S.-U.S.S.R. commercial relationship. According to this logic, events like Angola might have been avoided if the U.S.S.R. had had a stronger vested interest in trade with the United States. If the Soviets had a greater stake in trade, the argument went, then they would

be much more wary of exploiting instability in the world
and be hesitant to take other actions which might intensify
conflict with the U.S. and jeopardize a valued economic
connection. Despite the rapid growth of U.S.-Soviet trade
which began in 1972, existing trade levels were seen by
these executives as being too small to encourage Soviet
restraint.[7] In addition, under this line of reasoning,
it was viewed as necessary that Soviet-American trade
relations develop steadily and smoothly over a period of
time. Such a positive commercial atmosphere conducive to
world peace had not evolved, it was suggested, in large
part because of Congressional measures which precluded U.S.
Government implementation of the comprehensive Soviet-
American trade agreement signed in 1972. Consequently,
both the Jackson-Vanik Amendment to the 1975 Trade Reform
Act and the Stevenson and Church Amendments to 1975
Export-Import Bank legislation were not only seen as being
contrary to U.S. commercial interests, but apparently were
also viewed as inconsistent with the promotion of
international peace and security.

In summary, Angola and like developments were not
considered to be valid arguments for abandoning U.S.
Government attempts to cultivate economic interchange
between the U.S. and the Soviet Union. Rather, they were
regarded as examples of why such efforts should continue.

By fostering a less belligerent U.S.S.R., greater trade, not less trade, was seen as the way to more peaceful relations between the superpowers. (An attendant observation, of course, is that this train of thought strongly reflects the "web of interests" proposition that provided the foundation for the Nixon-Kissinger strategy of detente.)

Table 19 manifests a second intriguing response pattern. Some 37 executives (18.2% of the survey sample) voiced support for the trade-peace hypothesis and U.S. Government efforts to build commercial detente, but still indicated that they were somewhat unsettled by recent Soviet foreign policy behavior. In this connection, 18 businessmen responded that Angola and like developments had generated some uncertainty in their minds concerning their willingness to pursue Soviet business, whereas 19 executives actually said that they were now more reluctant to engage in U.S.-U.S.S.R. trade. Thus, although their confidence in the political desirability of Soviet-American trade does not appear to have been undermined by perceived Soviet actions in Angola, the Horn of Africa, etc., these executives nevertheless reported that such developments had exercised a deterrent effect on their own U.S.S.R. business activities. Personal interviews in 1976 with six SAEs

from this group provided a number of insights into this
seeming paradox.

Discussions with these six businessmen confirmed that
they, like their counterparts who said they had been
unaffected by recent Soviet foreign policy trends,
continued to believe that more trade between the U.S. and
the Soviet Union would act as an important force for world
peace which could possibly prevent future situations like
Angola from arising. However, while they continued to
support U.S.-Soviet trade in principle and as a political
ideal, these executives nonetheless said that recent
international events had raised a number of concerns which,
as practical businessmen concerned with the welfare of
their respective companies, they could not afford to
ignore. First, all six businessmen indicated that
perceptions of recent subversive activities by the U.S.S.R.
in Africa and/or West Europe had contributed importantly to
increased business uncertainty about the future direction
of U.S.-Soviet relations. This uncertainty, they said, had
caused them to revise upward their estimates of the
tangible risks of doing business with the U.S.S.R. It was
contended that any evidence of deterioration in Soviet-
American political relations necessarily increases the
chances that these adverse developments will spill over into
the commercial sphere; i.e., that one government or the

other will take economic reprisals that could adversely
affect on-going corporate activities.[8] Although noting
that such "political risk" dangers are often a factor in
U.S. company trading relationships with many countries,
three of the SAEs voiced the opinion that U.S. firms, in
deciding whether or not to pursue Soviet business
opportunities, are apt to be unusually sensitive to these
hazards for several reasons. In this regard, the long
adversary relationship of the superpowers, rooted in
fundamental conflicts of national interest, was viewed as
amplifying the probability that any single negative
political incident might also affect trading relationships. Additionally, it was emphasized that penetration of
the Soviet market is, for most U.S. companies, an unusually
expensive undertaking, typically requiring a 2-4 year
investment of time and energy in order to conclude a large
contract.[9] It follows that these two factors were
described as having a synergistic impact on executive
attitudes: In light of the high costs of Soviet business
and the relatively long period before a "pay out" can be
expected, the inherent political risks of Soviet-American
trade were seen as being magnified, causing most
businessmen to be exceptionally wary in making U.S.S.R.
business decisions. Viewed in the opposite perspective,

a stable political environment was regarded as especially important for U.S.-Soviet trade to flourish.[10]

Thus, four of the SAEs interviewed, who said that their firms were fulfilling Soviet contracts and/or had expended substantial sums in business development efforts, nonetheless said that the aforementioned international political events of 1975-1976 had caused them to advocate a "go-slow" policy toward the Soviet market. This recommendation, each said, had resulted in a company decision to maintain existing levels of business activity with the Soviets, but to rule out, at least temporarily, diversion of additional substantial resources to this aspect of the firm's business.

The remaining two executives who were interviewed said that, on their recommendation, their firms were actually scaling down Soviet business efforts. In their view, their companies' business development expenditures in the Soviet market were not yet high, and while a cutback in Soviet activities might result in this money being wasted, they felt that much more might be lost by continuing to invest in a prospective contract in a hostile international political climate. Pointing to Angola as a particularly disruptive international event, all six executives indicated that they were fearful of a further degeneration in U.S.-Soviet relations which might contribute, for example, to renewed U.S. export restrictions on sales to the U.S.S.R., or, alternatively, to a Soviet decision to divert additional business contracts away from U.S. companies to West European or Japanese suppliers.

Apart from such direct effects on businessmen's assessments of the practical business risks of U.S.-Soviet trade, the interviews also suggested that recent international political developments had affected these executives _indirectly_ as well. Already troubled by what they saw as U.S. business' unfavorable public image and lamenting that the occupation of "businessman" was not held in higher social esteem, they voiced great concern that Angola, Portugal, etc. had contributed to a worsening of the domestic political climate for Soviet-American commerce. Growing anti-Soviet sentiment among the American people, it was feared, might at some point result in a backlash by various segments of the U.S. public against those U.S. firms involved in Soviet business activities. The possibility of such a reaction was cited by these executives as yet another reason for their increased reluctance to invest corporate resources in U.S.-Soviet trade.[11] (SAEs' anxieties over a prospective domestic backlash, as well as their views on the forms which such a reaction might take, are discussed in further detail in Chapter VI.)

It deserves mention that all six executives said that
in arriving at their decisions to reduce or hold the line
on their Soviet activities, they had been conditioned by
the expectation that the importance of Soviet business to
their firms would likely remain limited, even under the
most optimistic economic and political circumstances.
Trade with the Soviet Union, they felt, would for a host of
reasons never approach the magnitude of their domestic
business nor, for that matter, the dollar volume of their
principal traditional foreign markets (e.g., Latin
America). Had they viewed the U.S.S.R. as a key growth
market, they suggested that their responses to the
above-noted adverse changes in the international political
environment might have been less cautious.

Again, referring to Table 19, yet another aspect of
business opinion can be discerned. A careful examination
of this table shows that 34 executives (17.9% of 1976
respondents) said they were either unsure of or opposed
continued U.S. Government efforts to build U.S.-Soviet
trade ties. At the same time, 19 of these businessmen also
indicated that recent Soviet international behavior had
generated doubts in their minds regarding their willingness
to do business with the U.S.S.R.; a position which was held
without major regard to their views on the legitimacy of
the trade-peace hypothesis. This finding tends to confirm

the validity of the inverse relationship noted earlier
(r = - .34) between businessmen's reactions to Angola,
etc., and their attitudes toward U.S. Government attempts
to strengthen commercial relations with the Soviets.
Although this connection appears weak and is the result of
the divergent opinions of a relatively small proportion of
the total 1976 survey sample, the nature and direction of
the relationship is nonetheless of considerable theoretical
importance.  Thus, at this juncture it is worth noting
several observations resulting from personal interviews
with 3 of the 19 executives whose responses to the 1976
survey fit the aforementioned pattern.  These discussions
disclosed that perceptions of Soviet misbehavior in Africa
and elsewhere had caused these executives, like others
noted above, to be more concerned about the practical
business risks of U.S.-U.S.S.R. commerce, as well as more
fearful of a possible domestic political backlash against
companies involved in trade with the Soviets.  However, an
added dimension was also evident in these interviews:  All
the executives indicated that they had become suspicious of
the Soviet Union's basic motives in pursuing trade and
detente with the United States, and they repeatedly
referred to events in Angola, and secondarily to communist
activities in Portugal, as fueling their mistrust.  Such
Soviet actions, they reasoned, are inconsistent with a

genuine commitment to a lessening of East-West tensions and violate what one executive termed the "spirit of detente." Hence, these businessmen felt that there was a substantial possibility that the U.S.S.R. was simply employing its declared policy of detente as a smokescreen for expansionist objectives. A corollary to this line of thought was a vague apprehension that the Soviets, in seeking more trade with the U.S., were somehow "up to something" which might ultimately prove detrimental not only to general U.S. business interests, but to overall U.S. national interests as well.[12] When pressed for specifics on this point, two of the three executives indicated that they harbored fears that transfers of U.S. manufacturing technology to the Soviets might transform the U.S.S.R. into a formidable competitor of U.S. business in international markets. In addition, all three expressed doubts that the benefits gained from trade with the U.S. would accrue mainly to the Soviet civilian population. Instead, they suspected that the principal Soviet goal in U.S.-U.S.S.R. trade was to obtain a quick infusion of American knowhow which would be diverted to strengthen the industrial and technological base of the Soviet military.

It therefore appears that Soviet international behavior during 1975-1976 not only caused some U.S. executives to be more hesitant to deal with the U.S.S.R.

for parochial reasons such as increased risk to the firm,
but also stimulated a small number of businessmen to
question the wisdom of their own involvement and the
country's involvement in U.S.-Soviet trade from a "national
welfare" perspective. Interestingly, this theme that
expansion of U.S.-Soviet trade might not be in U.S.
national interests was articulated in personal interviews
by two executives who nevertheless maintained that stronger
U.S. trade ties with the U.S.S.R. will contribute
significantly to world peace. Asked to resolve this
apparent inconsistency, both businessmen clarified their
position by saying that they continued to believe in the
trade-peace hypothesis in principle, but suggested that
Soviet activities in Angola and elsewhere had made them
hesitant to advocate U.S. Government trade initiatives
aimed at the U.S.S,R. at that time. Rather, it was
contended that it might be wiser for the U.S. Government to
defer any efforts to improve commercial relations with the
Soviets until the U.S.S.R. demonstrates its commitment to
detente by desisting from international adventurism.

To summarize the above data, several preliminary
statements can be made concerning the essence of the
relationships in 1976 between executives' reactions to
Soviet foreign policy, views on the trade-peace hypothesis,
and attitudes toward U.S. Government efforts to improve

trade relations with the U.S.S.R. First, there would appear to be no actual direct correlation between the Soviet foreign policy variable and responses on the trade-peace variable. Relevant to the absence of such relationship is the fact that the 1976 survey question that solicited executives' reactions to the Angola affair and like developments unquestionably measured, simultaneously, two qualitatively different business responses to these events. In the final analysis, however, the lack of a connection is attributable primarily to the remarkable stability of the conviction, held by most survey respondents, that U.S.-Soviet trade will contribute to world peace--if not in the short run, then in the long run.

All of this is not to say that there is not an indirect relationship between reactions to Soviet foreign policy and adherence to the trade-peace hypothesis. Indeed, such a roundabout connection is indicated and is the most plausible explanation as to why these two factors vary together weakly but significantly. In this regard, an intervening role is suggested for executives' attitudes toward U.S. Government trade initiatives directed at the U.S.S.R. This ensues from the fact that when this U.S. Government trade policy variable is used as a control, the correlation between the Soviet foreign policy variable and the trade-peace variable falls to virtually zero ($r = .04$).

Assuming that the strong correlation found between the U.S. Government trade policy variable and the trade-peace variable (r = .56) is not spurious, the preceding information obtained from personal interviews strongly suggests the following scenario: Soviet activities in Africa, Portugal, etc. during 1975-1976 evoked a "national welfare" response on the part of a small percentage of survey respondents, making them more reluctant to involve themselves in Soviet business and rendering them less supportive of U.S. Government efforts to build closer trade relations with the U.S.S.R. A lessening of support for U.S. trade initiatives, in turn, seemingly contributed to a slight reduction in enthusiasm for the trade-peace hypothesis.

Note that this interpretation of the data rejects the notion, advanced earlier, of an alternative causal path: that executives' doubts about the trade-peace connection resulted in similar doubts about the wisdom of U.S. Government efforts to improve U.S.-Soviet trade relations, which ultimately led to a more pronounced reaction to Soviet international behavior during 1975-1976. Apart from the above-noted findings of personal interviews, trends in survey data from 1975 to 1976 would appear to argue against this conception. Specifically, it is once again necessary to point out that the intensity of executives' enthusiasm

for the trade-peace hypothesis as well as their support for
U.S. Government trade initiatives towards the U.S.S.R. fell
only after the Soviet role in Angola and Portugal had become
a public issue in the U.S. This temporal sequence is an
important basis for inferring that executives' perceptions
of the aforementioned international events were independent
causal factors rather than dependent variables.

### The Impact of Background Variables on Executive Attitudes

As described in Chapter II, the International Trade
Politics Model assumes that relevant information gleaned
from the corporate environment exercises the principal
formative influence on SAE attitudes, beliefs, and perceptions concerning Soviet-American economic and political
matters. Conversely, the model largely discounts the
possible impact on executive orientations of sociological
and other background variables.[13]

The likely validity of this fundamental precept is
strongly indicated by results of both the 1975 and 1976
surveys. In particular, as noted earlier, the 1975 survey
questionnaire incorporated a substantial number of personal
and corporate background items the principal purpose of
which was to test for possible links between such variables
and businessmen's views on Soviet-American trade and
detente. Responses to the 1975 survey's background items

were first subjected to extensive crosstabulations and Pearson's correlations with key attitudinal variables. Next, the data were analyzed further employing canonical correlation (via the SPSS CANCORR program) in an effort to detect possible underlying relationships between patterns of background variables on the one hand, and patterns of attitudinal variables on the other. Finally, all attitudinal and background variables together were subjected to R-factor analysis in an attempt to identify even the most diffuse inter-correlations.

Despite this exhaustive treatment of the 1975 survey data, no statistically significant relationships were revealed between respondents' attitudes and a comprehensive series of personal background variables: education, age, birthplace, religion, political party preference, occupational position, and tenure at company post. Thus, a host of factors generally accepted as bearing on political and sociological research had no relevance in this instance. Indeed, although the Trade Politics Model makes allowance for possible conditioning influences of corporate background variables on executives' views, most company characteristics also were found to have no meaningful impact on attitudinal orientations. In this regard, no statistically significant correlations were disclosed between attitudes and the following corporate traits: size

of company, percentage of income derived from foreign sales,
corporate specialty (i.e., line of business), degree of
corporate multinationality, and whether or not the firm had
conducted business with the U.S.S.R. prior to World War II
or during the 1950-1965 "Cold War" period. Nonetheless,
several other company background variables appear to have
had some influence on respondents' views on a few specific
Soviet-American trade issues. (Discussion of these
relationships is deferred for the time being, since they
can best be understood in the context of data presented in
later chapters.)

In light of the substantial evidence from Survey 1
indicating the minimal theoretical importance of personal
background variables to this study, most of these items
were omitted from the second survey. Only 3 such variables
were retained, for the reason that they were judged to be
of potential substantive interest to some readers. In
contrast to personal variables, however, all corporate
background items were retained, again because these were
regarded as having practical value to certain audiences.

Just as in the case of the 1975 survey, responses to
Survey 2 were subjected to crosstabulations, Pearson's
correlations, canonical correlation, and factor analysis in
an attempt to locate possible relationships between
personal/corporate variables and attitudinal variables.

Once more, these efforts failed to establish any statistically significant connection between personal background and attitudes. Likewise, the corporate characteristics listed above were again found to exercise no influence on executives' views, although again a number of other company traits seemingly affected executives' attitudes on several discrete trade matters. (As was indicated for comparable findings for 1975, these relationships are examined in later chapters where appropriate.)

To conclude, the preceding exercise is a useful partial test of one of the central propositions of the International Trade Politics Model. While the elimination of one source of theoretical uncertainty does not furnish incontrovertible proof of the model's soundness, it nevertheless places the framework on firmer ground.

## Summary, Conclusions, and Theoretical Implications
### Synopsis

Survey and interview data presented in this chapter confirm that from July 1975 to July 1976 Soviet Area Executives remained solidly in favor of the development of U.S.-Soviet trade and detente. However, all evidence also indicates that some reduction in businessmen's enthusiasm occurred during the period being investigated. This is evident, for instance, in small but meaningful changes on

several key questions included in both the 1975 and 1976
survey questionnaires. These questions sought to obtain,
at the time of the respective surveys, SAEs' evaluations
of: (1) the continued desirability of U.S. Government
efforts to improve U.S.-U.S.S.R. trade relations, and (2)
the idea that stronger U.S. trade ties with the Soviet
Union will make a significant contribution to world peace.
Adverse shifts of opinion on these items are not only
apparent from Survey 1 to Survey 2, but, in the case of the
latter survey, negative responses on the aforementioned
variables are associated with unfavorable replies on
several other measures: Survey data for 1976, together
with results of personal interviews, show convincingly that
SAEs became somewhat more reluctant to pursue Soviet
business as a result of the U.S.S.R.'s interventionist
activities in 1975-1976 (e.g., Angola), and, secondarily,
in response to major political gains by "Eurocommunist"
parties during this time frame.

Soviet Area Executives' reactions to these
international developments were manifested in two
qualitatively different ways. First, a sizable minority of
businessmen evinced what may be termed a "protective"
response. While they continued to view U.S.-Soviet trade
and detente as being in U.S. national interests, these
executives nevertheless saw the above-noted events as

contributing to a worsening of relations between Moscow and
Washington. This, in turn, sparked fears of a further
deterioration in the East-West political atmosphere which
at some point might spill over into the commercial sphere
via tighter U.S. export controls, a Soviet decision to
direct contracts away from U.S. companies, etc.
Apprehensions over such "political risks" were amplified
by: (1) the long-standing adversary relationship between
the superpowers, which was seen as increasing the
probability that any single negative political incident
might also affect trading relationships, (2) the unusually
high costs of penetrating the Soviet market coupled with
the abnormally long period required to recoup these
expenses, and (3) SAEs' perception that the U.S.S.R. would
not become a major growth market even under the most
optimistic economic and political scenario. All the
preceding combined to magnify possibilities for losses
relative to prospects for profit. Consequently,
notwithstanding their support for U.S.-Soviet
trade/detente, numerous executives felt compelled by
degenerating international political conditions to adopt a
more cautious business stance vis-a-vis the Soviet Union.
Apart from the aforementioned political risks, a more
hesitant business posture towards the Soviet market also
followed from these SAEs' worries that the Angola episode,

the Eurocommunist movement, etc., had contributed to a less favorable domestic political climate for Soviet-American commerce. Growing anti-Soviet sentiment among the American people, it was feared, might at some point result in a backlash by various segments of the U.S. public against those U.S. firms involved in Soviet trade activities.

In addition to the "protective" response described above, a small group of SAEs also exhibited a "national welfare" response to Soviet interventionist behavior and, to a lesser extent, to political gains by West European communist parties. Again, these businessmen displayed heightened sensitivity to the political risks of U.S.-U.S.S.R. commerce and became more fearful of a domestic political backlash against companies involved in trade with the Soviets. However, unlike other SAEs, adverse international political trends seemingly caused these executives to question their own involvement and their country's involvement in U.S.-Soviet trade from the standpoint of the national interest. These businessmen manifested a nascent mistrust of the Soviet Union's basic motives in pursuing trade and detente with the United States; i.e., they apparently harbored emerging fears that the U.S.S.R. was using detente as a cover for expansionist objectives. As a result, these SAEs were less supportive than other executives of U.S. Government efforts to improve

U.S.-Soviet trade relations and were somewhat more
skeptical that closer trade ties with the U.S.S.R. would
contribute significantly to world peace. Likewise, they
were more apprehensive than other SAEs that transfers of
U.S. manufacturing technology to the Soviets might
transform the U.S.S.R. into a formidable business
competitor in world markets, and that the Soviet defense
establishment, not the Soviet civilian population, would be
the primary beneficiary of trade with the United States.

### Linkage Scenarios

Viewed in the perspective of the International Trade
Politics Model, findings presented in this chapter have
several theoretical implications. First of all, the fact
that most SAEs strongly supported U.S.-Soviet trade/detente
in both 1975 and 1976 is seemingly consistent with Linkage
Scenario 1, which is set forth in Chapter II. To
reiterate, this scenario postulated that attitudes towards
trade/detente held by Soviet Area Executives would motivate
overt corporate political action directed at the U.S.
Government with the objective of influencing U.S. trade
policy towards the U.S.S.R. Resulting changes in U.S.
policy were then hypothesized as affecting the U.S.S.R.'s
political and economic decision processes. It will be
recalled that this sequence of events was described as a
reactive international linkage process whereby direct

corporate outputs trigger direct internal inputs in the
U.S. Government, resulting in direct polity outputs which
in turn generate environmental inputs in designated Soviet
decision structures:

**Scenario 1**

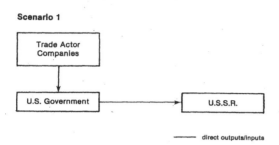

To some readers the above might seem to be a "common
sense" scenario. Given SAEs' overall advocacy of
trade/detente, one would logically anticipate U.S. firms to
lobby the U.S. Government for Soviet trade policies
consistent with American coporate interests. For example,
U.S. companies might naturally be expected to press hard
for the repeal of the much disliked Jackson-Vanik Amendment
as well as for the lifting of statutory restrictions on
Eximbank lending to the U.S.S.R.

However, although this line of reasoning may be
appealing, the fact remains that there is no historical
evidence to suggest that the U.S. business community was a
highly active force in the national debates on U.S.-Soviet

issues which took place throughout the latter half of the 1970s. By way of explanation, survey and interview data suggest another linkage scenario which may have contributed to a reduced level of U.S. corporate political activity on behalf of Soviet-American commerce.

Specifically, the above-noted reactions of SAEs to adverse international political trends in 1975-1976 may have helped to diminish company incentives to take part in pro-trade lobbying efforts. For instance, SAEs who manifested a "protective" response to then-recent international developments may have had a resulting tendency to view the potential liabilities of pro-trade political activities as exceeding the potential benefits of such activities. This follows from these executives' growing fears of a domestic political backlash against trade actor companies, their expectation of limited immediate monetary returns from U.S.S.R. business, and their preoccupation with the prospect of loss relative to prospects for profit. Likewise, the small group of SAEs who evinced a "national welfare" response to the Angola episode, the rise of Eurocommunism, etc. may have become less supportive of pro-trade corporate political activities because of their increasing skepticism about the U.S.S.R.'s motivations in seeking closer economic and political relations with the United States. Diagrammatically, the preceding hypotheses can be subsumed in the following

linkage scenario, which is the eighth postulated in this

study:

**Scenario 8**

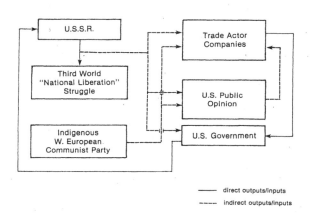

Note that Linkage Scenario 8 has certain similarities

with Linkage Scenario 3 (p. 55). Like Scenario 3, Linkage

Scenario 8 begins with Soviet actions not directly aimed at

trade actor companies nor at the U.S. political system

(i.e., material support of a Third World revolutionary

movement) but which nevertheless have a negative influence

on U.S. Government and public perceptions of the Soviet

Union. Soviet actions also have an unintended adverse

impact on SAEs' attitudes toward U.S.-U.S.S.R. trade. Some

executives see Soviet behavior as raising the political

risks of doing business with the U.S.S.R., and as

increasing the possibility for an anti-Soviet reaction against trade actor companies by various segments of the U.S. public. Also, some SAEs perceive Soviet actions as constituting an international communist threat contrary to U.S. national interests. Such anxieties are reinforced by other international events not directly related to Soviet behavior (i.e., major political gains in West Europe by indigenous communist parties), which further poison U.S. public opinion and adversely effect inter-governmental relations between the U.S. and U.S.S.R. As a result of all the preceding, Soviet Area Executives recommend to their directors that their companies reduce, terminate, or otherwise refrain from pro-trade political activities aimed at the U.S. Government. In view of the fact that the U.S. business community is a principal U.S. political constituency for U.S.-Soviet commerce, diminished pro-trade political efforts by American business give an added advantage to those U.S. political elements seeking a less compromising U.S. Government stand on Soviet-American economic and political issues. Consequently, U.S. Government policy outputs aimed at the U.S.S.R. become more contentious than would otherwise be the case.

Employing the concepts of the International Trade Politics Model, Scenario 8 begins with a reactive national-international linkage (i.e., a macro-linkage),

whereby direct polity outputs by the U.S.S.R. and indirect
polity outputs by Eurocommunist parties give rise to
indirect environmental inputs in the United States.  As in
Linkage Scenario 3 (p. 55), these environmental inputs
involve behavioral reactions within the U.S. Government,
U.S. public opinion, and trade actor companies (i.e.,
corporate inputs) as a result of perceptions of the
international environment.  Additionally, environmental
inputs to U.S. public opinion give rise to a micro-linkage
via indirect internal outputs (e.g., anti-Soviet press
stories) which in turn generate indirect internal corporate
inputs in trade actor companies (i.e., fear of a domestic
political backlash).  These indirect internal corporate
inputs combine with environmental corporate inputs from the
international arena to trigger a second micro-linkage:
Direct internal corporate outputs (i.e., reduced pro-trade
corporate political activity) result in direct internal
inputs in the U.S. Government (i.e., a more pugnacious
federal stance on various U.S.-Soviet issues).  At this
point, then, a second reactive macro-linkage is triggered
in the form of direct polity outputs by the U.S. Government
("hard line" policies directed at the U.S.S.R.) which end
in direct environmental inputs into the Soviet Politburo.
This terminal sequence, together with the initial reactive
national-international linkage, comprise what Rosenau terms

a "fused" linkage; i.e., there is a causal relationship between the two respective chains of events. Thus, Scenario 8 corroborates Linkage Scenario 7 (p. 60) which postulates the existence of fused linkages in the Soviet-American case.

Several additional fused linkages are indicated by the survey and interview data presented in this chapter. These relationships are shown in the following schema, which is designated Linkage Scenario 9:

**Scenario 9**

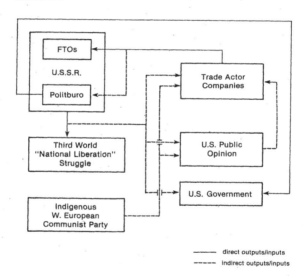

Linkage Scenario 9 is clearly a variate of Linkage Scenario 8. Once more, direct polity outputs by the U.S.S.R. (i.e., support for a Third World revolutionary

movement) and indirect polity outputs by Eurocommunist
parties stimulate indirect environmental inputs in U.S.
public opinion and trade actor companies (i.e.,
increasingly negative assessments of the political risks of
U.S.S.R. business, worries of a growing international
communist threat). Again, environmental inputs to U.S.
public opinion trigger a micro-linkage whereby indirect
internal outputs (e.g., anti-Soviet press stories) generate
indirect internal corporate inputs (i.e., fear of a
domestic political backlash) in trade actor companies.

At this juncture, the similarities with Linkage
Scenario 8 end. Instead of resulting in corporate
decisions to minimize pro-trade political activities aimed
at the U.S. Government, the various anxieties stimulated by
environmental and internal inputs culminate in decisions by
trade actor companies to slow the expansion of their
commercial relationships with the U.S.S.R, to cut back
Soviet business efforts, or to otherwise adopt a more
cautious stance toward opportunities in the Soviet market.
Such decisions, of course, constitute direct polity outputs
which result in direct environmental inputs in Soviet
foreign trade organizations (e.g., frustration at the
inability to conclude desired business deals). At the same
time, however, retrenchment by trade actor companies
fosters indirect environmental inputs in the Soviet

.Politburo. As a result of U.S. corporate actions, Soviet leaders begin to perceive American firms as unreliable business partners, and eventually conclude that the U.S.S.R. stands to gain less from trade with the United States than had originally been thought. Consequently, seeing itself as having a reduced vested interest in restraint in relations with the U.S., the U.S.S.R. subsequently begins to adopt less compromising stances on outstanding issues between the two countries. This, of course, involves a series of direct polity outputs aimed at the United States which triggers direct environmental inputs in various U.S. Government structures.

In sum, Linkage Scenario 9 can be characterized as a network of fused linkages, consisting of three identifiable and interrelated national-international sequences. In fact, the fused linkages depicted above closely correspond to those hypothesized in Linkage Scenario 7. Additionally, it merits attention that Scenario 9, like Scenario 8, shares a number of important characteristics with Linkage Scenario 3 (p. 55). Thus, Scenario 9 might best be described as a hybrid of Scenarios 3 and 7.

It should be self-evident that survey and interview findings thus far discussed are highly supportive of Scenario 9. Although SAEs reacted in two qualitatively different ways (i.e., the "protective" and "national

welfare" responses) to deteriorating East-West political
conditions during 1975-1976, both reactions seemingly
triggered the same inclination among businessmen; namely,
to adopt a more hesitant corporate posture towards Soviet
business.

Scenarios 8 and 9 are, of course, not mutually
exclusive but rather are complementary. Indeed, the
respective linkage diagrams may be superimposed on one
another, since both behavioral sequences initally flow from
identical international political stimuli. Taken together
the two scenarios comprise a set of hypotheses which may
provide a partial explanation for the failure of the U.S.
business community to perform as a forceful U.S. political
advocate of trade/detente throughout the last decade, for
the stagnation of non-agricultural U.S.-Soviet economic
relations which began in the mid-1970s, for the
increasingly strident posture of the U.S. Government from
1976 onward vis-a-vis a host of U.S.-Soviet economic and
political questions, and for the U.S.S.R.'s pursuit in the
late 1970s of a more adventurous and contentious foreign
policy. All of this is not just of historical interest.
Linkage Scenarios 8 and 9 warrant further investigation and
testing because they have fundamental implications for the
present and future course of U.S.-Soviet relations. If, as
the data suggest, U.S. business' willingness to participate

in and lobby for U.S.-U.S.S.R. commerce is unusually
susceptible to adverse developments in the East-West
political climate, then it will be extremely difficult ever
to establish an enduring and vigorous Soviet-American
trading relationship as the cornerstone of a superpower
detente.

A basic proposition of the hypothesis that trade can
have a "spill-over" or "ripple effect" on other aspects of
Soviet-American relations is that international trading
relationships, because they are founded on reciprocal
economic benefit, have an inherent stability not easily
disrupted by international political events. However,
Scenario 9, in conjunction with relevant survey and
interview findings, gives reason to doubt this assumption,
at least as far as Soviet-American relations are
concerned. Indeed, Scenario 9 suggests that the continuity
of U.S.-Soviet commerce may be affected by international
political events over which neither superpower has direct
control (e.g., West European political trends) but which
nevertheless can alter the business decision calculus of
American companies.

Similarly, Scenario 8 and associated research findings
undermine another fundamental premise of the "spill-over"
hypothesis. Central to this formulation is the idea that a
robust economic relationship will give both superpowers a

vested interest in cooperation and mutual restraint on non-commercial issues. Implicit in this proposition is the assumption that both the Soviet and American governments cannot fail to recognize and be responsive to their nations' vested economic interests as bilateral trade grows. As Scenario 8 suggests, such an assumption may be a gross oversimplification of reality. Given historically strong anti-Soviet sentiments in the United States and the pluralistic nature of the American political system, the U.S. Government's awareness of and sensitivity to commercial considerations in its relations with the U.S.S.R. would seem to be a function of the U.S. business community's willingness and ability to act as a consistent, forceful, and convincing advocate of the benefits of trade. However, U.S. businessmen's appetite for pro-trade political activity would appear to be limited by their intrinsically fragile commitment to the Soviet market, fears of a possible domestic political backlash against firms engaged in Soviet business, perceptions that Soviet business entails unusual "political risks," and nagging doubts about whether trade with the U.S.S.R. is in the national interest. Since there appears to be at least a moderate causal relationship between the East-West political atmosphere and the prominence of the preceding factors, it follows that periods of U.S.-Soviet tension

will tend to reduce the level of pro-trade political
behavior by U.S. business at the very time that such
activity could be especially helpful in promoting the
stability of U.S. commercial policies toward the U.S.S.R.
and in moderating U.S. Government political responses to
perceived Soviet threats.  One may therefore postulate that
any deterioration in the East-West political environment
will result in a strong propensity by U.S. policy-makers to
view trade relations with the U.S.S.R. as an instrument of
foreign policy rather than as a central concern of foreign
policy.  Likewise, there is always the significant
possibility that U.S. business may reduce its pro-trade
political activities and that the U.S. Government may adopt
a more muscular approach vis-a-vis the U.S.S.R. in response
to international political events over which neither
superpower has direct control.

   In sum, although numerous theorists have proposed that
a highly developed U.S.-Soviet economic relationship can
mitigate Soviet-American conflict in the political and
military spheres, data presented throughout this chapter
suggest that the "spill-over" mechanism may operate more
efficiently in reverse, at least as far as U.S. companies
and the U.S. Government are concerned.  This naturally
brings to mind a rather provocative proposition:  Given the
Soviet government's central control over the U.S.S.R.'s

foreign trade and the relative insulation of Soviet foreign
policy from capricious domestic political forces,
U.S.-Soviet trade may be more effective in fostering a
vested economic interest in restraint among Soviet leaders
than among their political counterparts in the U.S.

## Miscellaneous Theoretical Considerations

A basic tenet of the various economic influence
theories which argue that U.S. business constitutes a
ruling class or "power elite" in the United States is that
the political views and political behavior of senior-level
American businessmen are molded by economic self-interest.
Economic self-interest is usually equated with short-term
profit maximization and businessmen are usually depicted as
being consumed by avarice.[14] However, empirical data
presented in this chapter suggest that economic
self-interest may be a much more complex concept than has
been assumed by economic influence theorists. Although
further investigation is necessary, economic self-interest
must seemingly be defined in much broader terms than simply
profit and must incorporate concerns such as the "security
of the firm." Apart from prospects for profit, executives
discussed above were equally preoccupied with the economic
and political risks of the Soviet market as well as the
chances for an anti-Soviet domestic political backlash
against their companies. In other words, decisions on

Soviet business opportunities were evidently based on a
careful balancing of potential benefits against potential
liabilities--including political liabilities. It follows
that, given the innumerable and intangible potential
liabilities which a specific company may face from one
situation to the next, the general concept of economic
self-interest may well be indeterminate and impossible to
operationalize consistently for purposes of political
research. Thus, the notion of economic self-interest may
have only limited utility for predicting political
attitudes and behavior. For example, survey and interview
results recounted above suggest that a sizeable number of
businessmen viewed the U.S.S.R. as only a marginal growth
market. Nevertheless, despite the absence of a strong
pecuniary motive, these executives apparently were still
highly supportive of U.S.-Soviet trade and detente.

It deserves emphasis that the preceding interpretation
of the data is consistent with the findings of two
pioneering empirical studies of the political attitudes and
beliefs of American businessmen. In their landmark 1963
study of U.S. business views on foreign trade issues,
Bauer, Dexter, and Pool also found important evidence of
the indeterminacy of economic self-interest.[15] More
recently, Russett and Hanson, in their comprehensive 1975
study of the foreign policy beliefs of U.S. businessmen and

military officers, concurred that the concept of economic self-interest is inherently elusive and is a poor predictor of businessmen's general views on foreign affairs. Rather, Russett and Hanson determined that businessmen's conceptions of American national interests as well as U.S. business "ideology" have superior explanatory power vis-a-vis executives' foreign policy perspectives.[16] Several findings outlined earlier would seem to corroborate Russett and Hanson's conclusions and cast further doubt on the traditional economic influence theories.

First, it will be recalled that those executives who remained committed to U.S.-U.S.S.R. trade despite increasingly negative reports of Soviet international behavior defended their position by arguing that more trade, not less trade, will promote peace between the superpowers. On the other hand, as has been noted throughout this chapter, a small group of businessmen responded quite differently to the Angola episode and similar events. Such Soviet activities evidently caused these executives to doubt the wisdom of their own involvement and their country's involvement in trade with the U.S.S.R.; e.g., they evidently became more suspicious of Soviet motives for pursuing detente, become somewhat more dubious that trade would make a near-term contribution to world peace, became more apprehensive that trade would augment Soviet military power, and seemingly became more anxious that U.S. industrial knowhow might help establish the U.S.S.R. as a future competitor of American business.

In sum, no matter what their views were on the desirability of Soviet-American trade and detente, SAEs seemingly formulated their attitudes and beliefs on these issues within the context of U.S. national interests. Indeed, the fact that emerging doubts about detente evidently caused some businessmen to become more fearful of the Soviets as potential business competitors suggests that shifts in businessmen's conceptions of the national interest may, under certain circumstances, lead to important changes in executives' conceptions of their firms' economic self-interests.

Concerning Russett and Hanson's stress on the importance of "ideology" in executives' thinking, there is reason to believe that, apart from its major role in SAEs' perspectives on the national interest in U.S.-Soviet relations, the general idea that "trade will contribute to peace" may be a fundamental component of the political culture of senior level U.S. businessmen. In this connection, Russett and Hanson, as a result of their wide-ranging survey of vice presidents of major U.S. firms, found that 61.5% of their 567 respondents selected "trade, technical cooperation, and economic interdependence" as the

most important approach to world peace. This was the case
even though only 43.7% of the Russett-Hanson sample was
comprised of firms that might qualify as "trade actor"
companies. Thus, viewed together with the data collected
in the course of the present study, the Russett-Hanson
findings suggest that the belief that trade can mitigate
international conflict may be widely shared and deeply held
in the U.S. business community.[17] If the trade-peace
proposition is indeed an integral part of a broad U.S.
business ideology, this would explain why several
businessmen who manifested a "national welfare" response to
adverse East-West political trends during 1975-1976
seemingly retained faith in the trade-peace notion. As
noted earlier, a "national welfare" reaction to Angola,
etc., apparently resulted in these businessmen placing the
trade-peace hypothesis in a longer term perspective, but
did not cause them to abandon the idea in principle.

Finally, it merits attention that besides Russett and
Hanson other analysts have also identified a role for the
national or public interest (as opposed to selfish
corporate interests) in the political thinking of U.S.
businessmen.[18] For example, F. X. Sutton, in his
comprehensive 1956 investigation of American business
ideology, discerned a substantial and growing concern for
the public interest among U.S. business executives. This

tendency, which Sutton called the "managerial" strain of
U.S. business ideology, is perhaps most succintly described
by M. S. Seider, who found a similar school of thought in
his 1974 study of the ideological make-up of American big
business.[19] Specifically, Seider characterizes Sutton's
"managerial" ideology in terms of a "social responsibility"
position:

> Here a firm spokesman emphasizes the role of
> his business in fighting social problems,
> improving life for the community and for its
> workers, and generally being concerned with social
> areas not directly related to the pursuit of
> maximum profit. Social responsibility as a theme
> should be recognized as a major goal of business,
> not as an incidental byproduct of its day to day
> operations.[20]

Complementing the above, Bauer, Dexter, and Pool found that:

> Foreign travel introduced international
> political problems and America's relationship to
> them increasingly into the businessman's
> consciousness. As he traveled, he found himself
> being role-cast, not as the representative of a
> particular industry, but as an American. He found
> himself playing at being secretary of state and
> talking for his country, not for his firm.
> There was a shift in the center of gravity
> away from narrow parochial interests towards
> international interests, . . . Thus, foreign
> travel broadened the frame of reference in which
> the businessman considered the foreign-trade issue
> to one which took account of world political and
> economic circumstances. But the responses he gave
> to the facts he learned abroad were ones that his
> own domestic reference group would approve. The
> reference group perceived as relevant changed from
> a parochial to national one, but it remained a
> domestic one. . . .
> Foreign travel served to blunt the power of
> narrowly defined self-interest to shape a man's

views. Those men who had traveled extensively
seemed to be formulating their views with an eye
to the self-interest of the United States rather
than to the self-interest of a single product.[21]

The preceding findings of Bauer et al., Sutton, and

Seider provide further documentation that non-monetary

considerations may play a major role in shaping the

political attitudes and beliefs of U.S. businessmen.  Thus,

such studies lend further credibility to the survey and

interview results presented in this chapter and to the

theoretical interpretations attached to these data.

Conversely, the findings of this chapter would seem to lend

additional credibility to the work of the aforementioned

analysts.

FOOTNOTES

[1]For an explanation of the Detente Index, see Chapter 3, p. 93.

[2]These survey findings concerning the relationship between trade and human rights issues are perhaps best reflected in the writings of Donald Kendall, President of Pepsico:

"Let me emphasize right now that my strong criticism of Congress on [the Jackson-Vanik Amendment] does not indicate a lack of concern for human rights. In fact, I believe that trade is the most effective vehicle for creating an environment in which human rights and other important issues have a better chance of being resolved. . . .

. . . . . . . . . . . . . . . . . . . . . . . . . .

"I do not believe that advances in trade and economic cooperation should be held hostage to equal advances in the human rights area. Progress in one area will significantly improve the overall climate so that the chances for progress in other, more sensitive, areas will be enhanced." [Donald M. Kendall, "U.S.-Soviet Trade, Peace and Prosperity," in Common Sense in U.S.-Soviet Relations, ed. by Carl Marcy (Washington, D.C.: American Committee on East-West Accord, 1979), pp. 40, 42.]

Fairness requires attention to the fact that, from the earliest days of detente to the present, various segments of the U.S. public have disagreed with the preceding logic of Mr. Kendall. The alternative point of view is concisely summarized in the following statement submitted by Professor Gregory Grossman of the University of California-Berkeley to the Senate Committee on Commerce in 1977:

"From the Soviet point of view detente with the United States is . . . as much as anything an attempt to enlist American economic help for the solution of its mounting economic problems and for averting the closely related political risks. It follows that our own economic power gives us opportunities to advance our international interests vis-a-vis the U.S.S.R. in the many areas where we are in confrontation or contact with it. In my opinion, the United States has not made sufficient use of the economic instruments in this sense." (Statement by Gregory Grossman, University of California, in U.S.

Congress, Senate, Committee on Commerce, The American
Role in East-West Trade, 95th Cong., 1st sess., 1977, p.
38.)

Similar sentiments have been voiced by the Committee for
Human Rights in the Soviet Area:

"As long as the adversary relationship between the
Soviet Union and the United States prevails, simple
logic tells us that it is of no advantage to us to
strengthen the adversary economically and help him solve
his economic problems, unless he is willing, in
exchange, to agree to concessions mitigating the
adversary relationship." (Statement by the Committee
for Human Rights in the Soviet Area, in U.S. Congress,
House, Committee on Foreign Affairs, Detente, p. 606.)

For additional discussion of businessmen's views on the
linkage of human rights and trade questions in U.S.-Soviet
relations, see Chapter VI, pp. 398-402.

[3]Despite this moderate reduction in enthusiasm for
the trade-peace hypothesis, personal interviews during 1976
confirmed the continued popularity of the idea. For
example, note the following comments made by a senior
executive of a high-technology California company:

"Personally, I feel that trade will open up more
channels of communication between us and the Russians.
The more we communicate, the better we will understand
each other, and the less chance there will be that we
will end up fighting one another."

Similar sentiments were expressed by a representative of an
Ohio machinery manufacturer:

"Trade with the U.S.S.R. will help build human
understanding between our two countries, which will make
at least a small contribution to a reduction in world
tension and reduce the chances for a nuclear war."

Yet another businessman, when queried as to how trade would
foster peace, responded by arguing that:

"Businessmen are envoys of goodwill who will help
open up Soviet society to Western values. Trade
establishes personal communication at low levels, which
can contribute to international understanding and
indirectly to world peace."

It deserves attention that, apart from survey and interview results, the contention that Soviet-American trade will promote peace between the superpowers pervades writings and public statements made by numerous key U.S. business leaders during the 1970s. In this regard, William Verity, Chairman of the Board of Armco, Inc., has observed that:

"Increased trade with the Soviet Union will offer more than substantial economic benefits to the United States. As the people of our two nations increase their contacts, normal trade relations will have a moderating effect upon the Soviet view of the outside world. More trade may even ultimately contribute to a more stable world order." [William Verity, "Current Issues in U.S.-Soviet Trade," in Common Sense in U.S.-Soviet Trade, ed. Willard C. Matthias (Washington, D.C.: American Committee on East-West Accord, 1979), p. 7.]

"I think it has not been recognized that increased trade could possibly help the SALT talks and would certainly help the American people support the SALT agreement once it is reached." [William Verity, "Toward Trade Normalization," Journal of the U.S.-U.S.S.R. Trade and Economic Council 5 (January-February 1979): 14.]

Likewise, Donald Kendall, President of Pepsico and one of the U.S. business community's strongest proponents of trade with the U.S.S.R., has repeatedly indicated his strong belief in the trade-peace hypothesis:

". . . in terms of benefits to Americans, and to my mind, most important, increased trade between our two countries enhances the chances for an improved political climate. As trade relations develop, person-to-person contacts build mutual understanding. The more they know us and the more we know them, the better. As the Soviet economy becomes more interconnected with the world's economy, its stake in a stable international economic order is heightened. At the same time, it becomes increasingly difficult for its government to withdraw to an isolationist and belligerent status, thereby bettering the odds for world peace." (Donald M. Kendall, "Is the U.S.S.R. a Good Trading Partner?," in Matthias, Common Sense in U.S.-Soviet Trade, p. 12.)

"I am firmly convinced that increased U.S.-Soviet trade will threaten neither our economic system nor America's defense, but rather increase the chances for world peace, while providing significant commercial benefits." [Donald M. Kendall, "U.S.-Soviet Trade,

Peace, and Prosperity," in <u>Common Sense in U.S.-Soviet</u>
<u>Relations</u>, ed. Carl Marcy (Washington, D.C.: American
Committee on East-West Accord, 1978), p. 37.]

Armand Hammer, Chairman of Occidental Petroleum and a
pioneer of U.S.-Soviet trade, has also expressed opinions
consistent with those of Messrs. Verity and Kendall:

> "My part in . . . [fostering Soviet-American trade]
> . . . has . . . been to help create understanding
> between the USSR and the USA, to try to help avoid the
> ultimate clash between our ideologies through the common
> aim of beneficial trade. As Benjamin Franklin once
> said, 'Trading partners do not make war.' I believe
> that, and our experience in recent years suggests that
> it is a workable proposition." [Armand Hammer, "It's a
> Deal: A Personal History of Trade with the Soviet
> Union," <u>American Review of East-West Trade</u> 10 (May
> 1979): 34.]

Throughout the era of detente, the International Harvester
Company was one of the most vocal and articulate corporate
supporters of trade and detente with the U.S.S.R. It
follows that officials of that firm have been strong
adherents of the spill-over or trade-peace hypothesis.
This is evident, for instance, in the following remarks by
Robert J. McMenamin, Vice President of Harvester's Overseas
Division, before a 1974 session of the House Committee on
Foreign Affairs:

> ". . . International Harvester, under present world
> conditions, favors continuing efforts to build trade
> relations with the Soviet Union. The prime reason is to
> increase American production, jobs, corporate income,
> tax revenues, and in other words help the U.S. economy
> and balance of trade and balance of payments. Perhaps
> more important, it offers a chance or realistic
> opportunity to end the threat of total war, reduce
> tensions, and develop peaceful relations between the two
> superpowers which will benefit not only America and the
> Soviet Union but all the world. . . .
> . . . . . . . . . . . . . . . . . . . . . . . . . . . . .
> ". . . on the question of building up Soviet
> military power, we cannot avoid noting that both
> countries already have the military capability to
> destroy one another and the only real protection for the
> United States is maintaining a strong military posture
> ourselves while at the same time holding out the olive
> branch of detente to get a mutual lowering of military

strength and a lessening of tensions." (Statement by
Robert J. McMenamin, Vice President, Overseas Division,
International Harvester Co., in U.S. Congress, House,
Committee on Foreign Affairs, <u>Detente, Hearings before
the Subcommittee on Europe</u>. 93 Cong., 2d sess., 1974,
pp. 129-130.)

Another leading U.S. industrialist, Samuel B. Casey of
Pullman, Inc., has similarly argued that U.S.-Soviet trade
will promote peace via enhanced inter-societal
communication, and has argued that the alternative is to:

> ". . . allow the door to be closed . . . so that the
> only messages that can get through are carried on
> strategic missiles. . . .
> . . . . . . . . . . . . . . . . . . . . . . . . . . . . . . .
> ". . . trade is the way to understanding and peace
> throughout the world, no matter what the medium.
> Whether it's dollars, deutschemarks, rubles, dinars,
> shoes, steel, oil, gas or grain, any stimulus to trade
> will stimulate interdependent economies. Every nation
> will benefit." [Samuel B. Casey, "Pullman and World
> Trade in Perspective," <u>American Review of East-West
> Trade</u> 10 (May 1979): 40.]

Finally, William T. Ylvisaker, Chairman of Gould, Inc., has
observed that:

> ". . . tomorrow's security need not come from mutual
> fear of MIRVs and ICBMs, but rather from dependence of
> each country on the other's technological resources as
> well as natural resources and markets." [William T.
> Ylvisaker as quoted in "Gould Credits Technology for Its
> Soviet Success," <u>Journal of the U.S.-U.S.S.R. Trade and
> Economic Council</u> 2 (July-August 1976): 17.]

At this juncture an important caveat is in order:
Despite businessmen's strong advocacy of the spill-over or
trade-peace hypothesis, there is no consensus in the
academic community as to the validity of this proposition.
Critics of the idea have been apt to point to the high
levels of trade existing between Germany and France prior
to World War I and between Germany and the U.S.S.R. prior
to Hitler's invasion of the Soviet Union. Thus, various
U.S. interest groups have repudiated the spill-over
argument as a political basis for conducting economic
relations with the U.S.S.R. For example, note the
following statement submitted to the U.S. Congress in 1974
by the U.S. Committee for Human Rights in the Soviet Area:

"It is sometimes assumed, or argued, that there is a linkage between increased economic transactions as such, and pacification of international relations, but this was never satisfactorily demonstrated. It is therefore legitimate to tie economic concessions to explicit requests for counterconcessions of a political nature. If the Soviet government finds it unacceptable, that is no reason for dropping the demands and assisting our adversary economically in any event. It is important to adhere to these principles because of their psychological effect and educational value, even if the real contribution of increased economic transactions to Soviet capabilities seems negligible." (Statement by the Committee for Human Rights in the Soviet Area, in U.S. Congress, House, Committee on Foreign Affairs, Detente, p. 606.)

[4]For examples of adverse publicity of Soviet foreign policy activities during 1975-1976 see Angus Deming et al., "Tough Talk on Detente," Newsweek, September 1, 1975, pp. 14-15; "How Far Can Russia Push?," U.S. News and World Report, January 5, 1976, pp. 24-26; "Behind U.S. Threats to Cuba," U.S. News and World Report, April 5, 1976, pp. 21-22; and "Big Push for Detente: Is U.S. Moving Too Fast?," U.S. News and World Report, July 28, 1975, pp. 12-13.

[5]For examples of U.S. press coverage of the Eurocommunist movement during 1975-1976 see Daniel Seligman, "Communism's Crisis of Authority," Fortune, February 1976, pp. 92-95, 168-170, 172; Daniel Seligman, "Communists in Democratic Clothing," Fortune, March 1976, pp. 116-119, 188, 190, 192-193; and "How Far Can Russia Push?," pp. 25-26.

[6]Examples of such media reports include, "Portugal: A Test of Whether Moscow Will Keep Hands Off," U.S. News and World Report, July 28, 1975, p. 21; James Reston, "Detente--Soviet Style," Reader's Digest, November 1975, pp. 171-172; and "Big Push for Detente", p. 12.

[7]Such logic is mirrored in a 1977 statement submitted to the Senate Commerce Committee by the Chase Manhattan Bank:

"As an enlarged trading volume is achieved with the Soviet Union in the years ahead, and it is conceivable that such trading exchanges could reach $5 to $10 billion a year--certainly the trade itself will have a stabilizing influence on relations between the Soviet Union and the United States. At such a time, we would

have indeed some leverage because we would be partners
in trade in a major way, each of us would have to take
more into account the interests of the other partner in
our international relations with third countries."
(Statement by the Chase Manhattan Bank in U.S. Congress,
Senate, Committee on Commerce, The American Role in
East-West Trade, p. 50.)

[8]This perspective was set forth most succinctly by a
San Francisco executive:

"This whole Angola thing has definitely affected
business attitudes toward the Russians—if only because
of practical considerations. American companies, including our firm, are afraid that the political situation
may cause export licenses to be delayed, or that the
Russians may hold up contracts. I think most businessmen are aware of the moral questions presented by the
Soviets' recent mischief-making, but these concerns are
not dominant yet. It would take a lot more for business
to react in this way. Right now most businessmen are
mainly concerned that politics may destabilize
U.S.-Soviet trading conditions."

[9]Further discussion of the logistical difficulties
of doing business with the U.S.S.R. can be found in Chapter
V, pp. 233-237.

[10]The following statement made by an Ohio
businessman is typical of the opinions that were voiced
during personal interviews:

"The U.S.S.R.'s monkey-business in Angola and the
frustrating logistics of doing business with Soviet FTOs
are the two reasons why most American companies have
adopted a much more reserved attitude toward the Soviet
market over the last year."

[11]This point of view is best illustrated by the
following remarks made by a senior official of a
California-based industrial conglomerate:

"Angola has had a couple of different effects on
American companies. It's made businessmen more aware of
the fact that U.S.-Soviet trade is inherently risky
because it's based on a political house of cards. It
has also raised once again all the old 'trading with the
enemy' concerns; businessmen don't want to take part in
activities which they feel might be unpatriotic, or which
they think the public might see as being unpatriotic."

[12]For example, during a personal interview one Midwestern executive commented that:

"The U.S.S.R.'s activities in Angola have reminded a lot of businessmen that the Soviet Union's ultimate goal is still to crush the United States and all that it stands for. I think that quite a few businessmen are becoming disenchanted with detente."

Another Midwestern businessman, representing a major capital equipment manufacturer, remarked that:

"By their behavior in Africa the Soviets have created a serious image problem for themselves among businessmen as well as the general public. People have become much more skeptical about detente and are worried that the U.S.S.R. may promote further warlike activity against Israel or China. If the Soviets continue to fool around as they have recently, many American companies won't want to have anything to do with them."

[13]See pp. 44-67 for a thorough explanation of the International Trade Politics Model.

[14]See, for example, Mills, The Power Elite; Domhoff, Who Rules America?; and Horowitz, Corporations and the Cold War.

[15]Bauer, Pool, and Dexter, American Business and Public Policy, pp. 127, 142-143.

[16]Russett and Hanson, Interest and Ideology, pp. 248-249.

[17]Ibid., pp. 271-279.

[18]Francis X. Sutton et al., The American Business Creed (Cambridge, Mass.: Harvard University Press, 1956), p. 357.

[19]Maynard S. Seider, "American Big Business Ideology: A Content Analysis of Executive Speeches," American Sociological Review 39 (December 1974): 809-814.

[20]Ibid., p. 809.

[21]Bauer, Pool, and Dexter, American Business and Public Policy, pp. 169-170, 225.

CHAPTER V

FLOWS OF BENEFITS IN U.S.-SOVIET TRADE

Thus far, documentation has been provided with regard
to U.S. executives' fundamental support during 1975-1976
for close U.S.-Soviet economic and political ties, their
overall repudiation of the idea that U.S. trade policy
should be employed overtly as a lever to extract various
political concessions from the U.S.S.R., and their
principal political justification for pursuing Soviet
business, i.e., that increased U.S. trade with the Soviet
Union will engender more peaceful relations between the
superpowers. We have also investigated in some detail the
weak albeit apparently real impact on such views of the
deterioration in the international and to a degree the
domestic political environment for U.S.-Soviet trade which
took place during the period under investigation. Having
considered these basic political variables, it is next
necessary to explore businessmen's views on a central
question which has generated major political controversy in
the U.S. since the inception of detente in the early 1970s:
Namely, has the Soviet Union or the United States gained

222

the most from U.S.-U.S.S.R. trade? Or, to phrase the
matter in the rhetorical terms that have frequently been
used by domestic critics of U.S.-Soviet economic ties, how
did executives react to the charge that trade with the
U.S.S.R. is a "one-way street" with the benefits of
commerce accruing mainly to the Soviets?[1] Drawing upon
survey and interview data, the following text attempts to
provide a comprehensive record of businessmen's opinions on
this key issue, examining respondents' assessments of the
flow of U.S.-Soviet trade benefits from two different
perspectives. Specifically, attention is devoted to
executives' evaluations of the pros and cons of trading
with the U.S.S.R. from the standpoint of overall U.S.
economic welfare and vital U.S. national security interests.

### Economic Factors in U.S.-Soviet Trade

Contentions by U.S. businessmen that sustained
U.S.-Soviet trade will contribute to world peace and lead
to liberalization of the Soviet political system were
obviously not just part of an altruistic rationale for
doing business with the U.S.S.R., they were also arguments
that the United States will secure tangible political
benefits from U.S.-Soviet commerce. Likewise, 1975-1976
survey and interview data show that throughout this period
SAEs on the whole held the conviction that Soviet-American
commerce would also yield important economic benefits for

the United States. In this regard, an overwhelming 86% of the respondents to the 1975 survey said that increased trade with the U.S.S.R. will be "generally beneficial" to the U.S. economy, whereas only 10% were "not sure," and a mere 4% felt that the U.S. economy would not benefit (Table 20). In terms of specific economic plusses, many of those in Survey 1 pointed to the prospect that the U.S. might gain valuable access to abundant supplies of Soviet natural resources: Some 61% felt that stable long-term business deals for the import of Soviet raw materials to the U.S. are indeed possible, and that such imports would be advantageous in comparison with other world sources. Interestingly, when asked to elaborate on this response during personal interviews, most of the participants continually cited petroleum and natural gas as commodities which the U.S. could usefully import from the U.S.S.R. in large quantities. In this connection, repeated favorable references were made to then on-going negotiations between American firms and Soviet foreign trade officials aimed at launching several massive joint venture projects for the development and export to the U.S. of Siberian energy resources.[2] Did these businessmen see any inherent danger in the U.S. relying on its main international adversary for oil, gas, and other vital raw materials? When questioned on this point, most of those interviewed

TABLE 20

COMMERCIAL BENEFITS FROM U.S.-SOVIET TRADE, 1975-1976

(Percentaged Horizontally)

| | Agree Strongly | Agree But Not Strongly | Not Sure, Depends | Disagree, But Not Strongly | Disagree Strongly | (N)* |
|---|---|---|---|---|---|---|
| **1975 Survey** | | | | | | |
| Increased trade with the U.S.S.R. will be generally beneficial to the U.S. economy. | 53.7% | 32.4% | 10.2% | 3.7% | 0% | (108) |
| Stable long-term business deals for the import of Soviet raw materials to the U.S. are possible and will be advantageous in comparison to other world sources. | 15.9 | 44.9 | 29.0 | 10.3 | 0 | (107) |
| **1976 Survey** | | | | | | |
| The benefits gained from agricultural sales to the U.S.S.R. have outweighed the inflationary effects such sales have had on the Consumer Price Index. | 24.1 | 33.2 | 16.1 | 19.1 | 7.5 | (199) |

TABLE 20 (continued)

COMMERCIAL BENEFITS FROM U.S.-SOVIET TRADE, 1975-1976

(Percentaged Horizontally)

| | Agree Strongly | Agree But Not Strongly | Not Sure, Depends | Disagree, But Not Strongly | Disagree Strongly | (N)* |
|---|---|---|---|---|---|---|
| Trade with the U.S.S.R.'s planned economy has had a beneficial stabilizing effect on industries which are highly sensitive to fluctuations in the business cycle. | 17.3 | 26.2 | 23.6 | 23.6 | 9.4 | (191) |
| Your company's business with the U.S.S.R. has been profitable. | 32.0 | 39.4 | 9.7 | 9.1 | 9.7 | (175) |

*Variations in the number of cases (N) are attributable to "no answers" which are excluded from all calculations. Survey results reported for 1975 are based on a total N of 109 executives. Results for the 1976 survey reflect a total N of 203 executives.

responded that as long as the U.S. does not become
excessively dependent on the U.S.S.R. for natural
resources, there would be only a minimal risk that a sudden
cut off stemming from a political downturn could disrupt
the American economy.  In any event, it was argued that
Third World countries, and especially the OPEC nations,
cannot be regarded as highly reliable providers of raw
materials to the United States.  Indeed, some businessmen
contended that a case can be made that the Soviets might be
more dependable, given their widely known obsession with
fulfilling business contracts to the letter.  Consequently,
it was suggested that the U.S. could only gain from a mild
dependence on the U.S.S.R., because this would further
diversify U.S. sources of supply and thereby result in a
net reduction in the overall vulnerability of the U.S.
economy to external economic forces.[3]

It is important to note, however, that while most
executives in the 1975 survey sample viewed natural
resource imports from the Soviet Union as a desirable
possibility, a sizable 29% of the respondents reported that
they were "not sure" on this issue, and another 10% were
somewhat opposed to reliance on the U.S.S.R.  Like
reservations were expressed by a few executives during
personal interviews.  Although these businessmen
acknowledged that natural resource imports from the

U.S.S.R. likely would never amount to a significant
proportion of total U.S. imports of raw materials, they
were nonetheless concerned that the U.S. might, over time,
be lulled into undue dependence on the Soviets for specific
needs. Particularly worrisome to these executives was the
possibility that U.S. commodity imports from the U.S.S.R.
would become concentrated in a narrow range of key raw
materials, such as oil and gas, which are of pervasive
importance to the health of the American economy. Thus,
unlike most of those interviewed, this small group of
executives tended to look upon the prospect of joint
U.S.-U.S.S.R. energy development projects in Siberia with a
skeptical eye.

The natural resource question notwithstanding, survey
data for 1976 show that many businessmen felt that trade
with the U.S.S.R. could confer other economic benefits on
the United States. In this regard, respondents offered a
generally favorable assessment of the massive and highly
controversial sales of U.S. grain to the Soviet Union which
took place during 1972-1974. These sales, often referred
to as the "great grain robbery" in media reports of the
period, had been denounced by various domestic critics as a
destabilizing economic influence that had caused
considerable increases in U.S. food prices.[4] In
countering these charges, 57% of 1976 survey respondents

said that agricultural sales to the U.S.S.R. had yielded
certain benefits to the U.S. which outweighed the
inflationary effects which had resulted. When asked in
personal interviews to specify these benefits, most
executives consistently characterized the grain sales as a
boon to U.S. farmers and stated that they had had an
important positive impact on what was seen as an otherwise
dismal U.S. balance of payments picture. Nevertheless, it
is worth mention that those interviewed generally did not
disagree with one aspect of the charges leveled by critics
of the grain sales: Namely, that the Soviets had been able
to take unfair advantage of the highly competitive,
decentralized nature of the American grain market to
purchase needed foodstuffs at bargain prices. For the most
part, however, this and other negative effects of the grain
sales were viewed as an aberration: The U.S. Government,
several executives contended, shared culpability for
adverse consequences of the sales because it failed to
provide U.S. farmers and grain companies with timely
information that it had on hand concerning the nature and
vast extent of Soviet needs. Thus, it was argued, American
suppliers understandably were unable to make intelligent
pricing decisions when approached by Soviet authorities.
As one executive put it, the U.S. Government "was asleep at
the switch." It follows that steps taken by the U.S.

Government in the aftermath of the so-called "grain
robbery," notably efforts which ultimately resulted in the
Long-Term Grain Agreement with the U.S.S.R. signed in
December 1976, were seen as preventing future disruptions
of U.S. agricultural markets while simultaneously
guaranteeing continued large-scale U.S. export earnings
from farm sales to the Soviets.

On a somewhat different note, 43% of 1976 survey
respondents reported that trade with the U.S.S.R.'s planned
economy has had a beneficial stabilizing effect on those
American industries which are highly sensitive to
fluctuations in the U.S. business cycle.[5] Although this
view was held by only a minority of those in the survey
sample, this minority is nonetheless quite sizeable, and
the response raises the prospect that the decisions of many
SAEs to seek Soviet business in the mid-1970s may have been
primarily a response to the world recession of 1974-1975.
As a result of the contraction in demand for U.S.
industrial goods which took place in traditional domestic
and international markets during this time frame, a number
of U.S. businessmen, who might otherwise have been
reluctant to pursue Soviet business, may have seen the
U.S.S.R. as one antidote to their problems. In other
words, the Soviet market, with its centrally-directed
economy largely insulated from Western recessionary forces,

may have been looked upon by some executives as a safety
net which could help cushion them from the negative effects
of an international economic slowdown.

Such an interpretation is supported by the results of
personal interviews held with five executives. Two of
these businessmen represented large manufacturers of
machine tools, whereas the remaining three were employed by
medium-sized suppliers of foundry equipment and related
items used in basic industries. All of these executives
noted that although the quantity of business between U.S.
firms and the Soviets would likely stay relatively small in
terms of U.S. companies' aggregate business volume (and as
a percentage of overall U.S. GNP), U.S.-Soviet trade
recently had had a disproportionate positive impact on the
fortunes of their particular companies. In this
connection, all said that they had been operating under
Soviet contracts at some point during the 1974-1975
recession, and that this business had been especially
opportune in light of the evaporation of demand on other
markets. Observing that their areas of manufacturing
normally bear the brunt of any economic downturn, these
executives, under questioning, also acknowledged that their
firms' great susceptibility to the vagaries of the business
climate had figured prominently in their original decisions
to try to penetrate the Soviet market. In sum, then,

businessmen of certain U.S. industrial sectors, conditioned by the circumstances confronting their particular companies, evidently saw more benefits from trade with the U.S.S.R. than was the case for the 1976 survey sample as a whole.

## The Profitability of U.S.-Soviet Trade

Having considered U.S. executives' evaluations of the effects of U.S.-Soviet trade on American agriculture and certain segments of U.S. business, it is necessary at this point to take a look at their views on the larger question of the overall profitability of the Soviet market for U.S. industry in general. Throughout the 1970s, a persistent theme in public debates on the efficacy of Soviet-American commerce was whether or not U.S. companies were being exploited financially by the U.S.S.R. Various analysts have argued that because Soviet foreign trade organizations (FTOs) are national purchasing monopolies, they possess inordinate market power; i.e., that they are able to play off prospective sellers against one another to obtain maximum contract concessions.[6]

In an effort to explore the possibility that U.S. firms were, on the whole, being coaxed or pressured by their Soviet counterparts into economically disadvantageous deals, participants in the 1976 survey were simply asked if their companies' business with the U.S.S.R. had been profitable. In reply, 71% of the respondents said that, in their judgment, their firms' experience with the Soviets had been worthwhile. Thirty-five percent "agreed strongly" that their companies' Soviet business had been profitable, while 39% agreed but "not strongly" (Table 20). On the other hand, 10% indicated that they were "not sure" whether or not their company had made money in the U.S.S.R.; another 9% reported that for them Soviet business had been somewhat unprofitable; and 10% felt "strongly" that their U.S.S.R. business efforts had yielded significant losses.

Given the centrality of the profitability question to the issue of the flow of benefits in Soviet-American trade, executives were queried closely about the preceding response pattern during personal interviews. As a result, a number of insights were gained that are relevant here:

First of all, reflecting 1976 survey results, the large majority of those interviewed regarded the Soviet market as profitable. However, virtually all these individuals also harbored an intense dislike for the Soviet style of doing business, which was variously described as slow, frustrating, and expensive.[7] Consequently, five of these executives, who maintained that U.S.-Soviet trade is politically desirable and who also said they had not been adversely affected by the Angola affair and like developments, nevertheless imparted that they were becoming

increasingly reluctant to do business with the U.S.S.R.
They observed that even if they could conclude otherwise
successful Soviet contracts, enormous opportunity costs
would be incurred by continuing to put up with the time
consuming business practices of Soviet foreign trade
organizations.  Two executives of high-technology
electronics companies further noted that, for their firms,
such opportunity costs were of growing importance because
their traditional markets were recovering from recession.[8]  Since more attractive sales opportunities were
once again available, the risk of investing heavily in a
prospective Soviet deal, and then failing to win the
contract, was now seen as outweighing the benefits which
would stem from successful negotiations.  In other words,
impatience with Soviet negotiating tactics evidently caused
at least some executives to regard the U.S.S.R. as a
residual market, to be courted during bad economic times
but relegated to secondary importance during good times.
It follows that the five businessmen in this group seemed
willing to devote currently unused production capacity and
executive talent to service the U.S.S.R., but were
extremely wary of investing in new capabilities for this
purpose.[9]

Given their displeasure with respect to Soviet
bargaining methods, executives who regarded the Soviet

market as profitable were asked to comment on the ability
of Soviet FTOs to "whipsaw" American companies into
unfavorable transactions by playing them off against one
another and against foreign competitors.  Virtually all
were quick to acknowledge that the Soviets have a
considerable theoretical capability for effective
whipsawing.  However, they contended that this potential
often goes unrealized.  Speaking from their own
experiences, they pointed to a number of considerations
which they saw as placing practical limits on the ability
of the U.S.S.R. to take advantage of U.S. firms.  In
particular, these executives argued that they and other
U.S. businessmen have a strong aversion to signing
unprofitable contracts for the fundamental reason that
their firms would not stay in business for long.  Hence,
they contended that U.S. companies simply will not develop
sustained trading relationships with the U.S.S.R. unless
such trade stands the test of economics.[10]  It was also
suggested that if the U.S.S.R. truly wants to foster a
large-scale long-term relationship with U.S. industry, then
the Soviets are harming their own interests by the frequent
use of "whipsaw" and "wear-them-down" negotiating tactics.
As noted above, a number of executives said that such
methods had generated increased reluctance on their part to
pursue Soviet business, and had contributed to a tendency

to view the U.S.S.R. as a residual market. According to
this view, U.S. executives' goodwill toward their Soviet
counterparts was being eroded by the U.S.S.R.'s growing
reputation as a difficult business negotiator. As one
executive saw it, "the Russians are cutting their own
throats." This individual, as well as several others,
observed that in the early days of detente most U.S.
companies had been entranced by visions of a vast,
virtually unlimited Soviet market for American goods and
services. These expectations, they said, had now given way
to a more tempered and realistic appraisal of U.S.S.R.
business possibilities. Consequently, U.S. firms were seen
as having developed a much lower tolerance level for Soviet
whipsaw tactics and related negotiating techniques.
Confronted with the prospect of lengthy, frustrating talks
with Soviet trade officials, it was regarded as
increasingly likely that U.S. businessmen might simply
by-pass these business opportunities. Reflecting on the
obstinacy of Soviet negotiators, one executive succintly
summarized his own views on the matter when he said, "who
needs it?"[11]

Apart from executives' sheer unwillingness to enter
into disadvantageous deals, another factor was seen as
nullifying the theoretically superior bargaining power of
Soviet foreign trade organizations. A number of executives

maintained that their companies have the reputation of
producing the "best in the world" in their particular
product sectors. This, they said, coupled with the
Soviets' widely-known penchant for quality, had placed
their firms in an excellent negotiating position vis-a-vis
the U.S.S.R. In fact, several executives felt that it was
they, not the Soviets, who had the superior bargaining
leverage. To characterize the attitude of one
businessman: "If they want quality, they are going to have
to pay for it." This individual as well as several others
interviewed claimed that, far from taking a loss on their
Soviet contracts, they had been able to charge the Soviets
premium prices. Somewhat defensively, they explained that
it was necessary to include a "safety margin" in any prices
quoted to the U.S.S.R., in order to offset the unusually
high costs and risks of penetrating the Soviet market.
Thus, because most U.S. companies were seen as translating
the frustrations of dealing with the U.S.S.R. into higher
prices charged on U.S. exports to that country, Soviet
wear-them-down business tactics were once again viewed as
being counter-productive to Soviet interests.

A variant of the preceding line of thinking was
evident among executives of U.S. companies specializing in
high-technology goods and services. These executives were
apt to point out that the U.S. has a near-monopoly on world

markets in their product areas, notably in the "frontier" areas of electronic data processing, instrumentation, etc. They were also aware that the acquisition of such technology has been a high priority of Soviet trade officials. Recognizing that the Soviets are keenly interested in their wares, and highly cognizant of the fact that there are few, if any, alternative sources of supply in other Western countries, these executives felt they were in an extremely strong position to extract maximum earnings on sales to the U.S.S.R. Indeed, some of these business-men, like their counterparts mentioned above, maintained that they had actually obtained windfall profits from their Soviet business.[12]

It follows from the preceding that certain types of companies, notably those with no special "quality" or "technology" advantage vis-a-vis the U.S.S.R., would appear to be especially vulnerable to Soviet whipsaw tactics and other pressure techniques. Logic would also seem to dictate that the same would be true for medium-sized and small companies as opposed to large companies, which can presumably deal with Soviet FTOs on a more equal footing in terms of foreign trade experience, market research capabilities, and other organizational resources. However, the fact remains that executives of seemingly vulnerable companies had nearly the same propensity to evaluate their

Soviet business as profitable as businessmen of firms
having superior bargaining power.  What accounts for this
finding?

Interviews with executives of medium and small-sized
companies possessing only "conventional" technologies
suggest a possible explanation.  These businessmen said
that for them bargaining with a monopoly buyer such as a
Soviet FTO had not been an altogether unfamiliar
experience.  Rather, they felt that based on their
experiences, negotiating with the Soviets had placed them,
in terms of relative bargaining strength, in the same
inferior position that they had frequently encountered in
dealing with a number of U.S. and Western European
industrial giants.  Large Western companies, it was argued,
also employ whipsaw tactics in soliciting bids on supply
contracts.  Pointing out that they had learned how to
survive under such disadvantageous circumstances in both
domestic and traditional international markets, these
businessmen generally did not feel that the size and market
power of Soviet FTOs represented unique factors with which
they could not cope.[13]

A slight modification of the preceding theme also
merits attention.  Irrespective of company size or the
level of company technology, businessmen who were
interviewed sometimes noted that doing business with the

Soviet foreign trade monopoly is certainly no more difficult, and in certain cases may be less troublesome, than contending with U.S. Government contracting procedures. In terms of putting U.S. companies at a bargaining disadvantage and vigorously applying whipsaw tactics, the federal government was characterized by some as being the ultimate "monopoly buyer." In this regard, criticism was leveled most frequently at U.S. defense procurement practices.[14]

In closing our discussion of those executives who viewed the U.S.S.R. as a profitable market, a final observation is in order: Some executives who were interviewed were genuinely puzzled by U.S. Government and media attention to the whipsaw issue, as well as by the seeming importance which the interviewer attached to this subject. However, several others saw public concern over the whipsaw question as a natural outgrowth of media attention to the negative aspects of the 1972-1973 U.S.-Soviet grain deals. Publicity surrounding the "great grain robbery," they noted, had focused attention on Soviet business tactics and had given U.S.-Soviet trade a lasting and unfavorable U.S. public image. The public, they felt, now tended to equate all Soviet-American commerce with the grain deals, leading to the perception that trade with the U.S.S.R. is a "one-way street" with most of the benefits

accruing to Moscow. While admitting that the Soviets had
been able to whipsaw U.S. grain companies to obtain bargain
prices,[15] these businessmen nevertheless maintained that
the 1972-1973 grain sales were a unique episode. Apart from
citing the failures of the U.S. Government noted previously,
they observed that the U.S. grain trade is inherently more
susceptible to Soviet negotiating tactics than most sectors
of the U.S. economy. This vulnerability, they indicated,
stems from the sheer immensity of the Soviets' continuing
requirements for imported farm products coupled with the
unusual and extreme volatility of agricultural commodity
markets. In contrast, the executives emphasized that most
industrial companies involved with the U.S.S.R. simply do
not confront such conditions: Soviet demand is normally
small relative to most firms' total business volume and
manufacturing companies generally have considerable control
over the selling price of their goods and services in the
market place.

Notwithstanding the fact that the large majority of
executives who answered the 1976 survey evaluated the
Soviet market positively and downplayed Soviet capabilities
for taking advantage of U.S. firms, what can be said about
those respondents whose experiences with the U.S.S.R. were
less favorable? Eight such executives were interviewed, and

several observations derived from these sessions deserve
mention briefly.

First, concerning the 8% of the 1976 survey
respondents who said they were "not sure" whether or not
their companies' business had been profitable, discussions
with 4 businessmen indicated a variety of reasons behind
the uncertain survey replies:   (1) One executive said that
his company had broken even on its first deal with the
Soviets.  However, he also reported that his firm had been
promised a more profitable contract in the near future.
Thus, he remained hopeful that Soviet business would
eventually generate benefits for his company.  (2) One
businessman said that his firm had only recently begun
efforts to penetrate the Soviet market and that, as a
result, he had not yet concluded a Soviet contract.  Hence,
he felt it was too early to provide an accurate evaluation
of his firm's experiences in the U.S.S.R.  (3) One executive noted that his company is a subsidiary of an industrial
conglomerate, and although his division is allowed to make
major marketing decisions autonomously, the parent company
handles all accounting matters.  The conglomerate's book-
keeping practices, he pointed out, do not include procedures
for separating out and evaluating Soviet business.  Therefore, he indicated that it is difficult for him to know
with any precision the net profitability of this market.

(4) Another businessman said that, in the midst of the
1974-1975 recession, he had entered into several contracts
with the Soviets that he knew at the time would turn out to
be break-even or mildly unprofitable deals.  However, he
did so because he felt that these contracts would still
help his firm to avoid layoffs, a temporary shutdown, or
even bankruptcy.  Hence, he felt his company had derived
certain benefits from U.S.-Soviet trade that did not quite
fit the standard criterion of profit and loss.  Consequently, when asked on the 1976 survey to evaluate his
firm's Soviet experiences in terms of profitability, he had
replied that he was "not sure" in this regard.

Regarding the 17% of the survey sample that responded
that their business experiences with the U.S.S.R. had not
been profitable, four executives in this group were
interviewed.  Two of these executives, who like 8% of all
respondents evaluated the Soviet market as being mildly
unprofitable, indicated that they had invested considerable
executive talent and money in Soviet business efforts over
the previous two to three years without having yet landed a
contract.  Hence, they were becoming increasingly
discouraged about their companies' prospects in the U.S.S.R.
and were extremely hesitant to expend any more resources in
this market.  Two remaining businessmen, who like 9% of
survey respondents felt "strongly" that their Soviet

business had been unprofitable, confirmed during the
interviews that they had lost significant money on their
first Soviet contract(s).  Interestingly, although these
two executives felt that the Soviets had successfully
"whipsawed" them against their competitors, they did not
seem as troubled by the Soviets' use of these tactics per se
as they were by their own failure to anticipate and minimize
the effectiveness of such methods.  In particular, both
noted that the initial price quotations which they had
provided the Soviets had been far too low.  Grudgingly,
they admitted that they had greatly underestimated the
out-of-pocket costs of doing business with the U.S.S.R.
Additionally, however, they observed that a higher initial
bid price would have given them more leeway in dealing with
Soviet negotiators; i.e., they could have responded more
easily to Soviet demands for price cuts while at the same
time preserving an acceptable profit margin.  In essence,
then, these businessmen indicated that they had neglected
to build a sufficient "safety margin" into prices quoted to
Soviet trade officials.[16]  (As noted above, executives of
companies which had been successful in the Soviet market
often pointed out that a large price cushion can be highly
important to conducting business in the U.S.S.R. on a
profitable basis.)  When asked what their plans were
vis-a-vis further business ventures with the Soviets, the

two executives differed in their responses.  The first said
that having learned from the past his company was still
prepared to entertain Soviet contracts, but was reluctant
to make further large expenditures in pursuit of these
opportunities.  The second executive was much more negative
in his outlook.  Feeling that he had been "burned" in the
U.S.S.R., this businessman said that doing business with
the Soviets is "much too expensive and too much trouble."
Thus, he said that unless he perceives a lucrative and easy
opportunity for his company, he would not actually seek
Soviet business in the foreseeable future.  Instead, he
felt that his time and energy would be better spent servicing his existing clients in his traditional markets and in
trying to cultivate new customers in these familiar areas.

## Perceptions of Profit and Attitudes
## Toward Trade and Detente

The fact that in 1976 SAEs generally evaluated the
Soviet market as having been profitable for their companies
highlights a question of substantial theoretical
importance:  Namely, to what extent were perceptions of
profitability influential in shaping executive attitudes on
the key trade/detente variables discussed in Chapter IV?
To put it in a more straightforward manner, was SAEs'
strong support in 1976 for improved U.S.-U.S.S.R.

commercial and political relations simply a reflection of greed, or was it based on broader considerations?

In an effort to shed some light on these questions, 1976 survey responses on the profitability variable were correlated with responses on a select group of previously discussed survey variables that were intended to measure executives' general orientations on fundamental U.S.-U.S.S.R. economic and political issues (Table 21). Although results are not definitive, they strongly suggest that the formulation of SAEs' positions on central Soviet-American trade questions was not influenced to any greater degree by perceptions of market profitability than by other concerns less directly related to corporate self-interest. In this connection, those SAEs who reported that their experiences in the Soviet market had been profitable--when contrasted with those who said otherwise--had a slightly greater propensity to have:  supported continued U.S. Government efforts to build closer trade ties with the U.S.S.R. ($r = .22$), expressed faith in the idea that increased Soviet-American trade will contribute to world peace ($r = .22$), and indicated the belief that trade is a normal condition which should exist between nations having diplomatic relations and should not be conditional upon negotiable differences on world issues nor on either country's domestic political policies ($r = .13$).

TABLE 21

CORRELATES OF CORPORATE PROFITABILITY, 1976*
(Percentaged Horizontally)

| | Your Company's Business with U.S.S.R. Has Been Profitable. | | | |
|---|---|---|---|---|
| | Agree | Not Sure, Depends | Disagree | Pearson's r or (N) |
| Entire Sample | 71.4% | 9.7% | 18.8% | (175) |
| **At this time, the U.S. Government should try to improve trade relations with the U.S.S.R.** | | | | .24 |
| Agree | 72.0 | 9.8 | 18.2 | (143) |
| Not sure, depends | 71.4 | 9.5 | 19.0 | (21) |
| Disagree | 71.4 | 0 | 28.6 | (7) |
| **Stronger trade ties with the U.S.S.R. will contribute significantly to world peace.** | | | | .20 |
| Agree | 76.7 | 7.0 | 16.3 | (129) |
| Not sure, depends | 57.7 | 19.2 | 23.1 | (26) |
| Disagree | 57.9 | 15.8 | 26.3 | (19) |
| **Trade with the U.S.S.R. should not be conditional upon negotiable differences on world issues nor on Soviet domestic policies.** | | | | .18** |
| Agree | 75.0 | 9.4 | 15.6 | (128) |
| Not sure, depends | 63.2 | 15.8 | 21.1 | (19) |
| Disagree | 63.0 | 7.4 | 29.6 | (27) |
| **Recent Soviet foreign policy activities (e.g., Angola) have adversely affected your company's outlook on doing business with the U.S.S.R.** | | | | -.14** |
| Agree | 63.6 | 12.1 | 24.2 | (33) |
| Not sure, depends | 58.8 | 20.6 | 20. | (34) |
| Disagree | 79.0 | 5.7 | 15.2 | (105) |

TABLE 21 (continued)

CORRELATES OF CORPORATE PROFITABILITY, 1976*
(Percentaged Horizontally)

| | Your Company's Business with U.S.S.R. Has Been Profitable. | | | |
| --- | --- | --- | --- | --- |
| | Agree | Not Sure, Depends | Disagree | Pearson's r or (N) |
| The increased strength of Communist Parties in W. Europe has adversely affected your company's outlook toward trade with the U.S.S.R. | | | | -.09*** |
| Agree | 63.6 | 22.7 | 13.6 | (22) |
| Not sure, depends | 83.3 | 8.3 | 8.3 | (24) |
| Disagree | 71.8 | 8.1 | 20.2 | (124) |

*Cases are omitted from the respective crosstabulations where the respondent failed to answer one or both of the variables being compared. Unless noted otherwise, Pearson's correlations are significant at the p = .01 level.

**Significant at the p = .05 level.

***Significant at the p = .25 level.

By way of comparison, as noted earlier, negative business perceptions of an increasingly aggressive Soviet international posture seem to have been at least as important as market profitability in exercising a formative influence on overall SAE attitudes.  In this regard, it will be recalled that unfavorable SAE views of the Soviet intervention in Angola (as well as similar activities elsewhere) were significantly related to:  the tendency to question the wisdom of U.S. Government efforts to improve U.S.-Soviet commercial contacts ($r = -.34$), a more skeptical view of the trade-peace hypothesis ($r = -.25$), and less intense opposition to the linkage of U.S. trade policies toward the U.S.S.R. to Soviet performance on human rights matters and Soviet international behavior ($r = -.15$).

Of particular relevance to the preceding is the fact that executive perceptions of Soviet international behavior in 1976 do not appear to have been motivated principally by considerations of profit (i.e., these two variables appear to be largely independent of one another).  Those respondents who had been the least disturbed by then-recent trends in Soviet foreign policy displayed only a weak corresponding tendency to have evaluated the U.S.S.R. as a profitable market ($r = -.14$).  Stated differently, those who regarded U.S.S.R. business as highly profitable did not display a strong parallel inclination to downplay the

Angola affair and like examples of Soviet adventurism. On
a similar but slightly different note, no statistically
significant relationship is apparent between the
profitability variable and SAEs' reactions in 1976 to the
then-growing political influence of the principal West
European communist parties ($r = .03$). Finally, a
comprehensive series of crosstabulations and Pearson's
correlations between the profitability variable and a whole
host of other attitudinal variables in all cases revealed
insignificant or weak relationships.

In sum, then, the profit motive seemingly exercised
some influence in shaping executive attitudes on a number
of critical issues of trade and detente. However, this
influence apparently was moderate and certainly was no more
important than that of independent non-pecuniary variables,
such as, for example, SAEs' perceptions of Soviet
international behavior.

### Selling Technology to the U.S.S.R.: The Competitor Issue

The question of the profitability of the Soviet
market, while important, is nonetheless limited in the
sense that it addresses an essentially short-term
consideration. Immediate profit is only one aspect of
corporate self-preservation and, although a major factor,
is not the sole determinant of the U.S. business

community's position in world trade. An additional element
vital to sustaining a leading role in international
commerce is the maintenance of a competitive edge over
foreign business rivals. Hence, it is not surprising that
the sales of U.S. industrial technology to the U.S.S.R.
which began in the early 1970s generated considerable
national controversy before, during, and beyond the period
under investigation. Concerns centered on a fundamental
question having long-term implications for overall U.S.
commercial interests: In light of several historical
precedents, would the transfer of U.S. technology to the
Soviet Union help transform that country from a weak force
in world markets for manufactured goods into a formidable
competitor of U.S. business? Especially relevant to the
objectives of the present study is how U.S. executives
engaged in Soviet-American commerce viewed this possibility
during 1975-1976.

Survey data for 1975 clearly confirm that in that year
a large proportion of businessmen pursuing trade
opportunities with the U.S.S.R. at the same time harbored
anxieties concerning the competitor issue. In this
connection, one survey question reminded respondents that
"post-World War II sales of U.S. technology set up Japan
and West Europe as our competitors in international
markets" and asked participants for their opinions on the

likelihood of a similar result in the case of the U.S.S.R.
In reply, 50% of the entire sample said that there was
reason for worry, whereas another 26% indicated uneasiness
by saying they were "not sure" about the prospects for such
a development (Table 22).

As a follow-up to the 1975 survey, participants in the
1976 survey were also solicited for their views on the
competitor issue. However, unlike the 1975 effort, the
1976 survey attempted to achieve a greater degree of
specificity on the matter. Two separate items on the
competitor issue were included on the survey questionnaire,
asking respondents to assess the relative possibilities for
establishing the U.S.S.R. as an effective competitor of
U.S. business in Lesser Developed Countries (LDCs) versus
markets in Industrialized Western (IW) nations. In
response, 41% expressed the view that the U.S. business
community has legitimate reason to fear setting up the
U.S.S.R. as a future competitor in the LDCs, another 18%
said they were "not sure," and 42% discounted this
prospect. In contrast, executives were considerably more
skeptical about chances that transfers of American
technology might eventually transform the Soviets into
viable rivals of U.S. business in IW markets. A full 60%
majority of respondents discounted this as a realistic

TABLE 22

ATTITUDES TOWARD THE COMPETITOR ISSUE, 1976
(Percentaged Horizontally)

| | Agree Strongly | Agree, But Not Strongly | Not Sure, Depends | Disagree, But Not Strongly | Disagree Strongly | (N)* |
|---|---|---|---|---|---|---|
| **1975 Survey** | | | | | | |
| Although post-WWII sales of U.S. technology set up Japan and W. Europe as our competitors in international markets, we really don't have to worry about the same thing happening again in the case of the U.S.S.R. | 4.7% | 18.7% | 26.2% | 26.2% | 24.3% | (107) |
| **1976 Survey** | | | | | | |
| The U.S. business community has reason to fear setting up the U.S.S.R. as a future competitor in international markets in the lesser developed countries as a result of sales of American industrial knowhow to the Soviet Union. | 11.7 | 29.1 | 17.9 | 27.6 | 13.8 | (196) |

TABLE 22 (continued)

ATTITUDES TOWARD THE COMPETITOR ISSUE, 1976
(Percentaged Horizontally)

| | Agree Strongly | Agree, But Not Strongly | Not Sure, Depends | Disagree, But Not Strongly | Disagree Strongly | (N)* |
|---|---|---|---|---|---|---|
| The U.S. business community has reason to fear setting up the U.S.S.R. as a future competitor in international markets in the industrialized countries as a result of sales of American industrial knowhow to the Soviet Union. | 6.6 | 24.5 | 9.7 | 35.7 | 23.5 | (196) |
| The Soviets usually buy "proven" production technology from American vendors, which soon makes it outmoded in terms of the advances we are preparing to put on line. | 20.6 | 43.8 | 16.5 | 17.5 | 1.5 | (194) |

*Variations in the number of cases (N) are attributable to "no answers" which are excluded from all calculations. Survey results reported for 1975 are based on a total N of 109 executives. Results for the 1976 survey reflect a total N of 203 executives.

possibility. Still, a sizeable 32% of the sample perceived a genuine risk, and another 10% were "not sure."

The fact that many SAEs apparently dismissed the possibility of a future Soviet competitive threat, as well as the fact that the potential for future Soviet competition was viewed as being greater with respect to LDC markets, can be accounted for by results of personal interviews. During these discussions, it was apparent that most SAEs were keenly aware of the serious problems affecting the U.S.S.R.'s civilian industrial sector, and some were particularly cognizant of shortcomings in the Soviet research and development process. Thus, a commonly expressed opinion was that despite massive imports of technology the U.S.S.R. will still have great difficulty penetrating Industrialized Western markets, in large measure because Soviet industry will have considerable trouble using purchased technology effectively. The Soviets, it was frequently noted, have consistently shown an inability to produce manufactured goods of contemporary design which are quality-competitive in the West. Furthermore, even if Soviet industry is able to capitalize on imported technology so as to mass produce certain items which are saleable in the West, these items will remain competitive only for a brief time, because the U.S.S.R. will be too slow to modify its product designs to keep pace with rapidly changing Western industrial requirements and consumer tastes. Finally, even if the U.S.S.R. can overcome the preceding problems, many SAEs observed that the bureaucratic nature of Soviet FTOs has caused the U.S.S.R. to neglect developing a global service network for Soviet-made products. This historical inattention to questions of "aftermarket support," it was contended, is not easily rectified and for the foreseeable future will seriously handicap Soviet efforts to sell their goods in the West.

Interestingly, the aforementioned Soviet marketing problems were seen as being less of a factor in Soviet attempts to improve their sales performance in LDCs. Various executives noted that in LDC markets the price of a product is often the critical element in decisions to buy, whereas price is frequently of secondary importance in IW markets where contemporary product design and product quality are normally the key criteria for success. Thus, these executives observed that the Soviets have a potentially important competitive advantage in LDCs because the Soviet government maintains central administrative control over the convertible currency selling prices of Soviet products. This, it was pointed out, gives Soviet foreign trade organizations the capacity to undercut price quotations by U.S. and other Western companies.

A second factor was seen as improving Soviet business prospects in LDCs: Various executives observed that industrial requirements and consumer tastes typically evolve more slowly in developing countries than in advanced nations. As a result, marketing opportunities in LDCs were seen as being generally less dependent upon a given vendor's capabilities for dynamic product development. Consequently, certain SAEs felt that the Soviets' limited ability to modify rapidly their product designs is not a major impediment to success in these markets. Hence, if the U.S.S.R. successfully uses imported U.S. manufacturing technology to produce items for export to LDCs, some SAEs expressed the nagging concern that these products might have a long competitive life.

Notwithstanding the fact that many SAEs discounted the prospect that U.S. technology might help establish the U.S.S.R. as an effective international competitor of U.S. business, it remains that a substantial number of respondents to both Survey 1 and Survey 2 regarded the commercial threat as credible. It follows, therefore, that it is relevant at this point to explore how willing SAEs were to sell their companies' industrial technology to the U.S.S.R.

Pertinent to this question, of course, is an understanding of the term "technology." In its most general usage, the concept of "technology" refers to all those elements necessary to organize and maintain agricultural and industrial production. Individual technologies are usually classified according to their pace of development. "Stable" technologies progress only slowly over time, whereas "dynamic" lines of technology are characterized by rapid innovation. In a more specific sense, technology, from an analytical standpoint, can be broken down into two basic constituents: a human component of technical skill or "knowhow," which is vital for the manufacture and effective use of the second element, "hardware" (or product). It is generally recognized that a country seeking to enhance its economic efficiency and productivity through the acquisition of foreign technology is usually better advised to import technological knowhow via industrial licensing agreements rather than buy technology primarily in the form of products. In other words, the transfer of technological knowhow, as opposed to the transfer of technological hardware, is widely regarded as the more effective path to development, although an important caveat is that the importing nation must be capable of absorbing and making effective use of the technical expertise being purchased. In sum, then, the sale of American manufacturing knowhow to the U.S.S.R. carries with it the greatest danger of establishing the

Soviet Union as a business competitor of the United States
in any given product line.

With this background in mind, a new perspective is
gained on the original question posed above. It is not
sufficient simply to measure the willingness of American
businessmen to sell U.S. industrial technology to the
U.S.S.R. It must also be determined whether executives are
anxious to sell their firms' knowhow to the Soviets through
licensing agreements, or whether they are principally
interested in selling products.

Survey data for 1975 and 1976 reveal that in both
years, more than on any other issue, businessmen were
deeply divided in their assessments of the merits of
selling knowhow to the U.S.S.R. (Table 23). In 1975, a
55.8% majority of respondents said they favored licensing
their companies' latest technology to the Soviets, but some
43.2% opposed such agreements. Most remarkable, perhaps,
is that only one executive, representing a miniscule 1.1%
of the sample, said he was uncertain of his position; a
fact which is indicative of the degree of polarization on
this issue. Survey data for 1976 reveal a similar pattern,
although with one important change: A majority of 54.3%
were now against the sale of their firms' latest knowhow to
the U.S.S.R., whereas the share favoring such licenses
diminished to 44%. Again, a mere 1.6% were "not sure" of

TABLE 23

ATTITUDES TOWARD THE LICENSING AND SALE OF
U.S. TECHNOLOGY, 1975-1976
(Percentaged Horizontally)

|  | Yes | No | Don't Know | (N)* |
|---|---|---|---|---|
| Within limits set by export controls, do you personally favor <u>licensing</u> your firm's latest technology to the U.S.S.R.? |  |  |  |  |
| 1975 | 55.8% | 1.1% | 43.2% | (95) |
| 1976 | 44.0 | 1.6 | 54.3 | (184) |
| Within limits set by export controls, do you personally favor <u>product sales</u> to the U.S.S.R. incorporating your company's latest technology? |  |  |  |  |
| 1975 | 93.9 | 0 | 6.1 | (98) |
| 1976 | 89.6 | 2.2 | 8.2 | (182) |

*Variations in the number of cases (N) are attributable to "no answers" which are excluded from all calculations. Survey results reported for 1975 are based on a total N of 109 executives. Results for the 1976 survey reflect a total N of 203 executives.

their feelings on the matter. In sum, while opinion on the
licensing question remained split, opposition to the
transfer of U.S. industrial knowhow clearly grew between
the two surveys, with the end result being a complete
reversal in the proportions of respondents for and against
licensing.

In marked contrast with the major difference of
opinion evident on the licensing issue, almost all
respondents to both surveys had no objections to the sale
of U.S. industrial technology to the U.S.S.R. in the form
of hardware. An overwhelming 93.9% of executives in the
1975 sample reported that within limits set by U.S. export
controls, they personally favored selling the Soviets
products incorporating their firms' latest technology. The
comparable figure for the 1976 survey was 89.6%, indicating
that on this particular matter business opinion remained
highly stable during the period between the first and
second surveys.

Survey respondents' strong preference for selling
technology-as-product to the Soviets, as opposed to
providing the U.S.S.R. with technological knowhow, is
completely consistent with these executives' previously
noted fears of setting up the U.S.S.R. as a rival of
American industry. The response patterns imply clear
recognition of the fact that the licensing of technology

inherently involves a much greater risk of transforming a customer into a competitor. Hence, one would expect to find strong inverse correlations between the "competitor" variables and "licensing" variables for both surveys. Surprisingly, this is not the case (Table 24). In 1976, for instance, those who harbored fears of setting up the Soviet Union as a business competitor, when contrasted with those who dismissed this as a possibility, had only a mildly greater propensity to oppose licensing their firms' latest technology to the U.S.S.R. Furthermore, there was only an insignificant difference in the tendency to oppose licensing between those who saw the U.S.S.R. as a potential competitor in the LDCs ($r = -.19$), and those who saw the U.S.S.R. as a possible commercial threat in Industrialized Western (IW) markets ($r = -.17$). Even more remarkable, however, is that in the 1975 survey data the relationship between attitudes toward licensing and attitudes on the competitor issue is entirely absent ($r = -.04$). What accounts for these perplexing findings?

First, the survey data for 1975, and especially for 1976, indicate that a meaningful number of Soviet Area Executives did in fact oppose licensing their firms' latest technology to the U.S.S.R. principally because they feared that a long-term competitive threat might result. In this regard, 10% of the 1975 survey respondents stated that they

TABLE 24

CORRELATES OF ATTITUDES TOWARD TECHNOLOGY LICENSING, 1975-1976*
(Percentaged Horizontally)

| | Do You Personally Favor Licensing Your Firm's Latest Technology to the U.S.S.R.? | | | |
| | Yes | Not Sure, Depends | No | Pearson's r or (N) |
|---|---|---|---|---|
| **1975 Survey** | | | | |
| Entire Sample | 55.8% | 1.1% | 43.2% | (95) |
| Although post-WWII sales of U.S. technology set up Japan and West Europe as our competitors in international markets, we really don't have to worry about the same thing happening again in the case of the U.S.S.R. | | | | .05** |
| Agree | 60.9 | 0 | 39.1 | (23) |
| Not sure, depends | 52.2 | 4.3 | 43.5 | (23) |
| Disagree | 55.1 | 0 | 44.9 | (49) |
| **1976 Survey** | | | | |
| Entire Sample | 44.0 | 1.6 | 54.3 | (184) |
| The U.S. business community has reason to fear setting up the U.S.S.R. as a future competitor in international markets in the lesser developed countries as a result of sales of American industrial knowhow to the Soviet Union. | | | | -.21 |
| Agree | 34.2 | 1.4 | 64.4 | (73) |
| Not sure, depends | 41.4 | 0 | 58.6 | (29) |
| Disagree | 54.7 | 1.3 | 44.0 | (75) |

TABLE 24 (continued)

CORRELATES OF ATTITUDES TOWARD TECHNOLOGY LICENSING, 1975-1976*
(Percentaged Horizontally)

| | Do You Personally Favor Licensing Your Firm's Latest Technology to the U.S.S.R.? | | | |
| | Yes | Not Sure, Depends | No | Pearson's r or (N) |
| --- | --- | --- | --- | --- |
| The U.S. business community has reason to fear setting up the U.S.S.R. as a future competitor in international markets in the industrialized countries as a result of sales of American industrial knowhow to the Soviet Union. | | | | -.18 |
| Agree | 30.9 | 1.8 | 67.3 | (55) |
| Not sure, depends | 44.4 | 0 | 55.6 | (18) |
| Disagree | 50.5 | 1.0 | 48.6 | (105) |
| Recent Soviet foreign policy activities (e.g., Angola) have adversely affected your company's outlook on doing business with the U.S.S.R. | | | | -.09*** |
| Agree | 35.3 | 5.9 | 58.8 | (34) |
| Not sure, depends | 50.0 | 0 | 50.0 | (34) |
| Disagree | 46.2 | 0 | 53.8 | (106) |

*Cases are omitted from the respective crosstabulations where the respondent failed to answer one or both of the variables being compared. Unless noted otherwise, Pearson's correlations are significant at the p = .01 level.

**Significant at the p = .63 level.

***Significant at the p = .27 level.

were against licensing their firms' modern knowhow to the
U.S.S.R., and at the same time expressed fears that U.S.
companies might assist the Soviets, as they had West
Germany and Japan, in becoming an effective competitor of
American business.  More importantly, however, fully 26.6%
of respondents to the 1976 survey said they opposed
licensing their latest knowhow to the Soviets and also said
they were anxious about possible future Soviet business
competition in the LDCs. On a similar note, 21% of 1976
respondents saw prospects for Soviet competition in IW
markets and likewise indicated that they were not willing
to license up-to-date technology to the U.S.S.R.  In sum,
the executives who responded along the lines just described
seemingly drew a direct connection between the competitor
issue and licensing.  Indeed, this inference was confirmed
by follow-up personal interviews with relevant executives
from the 1976 survey.  Under questioning these businessmen
flatly stated that, partly due to competitive factors, they
had a deep aversion to licensing their latest technology to
the U.S.S.R. or, for that matter, to any other country.
For these executives, opposition to licensing was a matter
of principle.  It simply does not make sense, they argued,
for American companies to permit foreign firms to build
upon U.S. technology and to cede voluntarily potentially

lucrative overseas markets. Royalties from licenses, they contended, just do not offset these disadvantages.[17]

The preceding evidence, which strongly suggests that the willingness of many executives to license technology was indeed inhibited by the fear of setting up foreign competition, raises an important question: Why is this connection not apparent from the crosstabulations and Pearson's correlations of the survey data--i.e., what factors acted to obscure the linkage between these two issues?

A partial answer to this question is suggested by the fact that 44% of the 1976 survey respondents who dismissed the possibility of setting up the U.S.S.R. as a competitor in LDCs nevertheless still opposed licensing their latest technology to the Soviets. Likewise, 48.6% of those who dismissed the prospect of a future Soviet commercial threat in Industrialized Western markets also responded negatively to the licensing question. In essence, sizeable numbers of businessmen apparently opposed licensing their technology to the U.S.S.R. on grounds other than the fear of future Soviet competition, thereby helping to mask the link between these two questions. Personal interviews with 4 executives from this category revealed that their reluctance to sell knowhow to the U.S.S.R. was part of a general opposition to licensing which stemmed from several

narrow, pragmatic business concerns. These businessmen
pointed out that pricing a license so as to insure a fair
return is an extremely difficult process which frequently
relies more on judgment than on objective criteria. Thus,
earnings from licenses often fail to recoup an acceptable
share of the research and development costs of the
technology in question. Additionally, the executives noted
that the great care which must be taken to arrive at an
acceptable licensing arrangement means that licensing
negotiations are almost always unusually lengthy and
therefore expensive to conduct. Even if a contract can be
arrived at, they argued, the written agreement can provide
only a broad framework for the future relationship between
the licensor and the licensee. The intrinsically
complicated nature of a license, it was believed, usually
dictates that many details are left to be worked out as the
needs of both parties evolve. Thus, the success or failure
of a licensing agreement was seen by these businessmen as
being heavily dependent on the development and maintenance
of strong mutual trust between all participants.
Consequently, the executives said that in view of all the
possible complications, they had concluded that licensing
simply did not make good sense for their companies.
Instead, the straightforward sale of products, to the

U.S.S.R. as well as elsewhere, was seen as less risky, easier, and more profitable.

Personal interviews with 3 other executives revealed a variation on the preceding theme: These businessmen did not object to licensing generally, but were aware of the unique and complex character of licensing agreements. They went on to point out that, given the Soviets' reputation as difficult business negotiators, concluding even the most basic contracts for the sale of products to the U.S.S.R. is usually a drawn-out, tiresome affair. It follows that the Soviets' frustrating business habits were seen as greatly magnifying the complicated, knotty problems which are normally encountered in the negotiation of any license. Thus, these executives indicated a strong preference for limiting any future deals between their companies and the Soviets to straightforward sales of products, which they considered to be less troublesome to arrange and, hence, generally more profitable. In essence, then, displeasure with Soviet business procedures seemingly exercised a differential negative impact on the willingness of some executives to conclude licensing agreements with the U.S.S.R.[18]

Data from Survey 2 suggest that a second factor acted to obscure the connection between the competitor and licensing issues: Thirty-four percent of those respondents who acknowledged the potential for setting up the Soviets as competitors in LDC markets nevertheless expressed a willingness to license their latest technology to the U.S.S.R.  The same position was also voiced by 31% of those who perceived a possible future Soviet competitive threat in Industrialized Western markets.  Although this stance is seemingly irrational and contradictory, personal interviews with three SAEs who stated such views suggest several explanations:

First, the SAEs noted that American companies, especially those dealing in conventional as opposed to high-technology product lines, no longer have a near-monopoly on many kinds of industrial knowhow.  The West Europeans and Japanese, they observed, have developed many industrial processes which are often competitive with--and sometimes superior to--American techniques. Thus, the view was that if U.S. firms refuse to license non-exclusive U.S. technology, the Soviets will simply buy it from other Western sources.  As one executive put it, "If they are going to get it anyway, we might as well be the ones to get the business."[19]

The executives also pointed out that, while they are apprehensive that U.S. technology might help transform the U.S.S.R. into an effective international business competitor, most American firms interested in Soviet licensing intend to minimize the risk by confining the transfer of knowhow to <u>proven</u> technology.  In this regard, these three SAEs (as well as the majority of others interviewed who favored licensing but who discounted the Soviet competitive threat) expressed a strong preference for selectively licensing only those industrial processes that are in standard operation and to withhold innovations just emerging from research and development (R&D) and prototype stages.  Underlying this careful strategy was confidence in the continued ability of their companies' R&D to stay well ahead of the Soviets.[20]  Additionally, it was noted by various executives that Soviet industrial managers are inherently conservative and actually <u>prefer</u> proven technology, because it has been extensively tested in a production environment and is generally less likely to require maintenance.  (Reflecting such opinions, it should be noted that 64.4% of 1976 survey respondents were of the view that the Soviets do indeed have a penchant for buying proven technology from American vendors, which soon makes it outmoded in terms of the advances which U.S. firms are preparing to put on line.)[21]

Summing up the licensing-competition question, reluctance to help set up the U.S.S.R. as an effective future competitor of U.S. business in world markets evidently did exercise an important negative effect on many executives' willingness to license their companies' technology to the Soviet Union. However, this link is masked in correlations and crosstabulations of the survey data because, despite the analyst's painstaking efforts to the contrary, relevant survey variables were not phrased with sufficient precision to isolate the licensing-competition connection from extraneous albeit closely related influences.

A question previously raised but not directly addressed concerns the reasons behind the apparent decline during 1975-1976 of SAEs' willingness to license their latest technology to the Soviets. It will be recalled that whereas 55% of 1975 survey respondents were positively inclined toward licensing, this figure fell to 44% in 1976. While sampling error may account for some of this reduction, it is more likely that other, substantive factors were primarily responsible. Two possible influences have already been suggested: It is probable, for example, that the above-noted impatience with Soviet business habits contributed to growing SAE negativism with respect to licensing. Unfortunately, it is not possible to test this hypothesis fully, because neither the 1975 nor 1976 surveys incorporated variables designed to measure the frustration dimension. Likewise, a case can be made that at least part of the drop in SAEs' enthusiasm for licensing

can be attributed to executives' aforementioned
apprehensions about helping to establish the U.S.S.R. as a
competitive force in world markets. Again, however,
although the logic is appealing, it is also difficult to
establish empirically, since the 1975 and 1976 surveys
employed different methods to gauge anxiety on the
competitor issue. Thus, accurate identification of trends
on this matter is problematical.

Apart from the preceding, however, 1976 survey and
interview data provide evidence that a third factor
exercised a meaningful influence on the evolution of SAEs'
perspectives on licensing during 1975-1976: Some 59.8% of
those respondents to Survey 2 who said that their
willingness to do business with the U.S.S.R. had been
adversely influenced by then-recent Soviet foreign policy
activities (e.g., the Angola affair) likewise reported that
they opposed licensing their firms' latest technology to
the U.S.S.R. (Table 24). Indeed, insights gained from 4
personal interviews suggest that, although this category of
SAEs evidently had a diminished desire to pursue any kind
of business opportunity with the U.S.S.R., the Angola
affair and similar Soviet activities evidently had a more
pronounced adverse effect on the willingness to license
than on the inclination to enter into product
transactions. In other words, SAEs' perceptions of

expansionist Soviet international behavior during 1975-1976
seemingly had a differential negative impact on licensing
attitudes.

Of relevance here is that, as previously discussed in
Chapter IV, some executives interviewed who reported
unfavorable reactions to events like Angola also tended to
perceive the recent deterioration in the U.S.-Soviet
political climate as posing increased "political risks" to
companies doing business with the U.S.S.R.  To reiterate,
there were apparently growing fears that the worsening
state of Soviet-American relations would sooner or later
spill over into the commercial sphere and adversely effect
on-going U.S. corporate activities with the U.S.S.R. (e.g.,
via new U.S. export control restrictions).  Also, various
executives voiced the apprehension that at some point there
might be a domestic political backlash against U.S. firms
involved in Soviet activities.  In addition, as noted
earlier, some executives also indicated growing doubts
about their own involvement and the country's involvement
in U.S.-Soviet trade from a "national welfare" perspective;
i.e., they felt that recent Soviet foreign policy
activities had been inconsistent with the true spirit of
detente and, hence, they were concerned that the Soviets
might simply be employing detente as a smokescreen for
expansionist objectives.

With this background in mind, it is once again necessary to emphasize that many executives interviewed contended that successful licensing agreements, in contrast with straightforward contracts for the exchange of products, depend heavily on the development and maintenance of trust between the lessor and lessee for a long period. Mutual trust, it was pointed out, is an intangible and inherently fragile commodity. Thus, they observed, it is only logical that the above-noted fears and suspicions would have a more serious negative impact on executives' willingness to conclude licensing agreements with the Soviets than on their willingness to engage in product transactions.

Elaborating on this line of thought, several businessmen went on to say that U.S. companies normally conclude licensing agreements only with foreign partners whose governments have a stable and generally amicable relationship with the United States Government. Thus, a positive inter-governmental atmosphere was viewed as a necessary (but not sufficient) condition for the facilitation of licensing negotiations. Conversely, the decline or absence of inter-governmental trust was seen as undermining the relationship of trust which must exist between the parties to a licensing arrangement. In this regard, licensing negotiations with the U.S.S.R. were

considered to be unusually sensitive to negative
developments between Washington and Moscow, because, in the
case of the U.S.S.R., American businessmen can only deal
with Soviet government agencies and not with private
companies as is standard practice in non-communist
countries. In essence, the Soviet government's monopoly of
the U.S.S.R.'s foreign trade was seen as greatly magnifying
the possibility that any given U.S.-Soviet political
incident could affect Soviet behavior toward U.S.
companies, especially on licensing questions.

Lastly, commenting on the possibilities for a domestic
political backlash against U.S. companies involved in
Soviet business deals, various SAEs observed that one
aspect of this backlash was already becoming apparent:
namely, the inclination of the U.S. news media and the ·U.S.
public to label any licensing of U.S. technology to the
U.S.S.R. as being ipso facto a "giveaway." Hence, because
of their sensitivity to such criticism, these SAEs
generally indicated that they would be hesitant to grant
the Soviets any meaningful licenses even if these licenses
were desirable from a purely business standpoint.[22]

In view of the apparent impact of Soviet foreign
policy activities on SAEs' willingness to enter into
licensing agreements with the U.S.S.R., one would expect
that there would be a statistically significant correlation

between these two variables.  However, as is revealed in
Table 24, this is not the case (r = -.04).  A possible
reason for this paradox was indicated in a number of
personal interviews:  Specifically, Soviet foreign policy
behavior apparently influenced the business attitudes of
even those SAEs who stated in Survey 2 that they had not
been affected by events like Angola.  This does not mean
that these executives were untruthful in their survey
responses.  To the contrary, it appears that their overall
commitment to the Soviet market was in fact not diminished
by reports of expansionist Soviet activity.  Nonetheless,
while their general inclination to pursue Soviet business
apparently was unaffected, there seemingly was a shift in
emphasis in the kind of commercial opportunities that they
would henceforth consider.  In this connection, although
they were as eager as ever to sell products to the
U.S.S.R., licensing opportunities had become less
attractive.[23]  (In contrast, as noted above those
interviewed who said that Angola, etc., had resulted in a
reduced commitment to the Soviet market also indicated that
this applied to all types of U.S.-Soviet commerce, whether
involving product sales or licenses.)

Once again, then, SAEs' growing perceptions of the
political risks associated with Soviet-American trade,
coupled with unique features of licensing agreements,

seemingly combined to render SAEs' willingness to license
technology to the U.S.S.R. especially vulnerable to adverse
international political events.  Also, as a result of the
preceding, the connection between SAEs' licensing attitudes
and their reactions to Soviet foreign policy activities
during the period under study is not readily apparent
through statistical manipulation of the 1976 survey data.

Another fact which merits attention is that 1976
survey data indicate a moderate positive relationship
between executives' reactions to Soviet foreign policy
behavior and their views on the competitor issue ($r = .29$
with reference to possible future competition in LDCs;
$r = .33$ with regard to the Industrialized West).
Specifically, those executives who said that their
willingness to do business with the U.S.S.R. had been
affected adversely by reports of Soviet adventurism also
indicated a somewhat greater degree of apprehension that
transfers of U.S. technology might strengthen the
U.S.S.R.'s competitive position in world markets.  This, in
turn, evidently generated increased reluctance on the part
of some executives to license their industrial knowhow to
the Soviets.  Stated differently, negative perceptions of
Soviet behavior in Angola, etc., seemingly had an indirect
influence on attitudes toward licensing.  To illustrate,
Table 25 displays the relationship between the pertinent

TABLE 25

ATTITUDES TOWARD TECHNOLOGY LICENSING BY ATTITUDES TOWARD THE COMPETITOR
ISSUE, CONTROLLING FOR REACTIONS TO SOVIET FOREIGN POLICY, 1976*
(Percentaged Vertically)

| Within Limits Set by Export Controls, Do You Personally Favor Licensing Your Firm's Latest Technology to the U.S.S.R.? | Recent Soviet Foreign Policy Activities (e.g., Angola) Have Adversely Affected Your Company's Outlook on Doing Business with the U.S.S.R. | | | | | | | | | |
|---|---|---|---|---|---|---|---|---|---|---|
| | Agree | | | Not Sure | | | Disagree | | | |
| | Fear Setting Up U.S.S.R. as Competitor in LDCs. | | | Fear Setting Up U.S.S.R. as Competitor in LDCs. | | | Fear Setting Up U.S.S.R. as Competitor in LDCs. | | | |
| | Agree | Not Sure | Disagree | Agree | Not Sure | Disagree | Agree | Not Sure | Disagree | (N) |
| Yes | 25.0% | 60.0% | 44.4% | 35.7% | 33.3% | 75.0% | 41.2% | 38.9% | 50.9% | (76) |
| (N) | (5) | (3) | (4) | (5) | (2) | (9) | (14) | (7) | (27) | |
| Not Sure | 5.0 | 0 | 11.1 | 0 | 0 | 0 | 0 | 0 | 0 | (2) |
| (N) | (1) | (0) | (1) | (0) | (0) | (0) | (0) | (0) | (0) | |
| No | 70.0 | 40.0 | 44.4 | 64.3 | 66.7 | 25.0 | 58.8 | 61.1 | 49.1 | (93) |
| (N) | (14) | (2) | (4) | (9) | (4) | (3) | (20) | (11) | (26) | |
| Total | 100% | 100% | 100% | 100% | 100% | 100% | 100% | 100% | 100% | (171) |
| (N) | (20) | (5) | (9) | (14) | (6) | (12) | (34) | (18) | (53) | |

*Cases are omitted from the crosstabulation where the respondent failed to answer one or more of the three variables under consideration.
Partial correlation of the independent and dependent variables is r = -.18, which is significant at the p = .01 level.

survey variables by means of a three-way crosstabulation.
As is evident from this table, the principal effect of
executives' adverse reactions to Soviet foreign policy
behavior was to reduce greatly the percentage of SAEs who,
although fearing the U.S.S.R. as a potential future
business competitor, were nevertheless in favor of
licensing their latest knowhow to the Soviets.  In this
regard the table shows that, of those SAEs who reacted
negatively to Soviet international activities and who also
viewed the U.S.S.R. as a future competitive threat, only
25% still maintained a positive attitude toward licensing.
In marked contrast, the comparable figure was a
substantially higher 41% for those SAEs who saw the Soviets
as potentially effective competitors but who denied any
adverse effect of Angola, etc., on their willingness to do
business with the U.S.S.R.

The fact that executives' reactions to Soviet
international behavior seemingly helped to stimulate
opposition to technology licensing and magnify business
fears of setting up the U.S.S.R. as a global competitor of
American industry tends to complement certain findings
recounted in Chapter IV.  In this connection, it will be
recalled that a number of personal interviews indicated
that growing doubts about detente from the standpoint of
U.S. national interests had caused some businessmen to

become more fearful of the possibility of future Soviet business competition. Taken together, all these findings once again suggest the proposition that shifts in executives' perceptions of the national interest vis-a-vis the U.S.S.R. may have caused some businessmen to reformulate their conceptions of their corporate self-interests in Soviet trade.

To put the licensing issue in proper perspective a final observation is in order: Results of personal interviews strongly suggest that as of August-September 1976 not a great deal of licensing of American knowhow to the Soviets had taken place. Of those executives who said they had issued licenses to the U.S.S.R., most said that these arrangements had involved showing the Soviets how to run and care for machinery, not how to make it. Hence, the licenses were generally described as being relatively narrow in scope, and in most instances were characterized as a small but necessary part of a larger overall product transaction. Lastly, among those SAEs who said they were willing to license their latest technology to the U.S.S.R., very few reported that they were actually engaged in negotiations to do so. Thus, in drawing conclusions from the above data, care must be taken to distinguish between SAEs' expressed intent and their statements about on-going activities.

## Soviet-American Trade:   The National
## Security Dimension

Having investigated SAEs' views during 1975-1976 on

the economic plusses and minuses of U.S.-Soviet commercial

relations, it is now necessary to examine businessmen's

perspectives in yet another critical area:   To what extent,

if any, does trade with the U.S.S.R., and especially the

sale of American technology to the Soviets, pose a danger

to U.S. national security interests?   Conversely, does

U.S.-Soviet trade open up opportunities for enhancing U.S.

national security; for example, through the acquisition of

new technology from the U.S.S.R. or by fostering Soviet

technological dependence on the United States?   Executives'

views on these key questions and related issues are

explored in detail in the following text.

### The Impact of Soviet-American Trade on
### Soviet Military Capabilities

## The Effect of Trade on the
## Soviet Military Burden

One of the most basic concerns in the national

security area during 1975-1976 was the question of whether

or not Soviet access to U.S. goods and technology would, by

stimulating productivity in the U.S.S.R.'s civilian

economy, facilitate the diversion of additional economic

resources (either in terms of absolute volume or percentage

of GNP) to the Soviet military establishment.   With

reference to this controversial issue, 1976 survey data show that SAEs' opinions were extremely divided (Table 26). Some 31.9% of responding executives did acknowledge that, if U.S.-U.S.S.R. trade were to help the Soviet civilian economy, this might indeed encourage the U.S.S.R.'s leaders to increase resource allocations to the defense sector. On the other hand, 37.1% were "not sure" that greater Soviet military spending would result, and 30.9% felt that this was not a likely possiblity.

It might appear at first glance that the above pattern, indicating that 69% of 1976 survey respondents did not rule out the prospect that U.S.-Soviet trade might yield general economic benefits to the Soviet military, is evidence that most SAEs were remarkably insensitive to U.S. national security interests. If many felt that trade might contribute to Soviet military power, why then were these executives still willing to do business with the U.S.S.R.? In this connection, results of personal interviews suggest that most SAEs were acutely aware of and greatly concerned about the national security implications of their firms' actions. However, the overwhelming majority also felt that the military dangers often cited by critics of Soviet-American trade have generally been overstated and must be kept in perspective.

TABLE 26

EVALUATIONS OF THE IMPACT OF U.S.-U.S.S.R. TRADE
ON SOVIET ECONOMIC AND MILITARY CAPABILITIES, 1976
(Percentaged Horizontally)

| | Agree Strongly | Agree But Not Strongly | Not Sure, Depends | Disagree, But Not Strongly | Disagree Strongly | (N)* |
|---|---|---|---|---|---|---|
| If U.S.-U.S.S.R. trade were to help the Soviet civilian economy, this would not encourage Soviet leaders to increase allocations to the defense sector. | 7.2% | 23.7% | 37.1% | 17.5% | 14.4% | (194) |
| In terms of a "technology gap," the Soviet Union does not lag far behind the U.S. in the area of defense production; their main difficulty is the development and application of technology in the civilian sector with reference to problems of large-scale commercial production. | 45.4 | 39.7 | 7.7 | 4.6 | 2.6 | (194) |
| The sale of "sensitive" high technology to the U.S.S.R. (computers, programmed machine tools, etc.) will not necessarily endanger our national security if precautions are taken by U.S. firms involved. | 21.3 | 32.0 | 14.7 | 17.8 | 14.2 | (197) |
| U.S.-U.S.S.R. trade will have a significant beneficial impact on the Soviet civilian economy. | 18.7 | 50.5 | 16.7 | 12.1 | 2.0 | (198) |

*Variations in the number of cases (N) are attributable to "no answers" which are excluded from all calculations. Total N for the 1976 survey is 203 executives.

First, most of those interviewed--even those who felt trade might facilitate some additional Soviet military spending--believed that U.S. exports to the Soviet civilian economy would, at best, benefit the U.S.S.R.'s defense sector only minimally in terms of increased resource allocations. The overall view was that under any and all circumstances the Soviet government <u>always</u> gives the military establishment top priority access to scarce economic resources, and that the U.S.S.R.'s civilian sector simply receives any investment funds left over. Therefore, SAEs generally believed that because the Soviet military always gets what it wants anyway, any increases in Soviet productivity resulting from trade with the U.S. would likely have the greatest impact on the Soviet civilian economy, with the principal result being an increase in the living standards of the Soviet population. Thus, according to this logic, the Soviet people, not the Soviet military, would be the primary beneficiaries of commercial relations with the United States.[24]

A related view was also pervasive in executives' thinking: Many of those interviewed believed that while the U.S.S.R.'s leaders may be tempted by trade-induced increases in economic productivity to shift resources to defense production, the Soviet Politburo will be constrained from doing so to a significant degree by growing popular pressure for consumer goods. Thus, Soviet public opinion was perceived by SAEs as having a direct impact on policy-making at the highest levels of the Soviet government. Indeed, a widespread opinion held by those interviewed was that trade with the United States and the West, by bringing sizeable numbers of Soviet citizens into regular contact with Westerners and especially with Western goods, inevitably fuels popular expectations in the U.S.S.R. for greater material welfare. Thus, rather than making it easier for the U.S.S.R. to bear its massive defense burden, trade with the U.S. (and the West) may actually make it more difficult for Soviet leaders to gain the acquiesence of the Soviet people to continuing large defense budgets at the expense of national consumption. As one executive characterized the situation, "The Soviet people simply have not known any better. Now (because of increased Western contact) they are finally getting a glimmer of what they have been missing."[25]

Even if U.S. exports to the U.S.S.R. might facilitate some increases in Soviet military spending, almost all executives interviewed once again emphasized that if U.S. industry opts out of the Soviet market, the only purpose served would be to divert profitable business to foreign competition. The U.S., it was repeatedly stressed, is no longer the world's only viable source of advanced knowhow and equipment. Thus, whether or not U.S. firms withhold their wares from the U.S.S.R., in the final analysis this will have no impact on levels of Soviet military spending, simply because the Soviets will be able to purchase most needed items from alternative suppliers in Western Europe or Japan.

Relevant here is the opinion, held by a number of executives representing high-technology firms, that if U.S. industry is to remain at the leading edge of world technology, American companies cannot afford to abdicate completely any sizeable overseas market to foreign competition. To do so, it was argued, will make it even more difficult for U.S. industry to generate the huge cash flow it needs to fund continuous large investments in vital R&D activities. Conversely, by totally ceding the Soviet (or any other) market to foreign competition, U.S. firms will be enhancing the R&D support capabilities of West European and Japanese companies, while simultaneously providing the market incentive to develop export industries which may then challenge U.S. industry world-wide.[26]

Several executives, who felt that trade with the U.S.S.R. might well facilitate greater Soviet military spending and who were concerned about this possibility, nonetheless said that it would be an unsound business practice for U.S. companies unilaterally to forego

commercial relations with the Soviets due to the aforementioned risk. As one executive put it, "The business of
business is business." In this view, it is the responsibility of the U.S. Government, not American companies, to
determine what the national interest is and, subsequently,
to provide U.S. firms with clear policy guidance.[27]
Otherwise, it was argued, U.S. companies would in essence
be formulating their own foreign policies in specific
international situations. This, it was contended, would
not only be an undesirable practice, but would in fact be
highly dangerous. For example, it was noted by one senior
businessman that the economic power of many large U.S.
companies is such that, if they developed a penchant for
politically-motivated punitive behavior, they could collectively (and in certain cases individually) destabilize the
economic and political systems of more than half the
countries in the world. Consequently, the opinion of these
SAEs was that, until instructed otherwise by the federal
government, U.S. companies should continue to pursue
U.S.S.R. business opportunities as dictated by individual
corporate commercial self-interest and consistent with
existing U.S. statutes and export control regulations.

However, those SAEs who argued that U.S. companies
should not base purely business decisions on corporate
political preferences were also quick to chastise the U.S.

Government for a perceived failure to provide American industry with a set of unambiguous policy guidelines for conducting trade with the U.S.S.R. Most other SAEs echoed this criticism. Although all executives were aware of the U.S. Government's officially stated general support for mutually beneficial U.S.-Soviet economic relations, the interviewer was constantly subjected to tirades accusing federal policy-makers of failing to match their words with deeds. Oft criticized U.S. Government actions included the failure to ratify already-signed U.S.-U.S.S.R. trade and financial agreements, the Jackson-Vanik Amendment to the Trade Reform Act of 1975, and various then-new statutory restrictions on the extension of Export-Import Bank credits to the Soviets.

Most executives, particularly those from high-technology firms, also emphasized that the inconsistencies evident in general U.S. commercial policy toward the U.S.S.R. had been frequently reflected in the erratic application of U.S. export control regulations to specific Soviet-U.S. company transactions. These and other vagaries of federal policies on trade with the U.S.S.R. were cited by virtually all SAEs interviewed as having generated much uncertainty in business circles as to whether the U.S. Government in fact regarded Soviet-American commerce as being in the national interest. This uncertainty, the SAEs

contended, had caused many U.S. companies to become
increasingly reluctant to invest time, money, and energy in
developing Soviet business, because the normal response of
businessmen to uncertain conditions is to shy away from
taking risks. Finally, two executives noted that the
absence of clear direction from Washington had caused some
U.S. firms to fall back on their own perceptions of the
national interest in arriving at Soviet business decisions. Again, for reasons noted above, this development
was regarded as highly undesirable.

## Potential Diversion of U.S. Technology for Soviet Military Purposes

Another dimension of the national security question is
the extent to which U.S. knowhow and equipment exported to
the U.S.S.R. might be diverted for direct use by the Soviet
military. On this issue, the widely-shared opinion of SAEs
interviewed was that while many items sold to the U.S.S.R.
could be diverted to military use, and although some
undoubtedly would be, most Soviet purchases from the U.S.
will not be channeled into the defense sector. Underlying
this view was the belief, voiced by 85.1% of 1976 survey
respondents, that in terms of a "technology gap" the Soviet
Union does not lag far behind the U.S. in the area of
defense production; rather, the U.S.S.R.'s principal
difficulty is the development and application of technology

in the civilian economy to problems of large-scale
commercial production (Table 26).  In this regard, during
personal interviews SAEs of high-technology companies
frequently observed that because the defense sector has
priority access to the U.S.S.R's economic resources, the
Soviet military has been able to make massive investments
in defense-related R&D which have boosted the level of the
U.S.S.R.'s defense technology well above that prevailing
elsewhere in Soviet industry.[28]  A related opinion was
that one of the major problems of the Soviet civilian
economy is that it has usually been slow to benefit from
technological advances in the defense sector, because,
unlike the situation in the United States, responsibility
for Soviet military production is vested in elite and
specialized bureaucratic organizations which are tightly
insulated from non-defense areas of the economy.  In sum,
then, because Soviet and U.S. military technologies were
seen as being generally comparable, and because the
U.S.S.R.'s military was viewed as being already
well-supplied with high quality industrial hardware and
scientific instrumentation, most businessmen interviewed
felt that the Soviets do not have much need to divert
imported U.S./Western goods and knowhow to military uses.

Consistent with the above views, most SAEs interviewed
believed that the U.S.S.R.'s main objective in seeking

increased trade with the U.S. and the West is not to obtain
items that will directly enhance Soviet military
capabilities. Rather, the prevailing opinion was that the
Soviets' principal goal is to bolster the U.S.S.R.'s
stagnating civilian economy by means of large-scale
injections of Western goods and technology, so as to
improve the miserable lot of the frustrated Soviet
consumer. Hence, several executives pointed out that
despite popular impressions left by the U.S. news media,
Soviet purchases of U.S. and Western "frontier"
technology/equipment with potential direct military
applications have actually been quite small as a percentage
of the total dollar volume of Soviet imports of Western
manufactured goods. Instead, the Soviet buying strategy
has been aimed at achieving a rapid expansion of industrial
capacity in certain non-defense sectors via the acquisition
of Western mass production knowhow and equipment.[29]

Interestingly, many SAEs interviewed contended that
the Soviets usually do not end up purchasing the most
modern U.S. industrial processes, despite the fact that
Soviet foreign trade organizations almost always open talks
with U.S. companies by saying that they are interested only
in state-of-the art technology. Soviet FTOs were described
as often scaling down their requests during the course of
business negotiations for a variety of reasons: First, the

Soviet foreign trade bureaucracy, which arranges almost all the U.S.S.R.'s imports on behalf of end-users in Soviet industrial ministries and other state agencies, was seen as being under pressure from various quarters to maximize the technological return to the U.S.S.R. of every dollar spent on Western knowhow and equipment. On the other hand, as noted earlier, many SAEs felt that Soviet industrial managers (i.e., the end-users) generally like to buy less-sophisticated, proven technology which has been extensively tested in a production environment. These differences in approach, the SAEs said, are usually resolved in favor of the end-users, but normally only after a time-consuming campaign by industrial managers to impose their preferences on recalcitrant trade officials.

Another factor which was believed to influence Soviet purchasing patterns is the difficulty of integrating advanced U.S. and Western industrial hardware with existing installed Soviet manufacturing processes, which were generally characterized as obsolete. Hence, even in instances where Soviet managers would like to buy state-of-the-art Western production technology, many SAEs believed they are often constrained from doing so by practical realities.

Perspectives on the Export Control Process

Despite SAEs' general sentiment that most items imported by the U.S.S.R. will not be diverted to military uses, a majority of executives interviewed still acknowledged the need for an effective set of U.S. export controls to prevent the transfer to the Soviets of U.S. technologies which could have direct defense applications. In particular, executives of firms possessing high technology were apt to note that although Soviet imports of "frontier" technologies from the West have been small in relative dollar terms, Soviet FTOs have nevertheless often displayed great eagerness to acquire "sensitive" goods/ knowhow. This, they said, has been especially evident in Soviet negotiators' willingness in many cases to pay premium prices for U.S. computers, lasers, video recorders, etc. Consequently, SAEs representing high technology firms were almost universally suspicious of Soviet intentions behind purchases of certain kinds of U.S. technology.

However, although most executives interviewed saw U.S. Government export controls as a necessity, most were also quick to cite perceived shortcomings in the U.S. export control process: First, referring to competitive consider-ations noted earlier, many SAEs constantly grumbled that the federal government has maintained too many "unilateral" controls on U.S. goods/knowhow that the Soviets can obtain

elsewhere. The export control agencies of a number of
Allied Western nations, they argued, have a much less
restrictive idea of what is "defense-related"; and some
Allied governments, a few executives contended, are
frequently lax about enforcing controls on even those items
which are clearly sensitive and which appear on the multilateral Western export control list (i.e., the so-called
Free World Coordinating Committee or COCOM list). Additionally, several SAEs from high-technology companies indicated
their belief that the Soviets have been able to obtain a
substantial amount of embargoed technology from advanced
industrial nations which are avowedly neutral politically,
e.g., Switzerland, Sweden, and Finland. These countries,
the SAEs said, not only have provided the Soviets with
sensitive technologies generated by their own domestic
industries, but also have acted frequently as middlemen for
transshipment to the U.S.S.R. of advanced technology
originating elsewhere in the West. Finally, certain U.S.
and COCOM controls, such as restrictions on various
categories of electronic components, were simply seen as
unenforceable because of the ubiquitous nature of the items
and the great number of channels through which the Soviets
can obtain them.[30]

Therefore, a substantial portion of the SAEs
interviewed--and especially those from high-technology

companies--proposed a series of changes in U.S. and COCOM
export regulations intended to make these controls more
realistic as well as more equitable from a competitive
standpoint. A frequent suggestion was to reduce the number
of U.S. "unilateral" regulations so as to bring the U.S.
control list into close conformity with the multilateral
COCOM list. U.S. "unilateral" controls, SAEs argued,
should only be retained where no close foreign substitute
for the U.S. product is available. Secondly, executives
felt that the COCOM list should confine itself to
regulating truly sensitive technology. In this regard, a
widely-held opinion was that the COCOM list should be
revised more often to reflect the U.S.S.R.'s own
technological advances. It makes little sense, SAEs
reasoned, to control items which the Soviets have shown the
capacity to produce themselves. In addition, a few
executives argued that selected high-technology items,
which are militarily sensitive, should nonetheless be
dropped from the COCOM list because it is logistically
impossible to prevent their acquisition by the U.S.S.R.
According to this line of thinking, to retain controls on
such products simply compromises the overall credibility of
the COCOM list in the eyes of U.S. Allies, wastes limited
federal manpower on futile enforcement efforts, and, as a
result of the preceding, generally complicates the

effective implementation of multilateral controls on more
critical items.  Lastly, some SAEs felt that the U.S.
Government should take prompt action directed at Allied
governments to encourage more rigorous enforcement of
COCOM-controlled hardware/knowhow by their respective
export control agencies.  Similar action was also advocated
with respect to "neutral" Western countries, in order to
cut down on third-country transshipments as well as reduce
the quantity of indigenous technology provided to the
Soviets.

Apart from the perceived need for equitable
multilateral controls, during interviews most executives of
high-technology firms pointed to another major difficulty
with U.S. export regulations:  There are certain kinds of
technologies, they said, which all reasonable businessmen
agree should be subject to strict U.S. Government review
procedures.  In their view, however, federal review
procedures often produce inconsistent and vexing
decisions.  For example, a U.S. company might be given
permission to sell a particular product to the Soviets one
month, but the same firm might be denied an export license
for a follow-up purchase of the identical item several
months later.  This erratic behavior, the executives
bemoaned, stems primarily from capricious political
influences (see above, p. 288), and secondarily from the

burdensome case-by-case approach used in U.S. licensing
evaluations, which essentially requires exporters to prove
that the item being sold will be put to a verifiable
civilian "end-use." By its unpredictable nature, the SAEs
complained, the U.S. export control process has contributed
significantly to business uncertainty and the perception of
risks with respect to the Soviet market. Accordingly, it
was argued that many businessmen--most notably those in
high-technology firms--have become more hesitant to expend
significant corporate resources to develop Soviet contracts.

Finally, in addition to their litany of criticisms of
the U.S. export control process, many SAEs interviewed
(again, especially those of high-technology companies) felt
that U.S. Government officials, the U.S. news media, and
the general public have not fully appreciated the extent to
which many U.S. firms voluntarily maintain internal
controls on the transfer of their technology to the
U.S.S.R. as well as to foreign countries in general (e.g.,
standing policies against licensing, licensing only one's
latest "proven" technology, or, alternatively, licensing
only obsolete technology). Interestingly, a majority of
respondents to the 1976 survey evidently held a similar
view: Some 53.3% of the survey sample contended that sales
of "sensitive" high technology to the U.S.S.R. (computers,
programmed machine tools, etc.) will not necessarily

endanger U.S. national security if precautions are taken by
the U.S. firms involved (Table 12). Consistent with
interview findings, the survey data also show that SAEs
from high-technology companies had the greatest propensity
to believe in the efficacy of self-imposed restraints.
Whereas a strong 67.5% majority of respondents in this
category regarded internal corporate export controls as
credible, the comparable figure for SAEs representing
"conventional" technology companies was only 40.2%.[31]

### Impact of Soviet-American Trade on the U.S.S.R.'s Civilian Economy

As outlined above, many SAEs believed that most of any
benefits which the U.S.S.R. might receive from trade with
the U.S. will accrue mainly to the Soviet civilian
economy. The next appropriate step, then, is to explore
SAEs' views on the likely extent of such benefits. In this
connection, a 69.2% majority of respondents to Survey 2
agreed that U.S.-U.S.S.R. trade will have a "significant"
beneficial impact on the Soviet civilian economy, although
only 18.7% agreed "strongly" with this view, whereas 50.5%
agreed, but "not strongly" (Table 26). This pattern would
therefore seem to indicate that while most SAEs believed
that trade with the U.S. would have some positive effects
on the Soviet economy, the general impact of U.S.
goods/knowhow on the U.S.S.R.'s economic well-being will

not be major.

This interpretation of the survey data is strongly supported by the results of personal interviews. For the most part, SAEs voiced the opinion that the U.S.S.R. will continue to benefit from economic relations with the U.S. primarily in the agricultural area, as manifested in gradual improvements in the diet of the Soviet people. However, imports of U.S./Western industrial hardware and technological expertise were expected to result, at best, in only marginal increases in the general technological level of the U.S.S.R.'s civilian economy. Although it was generally acknowledged that certain select sectors of Soviet industry (e.g., petroleum production) had benefited and would continue to benefit importantly from equipment purchases, most SAEs also tended to feel that import-generated improvements in productivity would remain confined to a limited number of such narrow areas. Underlying this view was deep skepticism, expressed by many executives, with respect to the ability of the U.S.S.R.'s economy to absorb, reproduce, and build upon imported American and Western technology. The Soviet Union's civilian R&D system, it was contended, is grossly inefficient, and the bureaucratic nature of the Soviet economy places formidable and often insurmountable obstacles to innovation in the way of Soviet factory

managers. Elaborating on this highly negative assessment,
several SAEs from high-technology companies commented that
although the U.S.S.R. occasionally does make effective use
of imported equipment/knowhow in a particular factory or
industry, the resulting increases in productivity are
frequently dissipated by the immense waste that prevails
throughout the economy.[32]

The Potential for Technological Dependency

Given the aforementioned perceived weaknesses in the
U.S.S.R.'s economy, it should not be surprising that survey
and interview data reveal that many SAEs believed that
there is substantial potential for the gradual development
of a lasting Soviet technological dependency on the U.S.
and the West. In this regard, a 73% majority of
respondents to Survey 2 reported that solid prospects exist
for continuous Soviet reliance on U.S. industrial knowhow
in meeting practical everyday needs such as spare parts for
equipment exported to the U.S.S.R. (Table 27). A similar
view was held with respect to the possibilities for a more
meaningful long-term general dependency of Soviet civilian
industry on the superior capabilities of the R&D establish-
ments of the U.S. and other Western countries: Some 67% of
1976 survey participants said that if the Soviets buy
advanced Western technology for a period of time and
subsequently try to "go it alone," they will still find it

TABLE 27

EVALUATIONS OF PROSPECTS FOR SOVIET TECHNOLOGICAL DEPENDENCE ON
THE U.S., 1976

(Percentaged Horizontally)

|  | Agree Strongly | Agree But Not Strongly | Not Sure, Depends | Disagree, But Not Strongly | Disagree Strongly | (N)* |
|---|---|---|---|---|---|---|
| Prospects exist for continuous Soviet dependency on U.S. industrial knowhow in meeting practical everyday needs such as spare parts for equipment exported to the U.S.S.R. | 26.5% | 45.9% | 12.8% | 9.7% | 5.1% | (196) |
| If the Soviets buy advanced Western industrial technology for a period of time and then try to go it alone, they will find it impossible in their civilian economy to keep up with Western research and development. | 24.2 | 41.4 | 13.1 | 15.7 | 5.6 | (198) |
| The Soviets are likely to buy injections of Western technology for their civilian economy until they feel they have caught up, then try to go it alone. | 28.3 | 43.9 | 16.2 | 11.1 | 0.5 | (198) |

*Variations in the number of cases (N) are attributable to "no answers" which are excluded from all calculations. Total N for the 1976 survey is 203 executives.

impossible to keep up with Western research and development.[33]

Interestingly, most SAEs viewed the Soviet leadership's commitment to technological trade with the West as
being essentially short-term. Some 72% of respondents to
Survey 2 said that the Soviets are likely to buy injections
of Western hardware/knowhow for their civilian economy      .
until they feel there has been substantial progress in
closing the technology gap, and then try to terminate their
technological dependence on the West.

Why, then, did SAEs feel that a lasting Soviet
dependency on Western R&D processes is a probability?
Results of personal interviews suggest that the answer to
this question lies in SAEs' above-noted negative evaluation
of the U.S.S.R.'s system of industrial organization, and
the anticipated response of the Soviet leadership to
pressing problems of technical innovation. Many interview
participants believed that Soviet difficulties run so deep
that the Kremlin's traditional remedies for economic ills
(e.g., exhortation, cosmetic bureaucratic reorganizations)
are simply no longer viable and henceforth will not achieve
much. Rather, major progress in the U.S.S.R.'s civilian
economy was seen by these executives as dependent upon
radical changes in the economy's administrative apparatus
and upon substantial reallocations of managerial and

technical talent away from the military sector. Most of
these businessmen appeared keenly aware of the
intrinsically conservative and bureaucratized nature of the
Soviet system, and did not, therefore, think such changes
are likely. Thus, many SAEs interviewed seemingly had
arrived at the conclusion that although Soviet leaders are
intent on avoiding technological dependence on the West and
are probably seeking a one-shot "technology fix" for the
U.S.S.R.'s economy, this strategy will fail to rectify the
serious problems which afflict the Soviet R&D process.
Consequently, faced with the continued inability of Soviet
R&D to keep pace and rather than implement real and
effective reform, Soviet leaders will opt for technological
dependency on the West as the least onerous alternative.
Therefore, according to this reasoning, at some indefinite
point in the future the U.S.S.R. will be drawn reluctantly
into a permanent relationship with the Western research and
development process.[34] This R&D dependency, as suggested
earlier, will be forged on the acquisition of high-yield
productive capacity embodying the West's latest proven
technology, which will have its most tangible benefits in
certain select Soviet industrial sectors.

During personal interviews, executives were apt to
point out that a lasting Soviet dependence on U.S.
technology would have two tangible benefits for the United

States, one commercial and the other political. From a
strictly economic standpoint, SAEs contended that
technological dependence on the U.S. will generate
continuous and even increasing Soviet demand for American
exports. More importantly, however, from a political
perspective Soviet reliance on U.S. technology was seen by
some businessmen as contributing in a major way to the
"gulliverization" of the U.S.S.R.; i.e., that such
dependence would give the Soviet Union a powerful vested
interest in pursuing restraint in its relations with the
U.S. and would help build a web of cooperative interrelationships between the superpowers.

### Potential Transfer of Soviet Technology to the United States

Because the transfer of U.S. technology to the
U.S.S.R. consistently has been one of the most controversial issues in domestic debates on Soviet-American
economic relations, considerable attention has been devoted
to examining SAEs perspectives on this question. However,
as some SAEs noted in personal interviews, U.S. political
debates on technology transfer have left unaddressed the
possibility that the U.S. might be able to obtain useful
technology from the U.S.S.R. The common presumption,
certain executives observed, is that the stagnating Soviet
civilian economy has produced little if anything new which

could be of technological value to American business. This conventional wisdom, these SAEs contended, may in fact be incorrect.[35]

Data from Survey 2 indicate that the above sentiments were shared by a sizeable minority of respondents (Table 28). Some 24.5% of survey participants agreed with the proposition that Soviet industry possesses advanced technology already in operation (i.e., "on line") which, if acquired by American firms, could greatly benefit the U.S. economy. This view was particularly prevalent among SAEs representing firms which had signed "scientific-technical" (S&T) cooperation agreements with the U.S.S.R. In this category of respondents, 42.5% saw real potential for the acquisition of advanced on-line Soviet technology.

Perhaps even more remarkable is that 49.7% of all respondents to the 1976 survey expressed the belief that Soviet scientists and industrial engineers have some innovative ideas--as yet undeveloped--which U.S. companies could borrow and develop themselves to their substantial benefit. Once again, this view was most frequently held by SAEs from companies with S&T agreements. Indeed, a striking 67.5% majority of this sub-sample thought it likely that American industry could profit from new Soviet technological concepts.

## TABLE 28

### EVALUATIONS OF THE POTENTIAL FOR THE TRANSFER OF SOVIET TECHNOLOGY TO THE U.S., 1976
#### (Percentaged Horizontally)

|  | Agree Strongly | Agree But Not Strongly | Not Sure, Depends | Disagree, But Not Strongly | Disagree Strongly | (N)* |
|---|---|---|---|---|---|---|
| Soviet scientists and industrial engineers have some innovative ideas—as yet undeveloped—which we could borrow and develop here with substantial benefits for U.S. industry. | 11.9% | 37.8% | 25.9% | 16.6% | 7.8% | (193) |
| Soviet industry possesses advanced technology already on-line which, if acquired by American firms, could greatly benefit the U.S. economy. | 6.1 | 18.4 | 25.0 | 29.6 | 20.9 | (196) |

*Variations in the number of cases (N) are attributable to "no answers" which are excluded from all calculations. Total N for the 1976 survey is 203 executives.

Thus, quite a few executives apparently were of the opinion that massive Soviet R&D expenditures over the past several decades necessarily must have produced some concrete on-line results, despite the major bureaucratic barriers to innovation which exist in the Soviet civilian economy. Additionally, many SAEs evidently had considerable respect for the ability of Soviet scientific and engineering personnel to conduct creative basic research.[36] Given their awareness of the great difficulties which Soviet inventors face in trying to introduce new technologies into the economy, a considerable number of U.S. businessmen seemingly perceived the presence of many frustrated geniuses in Soviet research organizations. Consequently, many SAEs evidently believed that if regular access to imaginative Soviet R&D staffs could be gained by American companies, U.S. firms might well succeed in obtaining some original and worthwhile Soviet technological knowhow. In order to establish continuous contacts with Soviet research personnel, a "scientific-technical" cooperation agreement with the U.S.S.R. was clearly viewed as an important tool by SAEs of companies having such agreements.

In fact, personal interviews with 9 executives from companies with S&T pacts confirmed that an important U.S. corporate motivation in concluding these agreements was the hope that they would facilitate access to Soviet R&D staffs, as well as the discovery and subsequent licensing of advanced on-line Soviet technology presently underutilized in Soviet industry.[37]  However, SAEs cited another objective as their principal reason for entering into S&T agreements:  These agreements, the SAEs contended, can be convenient bases of operations from which to develop profitable sales contracts with Soviet foreign trade organizations.  It was frequently noted that Soviet business negotiators tend to favor American companies which have signed S&T pacts, because they perceive that the U.S. firms involved have been granted special high-level approval by Soviet political authorities.  In addition, several businessmen said that, because S&T agreements normally specify priority areas for future technical cooperation, U.S. companies can often get a more precise idea of where Soviet buying interests really lie.  This was described as being of considerable help in designing Soviet sales campaigns, and as one way to reduce the typically high costs of penetrating the Soviet market.[38]

## S&T Agreements as a Vehicle for Technology Transfer

In view of prominent media attention devoted throughout the 1970s to alleged "giveaways" of U.S. technology to the U.S.S.R., SAEs' evaluations of their

experiences with S&T agreements are especially relevant to
this analysis. Have S&T agreements indeed been a "one-way
street" for the unrestricted flow of U.S. technology to the
Soviets, as critics have charged? What types of U.S.
technology have been transferred to the Soviets? To what
extent have S&T agreements actually resulted in the
acquisition of innovative Soviet technology by U.S. firms?
Do S&T agreements normally yield substantial commercial
benefits to American companies, or does this occur only in
isolated instances? Survey and interview data suggest some
answers to these questions.

At first glance, survey data for 1976 seem to confirm
the widely-held suspicion that the U.S.S.R. has been the
primary beneficiary of S&T agreements with U.S. firms
(Table 29). A total of 47 respondents reported the
existence of an S&T pact between their companies and the
Soviets, and of this number only 17% stated that their
firms had benefited from the agreement via acquisition of
new technology from the U.S.S.R. In marked contrast, 45.3%
indicated that the Soviets had benefited through the
transfer of technology from their companies. To place the
matter in a somewhat different perspective, of the 16
businessmen who reported that the U.S.S.R. had obtained
technology from their firms, 81.3% said they had not gotten
any new Soviet technology in return. Finally, a

TABLE 29

EVALUATIONS OF SCIENTIFIC-TECHNICAL COOPERATION AGREEMENTS, 1976
(Percentaged Horizontally)

|  | Yes | Not Sure, Depends | No | (N)* |
|---|---|---|---|---|
| Has your company benefited from its scientific-technical cooperation agreement via acquisition of new technology from the U.S.S.R.? | 15.0% | 2.5% | 82.5% | (40) |
| Has your company benefited from its scientific-technical cooperation agreement via a larger dollar volume of trade with the Soviets? | 33.3 | 5.1 | 61.5 | (39) |
| Has the U.S.S.R. benefited from its scientific-technical agreement with your company via acquisition of technology from your firm? | 45.0 | 2.5 | 52.5 | (40) |

*Variations in the number of cases (N) are attributable to "no answers" which are excluded from all calculations. Results reported are based on a total N of 47 executives from 47 companies that had scientific-technical cooperation agreements with the U.S.S.R. at the time of the 1976 survey.

surprisingly low 32% of those reporting S&T pacts felt that
the agreements had benefited their firms indirectly by
generating a larger dollar volume of trade with the Soviets.

Thus, to the casual observer it would appear that S&T
agreements have in fact been largely one-way affairs
resulting in transfers of knowhow to the U.S.S.R. without a
technological quid pro quo. However, this adverse picture
becomes less straightforward upon a more careful
examination of the data. For example, 62.5% of those SAEs
who said that the Soviets had benefited technologically
from their companies likewise indicated that their S&T
agreement had resulted in an increased amount of Soviet
business for their firm (Table 30). Conversely, 74% of
those who said that their S&T agreement had not stimulated
a greater volume of trade with the U.S.S.R. also reported
that the Soviets had failed to obtain any new technology
from their companies. Lastly, of those 21 businessmen
whose companies had not secured either technological or
trade benefits from S&T pacts with the Soviets, 76.2%
reported that they had not transferred any technology to
the U.S.S.R. as a result of these agreements.

Basically, the preceding response pattern points to a
strong inclination by SAEs to secure adequate monetary or
technological compensation for any U.S. corporate
technology transferred to the U.S.S.R. Indeed, this

TABLE 30

ASSESSMENTS OF THE BALANCE OF BENEFITS FROM SCIENTIFIC-TECHNICAL
(S&T) COOPERATION AGREEMENTS, 1976*
(Percentaged Vertically)

U.S.S.R. Has Benefited from Its S&T Agreement Via New Technology from Your Firm.

|  | Yes | Not Sure, Depends | No |
|---|---|---|---|
| Has your company benefited from its S&T agreement via acquisition of new technology from the U.S.S.R.? | | | |
| Yes | 18.8% | 0% | 9.5% |
| Not sure, depends | 0 | 100.0 | 0 |
| No | 81.3 | 0 | 90.5 |
| (N) | (16) | (1) | (21) |
| [r=.14, p=.21] | | | |
| Has your company benefited from its S&T agreement via a larger dollar volume of trade with the Soviets? | | | |
| Yes | 62.5 | 0 | 10.0 |
| Not sure, depends | 0 | 100.0 | 5.0 |
| No | 37.5 | 0 | 85.0 |
| (N) | (16) | (1) | (20) |
| [r=.53, p=.01] | | | |

*Cases are omitted from the respective crosstabulations where the respondents failed to answer one or both of the variables being considered. Results reported are based on a total of 47 executives from 47 companies that had scientific-technical cooperation agreements with the U.S.S.R. at the time of the 1976 survey.

attitude was continually manifested throughout the 9
personal interviews with executives whose companies had
concluded S&T pacts.  The furthest thing from their minds,
all of them maintained, is to facilitate the unrestricted
flow of their companies' technology to the Soviets.  To the
contrary, all said that they had sought to employ S&T
agreements to their own advantage, by using the agreements,
as described earlier, as marketing platforms as well as to
gain access to Soviet R&D staffs and potentially useful
advanced Soviet on-line technology.[39]

Additionally, of those SAEs who said that their S&T
agreement had resulted in a technological benefit to the
Soviets, most said that the technology that had been
transferred had not been of major importance to their
firm.  The bulk of the technology provided to the Soviets,
they indicated, had been in the form of products embodying
their companies' latest "proven" technology.  Most said
they had engaged in little if any licensing of their firms'
technological knowhow, and those who had signed licenses
generally said that these contracts had been a small part
of an overall product transaction and had been necessary to
show the Soviets how to run and care for purchased
machinery.  In sum, these SAEs indicated that their
licensing activities under S&T agreements had been
relatively limited in scope and generally confined to

"conventional" technology (as opposed to advanced "frontier" technology just emerging from U.S. corporate research and development).

### Impact of Soviet Foreign Policy Activities on "National Security" Variables

Throughout this study, 1976 survey and interview findings have consistently pointed to a "national welfare" response by a small but important number of SAEs to perceptions of Soviet expansionism during 1975-1976 in Angola, the Horn of Africa, etc. To repeat an earlier observation, as a result of media reports of the aforementioned Soviet activities, certain businessmen indicated growing doubts about the wisdom of their own involvement and their country's involvement in trade with the U.S.S.R from the perspective of the common good of the United States. As has been shown, these nascent anxieties apparently contributed to a more skeptical view of the possibilities for engendering peace through trade, to reduced support for U.S. Government efforts to build closer U.S.-U.S.S.R. commercial ties, to a lessening of resistance to the idea of using economic "leverage" to influence Soviet policies, and to increased fears that transfers of U.S. manufacturing technology to the Soviets might transform the U.S.S.R. into a formidable international competitor of U.S. business (and, hence, to greater reluctance to license U.S. industrial

knowhow to the Soviets). In Chapter IV, it was noted that
during personal interviews the few SAEs who evidenced the
preceding tendencies likewise shared an emerging suspicion
that the U.S.S.R. was simply employing its declared policy
of detente to camouflage its aggressive intent to widen the
sphere of Soviet international influence by means of
subversive and interventionist tactics.

Thus, it should not be surprising that, as was
mentioned in Chapter IV, SAEs interviewed who indicated the
above views were also somewhat more concerned than other
businessmen about the potential dangers to U.S. national
security posed by a growing volume of trade with the
U.S.S.R. Specifically, these executives seemingly harbored
a nagging worry that a principal Soviet goal in fostering
economic relations with the U.S. (and the West) is to obtain
a rapid and large-scale injection of advanced technology in
order to strengthen the industrial and technological base
of the U.S.S.R.'s defense establishment.

These sentiments are clearly reflected in the data
from Survey 2 (Table 31). Specifically, those SAEs who
reported that their willingness to do business with the
U.S.S.R. had been adversely affected by then-recent Soviet
foreign policy activities, also indicated a weak but
statistically significant propensity to believe that
U.S.-U.S.S.R. trade, if it should help the Soviet civilian

TABLE 31

ATTITUDES TOWARD NATIONAL SECURITY ISSUES BY REACTIONS TO
SOVIET FOREIGN POLICY, 1976*
(Percentaged Horizontally)

Recent Soviet Foreign Policy Activities
(e.g., Angola) Have Adversely Affected Your
Company's Outlook on Doing Business with
the U.S.S.R.

|  | Agree | Not Sure, Depends | Disagree | Pearson's r** or (N) |
|---|---|---|---|---|
| Entire Sample | 20.3% | 18.8% | 61.0% | (192) |
| If U.S.-U.S.S.R. trade were to help the Soviet civilian economy, this would not encourage Soviet leaders to increase allocations to the defense sector. |  |  |  | -.20 |
| Agree | 10.5 | 26.3 | 63.2 | (57) |
| Not sure, depends | 22.5 | 14.1 | 63.4 | (71) |
| Disagree | 30.4 | 17.9 | 51.8 | (56) |
| The sale of "sensitive" high technology to the U.S.S.R. (computers, programmed machine tools, etc.) will not necessarily endanger our national security if precautions are taken by U.S. firms involved. |  |  |  | -.27 |
| Agree | 13.6 | 16.5 | 69.9 | (103) |
| Not sure, depends | 25.0 | 17.9 | 57.1 | (28) |
| Disagree | 30.4 | 23.2 | 46.4 | (56) |

*Cases are omitted from the respective crosstabulations where the
respondent failed to answer one or both of the variables being
considered.

**All Pearson's correlations are significant at the p=.01 level.

economy, might well encourage Soviet leaders to increase
resource allocations to the defense sector (r = -.20).
Also, businessmen who replied that Angola and similar
Soviet behavior had reduced their desire to engage in
Soviet trade, likewise had a moderate corresponding
tendency to be skeptical that self-imposed precautions
taken by U.S. companies will be effective in safeguarding
U.S. national security with respect to sales of "sensitive"
high technology to the U.S.S.R. (computers, programmed
machine tools, etc.) (r = -.27).

Summary, Conclusions, and Theoretical Implications

Synopsis

Findings presented in this chapter clearly show that during 1975-1976 Soviet Area Executives on the whole viewed trade with the U.S.S.R. as anything but a one-way street benefiting the Soviet Union.  In particular, in addition to believing that the U.S. would secure political benefits from trade with the U.S.S.R. (see Chapter IV), SAEs also held the conviction that Soviet-American commerce would yield important economic benefits to the United States. Specifically, sizeable majorities of participants in the study felt that increased trade with the Soviet Union will be "generally beneficial" to the U.S. economy, that large-scale agricultural sales to the U.S.S.R. had been and would continue to be extremely helpful to American farmers and the U.S. balance of payments, and that stable long-term deals for the import of Soviet raw materials would be advantageous for the U.S. and would further diversify U.S. natural resource supplies.  In fact, some businessmen contended that the Soviets, given their well-documented obsession with fulfilling business contracts to the letter, might be more reliable providers of raw materials than many Third World nations.  On a somewhat different note, a considerable number of businessmen felt that trade with the U.S.S.R.'s planned economy can have a beneficial stabilizing

effect on those American industries which are highly
sensitive to fluctuations in the U.S. business cycle.

Consistent with their upbeat views on the desirability
of U.S.-Soviet commerce from an economic standpoint (and
complementing their endorsement of trade on political
grounds), SAEs displayed a corresponding tendency to play
down certain potential liabilities of an expanded Soviet-
American economic relationship. For example, reflecting
the fact that 71% of respondents to Survey 2 reported that
their Soviet business had been profitable, SAEs generally
rejected the popular notion that "monopoly" Soviet foreign
trade organizations can easily "whipsaw" American companies
into unfavorable transactions. Although the U.S.S.R. was
viewed as having a considerable theoretical capability for
playing off U.S. companies against each other and against
foreign competition, a number of factors were seen as
placing practical limits on the ability of the U.S.S.R. to
take advantage of U.S. firms.

Apart from the whipsaw question, SAEs also did not
seem particularly alarmed about the prospect that U.S.-
Soviet trade might make it easier for the U.S.S.R. to
increase defense spending. The prevailing opinion seemingly
was that although trade with the U.S. might result in some
economic benefits to the Soviet military, U.S. exports to
the U.S.S.R. would, at best, generate only minimal increases

in resources devoted to the Soviet defense effort.  The overall view was that the Soviet government always gives the military establishment top priority access to scarce economic resources, and that the U.S.S.R.'s civilian sector simply receives any investment funds left over.  Thus, because the Soviet military always gets what it wants anyway, SAEs generally felt that the Soviet consumer would likely be the primary beneficiary of any Soviet economic gains resulting from trade with the U.S.  A common variation on this theme was that, while Soviet leaders may be tempted by trade-induced increases in economic productivity to shift resources to defense production, they will be constrained from doing so by growing popular pressures in the U.S.S.R. for more consumer goods.  Rather than making it easier for the Soviet Union to bear its massive defense burden, trade with the U.S. and the West, by fueling the material aspirations of the Soviet citizenry, may actually render it more difficult for Soviet leaders to gain the acquiescence of the Soviet people to continuing large defense budgets at the expense of national consumption.

SAEs also did not seem greatly troubled by the possibility that U.S. knowhow and equipment sold to the U.S.S.R. might be diverted for direct use by the Soviet military. Underlying this view was the belief that Soviet and U.S. military technologies are generally comparable; i.e., that

the U.S.S.R.'s technological problems lie primarily in the
civilian economy, which is tightly insulated from the
defense sector and therefore does not benefit from heavy
Soviet investments in military R&D.  Thus, because the
Soviet defense establishment was seen as being already well
supplied with high quality industrial hardware and scientific instrumentation, businessmen for the most part thought
that the Soviets do not have much need to divert imported
technology to military purposes.  Nevertheless, as a
precautionary measure, SAEs generally acknowledged the need
for an effective set of U.S. export controls to prevent the
transfer to the Soviets of advanced U.S. technologies which
could have direct defense applications.

Interestingly, although most SAEs reported that a major
expansion in U.S.-U.S.S.R. trade would likely result in a
"significant" positive effect on the U.S.S.R.'s civilian
economy, most also evidently believed that the beneficial
impact on the Soviet Union's economic well-being would not
be major.  Because of gross deficiencies in Soviet industrial organization and formidable obstacles to innovation,
imports of U.S. industrial hardware and technological
expertise were expected to result in only marginal
increases in the general technological level of Soviet
civilian industry.  In fact, some SAEs argued that even
when the U.S.S.R. manages to make effective use of imported

equipment/knowhow in a particular factory or industry, the resulting increases in productivity are frequently dissipated by the immense waste that prevails throughout the rest of the economy. Given the deep-seated structural problems of Soviet industry, many SAEs felt that the U.S.S.R. might gradually develop a lasting technological dependence on the U.S. and the West; which was seen as both politically and economically beneficial to the United States.

Addressing critics of U.S. corporate activities with the U.S.S.R., some SAEs pointed out that American companies cannot afford to abdicate any sizeable overseas market to foreign competition, because to do so is to make it even more difficult for U.S. industry to generate the huge cash flow it needs to fund continuous large investments in vital R&D activities. Conversely, by totally ceding the Soviet (or any other) market to foreign competition, it was felt that U.S. firms would be enhancing the R&D base of West European and Japanese companies, while simultaneously providing them with incentives to develop export industries which might then challenge U.S. industry world-wide.

Economic relations with the U.S.S.R. were seen as potentially advantageous in yet another respect: Nearly half of all respondents to the 1976 survey believed that Soviet scientists and engineers have some innovative ideas--

as yet undeveloped--which U.S. companies could borrow and develop themselves to their substantial benefit. Many SAEs believed that if regular access to imaginative Soviet R&D staffs could be gained by American companies, U.S. firms might well succeed in obtaining some original and worthwhile Soviet technological concepts. In order to establish continuous contacts with Soviet research personnel, a "scientific-technical" (S&T) cooperation agreement was viewed as an important tool by executives of companies having such agreements. It merits emphasis that SAEs whose firms were involved in S&T pacts categorically denied that these agreements had facilitated the unrestricted flow of their companies' technologies to the U.S.S.R. To the contrary, there was a strong inclination to secure adequate monetary or technological compensation for any U.S. corporate technology transferred to the Soviet Union. Additionally, of those SAEs who said that their S&T agreement had resulted in a technological benefit to the Soviets, most indicated that the technology transferred had not been of major importance to their firm.

## Miscellaneous Theoretical Considerations

As suggested by the preceding summary, survey and interview data presented in this chapter tend to corroborate the observation, initially reported in Chapter IV, that executives' principal frame of reference for views on

U.S.-Soviet trade/detente was the broad national interests
of the United States rather than the narrow interests of
their individual companies. Additional support for this
conclusion lies in the fact that the profitability of trade
with the U.S.S.R., as measured by Survey 2, did not
correlate strongly with trade/detente attitudes. This is
not to say that profit did not exercise any influence in
shaping SAEs' attitudes on critical U.S.-Soviet issues, but
only that this influence apparently was moderate and no
more important than a number of other factors, such as, for
example, SAEs' perceptions of Soviet international behavior.
Relevant here, of course, is that SAEs' perceptions of
Soviet international behavior were also largely independent
of perceptions of profit; i.e., those who regarded U.S.S.R.
business as highly profitable did not display a strong
parallel inclination to play down the Angola episode and
similar examples of Soviet expansionism. Again, this is a
further indication of the role that conceptions of the
national interest seemingly played in SAEs' thinking during
1975-1976. Lastly, the failure to identify a powerful
influence for the profit motive on SAEs' views toward
Soviet-American trade/detente is additional reason to
question the traditional economic influence theories noted
earlier, and is consistent with the proposition, advanced

in the previous chapter, that "economic self-interest" is
an inherently complex and amorphous concept.

## Linkage Scenarios

It deserves emphasis that none of the findings of this
chapter conflicts with the linkage scenarios postulated in
Chapter IV. Indeed, there is additional support for
Linkage Scenario 9, which is reproduced below:

**Scenario 9**

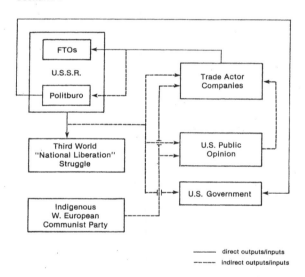

To reiterate, in this scenario direct polity outputs
by the U.S.S.R. (e.g., support for a Third World
revolutionary movement) and indirect polity outputs by
Eurocommunist parties stimulate indirect environmental

inputs in U.S. public opinion and trade actor companies
(e.g., increasingly negative assessments of the political
risks of U.S.S.R. business, worries of a growing
international communist threat). Environmental inputs to
U.S. public opinion trigger a micro-linkage whereby
indirect internal outputs (e.g., anti-Soviet press stories)
generate indirect internal corporate inputs (e.g., fear of
a domestic political backlash) in trade actor companies.
Subsequently, the various anxieties stimulated by
environmental and internal inputs culminate in decisions by
trade actor companies to slow the expansion of their
commercial relationships with the U.S.S.R., to cut back
Soviet business efforts, or to otherwise adopt a more
cautious stance toward Soviet business opportunities.
These direct polity outputs aimed at Soviet foreign trade
organizations also generate indirect environmental inputs
in the Soviet leadership which cause the U.S.S.R. to become
less forthcoming in its relations with the U.S. (i.e.,
direct polity outputs are triggered on the Soviet side).

What relevance do the findings of this chapter have
for the preceding scenario? Interview data outlined above
strongly indicate that, when adopting a more careful
business posture towards the U.S.S.R. as a result of
deteriorating East-West political conditions, U.S.
businessmen are much more likely to scale back licensing

activities relative to straightforward product deals.  In
other words, transactions involving transfers of industrial
knowhow to the U.S.S.R. appear to be much more sensitive to
adverse East-West political trends than transactions
consisting primarily of equipment.

The primary reason for this seems to be that licensing
agreements, in contrast with most contracts for the exchange
of products, depend heavily on the development and maintenance of trust between the licensor and licensee for a long
period.  Such trust is inherently fragile and is therefore
highly susceptible to negative developments between
Washington and Moscow.  As a result, interview results
indicate that East-West political developments during
1975-1976 contributed to a reduced desire to license even
among those SAEs who reported on Survey 2 that they had not
been affected by events like Angola.  Although these
businessmen were as eager as ever to sell products to the
U.S.S.R., licensing opportunities became less attractive; i.e., there was a shift in emphasis in the kind of
commercial opportunities that they would henceforth
consider.  Thus, it would appear that Soviet activities in
Angola, the Horn of Africa, etc., as well as the then-
growing power of Eurocommunist parties may have had a
substantially greater impact on U.S. businessmen's
inclinations to do business with the U.S.S.R. than is

indicated by responses to 1976 survey variables intended to measure such effects.

Complementing Scenario 9, survey and interview data outlined in this chapter suggest yet another linkage scenario which incorporates elements of Linkage Scenario 7 (Chapter II) and Linkage Scenario 8 (Chapter IV):

**Scenario 10**

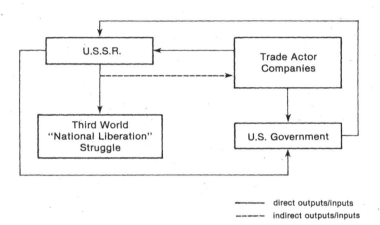

——— direct outputs/inputs
– – – indirect outputs/inputs

The above scenario stems from the finding that negative perceptions of Soviet activities in Angola, etc., evidently had a degree of indirect influence on SAEs' views on licensing technology to the U.S.S.R. Specifically, in Scenario 10 Soviet support for Third World revolutionary movements stimulates U.S. businessmen's fears that the

U.S.S.R. might misuse licensed American technology to compete with U.S. companies for world markets. Such fears may flow from either a "protective" response (i.e., perceptions of increased risk to the firm) and/or a "national welfare" response (i.e., fundamental doubts about the desirability of trade/detente) to Soviet activities. In any case, at the urging of their SAEs, trade actor companies become more reluctant to participate in licensing agreements with the U.S.S.R. Likewise, trade actor companies scale down their pro-trade political activities directed at the U.S. Government. In particular, U.S. firms become less aggressive in seeking more liberal and consistent federal policies in the export control area. As a result of the diminished political role of U.S. business, domestic political forces demanding restrictive Soviet trade policies--especially tighter export controls--become more influential. Consequently, the U.S. Government adopts a less compromising stand on Soviet-American economic and political issues, especially on questions of technology transfer. The tougher U.S. Government stand, together with the increased reluctance of U.S. firms to license technology to the U.S.S.R., causes Soviet leaders to doubt that substantial technological gains can be achieved through trade with the United States. Consequently, seeing itself as having a reduced vested interest in restraint in relations with the U.S., the U.S.S.R. also begins to adopt less compromising positions on outstanding issues between the two countries.

In the lexicon of the International Trade Politics Model, the preceding scenario is initially triggered by direct polity outputs by the U.S.S.R. not intended to affect Soviet relationships with U.S. companies. Nevertheless, Soviet actions generate indirect environmental inputs in American trade actor firms, which give rise to several behavioral sequences. First, a second macro-linkage is triggered involving direct polity outputs by trade actor firms which stimulate indirect environmental inputs in the Soviet leadership. At the same time, a micro-linkage results whereby direct internal outputs by U.S. companies result in direct internal inputs in the U.S. Government. This, in turn, precipitates the initial stage of a third macro-linkage which generates direct environmental inputs in the Soviet political leadership. Subsequently, Soviet leaders, responding to a combination of direct environmental inputs from the U.S. Government and indirect environmental inputs from trade actor companies, instigate a fourth macro-linkage consisting of direct polity outputs aimed at the United States. In sum, then, Scenario 10 is comprised of a series of "fused" linkages which is initially triggered by the Soviet side.

Scenarios 9 and 10, together with survey and interview data presented in this chapter, suggest a rather ironic conclusion:  The Soviet Union, in pursuing interventionist foreign policies during 1975-1976, may have inadvertently albeit seriously undercut its own efforts to license industrial knowhow from American companies.  Once again, such a finding has great relevance for the present and future course of U.S.-Soviet relations.  The apparent hypersensitivity of U.S. business attitudes toward licensing to fluctuations in the East-West political climate graphically illustrates how international political influences may make it problematical ever to establish a stable, broad-based commercial relationship as a foundation for a superpower detente.  Stated differently, the findings of this chapter reaffirm the proposition (first advanced in Chapter IV) that the so-called "spill-over" effect, which postulates that closer economic relations with the U.S.S.R. can help to control U.S.-Soviet political and military competition, may operate more efficiently in reverse.

Notwithstanding the impact that an adverse East-West political climate may have on the willingness of U.S. businessmen to sell knowhow to the U.S.S.R., there is reason to believe that even under extremely positive U.S.-Soviet political circumstances a great many American businessmen would still be inhibited from licensing knowhow to the Soviets. Indeed, even if most existing national security controls on U.S. exports to the U.S.S.R. were abolished, it is probable that many U.S. companies interested in entering into product transactions with the Soviets would still balk at getting involved in licensing arrangements. The likelihood of such self-restraint stems in large measure from numerous executives' fundamental disapproval of licensing--not just with respect to the U.S.S.R. but as a matter of general principle--because of the unusually complicated and long-term nature of licensing contracts, major difficulties in pricing licenses to insure a fair return, and deep-seated fears that transfers of industrial knowhow may one day transform one's customers into viable competitors. Even among those businessmen not irreconcilably opposed to licensing, there would still likely be substantial reluctance to pursue license negotiations, because of the Soviets' reputation as difficult business negotiators and executives' perceptions that this would magnify the knotty problems normally connected with any license.

Two additional and closely related linkage scenarios are implicit in the preceding propositions. These scenarios, designated 11A and 11B, can be represented as follows:

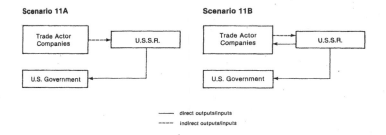

In Scenario 11A, U.S. businessmen's inherent
reluctance to license knowhow to the U.S.S.R. triggers
indirect polity outputs which result in indirect
environmental inputs in the Soviet leadership.
Specifically, Soviet political authorities become
increasingly disillusioned with U.S. companies' aversion to
licensing, and as a result they lower their expectations
for obtaining a massive infusion of industrial technology
from American firms. The Soviet government therefore
concludes that the U.S.S.R. stands less to gain from trade
with the United States than had originally been thought.
Consequently, seeing itself as having a reduced vested
interest in restraint in relations with the U.S., the
U.S.S.R. subsequently begins to adopt less compromising
stances on contentious issues dividing the two powers. Of
course, any such shifts in Soviet positions constitute

direct polity outputs intended to generate direct environmental inputs in the U.S. Government.

Scenario 11B is virtually identical to Scenario 11A
except for one important difference:  In Scenario 11B, U.S.
businessmen's recalcitrance with respect to Soviet licensing
is fueled by the U.S.S.R.'s frustrating business habits.
Inflexible and time-consuming Soviet negotiating tactics,
designed to shave Western profit margins and secure the
most advantageous contracts possible, result instead in a
heightened U.S. business reluctance to get involved in
complicated deals with the U.S.S.R.  Thus, direct polity
outputs by Soviet foreign trade organizations stimulate
direct environmental inputs in American firms, although the
actual effects on U.S. companies are not those that were
intended by Soviet officials.  Consequently, the aforementioned environmental inputs help to trigger the chain of
events described by Scenario 11A.  Once again, as in
Scenarios 9 and 10, Soviet actions inadvertently prove to
be counter-productive to the U.S.S.R.'s own efforts to
obtain U.S. industrial technology.

Note that Scenarios 11A and 11B, like Scenarios 8, 9,
and 10, are fused linkages as defined by Rosenau.  Also, it
merits emphasis that the two preceding scenarios, like
others postulated above, have important implications for
the continued development of Soviet-American commercial and

political relations. In particular, both scenarios cast
additional light on the difficulties inherent in any
attempt to establish a vigorous U.S.-U.S.S.R. economic
relationship as the basis for increased Soviet-American
cooperation in non-commercial areas.

Survey and interview data presented in this chapter
suggest a twelfth linkage scenario, which is shown below:

**Scenario 12**

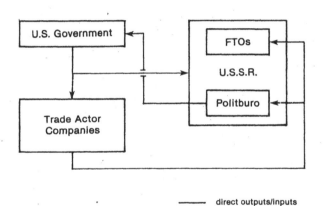

—— direct outputs/inputs
------ indirect outputs/inputs

The above network of relationships bears a strong resemblance to a pattern hypothesized in Linkage Scenario 5, which is delineated in Chapter II. Specifically, in Linkage Scenario 12, the U.S. Government pursues increasingly restrictive trade policies toward the U.S.S.R. in an effort to influence Soviet behavior and/or to prevent Soviet acquisition of U.S. technology. However, these direct polity outputs aimed at the Soviet Union also generate indirect internal outputs which give rise to indirect internal inputs in trade actor companies (i.e., a micro-linkage). As a result of perceived inconsistencies in overall federal commercial policies toward the U.S.S.R. and the erratic application of U.S. export control regulations to specific Soviet-U.S. company transactions, U.S. businessmen become increasingly unsure as to whether the U.S. Government in fact regards U.S.-Soviet trade as in the national interest. Given their growing uncertainty, American executives become more reluctant to invest time and money in the Soviet market, with the result that numerous U.S. companies decide to slow the expansion of their commercial relationships with the U.S.S.R., actually cut back their Soviet business relationships, or otherwise adopt a more cautious stance toward opportunities in the Soviet market. Collectively, these U.S. corporate actions comprise direct polity outputs which stimulate direct

environmental inputs in Soviet foreign trade organizations
(i.e., frustration at not being able to conclude desired
business deals). Simultaneously, however, the increasingly
hesitant behavior of U.S. companies generates indirect
environmental inputs among Soviet political leaders.
Soviet authorities begin to view American firms as
unreliable business partners, and ultimately revise
downward their estimation of the likely benefits of trade
with the United States. Consequently, the U.S.S.R.
perceives itself as having a reduced vested interest in
restraint in relations with the U.S., and begins to take
less compromising positions on unresolved political
differences between Moscow and Washington. This, of
course, involves a series of direct polity outputs aimed at
the United States which triggers direct environmental
inputs in various U.S. Government structures.

Again, Scenario 12, like previous scenarios,
graphically illustrates the evident sensitivity of U.S.
companies to various political factors and further suggests
a role for perceptions of the "national interest" in
businessmen's decision calculus. Perhaps more important,
however, is the relevance of Scenario 12 to the continuing
evolution of U.S.-Soviet relations. This scenario,
together with supporting data presented earlier, strongly
suggests and clearly outlines how any attempt by the U.S.

Government to calibrate or link its Soviet trade policies
to specific Soviet political actions may have unforeseen
side effects injurious to the fabric of the overall
Soviet-American relationship.  Indeed, such effects may be
lasting and not easily reversed.  For example, after
scaling back their Soviet business efforts in response to
perceived adverse shifts in federal policy, U.S. firms
might well be reluctant to respond to a future warmup in
U.S.-U.S.S.R. relations should one occur.  Having
experienced one major U.S. policy change, American
companies may develop an acute fear of possible future
policy reversals, and therefore will likely be hesitant to
invest heavily in Soviet business despite substantial
improvements in superpower relations.  If the preceding
proposition is valid, then any U.S. Government efforts to
fine-tune Soviet-American trade in accordance with broad
U.S. policy objectives may be doomed to ineffectiveness.
While U.S.-Soviet trade may be calibrated downward rather
easily, it may be much more difficult to calibrate trade in
an upward direction.

   Lastly, survey and interview data presented in this
chapter indicate that during 1975-1976 many U.S. companies
tended to view the U.S.S.R. as a residual growth market;
i.e., the Soviet Union was looked upon as a customer to be
courted during bad economic times but relegated to

secondary importance during good times. This finding is
clearly consistent with the network of relationships
postulated in Linkage Scenario 6 (outlined in Chapter II).
However, it would seem that Linkage Scenario 6 can be
subsumed by two broader scenarios, designated 13A and 13B,
which are sketched below:

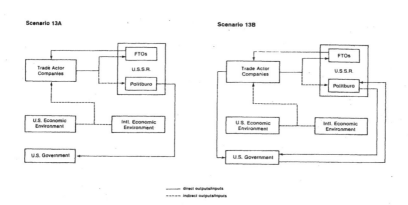

In Scenario 13A, indirect internal outputs from the
U.S. economic system, indirect environmental outputs from
the international economic system, and direct polity
outputs from the U.S.S.R. combine to generate indirect
corporate inputs in trade actor firms. Specifically, U.S.
businessmen perceive their traditional markets as expanding

due to improving domestic and world economic conditions.
Also, because of the Soviets' time consuming and inflexible
negotiating practices, the U.S.S.R. is viewed by many
executives as a troublesome and expensive place in which to
do business. As a result of all the aforementioned
factors, businessmen begin to regard the Soviet market as
of diminishing importance to their firms' immediate
fortunes. Indeed, some executives, confronted with growing
demands from priority customers and constrained by limited
company resources, may come to see their firms' Soviet
business activities as a burden which absorbs a
disproportionate amount of corporate time and talent.
Consequently, trade actor companies decide to slow the
expansion of their commercial relationships with the
U.S.S.R., or actually cut back their Soviet business
efforts. Such moves constitute direct polity outputs aimed
at the Soviet Union and subsequently generate direct
environmental inputs in Soviet foreign trade organizations
(e.g., frustration at the inability to conclude desired
business deals). However, as in other scenarios previously
described, the increasing recalcitrance of U.S. companies
simultaneously generates indirect environmental inputs
among Soviet political authorities, causing them to arrive
at a more negative assessment of the potential gains from
trade with the United States. As a result, the Soviet

Union, viewing itself as having a reduced stake in a
conciliatory relationship with Washington, initiates direct
polity outputs aimed at the U.S., which take the form of
tougher stances on a host of issues dividing the superpowers.

Like Scenarios 8 and 9, Scenario 13A illustrates how
events not under the direct control of either the Soviet or
American governments may complicate the development and
maintenance of strong, lasting, and broad-based commercial
ties between the U.S. and U.S.S.R. However, whereas in
Scenarios 8 and 9 the exogenous variables have a political
character, in Scenario 13A the external factors affecting
U.S. firms are economic in nature. It follows that
Scenario 13A strongly suggests that, even if an ideal
political atmosphere for U.S.-Soviet trade could somewhow
be created, it might still be problematical to establish a
consistent and robust Soviet-American trading
relationship. Of course, much depends on whether Soviet
foreign trade officials remain wedded to the stubborn
business style that has been their hallmark since the
1920s. Because such intransigence seemingly magnifies
other negative factors in the minds of American
businessmen, one would expect that, other things being
equal, a more relaxed Soviet business manner could go a
long way toward placing U.S.-U.S.S.R. trade on a more even

keel. Viewed from a somewhat different perspective, Scenario 13A, like Scenarios 9, 10, and 11B, shows once again how Soviet behavior may inadvertently undermine the U.S.S.R.'s own goals vis-a-vis trade with the United States.

Scenario 13B differs from 13A in one key respect: In responding to frustrating Soviet business habits and the expansion of traditional markets, U.S. companies not only give a lower priority to Soviet business activities, but also scale down any on-going political efforts on behalf of U.S.-U.S.S.R. commerce. This reduction in pro-trade political activity constitutes direct internal outputs which give rise to direct internal inputs in the U.S. Government (i.e., a micro-linkage). Specifically, in the absence of countervailing political pressure from the business community, domestic political forces advocating a tougher U.S. Government stance toward the U.S.S.R. become more influential. As a result, the U.S. Government initiates direct polity outputs which take the form of less compromising positions on a wide range of U.S.-Soviet economic and political issues. Next, these adverse signals from the U.S. Government, in conjunction with the increased reluctance of American companies to pursue Soviet business, yield the environmental inputs in the Soviet leadership that were described in Scenario 13A. Once again, as in 13A, the U.S.S.R.'s growing pessimism regarding the potential for trade with the U.S. results in an increasingly aggressive Soviet posture on various outstanding U.S.-Soviet issues.

Note that Scenario 13B, just like Scenario 10, supplements and is consistent with Scenario 8 (outlined in Chapter IV). The primary importance of 13B lies in the proposition that, even if a positive U.S.-U.S.S.R. political climate conducive to trade could one day be established, this fragile policy environment could well be difficult to maintain for long, since fluctuating U.S. and global business conditions might help to destabilize the underlying balance of political forces in the United States.

In concluding this chapter it is necessary to emphasize once again that the preceding linkage scenarios and associated propositions are meant to be heuristic, not definitive. They should therefore be viewed as sets of hypotheses deserving of further investigation and testing. However, with this qualification in mind, it can still be said that the above behavioral sequences, together with supporting survey and interview data, provide a plausible partial explanation for certain aspects of the evolution of superpower relations during the past decade. Relevant here is that Scenarios 9-13B are not mutually exclusive, but rather are complementary chains of events capable of synergistic interrelationships. Viewed collectively, these scenarios (together with Scenario 8 outlined in the previous chapter) can partly account for the failure of the U.S. business community to pursue a strong pro-trade political strategy during the latter half of the 1970s, for the stagnation in non-agricultural U.S.-Soviet trade which began about 1976, for the increasingly strident posture of the U.S. Government from 1976 onward vis-a-vis a host of U.S.-U.S.S.R. economic and political questions, and for the Soviet Union's pursuit from 1975 to the present of an increasingly contentious and adventurous foreign policy. Finally, apart from their historical interest, Scenarios 9-13B clearly have relevance for the present and future course of Soviet-American relations. Fundamentally, they further suggest that the dynamics of U.S. corporate behavior may make it extremely difficult ever to facilitate a trading relationship sufficient to give both superpowers a vested interest in moderation and restraint in their bilateral relations. Thus, the scenarios highlight additional weaknesses in the so-called "spill-over" hypothesis.

FOOTNOTES

[1]For examples of press articles that characterize
U.S.-Soviet trade and detente as a "one-way street" see
Howard Flieger, "Moscow's One-Way Road," U.S. News and World
Report, May 19, 1975, p. 80; "Detente:  Loaded in Russia's
Favor?," U.S. News and World Report, December 8, 1975, pp.
21-22 (Interviews with Sens. Henry M. Jackson and Charles
Mathias, Jr.); Theodore Draper, "Appeasement and Detente,"
Commentary, February 1976, pp. 27-38; "It's Russia's Turn
to Give," U.S. News and World Report, August 11, 1975, pp.
11-12, 14; "The West Gives Everything Away," U.S. News and
World Report, March 15, 1976, p. 23 (Excerpts from an
interview with Alexander Solzhenitsyn on BBC television).

[2]Relevant here is a comment made to the analyst by
an Ohio businessman:

"A moderate economic interdependency between the
U.S. and U.S.S.R. would work to the benefit of world
stability and peace.  For this reason, I think that a
limited reliance by the U.S. on Soviet natural resources
would be a good thing."

Complementing the above view, Samuel Casey, President of
Pullman, Inc. has written that:

"In the area of energy, for example, it actually is
in the best long range interests of the U.S. to work
with the Soviet Union and Eastern Europe.  Assisting
them in resource development and energy production will
increase the usable supply of gas and oil to the world
as well as keep them from becoming a net importer of
energy with a resultant further increase in the world
market price for these items."  (Casey, "Pullman and
World Trade", p. 40.)

[3]Executives concurring with this reasoning include
Donald Kendall of Pepsico:

"Is there any danger of the U.S. becoming too
dependent on Soviet imports?  The answer is, highly
unlikely.  When one considers the fact that East-West
trade currently represents about 1% of total U.S. trade,
it is obvious that increasing imports from the Soviet
Union can only serve to diversify U.S. sources of
supply."  (Kendall, "Is the U.S.S.R. a Good Trading
Partner?," in Matthias, Common Sense in U.S.-Soviet
Trade, p. 10.)

Similarly, Armand Hammer of Occidental Petroleum has argued
that:

> "Here, once again, we have that common denominator
> of decent men and women working together. On the one
> hand, the involvement of those of us from the U.S. will
> help the Soviet Union to develop the richness of
> Siberia. On the other, the development of Siberia will
> help to give the people of America a secure supply of a
> needed energy source without concern to any element that
> can from day to day change the rules and prices."
> [Armand Hammer, "Improved Relations Through Trade,"
> Journal of the U.S.-U.S.S.R. Trade and Economic Council
> 2 (January-February 1976): 15.]

[4]Representative background articles and reports on
the 1972-1973 U.S.-Soviet grain deals include, "The Grain
Drain," Newsweek, September 18, 1972, pp. 77-78; "The Great
Grain Robbery," America, October 14, 1972, p. 279; "All
About That Soviet Wheat Deal," U.S. News and World Report,
October 9, 1972, pp. 28-30. Also see U.S. Congress,
General Accounting Office, Exporters' Profits on Sales of
U.S. Wheat to Russia, GAO Report No. B-176943, February
1974.

[5]In this connection, during the course of a personal
interview, a senior executive of a major U.S. industrial
conglomerate made the following observation: "Once you can
get your company plugged into the Soviet Five-Year Plan,
you are almost guaranteed to get consistent business."

[6]For analyses of FTO "monopoly" market leverage,
which should properly be termed monopsony, see the
following: Marshall I. Goldman, Detente and Dollars (New
York: Basic Books, 1975); Glen A. Smith, Soviet Foreign
Trade: Organization, Operations, and Policy, 1918-1971
(New York: Praeger, 1973); Christopher E. Stowell et al.,
Soviet Industrial Import Priorities with Marketing
Considerations for Exporting to the U.S.S.R. (New York:
Praeger, 1975); U.S. Congress, General Accounting Office,
The Government's Role in East-West Trade--Problems and
Issues, GAO Report No. ID-76-13A, February 1976; U.S.
Department of Commerce, Bureau of East-West Trade, Office
of East-West Policy and Planning, U.S.-U.S.S.R. Trade and
the Whipsaw Controversy, ed. William F. Kolarik, Jr.,
excerpts from the March 30, 1977 meeting of the Advisory
Committee on East-West Trade, Washington, D.C., 1977.

[7]The following commentaries by three executives are
fairly typical of those interviewed:

"On the average, in the U.S. it takes only 1.5 phone
calls to reach the business contact that you want to
speak with. From my experience in Moscow, I would say
that the comparable figure for the U.S.S.R. is 15 phone
calls."

"The hassles of negotiating with the Soviets aren't
worth the reward--even though we mark up our prices to
cover the increased cost of doing business with them.
Their bureaucracy is hell to deal with, and they don't
seem willing to change their business practices to
accommodate U.S. firms."

"The Soviets cling to a dangerously narrow
interpretation of contract language. I just do not feel
comfortable doing business under such circumstances."

[8]One such executive, who happens to be one of
America's foremost scientist-businessmen, remarked that:

"As far as the U.S. electronics industry is
concerned, the Soviet Union does not represent a
significant growth market; particularly when one factors
in the costs which must be invested to develop Soviet
business. In order to remain competitive, we can't
waste sales dollars on a low volume market like the
U.S.S.R. During good economic times we have to chase
after other international markets which are much more
attractive."

[9]One executive who was interviewed related that
Soviet foreign trade officials had expressed unhappiness at
his company's tendency to regard the U.S.S.R. as a
secondary market:

"Fluctuations in U.S. economic conditions have
definitely made it harder for the U.S.S.R. to conduct
trade with this country. Soviet officials have
repeatedly complained to me that, 'You only want to deal
with us when your other business is poor.'"

[10]This view is clearly reflected in the following
public statement by Brooks McCormick, Chairman of
International Harvester Co.:

"If the extensive business International Harvester
has conducted with the Soviet Union did not benefit both

IH and the United States, my company would not enter into such trade." [Brooks McCormick, "IH's Involvement in Soviet Trade," Journal of the U.S.-U.S.S.R. Trade and Economic Council 3 (October-November 1977): 18.]

[11]Relevant here is a series of opinions voiced by four executives who were interviewed:

"Trying to cut a deal with the Russians is terribly fatiguing and costly. I think a lot of guys in a lot of companies are beginning to get fed up with it. If the Soviets keep on being difficult to deal with a lot of firms are just going to tell them to go to hell and refuse to do business with them."

"Concluding a contract with the U.S.S.R. is usually a 3-5 year proposition. In our view, it's almost impossible to plan business safely beyond 4 years, and if you can't do something in 4 years or less, you have to wonder whether its worth doing. If the Soviets keep on conducting business as they have, in the future they may have a hard time finding someone in this country to trade with."

"Now that we're into what looks like an economic boom, many companies figure that they no longer have to put up with the Soviets' antics. We can sell the same products for the same money with a lot less trouble here at home or in other international markets."

"How many years are you going to beat your head against the wall before you decide to quit?"

[12]One of these executives described his company's experience in the Soviet market as follows:

"We usually quote a price 55% higher to the Soviets than for our regular customers. We have to do that to make sure we cover the high costs of doing business with those guys."

Another executive from a high-technology firm indicated that his company's Soviet operations had been unusually lucrative:

"Our Soviet and other East bloc sales give us our highest profit margin. They never quibble about price."

[13]According to one businessman who was interviewed: "Dealing with Soviet FTOs is very much like dealing with Japanese industrial cartels."

[14]In a letter to the analyst subsequent to a personal interview, one executive summed up his views on FTO bargaining leverage as follows:

"I would strongly disagree that the FTOs have any unusual clout. For instance, our own Government's bids are publicly opened and similar bids often repeated in short intervals. This exerts much more pressure on the seller to engage in cutthroat competition. Dealing with the FTO, the seller is in full control of what terms and prices he is willing or not willing to agree to. It is no different than dealing with any large customer."

Similar sentiments are voiced by an executive who took part in a 1977 Commerce Department study of Soviet business negotiating tactics:

"The 'wear them down' negotiations certainly are true. I think, however, the delays are not just for negotiating purposes but rather because you're dealing with a highly bureaucratic organization on the other side. In our projects we normally think we will work from 1 to 3 years from inception to final contract. I could add facetiously that if an American company had as its negotiating partner some U.S. Government agency, I can see even greater delays!" (U.S. Department of Commerce, Office of East-West Policy and Planning, Whipsaw Controversy, pp. 8-9.)

[15]See "Cargill Claims Loss on Russian Wheat Sale of Almost Cent a Bushel, Rebutting Critics," Wall Street Journal, 3 November 1972, p. 4; and U.S. Congress, General Accounting Office, Exporters' Profits on Sales of U.S. Wheat to Russia.

[16]For example, one of these executives reported the following:

"Our deal was 'skinny' in the first place. We should have built more fat into our quotations. The thing that really hurt us is that we made a number of equipment guarantees without pressing the Soviets to allow our personnel to oversee installation of the machinery. Later we had to send some of our best people over to the U.S.S.R. to straighten everything out, and this cut heavily into our profits."

[17]Elaborating on his fundamental opposition to licensing, one executive said: "One problem with licensing is that our restraint of trade laws make it difficult for us to limit the markets of our licensees."

[18]One businessman who had been involved in license negotiations with the U.S.S.R. estimated that the cost of the effort had been perhaps four times higher than working out a similar agreement elsewhere. Other executives made the following interesting observations on the unique problems associated with Soviet licensing:

"You don't know your cost curves as well when licensing. It's especially difficult to estimate start-up and technical update expenses. Also, the Russians are much tougher in writing up licensing agreements compared with product contracts. They usually want to make a lump sum payment for the technology and generally resist any kind of long-term royalty arrangement. The lump sum payment initially seems attractive to U.S. companies but the profit margin on such deals can easily be eroded over time as the American firm is forced to provide servicing, technical updates, etc. On the other hand, royalty schemes present other special problems. In particular, it's virtually impossible to monitor the U.S.S.R.'s compliance with such agreements. In my view, it's a whole lot easier and a lot more profitable to concentrate on product sales to the Soviets and to avoid licenses altogether."

"The Soviets always try to put conditions in licensing contracts that are unacceptable to most companies. For example, they want continual updatings of the technology without making additional payments for them. Also there has to be more flexibility in a license agreement than in a regular contract. The Russians' insistence on sticking to the letter of the contract--which is always very detailed--doesn't provide us with the flexibility we need."

"You have to remember that the Soviet track record in honoring patents hasn't been that great. When you grant a license to the U.S.S.R., you essentially give up control over the technology, both legalistically and physically. This is because monitoring the license is much more difficult than almost anywhere else."

"Licenses are very hard to police in general--and especially so in the U.S.S.R. Another problem is the

Russians' obsession with writing everything into the
Contract. You've got to have flexibility of
interpretation in a license agreement, and the Soviets
don't like to conclude deals on such a basis."

"One difficulty in negotiating a license with the
Soviets is that they refuse to agree to a price
escalation formula for very long-term agreements. The
fact that they base their entire economy on a Five-Year
Plan simply does not permit this."

[19]Echoing this view, Samuel Casey of Pullman, Inc.,
and Donald Kendall of Pepsico have written that:

"The Soviet Union and the nations of CMEA will
either purchase from other countries, develop on their
own or do without that which is not available from the
U.S. whether it be financing, technology or equipment."
(Casey, "Pullman and World Trade," p. 39.)

"Another issue of concern to many is the whole area
of technology: by selling our technology to the Soviet
Union, are we aiding them to our own detriment? The
fact is, the U.S. does not possess a monopoly on
technology. Most of the technology which the Soviets
need and cannot obtain directly from us, they can
purchase from the Japanese, the Germans, or the
Italians." (Kendall, "Is the U.S.S.R. a Good Trading
Partner?," in Matthias, Common Sense in U.S.-Soviet
Trade, p. 11.)

[20]Reflecting this perspective, George Prill, former
President of Lockheed Aircraft International, has advocated
the following as the optimal licensing strategy:

"The ideal marketing scenario for any manufacturer
is one in which, through licensing, he siphons off the
funds that his competitor needs for the development of
products and uses those funds for his own next
generation. This leaves the competition building the
earlier generation, and building it at a higher cost."
(George Prill, "Can We Trade Commercial Aircraft?," in
Matthias, Common Sense in U.S.-Soviet Trade, p. 77.)

[21]Commenting on the preference of Soviet industrial
managers for proven technology, one executive stated the
following opinion in the course of an interview:

"They talk about it a lot, but the Soviets run away from advanced technology. It represents risk. Our technology won't fit well into their backward industrial set-up. They're not geared up for our latest stuff."

Another businessman, having spent significant time in Soviet production facilities, speculated:

"I get the feeling that they don't trust their own people. I think they like a piece of equipment to be foolproof because they don't trust their help to use it. They have incredibly lazy and incompetent line personnel. It was not unusual for me to find men literally sleeping on the job."

[22]The following comments by three executives who were interviewed will serve to illustrate the impact of the deteriorating East-West political climate on businessmen's willingness to license technology to the U.S.S.R.:

"The degenerating political situation, especially this business in Africa, has made American firms much more cautious about issuing licenses to the Soviets. In the current atmosphere, policing licenses becomes of greater concern to the average businessmen. This is because licenses are heavily based on trust between the parties involved; and as inter-governmental trust deteriorates this often has an effect on commercial trust as well. This is especially true in the Soviet case because American companies are signing contracts with Russian government agencies, not private companies. Businessmen are now more worried than they were a year or so ago that the U.S.S.R. might use American technology to compete with us in world markets, or that they might simply cheat on license royalty payments."

"Distrust of the Soviets is growing in this country, and this public mood is having a spill-over effect on business executives. This has had the greatest impact on the willingness of U.S. companies to consider licensing deals with the Russians."

"U.S. firms are definitely more reluctant now than they were a year ago to license technology to the Soviets. This development, I think, has mainly been a response to a deteriorating political climate. Companies have become especially sensitive to all the bad publicity in this country about so-called

'technology giveaways' to the Russians. Licensing
agreements are difficult to arrange even under the best
of circumstances, much less under these kind of
political conditions.

[23]This attitude perhaps is best illustrated by one
executive's comments during an interview:

"In our company we have never been particularly fond
of licensing, but we will consider granting licenses
under certain conditions. Before Angola, we would have
at least entertained the idea of issuing a license to
the Soviets. Now, however, it's out of the question.
We're perfectly willing to continue selling products to
the U.S.S.R., but the political fall-out from Angola has
created too much risk and uncertainty for us to get
involved in a tricky licensing deal."

[24]Typical of this view is the following opinion
which was expressed by an East Coast manufacturer of
scientific instruments:

"The Soviet military always gets first call on
economic resources anyway, so its unlikely that trade
with the U.S. and the West will result in bigger Soviet
military budgets. There might be a little increase in
Soviet defense spending, but not much."

[25]Other relevant comments include the following
statements by five businessmen who were interviewed:

"Soviet leaders may well want to boost their
military spending even more, but trade with the West may
make this more difficult and not easier. East-West
trade is opening up Russian society to a lot of new
Western influences and is exposing the Russian people to
a better standard of living than they have known. This
is going to place a lot of indirect consumer pressure on
the government and is going to make it harder for Soviet
leaders to boost weapons spending."

"There is a fantastic consumer demand over there
which will be intensified by growing contacts with the
West. That is going to put a lot of pressure on
Brezhnev to beef up the civilian sector--which is going
to make military spending a lot more difficult. In
fact, I think the Soviets' real motive in trade with the
West is to improve the Soviet standard of living, not to
expand military capacity."

"The Soviets could divert additional resources to the military as a result of trade, but I don't think that will happen. The Soviet population, especially the youth, are going to press the regime into raising living standards."

"Trade with the West will make the Soviet population more materialistic, which is going to put some pressure on the Soviet government to rearrange its priorities to favor consumer goods at the expense of military goods."

"I believe that the Soviets' main goal right now is to boost their civilian economy through Western trade. Clearly, their main motive is to increase the material standard of living of the average Russian. Trade with the West may help the Soviet military a little, but they'll continue directing most foreign purchases into civilian areas. If you visit Moscow, you can already see that the Soviet people are benefiting from expanded Western commercial contacts. Compared with my first trip over there a few years ago, people are a lot better dressed now."

[26]The most cogent presentation of this point of view was made by a senior executive of a West Coast manufacturer of advanced electronic equipment:

"Our industry's survival depends on increasing our market share on a world-wide basis. By forbidding companies like ours from selling products in the U.S.S.R., the U.S. Government is giving our competitors a protected market in which they can gain time to learn from their mistakes and upgrade their products to the point where they can challenge us in non-protected markets. It's my view that the way in which U.S. export controls are administered will ultimately damage U.S. national security in very basic ways: The Russians are going to get what they need anyway, European and Japanese industry will gain technological experience and jobs, and the vitality of American industry will be reduced."

Lester Hogan, Chairman of Fairchild Camera and Instrument, has argued along similar lines:

"What would happen if the U.S. elects not to pursue the Eastern European market? Quite simply, our competitors in Japan and Western Europe will. If this Eastern European business should go outside the U.S., this would deny us the opportunity to increase our research and development capability, broaden our cost base, and thus continue strengthening our position in the world market." (C. Lester Hogan, "Semiconductors: The Positive Advantages of Controlled Trade," in Matthias, Common Sense in U.S.-Soviet Trade, p. 71.)

[27]Exemplifying this attitude is the following statement made by one executive during the course of a personal interview:

"It's possible that trade with the Soviets might help them to increase defense spending, but it's not my place to worry about that. My government has given me the green light to do business over there, so I'm not going to lose any sleep over such issues."

[28]Executives' recognition of the achievements of the Soviet military economy is vividly illustrated by the ensuing remarks made by a Midwestern manufacturer of sophisticated machine tools:

"Our company agonized over whether or not to do business with the U.S.S.R. because our products have munitions manufacturing potential. We finally decided to go ahead because in our field the Soviets are close to technological parity in the military sector. We figure that most if not all of our stuff will be put to non-defense applications. Also, the equipment we sell is available to the Soviets from foreign suppliers, so we felt that we would be stupid if we didn't try to get our fair share of the market."

[29]As one executive put it:

"I think all the talk of the Soviets buying technology from the U.S. is off the mark. The Soviets are not as interested in purchasing advanced technology as they are in getting standard equipment to increase their production capacity. If you look at the machinery they've been buying from U.S. companies, most of it certainly doesn't qualify as advanced technology. What a lot of people don't understand is that the Soviets have only a limited ability to assimilate and utilize technology in their civilian economy."

Supplementing this view two additional businessmen said:

"If you take a careful look at the last two Five-Year Plans, it's obvious that the Soviets are

mostly concerned with increasing productivity in their
civilian economy. While Soviet purchases from the West
might result in some benefit to Soviet defense
production, it won't be of any real significance."

"The Soviets' number one priority is to maximize
output in their civilian economy, and imported
manufacturing technology is going to be the vehicle for
accomplishing this goal."

[30]One executive who was interviewed voiced his
dissatisfaction with export controls as follows:

"It's incredibly frustrating dealing with U.S.
export control procedures. In my opinion, it's not
worth the investment of selling energy."

The same executive went on to note that:

"Any Soviet currently residing in the U.S. can
purchase sophisticated microminiaturized LSI chips at
any electronics supply house and then transport those
components out of the country via diplomatic pouch."

Another businessman indicated his unhappiness with export
controls when he remarked that:

"I'm sick and tired of dealing with all the
governmentese connected with export controls. The
regulations are complex, conflicting, and vague. You
can only put up with it for so long before you just give
up trying."

[31]On the subject of self-imposed corporate
restraints on transfers of industrial technology, George
Prill, former President of Lockheed Aircraft International,
has argued that:

"As a rule--indeed as a conditioned reflex--the
managers of American high technology industries are very
careful with proprietary information, whether it
concerns patents, drawings, know-how, or marketing and
sales data. Far from being willing to 'give away'
proprietary data to the Soviet Union, they are not
willing to make these available to Western European,
Canadian, and Japanese companies, or to each other,
without substantial compensation.

". . . no successful manufacturer, American or otherwise, releases full technical information to his customers. An engine manufacturer is not prepared to transfer his manufacturing skills to the airframe company that installs the engine in a transport. These skills are not needed for operation or maintenance, and they are not a part of the sale. The same holds true in the relationship between the suppliers of accessories and the engine manufacturers and so on down the chain to the companies that supply raw materials. In other words, you do not have to be an expert in the smelting of steel to build an airplane with steel turbine blades or steel landing gear." (Prill, "Can We Trade Commercial Aircraft?," in Matthias, Common Sense in U.S.-Soviet Trade, p. 77.)

[32]When asked to evaluate the likely impact of imported Western technology on the Soviet economy, six executives interviewed responded as follows:

"The Soviets are often unable to utilize technology effectively because their society is so cumbersome. Sometimes I think that actually using purchased technology is of secondary importance to Soviet industrial ministries. Instead, all they frequently seem to care about is the possession of imported technology, because it's prestigious to have the latest U.S. equipment.

"The Soviets don't seem to do too much with the stuff we sell them. They want technology for prestige reasons, but they have a great deal of trouble using it as its supposed to be used."

"There are fantastic impediments to innovation. And when they finally do make a 'go' decision they try to make a quantum jump from small pilot plants to full-blown giant plants. Then they have problems. So all of a sudden there's great bureaucratic pressure to get things on-line fast, regardless of cost."

"Even licenses won't achieve what the Soviets want. You can't help them enough to make up for their lack of experience."

"Purchasing technology won't help the Soviets that much. Transplants are a poor substitute for organic growth."

"As far as the U.S.S.R.'s civilian sector is
concerned, quantum jumps in Soviet technological levels
are not likely to take place on a significant scale as a
result of East-West trade. Even if quantum jumps are
possible in selected areas, by the time the imported
technology 'takes' that level of technology will be
commercially obsolete in the West, where the
state-of-the-art changes almost daily due to an intense
competitive environment."

[33]Commenting on the prospects for engendering Soviet
technological dependence on the U.S. and the West, one
executive interviewed put forth his views in a particularly
straightforward manner:

"The more you sell to them [the Soviets] the more
they will rely on you for spare parts and technical
expertise. Our objective should be to get the bastards
hooked on our technology."

Another businessman interviewed observed that the
alternative to Soviet technological dependence on the West
may be the enhancement of Soviet research and development
capabilities:

"If the U.S. and the West refuse to sell the Soviets
the technology they want, then they will develop it
themselves. In terms of our national interests this
would really be bad, because the Soviets would not only
end up with the technology, but they would also end up
with the industrial infrastructure needed to support it."

Also relevant here are the published remarks of Lester
Hogan, President of Fairchild Camera and Instrument:

"With the dollar flow from the sale of technology
and share of market, the selling country has more money
to plow into research and development for new
technologies and for reduced manufacturing costs. In
addition, the seller has made the receiving country
dependent upon it not only for products but for
continuing technology. By not developing it in the
first place, the buyer denies his own engineers the
opportunity of learning by doing." (Hogan,
"Semiconductors: Positive Advantages of Controlled
Trade," in Matthias, Common Sense in U.S.-Soviet Trade,
p. 70.)

[34]This perspective is best illustrated by the following comment made by an executive of a high-technology company during the course of an interview:

"The Russians have bought technology from the West off and on many times before. What we're betting on is that this time they won't be able to taper off completely."

[35]It merits attention that this view is supported by findings of an extensive 1977 study funded by the U.S. Department of State and the National Science Foundation. See U.S. Department of State, Bureau of External Research, Report on the Potential for Technology Transfer from the Soviet Union to the United States, by John W. Kiser III, Contract 1722-620217, July 1977.

[36]On this issue the published views of William Norris, President of Control Data Corporation, are illustrative of the attitudes of many SAEs:

"The Soviet Union has more scientists and engineers at work than any other country, and it is producing vast amounts of basic technology. The Soviets have not been very effective in the application of technology to production, whereas Western countries have emphasized the application of technology to production. There is, then, the basis for a natural division of work in what can result in very productive cooperation." (William C. Norris, "Transfer of Commercial Technology: Harmful or Helpful?," in Matthias, Common Sense in U.S.-Soviet Trade, p. 29.)

Similar thoughts have been voiced by Paul Stroebel and E. N. Brandt, senior executives of Dow Chemical Corporation:

"The application of scientific developments to industrial production has been a forte of U.S. chemical companies, and it is in this area that more and better communication with the West could greatly strengthen the contribution of Soviet science to the economy. In turn, the cross-fertilization which would occur between scientists could increase the flow of Soviet technology to the U.S. beyond that already occurring . . ." (Paul G. Stroebel and E. N. Brandt, "Chemicals: Developing a Trade Relationship," in Matthias, Common Sense in U.S.-Soviet Trade, p. 57.)

[37]In this connection, one executive reported that his company had been trying to develop a symbiotic relationship with Soviet scientific and engineering personnel:

"The Soviets are trying to plug into U.S. industrial R&D labs. Under our S&T agreement with them they send prototypes and prototype ideas to our R&D facility. Then it's our job to think up some practical industrial applications for the stuff, which the Soviets subsequently can buy back. Basically, they want us to help them bridge the gap between theory and practice. Their labs can't do this by themselves, because they're usually insulated bureaucratically from a production setting."

[38]Four executives who were interviewed justified their companies' S&T agreements as follows:

"A scientific-technical agreement is a passport to prospects for future business. It makes the bureaucracy easier to deal with. They get the idea that the political leaders have said it's okay to deal with you."

"It expands your market and gives you acceptability with the Soviet bureaucracy. Besides, if your company doesn't sign one, somebody else [i.e., a competitor] will."

"An S&T agreement is an umbrella. It means nothing until you sign a subsidiary agreement. It also gives you an acceptability with the Soviet bureaucracy that you don't have otherwise."

"Rather than put together a costly marketing campaign for our entire product line, . . . our S&T agreement specified a number of areas they [the Soviets] were interested in. This way we concentrated our efforts and maintained a base from which we could operate."

[39]For example, one executive described his company's experience with its S&T agreement as follows:

". . . we've played it pretty cagey. At first we managed to show the Russians as little as we could while trying to pick their brains."

Two other executives indicated that American companies'
careful attitude toward S&T agreements had provoked Soviet
displeasure:

"The [Soviets] feel we haven't performed on
scientific and technical agreements. I've heard them
say that we're trying to 'sucker them,' that we just
sign the things to get more business."

"I think there have been different interpretations
to scientific-technical agreements by the parties
involved. American companies tend to view them as a
step to future business and as a basis for commercial
proposals regarding U.S. technology. On the other hand,
the Soviets see scientific-technical agreements
idealistically: as a commitment to engage in open-ended
discussion along technical lines. They don't understand
that U.S. companies have to make a profit on everything
they do. We just can't send our talented science and
engineering people over to Moscow for a month to swap
ideas for the fun of it . . . and they get disillusioned
when we don't. The Russians are able to do that sort of
thing because there's no profit motive over there and
they have far more people on a given industrial R&D
project than we do. They can waste time and manpower
like crazy."

CHAPTER VI

## THE DOMESTIC POLITICAL ENVIRONMENT
## FOR U.S.-SOVIET TRADE

In previous chapters, strenuous efforts were made to
provide an exhaustive description and analysis of SAEs'
attitudes and opinions on central issues of Soviet-American
economic and political relations. As a result of this
comprehensive inventory, it has been established that the
great majority of U.S. businessmen who were engaged in U.S.-
U.S.S.R. commerce during 1975-1976 considered their
activities to be in the U.S. national interest. The steady
development of trade relations with the Soviet Union, it
was believed, will yield important tangible political and
economic benefits to the United States. Perhaps more
importantly, a corollary view held by most SAEs was that
the U.S.S.R. would not obtain substantially <u>greater</u> benefits from Soviet-American commerce than the U.S. In other
words, trade with the Soviet Union was generally seen as
anything but a "one-way street." Trade, these businessmen
reasoned, is inherently reciprocal and mutually beneficial.

Immediately apparent from the preceding encapsulated
summary, as well as from a cursory reading of Chapters IV
and V, is the self-conscious, defensive quality of SAEs'

stated attitudes and opinions. Explicitly and implicitly, the data which have been presented clearly show that survey and interview participants were acutely aware of the fact that many elements in the American political system strongly disagreed with (and to a great extent still disagree with) their views. Similarly, many SAEs were obviously concerned by what they perceived to be an unsettled and increasingly hostile domestic political environment for trade with the Soviet Union.

In view of the above-noted anxieties, it would therefore seem appropriate at this juncture to examine more closely a number of questions, several of which have been touched upon throughout this study. Specifically, during the period under investigation, how did SAEs see themselves as relating to the broad U.S. political context? In particular, what impact did they perceive the domestic political environment as having on their companies' orientations vis-a-vis Soviet trade? Finally, to what extent did SAEs perceive a need for corporate political action aimed at modifying the U.S. political climate for Soviet-American commerce?

### The Governmental Environment: Perceptions of Federal Policy on U.S.-U.S.S.R. Commerce

It was previously noted in Chapter V that during personal interviews, SAEs continually complained about a

perceived dichotomy in U.S. Government trade policy toward
the Soviet Union:  During these discussions, it was
apparent that all the businessmen were fully cognizant of
the federal government's then-existing officially stated
policy which supported in principle the development of
mutually beneficial economic relations between the United
States and the Soviet Union.  At the same time, however,
most of the SAEs also felt that the U.S. Government's
historical support for U.S.-Soviet trade had not been
translated into concrete actions on a practical business
level.  In other words, there was a widespread perception
that the U.S. Government had failed to follow through on
and operationalize its positive public posture on Soviet
trade.  Indeed, the federal government was frequently
characterized as being blatantly obstructionist.  In this
connection, SAEs frequently cited the then-recent
implementation of a host of statutory restrictions on
lending to the U.S.S.R. by the Export-Import Bank; the
passage and entering into force of the Jackson-Vanik
Amendment to the Trade Reform Act of 1975, which made U.S.
tariff policies toward the U.S.S.R. conditional upon the
emigration of ethnic/religious minorities from the Soviet
Union; the failure to ratify U.S.-U.S.S.R. trade and
financial agreements signed during 1972-1974; and the
alleged erraticism of the U.S. export control process.[1]

Although research findings reflecting the preceding sentiments have been reported at various points throughout this study, some additional survey results will serve to illustrate further the extent of SAEs' aggravation with federal authorities. For example, a large 72.2% majority of respondents to Survey 1 agreed with the proposition that efforts of American businessmen to improve U.S.-Soviet trade have been seriously undercut by inconsistent U.S. Government trade policies toward the U.S.S.R. Only a meager 5.6% of respondents actually disagreed with the proposal, whereas the remaining 22.2% of the SAEs said they were "not sure" (Table 32).

Also, a strong 69.4% majority of 1975 survey respondents complained that the U.S. Government is damaging the competitive position of American business by its restrictive trade policies toward the U.S.S.R., because the Soviets can buy most of what they need in West Europe and Japan. A similar view on the question of foreign competition was also expressed by participants in Survey 2. An overwhelming 87.1% of 1976 survey respondents voiced the opinion that current U.S. tariff policy toward the U.S.S.R. and restrictions on Eximbank credit are, for financial reasons, forcing the Soviets to move away from American suppliers and back toward the West Europeans and Japanese, whose governments offer the U.S.S.R. better terms

TABLE 32

EVALUATIONS OF U.S. GOVERNMENT TRADE POLICY TOWARD
THE U.S.S.R., 1975-1976
(Percentaged Horizontally)

| | Agree Strongly | Agree But Not Strongly | Not Sure, Depends | Disagree, But Not Strongly | Disagree Strongly | (N)* |
|---|---|---|---|---|---|---|
| **1975 Survey** | | | | | | |
| Efforts of American businessmen to improve U.S.-Soviet trade have been seriously undercut by inconsistent U.S. Government trade policies toward the U.S.S.R. | 36.1% | 36.1% | 22.2% | 5.6% | 0 | (108) |
| Our government is damaging the competitive position of American business by its restrictive trade policies toward the U.S.S.R. because the Soviets can buy most of what they need in West Europe and Japan. | 49.1 | 20.4 | 12.0 | 13.9 | 4.6 | (108) |

TABLE 32 (continued)

EVALUATIONS OF U.S. GOVERNMENT TRADE POLICY TOWARD
THE U.S.S.R., 1975-1976
(Percentaged Horizontally)

| | Agree Strongly | Agree But Not Strongly | Not Sure, Depends | Disagree, But Not Strongly | Disagree Strongly | (N)* |
|---|---|---|---|---|---|---|
| **1976 Survey** | | | | | | |
| Current U.S. tariff policy toward the U.S.S.R. and restrictions on Eximbank credit are, for financial reasons, forcing the Soviets to move away from American suppliers and back toward the West Europeans and Japanese whose governments offer the U.S.S.R. better terms of trade. | 58.2 | 28.9 | 8.2 | 3.6 | 1.0 | (194) |
| The U.S. Government lacks a clear policy on technology transfer between American companies and the U.S.S.R. | 36.2 | 37.2 | 11.7 | 8.7 | 6.1 | (196) |

*Variations in the number of cases (N) are attributable to "no answers" which are excluded from all calculations. Survey results reported for 1975 are based on a total N of 109 executives. Results of the 1976 survey reflect a total N of 203 executives.

of trade. It is notable that 58.2% of the sample held this view "strongly," whereas a mere 4.6% believed to the contrary (Table 32).

Consistent with the frustration indicated in Chapter V with respect to U.S. export control procedures, a substantial 73.5% of 1976 survey respondents stated their perception that the U.S. Government lacks a clear policy on the transfer of technology between American companies and the U.S.S.R. Not surprisingly, this view was most prevalent among SAEs from high-technology firms. Whereas 81.1% of these businessmen described U.S. technology-transfer policy as being unclear, the comparable figure for SAEs from conventional technology companies was 68.0%.

It follows from the preceding data that throughout personal interviews virtually all SAEs cited ambiguities and inconsistencies in federal trade policies toward the U.S.S.R. as having generated major uncertainty in the U.S. business community with respect to the Soviet market. This uncertainty, in turn, was usually described as having been manifested in several different ways, with the result that U.S. companies were seen as becoming more reluctant to get involved in U.S.S.R. business and more hesitant to commit scarce corporate resources to pursue Soviet commercial opportunities.

For example, in elaborating on their above-noted objections to then-new legal restrictions on Eximbank lending to the Soviets, many SAEs said that without Eximbank support they were uncertain whether any bids they might offer to Soviet foreign trade organizations would be financially competitive with alternative overseas suppliers. Given this increased uncertainty, a number of businessmen maintained that it simply does not make sense to even take a chance in developing an expensive contract proposal for the Soviet market. In other words, the elimination of Eximbank from the U.S.-U.S.S.R. trade picture was viewed as amplifying the economic risks to the firm of pursuing Soviet business.

Additionally, as was mentioned in Chapter V, almost all SAEs observed that erratic federal policies toward trade with the U.S.S.R. had caused much uncertainty in business circles as to whether the U.S. Government in fact regarded Soviet-American commerce as being in the national interest. The absence of clear direction from Washington, it was contended, had caused many U.S. businessmen to refrain altogether from participation in trade with the U.S.S.R. In this connection, SAEs repeatedly stressed that the vast majority of U.S. businessmen and their firms aspire to be good and loyal citizens of the United States. Thus, before embarking upon any major effort to develop

business in a new and politically controversial foreign
market, the first step normally taken by a U.S. company is
to make certain that its plans have the blessing of U.S.
Government policy, or, at a minimum, do not conflict with
U.S. policy. Interview participants were apt to point out
that this is not only a civic responsibility, but to do
otherwise is to ignore possible political risks to one's
business venture (e.g., a possible future U.S. Government
trade embargo or other adverse measure). To determine
whether corporate plans are consistent with federal policy,
SAEs intimated that most businessmen rely on a variety of
indicators, some of which are primarily symbolic (e.g.,
official U.S. Government statements supporting trade) and
others which are substantive (e.g., a country's access to
Eximbank, an operative inter-governmental trade agreement).
Consequently, due to the glaring conflict between symbolic
and substantive signals on U.S.-U.S.S.R. trade coming out
of Washington during 1975-1976, SAEs generally observed
that it is only natural that companies not already committed
to this market would now hesitate to become involved. In
essence, businessmen's natural response to uncertainty is
to "avoid risks." (As was noted in Chapter IV, several SAEs
voiced the opinion that U.S. firms, in deciding whether or
not to pursue Soviet business opportunities, are likely to
be unusually sensitive to political risks. In this regard,

the long adversary relationship of the superpowers, rooted in fundamental conflicts of national interest, was viewed as amplifying the probability that any given political incident might spill over into the commercial sphere and affect on-going company activities.)

Apart from the fact that many SAEs saw political uncertainty generated by federal policies as deterring companies unfamiliar with the Soviet market from approaching that market, about 40% of executives interviewed indicated that despite their significant experience with U.S.S.R. business, they too had become more reluctant to invest in the Soviet market as a result of the aforementioned uncertainty. These businessmen were apt to point out that although U.S. trade policy vis-a-vis the Soviet Union had had its ups and downs, it had become obvious that the overall federal policy environment for Soviet-American trade was rapidly getting worse and showed no promise of improving soon. Thus, in addition to their concern over existing U.S. Government policies, these SAEs were particularly apprehensive about perceived negative trends in policy and about possible future adverse developments. Most of these executives therefore indicated that their anxieties about the direction of U.S. trade policy had contributed importantly to their adoption of a "go slow" stance with respect to Soviet business. At this

point, it merits emphasis that those SAEs who indicated
growing hesitancy vis-a-vis the Soviet market as a
consequence of uncertainty caused by federal trade policies
also indicated awareness of a variety of capricious forces
acting on U.S. Government policy from both within and
outside of the United States. For example, in Chapter IV,
considerable effort was devoted to describing how certain
SAEs perceived aggressive Soviet activities in Angola as
raising the risk that the U.S. Government might at some
point take economic reprisals aimed at discouraging
interventionist Soviet behavior (e.g., implementation of
tighter export controls). Also, Angola was viewed as
having contributed to a worsening of the domestic political
climate for Soviet-American commerce. This, in turn, was
seen having provided a number of anti-Soviet interest
groups in the U.S. with additional ammunition for use in
domestic political debates on U.S.-U.S.S.R. commercial
matters. The primary effect of this, it was felt, had been
to reduce further the slim existing possibilities for
near-term Congressional repeal of the Jackson-Vanik
Amendment and statutory restrictions on Eximbank lending to
the U.S.S.R. Conversely, it was believed that forces
seeking to undermine U.S.-Soviet economic relations might
have new success in engendering further federal
restrictions on trade with the U.S.S.R. In this regard,

the day-to-day application of export control regulations
was cited as being especially vulnerable to political
pressures by hostile anti-trade elements.

Of course, the inconsistency and growing negativism of
U.S. Government commercial policy toward the U.S.S.R. was
not viewed as solely the product of external events like
the Angola episode. Indeed, most SAEs who indicated during
interviews that they had become more reluctant to pursue
Soviet business did not seem preoccupied with the
implications of Angola for U.S. policy and the domestic
political context. Instead, it appeared throughout
personal interviews that the overwhelming majority of SAEs
were most deeply disturbed by the perceived gradual
re-emergence of an historical, indigenous, and almost
visceral anti-Soviet sentiment in American public opinion.
This trend, several SAEs pointed out, had made passage of
the Jackson-Vanik Amendment possible in the first place.
It was noted that more recently media diatribes had
resulted in renewed U.S. export controls on sales to the
U.S.S.R. of crime control and surveillance gear, because of
unsubstantiated charges that such equipment was being
purchased for use against Soviet dissidents. In sum, SAEs
evidently regarded the anti-Soviet groundswell as having a
momentum entirely of its own, although certain hard-core

anti-Soviet interest groups in U.S. society were clearly
seen as actively encouraging the trend.

### Political Cognition:  Businessmen's Evaluations
### of U.S. Government Institutions

From the above it should be apparent that businessmen
interviewed for the most part intuitively recognized that
recent ambiguous and adverse federal trade policies toward
the U.S.S.R. represented the outcome of an impersonal
political process; i.e., that the U.S. Government simply
had been responding to the interplay of various political
forces.  Nevertheless, throughout almost every personal
interview, SAEs' complaints against the federal government
were clearly tinged by a deep personal resentment of
Washington policy-makers, which repeatedly found expression
in comments having powerful overtones of political cynicism
and alienation.[2]  Reflecting this strong anti-Washington
bias, the nation's officials were often stereotyped as
being spineless, lacking character, and incapable of
independent thought on U.S.-Soviet trade issues.
Executives typically agonized that the U.S. Government had
responded shamelessly and irrationally to domestic
political pressures brought to bear by U.S. interest groups
seeking restrictions on Soviet-American commerce.  U.S.
policies toward the Soviet Union, they bemoaned, were
increasingly being made on the basis of emotionalism rather

than being governed by a clear, logical, and consistent concept of the long-term national interest. Needless to say, for reasons stated in previous chapters, most executives held the conviction that the steady development of U.S.-U.S.S.R. trade is in the best interests of the United States.

Interestingly, although general condemnation of Washington was pervasive throughout personal interviews, other interview data as well as results of the 1976 survey point to a certain degree of ambivalence in executives' attitudes toward the U.S. Government. In personal interviews, as well as on the 1976 survey questionnaire, a series of questions were posed asking businessmen to evaluate the role of specific governmental institutions in the development of U.S.-Soviet commercial relations. The basic finding was that certain federal institutions, especially agencies of the Executive branch, were regarded favorably despite executives' deep-seated anti-Washington feelings.[3]

For example, consistent with statements made during personal interviews, a large 70.3% majority of respondents to Survey 2 were of the opinion that both Presidents Nixon and Ford had made positive contributions toward improving U.S.-Soviet trade relations (Table 33). A similar positive contribution by the Department of State was acknowledged by

TABLE 33

EVALUATIONS OF U.S. GOVERNMENT INSTITUTIONS WITH RESPECT
TO SOVIET-AMERICAN TRADE, 1976
(Percentaged Horizontally)

| | Agree Strongly | Agree But Not Strongly | Not Sure, Depends | Disagree, But Not Strongly | Disagree Strongly | (N)* |
|---|---|---|---|---|---|---|
| Since 1972, both Presidents Nixon and Ford have made positive contributions toward improving U.S.-Soviet trade relations. | 31.3% | 59.4% | 6.3% | 2.6% | 0.5% | (192) |
| Since 1972, the U.S. Department of State has made a positive contribution toward improving U.S.-Soviet trade relations. | 21.3 | 53.7 | 14.4 | 9.0 | 1.6 | (188) |
| Since 1972, the U.S. Commerce Department has generally made a positive contribution toward improving U.S.-Soviet trade relations. | 22.6 | 58.1 | 11.8 | 5.9 | 1.6 | (186) |
| Information supplied by the Commerce Department's Bureau of East-West Trade is helpful in analyzing your company's marketing prospects in the U.S.S.R. | 11.1 | 45.8 | 15.8 | 18.9 | 8.4 | (190) |
| Since the inception of detente, the U.S. Export Administration Office has made a positive contribution toward improving U.S.-Soviet trade relations. | 5.3 | 37.4 | 35.1 | 19.3 | 2.9 | (171) |

TABLE 33 (continued)

EVALUATIONS OF U.S. GOVERNMENT INSTITUTIONS WITH RESPECT
TO SOVIET-AMERICAN TRADE, 1976
(Percentaged Horizontally)

| | Agree Strongly | Agree But Not Strongly | Not Sure, Depends | Disagree, But Not Strongly | Disagree Strongly | (N)* |
|---|---|---|---|---|---|---|
| Compared to the pre-detente period, there is today a much higher probability of eventually obtaining a validated export license for a sale to the U.S.S.R. | 23.8 | 50.8 | 17.1 | 6.6 | 1.7 | (181) |
| The turnaround time for obtaining a "yes" or "no" from the Export Administration Office on an application for a validated export license has been shortened considerably over the past few years. | 13.4 | 37.2 | 34.1 | 7.9 | 7.3 | (164) |
| From 1968 until 1972, the U.S. Congress generally made a positive contribution toward improving U.S.-Soviet commercial relations by revising restrictive export control legislation. | 11.0 | 59.3 | 13.7 | 11.0 | 4.9 | (182) |
| Since the late '60s the influence of the U.S. business community on Congressional policy toward the U.S.S.R. has generally declined. | 18.2 | 27.3 | 20.9 | 31.6 | 2.1 | (187) |

TABLE 33 (continued)

EVALUATIONS OF U.S. GOVERNMENT INSTITUTIONS WITH RESPECT
TO SOVIET-AMERICAN TRADE, 1976
(Percentaged Horizontally)

| | Agree Strongly | Agree But Not Strongly | Not Sure, Depends | Disagree, But Not Strongly | Disagree Strongly | (N)* |
|---|---|---|---|---|---|---|
| Since the beginning of detente, the U.S. House of Representatives has generally made more contributions to improving U.S.-Soviet commercial relations than the Senate. | 3.2 | 29.0 | 51.0 | 11.0 | 5.8 | (155) |
| The member of the U.S. House of Representatives from the Congressional district in which your firm is headquartered has not been responsive to your company's views on U.S.-Soviet trade. | 7.3 | 15.3 | 39.3 | 26.0 | 12.0 | (150) |
| Senators who represent the State in which your company is headquartered have not been responsive to your firm's views on U.S.-Soviet trade. | 11.6 | 24.5 | 34.8 | 23.2 | 5.8 | (155) |

*Variations in the number of cases (N) are attributable to "no answers" which are excluded
from all calculations. Total N for the 1976 survey is 203 executives.

75.0% of 1976 survey respondents. However, the most

plaudits were given to the Department of Commerce: Some

80.6% of the 1976 survey sample believed that Commerce had

helped to strengthen trade ties with the U.S.S.R. Within

Commerce, 56.8% of SAEs reported that information supplied

by the Department's Bureau of East-West Trade had been

helpful in analyzing their companies' Soviet marketing

prospects.

Of particular interest is that Commerce's image does

not seem to have been tarnished by its bureaucratic

responsibility for the administration of U.S. export

control regulations. Businessmen's aggravation with export

controls has been documented throughout this study.

Despite this frustration, however, fully 42.7% of

respondents to Survey 2 indicated that the Commerce

Department's Export Administration Office had played a

positive role in improving U.S.-Soviet trade relations, and

only 22.2% disagreed with this proposition. This apparent

paradox can be explained by the fact that executives

interviewed tended to view the Export Administration Office

as a victim of anti-trade forces elsewhere in the federal

establishment. Although the Commerce Department was seen

as the administrator of U.S. export control policy, it was

not considered to be at the helm of policy. Export control

recommendations of the Department of Commerce, it was

contended, are frequently overruled in inter-agency
committees dominated by the Department of Defense, or are
revised under Congressional pressure. Thus, Commerce was
often described as being on the defensive and as expending
its limited resources to fend off restrictive proposals
made from outside. Looking at it another way, certain
executives saw the Export Administration Office as
representing U.S. business' point of view in a complex and
murky regulatory process; although these same businessmen
were quick to criticize Commerce for often displaying
timidity in the performance of this function. Nonetheless,
respondents to Survey 2 evidently credited Commerce with
some important successes: A large 74.6% of the survey
sample reported that, compared to the pre-detente period,
there had recently been a substantial improvement in the
probability for eventually getting an export license for a
sale to the U.S.S.R. In addition, 50.6% said that the time
required for obtaining a yes or no on a license application
to the Export Administration Office had been shortened
considerably over the past few years.[4]

During interviews, the Congress was the U.S. political
institution usually singled out by businessmen for special
criticism, particularly with respect to the passage of the
Jackson-Vanik Amendment and legislative restrictions on
Eximbank lending to the U.S.S.R.[5] These verbal

denunciations, however, are not fully reflected in
collected survey data for 1976. For instance, a large
70.3% majority of respondents to Survey 2 felt that from
1968 to 1972 the U.S. Congress generally had made a
positive contribution to U.S.-Soviet commercial relations
by revising and liberalizing restrictive U.S. export
control statutes. Especially puzzling is that 33.7% of
survey participants reported that, in their opinion, the
U.S. business community's ability to influence Congressional
policy toward the U.S.S.R. had not declined since the late
1960s; and another 20.9% were "not sure" in this regard.
Also, perhaps most surprising is that survey participants
displayed a remarkable inability to differentiate between
the two chambers of Congress in terms of their respective
performances on Soviet trade issues. When asked to evaluate
the relative contributions of the House and the Senate to
the recent development of U.S.-Soviet commercial relations,
an extraordinary 51% of survey respondents said they were
"not sure" which had made the greater contribution (or,
conversely, which had been the most obstructionist). This
finding is nothing short of astonishing in view of Senator
Henry Jackson's well-publicized leading role during
1975-1976 in mobilizing Congressional support for
restrictive U.S.-Soviet trade legislation. Finally,
despite their direct interest in U.S.-U.S.S.R. commercial

matters, a surprisingly large percentage of 1976 survey
participants indicated that they were ignorant of positions
taken on Soviet-American trade issues by their Congressional
representatives.  A striking 39.3% reported that they were
"not sure" whether or not the Congressman representing
their company's Congressional district had been responsive
to their firm's views on U.S.-U.S.S.R. trade (whereas 22.7%
regarded their Congressman negatively, and 38.0%
positively).  Similarly, 34.8% indicated uncertainty as to
whether their state's Senators had been responsive to
company perspectives on Soviet-American economic relations
(whereas 36.1% viewed their Senators negatively and 29.0%
positively).  Of course, the preceding survey questions
presupposed that most SAEs had made an effort to express
company opinions to their elected legislative officials.
In fact, however, during personal interviews about half the
businessmen stated that their companies had not tried to
communicate directly with Congressional representatives.
Careful follow-up questioning revealed a series of
seemingly interrelated reasons for the failure to do so:  A
few businessmen simply did not know the names of their
Senators and Congressmen.  Some also said that they thought
it best to leave such political activities to their
industry's trade associations or lobbies like the National
Association of Manufacturers and the U.S. Chamber of

Commerce. Certain executives just did not recognize a
connection between their business activities and the need
for political action. Others who did see such a link often
felt that it would not be wise for individual U.S. firms to
play a highly visible political role on Soviet trade
questions. Finally, a pervasive undercurrent throughout
the conversations was the belief by many executives that
any political input by them on key U.S.-Soviet economic
issues would be an exercise in futility. (These and other
business perspectives on political action are explored in
greater detail in a later section.)

### The Anti-Soviet Impulse: Interest Groups, Public Opinion, and the Mass Media

Throughout this study repeated references have been
made to executives' concerns, expressed in personal
interviews, about a perceived deterioration during
1975-1976 in the domestic political climate for Soviet-
American commerce. In this connection, it was noted
earlier that a sizeable number of businessmen interviewed
indicated that adverse trends in the U.S. political
atmosphere, by contributing to the uncertainty of federal
trade policies, had indirectly encouraged them to pursue
more cautious business strategies with respect to the
U.S.S.R. However, perceptions of an increasingly hostile

U.S. political environment also apparently influenced executives' thinking in other, more immediate ways: During personal interviews SAEs imparted a growing sensitivity to possible direct criticism of their firms' Soviet business activities from a variety of sources. One executive, for example, feared that if the extent of his company's dealings with the U.S.S.R. were to become known in his community, local Jewish groups might respond by picketing his factory. Another businessman volunteered that he had become paranoid about the possibility of a reaction from the intensely anti-Russian Lithuanian-American population predominating in the neighborhood around his plant. Similar anxieties over a possible backlash by ethnic and/or religious groups were echoed by other executives. In addition, several businessmen expressed concern over the prospect that growing anti-Soviet sentiment in the U.S. might at some point provoke the nation's consumers to boycott products manufactured by American companies involved in trade with the U.S.S.R. One of these executives, whose company produces capital goods, was especially fearful of the possibility of a future boycott by his firm's industrial customers, who were generally characterized as being very conservative politically. It should be self-evident that SAEs who expressed the aforementioned views also indicated a strong preference for

keeping their companies' Soviet business out of the public
eye; and where secrecy was considered impossible,
unspecified public relations ("PR") measures were seen as
desirable to minimize possible problems. Reflecting such
opinions, 31.3% of 1976 survey respondents reported that
they thought it best to keep information about their firms'
business relationships with the U.S.S.R. to a minimum in
local news media (Table 34). Likewise, 27.8% thought it
important to keep their regular customers fully informed of
the nature of their companies' Soviet business deals.[6]
(Note that the importance of the preceding survey data is
not immediately apparent, given the relatively low
percentages indicated. Rather, the real meaning of the
survey results is revealed only when viewed in the context
of interview findings; i.e., the interviews enabled the
analyst to identify an emerging phenomenon that otherwise
would have been missed.)

Apart from their growing uneasiness over a possible
backlash from religious, ethnic, or consumer forces,
several SAEs interviewed whose companies were then
fulfilling Soviet contracts indicated increasing concern
over the strong, well publicized anti-Soviet posture of
George Meany, the late president of the AFL-CIO.
Opposition to U.S.-Soviet commerce by national labor
figures like Meany, it was feared, might at some point

TABLE 34

EVALUATIONS OF THE CORPORATE POLITICAL ENVIRONMENT
FOR U.S.-SOVIET TRADE, 1976
(Percentaged Horizontally)

| | Agree Strongly | Agree But Not Strongly | Not Sure, Depends | Disagree, But Not Strongly | Disagree Strongly | (N)* |
|---|---|---|---|---|---|---|
| It is best to keep news of your firm's business relationships with the Soviets to a minimum in the local news media. | 6.1% | 25.3% | 17.7% | 34.8% | 16.2% | (198) |
| It is important to the success of your company's business with the Soviets that your firm's regular customers fully understand the nature of deals with the U.S.S.R. | 10.8 | 17.0 | 20.1 | 33.5 | 18.6 | (194) |
| It is important to the success of your company's business with the Soviets that your firm's employee unions fully understand the nature of deals with the U.S.S.R. | 11.4 | 31.8 | 17.6 | 23.3 | 15.9 | (176) |
| On the whole, publications of the U.S. business community (Business Week, Fortune, etc.,) have proved to be objective sources of information on matters pertaining to U.S.-Soviet relations. | 10.2 | 66.5 | 12.2 | 9.1 | 2.0 | (197) |

TABLE 34 (continued)

EVALUATIONS OF THE CORPORATE POLITICAL ENVIRONMENT
FOR U.S.-SOVIET TRADE, 1976
(Percentaged Horizontally)

| | Agree Strongly | Agree But Not Strongly | Not Sure, Depends | Disagree, But Not Strongly | Disagree Strongly | (N)* |
|---|---|---|---|---|---|---|
| On the whole, the American national popular press has proved to be an objective source of information on matters pertaining to U.S.-Soviet relations. | 1.6 | 18.7 | 14.0 | 33.7 | 32.1 | (193) |
| On the whole, the American radio and television media have proved to be objective sources of information on matters pertaining to U.S.-Soviet relations. | 1.0 | 22.6 | 19.5 | 32.8 | 24.1 | (195) |
| Since the inception of detente, the Executive Branch of the U.S. Government has tended to ignore the advice of the business community when forming export control policy. | 16.2 | 31.9 | 16.8 | 27.6 | 7.6 | (185) |

*Variations in the number of cases (N) are attributable to "no answers" which are excluded from all calculations. Total N for the 1976 survey is 203 executives.

precipitate spontaneous refusals by union locals to work on Soviet contracts; or, alternatively the AFL-CIO might conceivably seek to organize strike action aimed at the U.S.S.R. on a nationwide scale. In any event, those executives who indicated that they were worried about possible labor problems also tended to say that they were taking certain measures to minimize the likelihood of trouble with their unions. Such measures were usually characterized as careful attempts to explain to one's employees the reasons behind management decisions to pursue Soviet business, and as efforts to convince workers of the benefits to the firm of U.S.S.R. contracts (e.g., additional man-hours of employment generated). Of relevance here is that a sizeable 43.2% plurality of respondents to Survey 2 evidently also saw a need for these preventive tactics, having indicated that they thought it important that their firms' employee unions fully understand the nature of any deals with the U.S.S.R. (Table 34).

Without a doubt, during personal interviews the most common thread running throughout executives' commentaries on the U.S. political climate was their growing sensitivity to possible criticism of their firms' Soviet business activities by corporate shareholders and directors. Although these individuals do not normally play a role in running the day-to-day affairs of most American companies, many SAEs pointed out that the management team of every U.S. public corporation must justify its activities to stockholders and the board of directors at least once a year. Thus, a corporation's managerial officials must continually remain responsive in a general way to concerns indicated by the company's owners and their elected representatives. In this connection, businessmen frequently stated that defending their companies' Soviet business efforts had become an increasingly worrisome issue because of the staunchly anti-communist politically conservative views held by certain key stockholders and corporate directors. Several executives even said that they had taken great pains to edit their annual corporate reports to shareholders so as to camouflage the extent of their business dealings with the U.S.S.R.

Interestingly, however, when pressed for specifics only a few businessmen actually reported a recent upsurge in complaints about their firms' Soviet business from stockholders and directors. As a matter of fact, under questioning almost all executives were also hard put to cite actual instances of an anti-Soviet backlash among their employees, customers, or local ethnic/religious groups (although two SAEs did report receiving hate mail from unspecified community elements). Rather, it seems

that the possibility and not the reality of negative
reactions from the aforementioned sources was pre-eminent
in executives' thinking, and that fears of this possibility
had been greatly magnified by the perceived deterioration
in the domestic political environment for U.S.-Soviet
commercial relations.

It merits attention that besides the worsening U.S.
political atmosphere, another factor unquestionably acted
to intensify executives' fears of a potential anti-Soviet
political backlash. Several SAEs related that until
recently they had felt confident that they could defend
against any criticism of corporate activities with the
U.S.S.R. (especially by stockholders and directors) by
pointing to the U.S. Government's policy of support for
U.S.-Soviet trade. However, given the recent inconsistency
and negativism of federal policies on Soviet trade, this
defense was regarded as increasingly untenable; thereby
leaving American firms more and more vulnerable to
potential attack by those opposing U.S.-U.S.S.R. commerce.
In sum, SAEs not only anticipated that their firms' Soviet
business dealings would be subjected to ever more frequent
criticism, but they also saw themselves as becoming less
able to ward off such assaults.

Another observation is relevant here. It will be recalled that in Chapter V several businessmen argued that in

the absence of clear, consistent policy guidance from Washington, U.S. firms would tend to fall back on their own perceptions of the national interest in arriving at Soviet business decisions. After some probing on this point, these executives further acknowledged that, absent a strong and unwavering pro-trade stance by federal authorities, many firms' concept of the "national interest" in U.S.-U.S.S.R. trade is likely to be shaped increasingly by the powerful anti-Soviet sentiments which pervade American society, especially when such views are held by corporate stockholders and directors. This means that SAEs' personal views on the benefits of Soviet-American commerce (its potential contribution to world peace, beneficial effects on the U.S. balance of payments, etc.) will become subordinated to other considerations. According to this reasoning, then, the natural inclination of U.S. companies in an uncertain government policy environment will be to shy away from business involvement with the U.S.S.R.

Although repeated references have been made to SAEs' growing disquiet over a perceived deterioration in the U.S. political climate for trade with the Soviet Union, little has been said thus far about the basis of these perceptions. To be specific, what factors did SAEs see as being primarily responsible for the worsening domestic atmosphere? A partial answer, readily apparent from data presented in previous chapters, is that some SAEs undoubtedly viewed the U.S.S.R.'s interventionist activities in Angola, the Horn of Africa, etc. as having had an important negative impact on U.S. public opinion. However, the fact remains that most executives who indicated during personal interviews that they had become more reluctant to pursue Soviet business did not seem preoccupied with the implications of Angola for the domestic political context. This does not mean that they were not concerned about U.S. political trends, but only that the Angola affair was regarded as only a minor influence on the recent evolution of the public's perspectives on trade with the U.S.S.R. Rather, a host of other factors was seen as fueling a resurgence of deep-rooted, traditional anti-Soviet feelings among the American people. Considerable anxiety over this development was displayed not only by SAEs who had recently scaled down their Soviet business efforts, but also by businessmen who had not yet opted for a more cautious corporate strategy vis-a-vis the U.S.S.R.

Asked to enumerate the factors which had contributed to recent adverse trends in U.S. public opinion, executives interviewed were virtually unanimous in citing the so-called "great grain robbery" of 1972-1973 as having been the turning point in national attitudes toward

Soviet-American commerce. The grain deals, it was contended, had left a lasting negative impression on the American public which had been manifested in several ways. First, adverse publicity associated with the grain sales was seen as having reinforced the Soviets' image as implacable and tough negotiators who, for mysterious reasons, are always able to take advantage of their U.S. counterparts. In this regard, the U.S. Government's inept performance in initial grain talks with the Soviets was alleged to have convinced many Americans that federal authorities are somehow not up to the task of protecting U.S. national interests in economic as well as political agreements concluded with the U.S.S.R. Similarly, because certain U.S. grain companies had sustained losses or had profited only minimally from their Soviet contracts, SAEs generally believed that the grain sales had contributed to the popular notion that U.S. companies are inherently at a bargaining disadvantage when confronted with the raw market power of the U.S.S.R.'s national foreign trade monopoly. In addition, businessmen pointed to another harmful effect of the grain episode: The U.S. public, they noted, had been justifiably incensed over the inflationary impact on U.S. food prices of the massive Soviet purchases; and this was generally viewed as the most damaging consequence of all. Numerous executives observed that although most

Americans neither care about nor fully understand the complexities of U.S.-Soviet relations, the average citizen instinctively reacts against anything which hurts his pocketbook. Thus the "grain robbery," by causing many Americans to associate U.S.-Soviet commerce with a threat to their economic well-being, was seen by many executives as severely undermining national support for trade with the U.S.S.R. In sum, SAEs felt that the controversial 1972-1973 grain sales had fostered continuing public skepticism of all forms of economic cooperation between the United States and the Soviet Union.[7]

Besides the "grain robbery" and Soviet activities in Angola, during personal interviews a variety of additional influences were recounted as having had an adverse impact since 1972 on public attitudes toward U.S.-Soviet trade and detente. For instance, some executives believed that many Americans had perceived a major Soviet role in the Arab-Israeli war of 1973. This event, it was contended, had planted the first real seeds of public doubt about the wisdom of a political and economic rapprochement with the U.S.S.R. Another frequently expressed view was that because of former President Nixon's close identification with the policy of detente, the Watergate-related demise of his presidency in August 1974 had permanently tarnished detente's image among the American people. Many executives also said that the public had reacted negatively to reports throughout 1975 of Soviet attempts to exploit political instability in Portugal. Similarly, SAEs often said that anti-Soviet feelings among the American people had been stirred by the collapse of South Vietnam in 1975 and the political successes of the French and Italian communist parties during 1975-1976. An additional factor cited was persistent adverse publicity concerning the U.S.S.R.'s continuing military buildup in both strategic and conventional arms. This, various businessmen observed, had caused many Americans to wonder about the Soviets' true intentions in seeking detente with the U.S. Lastly, several executives noted that the then-recent signing of the Helsinki Accords on Security and Cooperation in Europe had resulted in considerable unfavorable press in the U.S.; i.e., charges by critics that without receiving anything in return the U.S. had capitulated to Soviet desires for official Western recognition of their de facto domination over Eastern Europe. Whether or not legitimate, these businessmen felt that the aforementioned charges had reinforced public perceptions that well-intentioned American negotiators invariably come out second best when dealing with the wily and opportunistic Soviets.[8]

Despite differing assessments of the factors most responsible for negative trends in U.S. public opinion,

almost all executives interviewed were apparently in
agreement that the national reaction to the above-noted
developments had been far more pronounced than warranted by
events. The American people, many executives observed,
have an almost inborn impulse to embrace and exaggerate
anything which is anti-Soviet in nature. By way of
illustration, several executives pointed to the major
attention which had recently been given to a single
incident of cheating by a Soviet fencer at the Montreal
Olympic Games. This isolated event, it was argued, had
been blown way out of proportion by most Americans, and had
contributed greatly to a nascent public tendency to regard
all Soviets as dishonest and untrustworthy. Similarly,
several executives commented that the recent elevation to
national prominence of Soviet exile Alexander Solzhenitsyn
could only be explained in terms of the visceral appeal of
his strident anti-Sovietism to most Americans. Implicit
throughout most executives' remarks was the perception that
the recent decline in popular support for Soviet trade and
detente had been the result of a cumulative and synergistic
process, whereby the U.S. public's emotional response to
each negative incident (e.g., Angola) had amplified the
adverse impact on national opinion of subsequent incidents.

It follows from the preceding views that most
executives also lamented what they perceived to be the

inherent inability of the average American to appreciate
the subtle and multi-faceted nature of the U.S.-Soviet
relationship.  Asked to elaborate on this opinion, SAEs
were apt to note that the Nixon-Kissinger strategy of
detente had not assumed that conflict between the U.S. and
the U.S.S.R. would end, but that new cooperative aspects of
superpower relations (especially trade) would gradually
promote moderation in Soviet behavior.  The general public,
however, was described as having been unable to grasp this
dichotomy.  Most Americans, it was contended, had
originally taken detente to mean a new era of Soviet-
American friendship.  This misinterpretation, by fostering
unreasonably high initial expectations, was characterized
as having subsequently contributed in a major way to the
public's growing disillusionment with the detente process.

Although much of the recent deterioration in public
support for U.S.-Soviet trade was ascribed to the impulsive
anti-Sovietism of the American people, many executives were
also deeply resentful of perceived attempts by certain
elements in U.S. society to fan the flames of discontent.
For example, it was felt that national Jewish
organizations, by popularizing the plight of Soviet Jews
and dissidents, had focussed undue national and
Congressional attention on these issues.  This campaign,
the businessmen generally believed, had not only undermined

public support for U.S.-Soviet trade, but had been
instrumental in the passage of the Jackson-Vanik Amendment
to the Trade Reform Act of 1975. As has been noted
throughout this study, the Jackson-Vanik legislation was
viewed negatively by most executives interviewed, as well
as by the majority of participants in the 1975 and 1976
surveys. After denouncing the Jackson-Vanik Amendment
during personal interviews, executives were apt to deny
hastily any anti-semitic inclinations, and they generally
felt that U.S. Jewish groups were pursuing a noble goal in
seeking freer emigration of Jews from the Soviet Union.
Nonetheless, businessmen for the most part looked upon
Jackson-Vanik as the wrong means to achieve a desirable
end. Several criticisms were expressed by numerous
executives throughout a host of conversations.

First, citing various news reports, most executives
were of the view that the Jackson-Vanik Amendment had
actually been counterproductive to its objectives, because
emigration of Jews from the U.S.S.R. had dropped
precipitously since the the passage of the Trade Reform
Act. The Soviets, it was contended, had been incensed over
what they perceived to be a blatant U.S. Government attempt
to interfere in the U.S.S.R.'s internal political affairs
through the overt and highly visible use of economic
leverage. In fact, most businessmen seemingly agreed with

the Soviets' evaluation of the situation. No self-
respecting sovereign nation, SAEs frequently argued, could
tolerate or be seen as complying with the terms of the
Jackson-Vanik Amendment. Indeed, several executives added
that the Soviets had been embarrassed and felt stigmatized
by the Jackson-Vanik legislation, especially since the
United States over the years has extended Most-Favored-
Nation (MFN) tariff treatment to virtually every country on
earth.[9] Reflecting this view, it should be noted that
75.0% of 1976 survey respondents similarly reported that
eliminating what the Soviets see as unfair and unequal
treatment is just as important to the U.S.S.R. as the
financial benefits to be gained from the acquisition of MFN
status.

However, besides viewing the Jackson-Vanik Amendment
as an ineffective and self-defeating tactic for promoting
the emigration of Jews from the U.S.S.R., most executives'
primary objections to this legislation were more
fundamental in nature. Under questioning, most executives
acknowledged the fact that the language of the
Jackson-Vanik Amendment does not apply just to Soviet Jews,
but instead supports free emigration as a general
principle; i.e., that any person, regardless of ethnic or
religious background, should be able to leave the U.S.S.R.
of his or her own free will.

Nonetheless, businessmen generally dismissed this as a weak cosmetic attempt to obfuscate what was perceived as a legislative initiative instigated by American Jews and designed primarily to benefit Soviet Jews. Many executives were apt to point out that in debates leading up to the passage of Jackson-Vanik neither the U.S. Congress, the U.S. Administration, nor the national news media had given much attention to Soviet Latvians, Estonians, Lithuanians, or members of other groups that might wish to leave the U.S.S.R. In sum, most executives interviewed were greatly troubled by the perception that a single special interest group had been able to exercise a disproportionate influence on the formulation of a key element of the nation's foreign policy towards the U.S.S.R. It follows, of course, that executives were also of the opinion that the recent national preoccupation with Soviet Jews had caused both the public and the U.S. Government to lose sight of broader and longer term considerations of the national interest in U.S. relations with the U.S.S.R. As one might infer from observations made earlier, such views were usually intermixed with unmistakable overtones of political cynicism and alienation; i.e., that by passing the Jackson-Vanik Amendment, the nation's lawmakers had shown themselves incapable of independent thought, and had responded shamelessly to emotional appeals.

A final note is in order with respect to executives'
antagonism towards Jewish groups and the Jackson-Vanik
Amendment.  Instead of bluntly and publicly using U.S.
Government trade policy as a lever to extort concessions
from the U.S.S.R. on human rights issues such as Jewish
emigration, many executives interviewed thought an
alternative strategy would be both more effective and less
disruptive to overall U.S.-U.S.S.R. relations.
Specifically, SAEs generally thought that an approach
emphasizing quiet diplomacy and holding out the prospect of
U.S. trade concessions would be a more productive way to
promote the emigration of Soviet Jews, as well as to
encourage less repressive treatment of Soviet dissidents.
In effect, then, they advocated the use of trade as a
"carrot" rather than as a "stick" in pursuing U.S. foreign
policy goals vis-a-vis the Soviet Union.  Also, a second
line of thought often surfaced during personal
discussions.  Many businessmen interviewed stated their
belief that the continued growth of U.S./Western trade with
the U.S.S.R. will, over time, help break down barriers to
Western ideas which exist in Soviet society.  Executives
repeatedly argued that trade, by engendering face-to-face
contacts between Westerners and Soviet citizens, can open
up new lines of communication with a traditionally isolated
country.  This, in turn, was seen as contributing

meaningfully to the gradual permeation of Soviet culture by
Western values and to the eventual liberalization of the
Soviet political system. All executives who voiced the
preceding hypothesis readily admitted that it is an
extremely long term proposition, but they nonetheless felt
it to be an important political and moral justification for
building a strong U.S.-Soviet commercial relationship.[10]
Mirroring such sentiments, it is appropriate to recall from
Chapter IV that a 54% majority of 1975 survey respondents
indicated their belief that closer U.S.-Soviet trade ties
can help eliminate the worst features of the Soviet system,
because continuous trade will help it to evolve in a slow
but steadily positive manner.

Notwithstanding SAEs' criticism of U.S. Jewish groups
for allegedly fueling anti-Soviet feelings in the U.S. for
their own purposes, businessmen interviewed usually
reserved their most vehement attacks for the nation's news
media. The country's journalists, executives repeatedly
argued, had shown themselves to be all too eager to pour
gasoline on the U.S. public's smouldering anti-Soviet
sentiments, and to lend support to interests desiring
restrictions on U.S.-U.S.S.R. trade. Some SAEs felt that
the national media had been deliberately trying to sabotage
Soviet-American trade and detente. Most, however, believed
that news reporters had not been acting with malicious

intent, but had simply been following their natural journalistic instinct to give the public what it wants; i.e., that reporters had perceived a huge market for anti-Soviet stories among the American people. Whatever SAEs' views on the motivations of the nation's journalists, almost all executives regarded the U.S. news media with contempt and condemned the way that U.S.-Soviet issues had been covered since 1972. It was generally and strongly believed that news reports on U.S.-Soviet economic and political matters had usually been sensationalist and biased, and that they had frequently been blatantly inaccurate. Such reporting, executives often contended, had been a major contributing factor to the recent reduction in public support for U.S.-Soviet trade, and had been instrumental in promoting and giving credibility to the idea that detente is a "one-way street" that benefits only the U.S.S.R.

It must be emphasized, however, that executives' blasts at the national news media were not directed at business publications such as Fortune, the Wall Street Journal, Business Week, etc. Indeed, coverage of U.S.-Soviet issues by business-oriented media was widely regarded as having been objective and fair. Rather, businessmen's ire was aimed exclusively at media intended for national popular consumption; for example, magazines

like Time, Newsweek, etc., as well as broadcasts by
national television and radio networks. This
differentiation came through clearly not only during
personal interviews, but is also readily apparent in the
1976 survey data: Some 76.6% of respondents to Survey 2
reported that, in their opinion, publications of the U.S.
business community had proven to be objective sources of
information on matters pertaining to U.S.-Soviet
relations. In contrast, 65.8% indicated that the national
popular press had failed to be objective, and 56.9% felt
the same way about American radio and television (Table 34).

A number of specific criticisms were directed at the
popular media. First, as might be inferred from
observations made earlier, SAEs for the most part believed
that too much emotional publicity had been given to the
plight of Soviet Jews. It was contended that by
transforming the Jewish emigration question into a national
cause, the media had irresponsibly focussed on a narrow
issue at the expense of rational discussion of the United
States' broad long-term interests in its relations with the
U.S.S.R. Indeed, several executives felt that, by failing
to report on U.S.-U.S.S.R. issues fairly and accurately,
the U.S. news media were partly to blame for the perceived
inability of the U.S. public to grasp the dichotomous
nature of Soviet-American detente. Again, SAEs who voiced

the preceding views were apt to disavow hastily any
anti-semitic sentiments. Rather, the prevailing opinion
seemingly was that even if the Jewish emigration issue were
to disappear, the media would just find another anti-Soviet
cause to advocate. In this connection, many executives
cited the increasing national publicity being given to
Soviet dissidents such as Alexander Solzhenitsyn. The
recent and growing attention to Soviet dissidents,
executives constantly contended, was simply the latest
example of the media's historical tendency to emphasize and
exaggerate anything reflecting badly on the U.S.S.R.
However, some executives qualified such remarks, noting
that the media's approach to U.S.-Soviet affairs had been
typical of news coverage of any issue, specifically, that
the media's standard procedure is to report facts
selectively and dwell on the negative. In any case, apart
from the Jewish emigration and dissident questions, many
SAEs felt that the U.S.S.R. had recently been the target of
an unjustified amount of adverse publicity on several other
non-commercial issues. The media, many argued, had greatly
magnified the importance of the recent incident of cheating
by a Soviet fencer at the Montreal Olympic games, and had
given the U.S. public a distorted picture of the recently
signed Helsinki Accords on Security and Cooperation in
Europe. In fact, a few executives said that undue media

attention had been given to on-going Soviet interventionist behavior in Africa, the continuing Soviet military buildup, and alleged Soviet subversion in Portugal. When asked to elaborate on such opinions, these businessmen usually related that the U.S. is always engaged in similar pursuits, and that the aforementioned Soviet activities must therefore be viewed philosophically as part of the superpowers' continuing jockeying for position in the world.

As might be expected, during personal interviews executives' most vociferous and anguished complaints against the U.S. news media pertained to reporting on U.S.-Soviet trade and economic issues. The news media, businessmen frequently lamented, had grossly misrepresented U.S.-Soviet trade to the American people. It was contended that one never hears or reads about the benefits of trade with the U.S.S.R., but only about unfavorable and atypical aspects of this commercial relationship. SAEs commonly charged that the media had ignored positive effects from Soviet trade such as the jobs created in stagnating U.S. manufacturing industries, the important contribution to U.S. farm income of grain sales to the U.S.S.R., and the healthy impact of exports to the Soviets on an otherwise dismal U.S. balance of payments outlook. Additionally, businessmen frequently griped that the media, in coverage leading up to the Jackson-Vanik Amendment and legislative

limits on Export-Import Bank activities with the U.S.S.R.,
had failed to give adequate attention to the argument that
the principal effect of such restrictive measures would be
to divert Soviet business to U.S. business' foreign
competitors.  Also, it goes without saying that the news
media were roundly criticized for displaying a rabid
eagerness to publicize certain negative features of the
1972-1973 U.S.-Soviet grain deals.  However, executives
generally seemed to be most disturbed by what they
perceived to be the media's readiness to utilize
unsubstantiated or totally inaccurate information in
stories prejudiced against Soviet-American commerce.  For
example, many executives, particularly those from
high-technology companies, contended that without due cause
the media had given the U.S. public false impressions of
the amount and kind of sophisticated U.S. technology being
sold to the U.S.S.R., and had fostered the myth that U.S.
firms are "giving away" vast quantities of valuable
American knowhow to the Soviets.  Similarly, most of the
businessmen interviewed believed that largely as an
outgrowth of adverse publicity surrounding the 1972-1973
U.S.-Soviet grain deals, the media had unjustifiably
magnified the so-called "whipsaw" issue and had given the
American people the inaccurate notion that U.S. companies
inevitably come out second best in business negotiations

with the U.S.S.R. Furthermore, various executives bemoaned
that the U.S. media had depicted U.S. companies involved in
Soviet business as being avaricious, amoral, and
insensitive for trading with a repressive communist
regime. Such businessmen were apt to point out defensively
that their initial decision to open up Soviet commercial
contacts had been based on the understanding that the U.S.
Government supported and regarded such activity as being in
the national interest. Finally, several of these
executives said that it was ironic that the media had been
portraying U.S. firms as greedy profit-seekers, while
simultaneously projecting the idea that many American
companies had lost money on their Soviet contracts.[11]

## Executive Attitudes Toward Political Action

In view of their wide-ranging complaints about the
national news media, public opinion, and the U.S.
Government, one might expect that SAEs would have perceived
a need for and advocated U.S. corporate political action
aimed at improving the domestic political environment for
U.S.-Soviet commerce. Specifically, given their
unhappiness and criticism of the status quo, it only seems
logical that executives interviewed should have been strong
proponents of lobbying and public relations efforts by the
U.S. business community to promote a more accurate national
understanding of the nature of detente, to clear up alleged

misconceptions about the transfer of U.S. technology to the
U.S.S.R., to point out the benefits of U.S.-Soviet
commerce, and to mobilize political support for the repeal
of existing statutory barriers to trade.

In fact, however, personal interviews with businessmen
revealed a total absence of any well-defined sense of
political direction. Despite their worry and frustration
over recent trends in the political atmosphere and U.S.
Government policy, executives on the whole had no clear
concept of a political role for individual companies or the
U.S. business community in national debates on U.S.-Soviet
economic and political issues.

For example, a few executives interviewed, who for the
most part represented small and medium-sized companies,
clearly displayed what can only be labelled a "parochial"
mentality. When queried for their views on the need for
corporate political action, these businessmen appeared
confused by such questions. It was abundantly clear from
their responses that they did not conceive of their firms
as being active participants in the U.S. political system,
at least as far as U.S.-Soviet issues are concerned.
Stated differently, the idea that their companies should or
could play a role in formulating national policy on
U.S.-Soviet trade seemed totally alien to these
executives.[12] Instead, they perceived their firms

principally as _objects_ of the political system.  Thus,
despite their gripes about recent trends in public opinion
and U.S. Government policy, these businessmen were
nonetheless passive and acquiescent.

A somewhat different school of thought was much more
prevalent among those interviewed.  Many businessmen
indicated that the primary role of U.S. business in
American society is to provide jobs and produce goods and
services, not to meddle in political affairs.  Corporate
political activity, these SAEs believed, is only
appropriate and justifiable on select issues where a firm's
central interests are directly involved.  Even then, where
feasible it is preferable that any political activities
should be undertaken by U.S. business trade associations,
lobbies, etc., rather than by individual companies.  Thus,
although these executives perceived a role for American
business in the U.S. political process, they saw this role
as being carefully circumscribed and tended to view
political activity as a necessary evil.  It follows that
such executives typically went on to characterize the
current and prospective levels of their firms' U.S.S.R.
business as being of insufficient importance to overcome
their natural reluctance to involve their companies in
political debates on U.S.-Soviet issues.

A variation on the preceding attitude was also
apparent. Indeed, it was the dominant theme: Echoing
their above-noted counterparts, many businessmen saw a
circumscribed role for U.S. business in the U.S. political
process and thought that overt political activities by U.S.
firms should be the exception rather than the rule.
However, under questioning, these executives did not
repudiate in principle the idea of corporate political
action on behalf of U.S.-Soviet commerce, and they regarded
such trade as having important benefits for the United
States and/or for their firms (e.g., contributions to
"world peace," the U.S. balance of payments, corporate
profitability). Nonetheless, these businessmen generally
indicated that their firms had engaged in little if any
political activity with respect to U.S.-Soviet economic and
political issues. This apparently pertained to indirect
political action (e.g., encouraging lobbying by trade
associations) as well as to direct political activity by
the companies themselves (e.g., public relations efforts by
individual firms). A partial explanation for this
perplexing finding seemingly lies in several interrelated
and sometimes conflicting strands of thought that were
detected during interviews: First, a host of executives,
although they apparently thought corporate political action
to be desirable, conveyed the impression that they were

intimidated by the gravity of U.S.-Soviet political and economic issues. These businessmen seemingly felt that, given deep U.S.-Soviet political differences and the fundamental national security questions involved, it would somehow be improper or immoral for the U.S. business community to influence U.S. Government decisions on basic policies toward the U.S.S.R. Executives who harbored such feelings evidently believed that American companies should confine any political activities to narrow U.S.-Soviet questions having immediate practical importance to the firm (e.g., making export control regulations more realistic, and insuring their equitable and consistent application), and should shy away from issues having broad political ramifications. Interestingly, such sentiments were closely associated with the view, noted in Chapter V, that U.S. companies should not follow their own political inclinations when making business decisions vis-a-vis other countries, because to do so is to assume a foreign policy role which does not rightfully belong to American business; i.e., that it is the responsibility of the U.S. Government to determine the national interest and to provide clear policy guidance to U.S. firms. In sum, then, it appears that certain executives were torn between a desire to promote U.S.-Soviet trade/detente, and a conflicting instinct which might be labelled a "subject" mentality.

As might be expected, executives frequently indicated that another factor had acted to inhibit political action by their companies: Many businessmen said that it would be unwise for individual American firms or business trade associations to become highly visible on U.S.-U.S.S.R. issues, since this would greatly increase the chances for an anti-Soviet backlash against U.S. companies by the news media, ethnic/religious groups, consumers, and stockholders. Several executives also noted that recent downward U.S.-Soviet political trends (e.g., Soviet subversion in Portugal, interventionist activities in Africa) had raised the possibility of an eventual return to a "Cold War" atmosphere. This prospect, they contended, had contributed greatly to U.S. business' reluctance to give active political support to detente and trade. American business, they suggested, does not want to take a political lead in U.S.-Soviet affairs, because if superpower relations collapse U.S. companies would be left out on a political limb and would be open to fire from all sides.

Executives also often lamented the perceived absence of an effective political vehicle for expressing corporate views on U.S.-Soviet issues.[13] In general, traditional business lobbies and trade associations (e.g., the U.S. Chamber of Commerce, the National Association of

Manufacturers) were characterized as hesitant to get
involved in U.S.-Soviet matters because of the broad and
heterogeneous nature of their corporate memberships. Such
organizations, executives repeatedly noted, tend to focus
on general issues having wide membership appeal (e.g.,
product liability legislation). Conversely, they were
described as having a strong tendency to avoid narrow and
controversial issues which might offend some members. In
this connection, businessmen frequently remarked that firms
involved in Soviet business comprise only a small minority
in the membership of most large U.S. business associations.
Instead, numerous small companies, many with strong
anti-Soviet sentiments, were seen as dominating these
organizations.

In response to the above comments, executives were
asked why their companies did not resort to direct
advertising as a method for influencing public opinion and
governmental policy on U.S.-Soviet questions.
Interestingly, some businessmen said that this idea had not
occurred to them. However, most executives dismissed the
suggestion in an offhand manner and typically cited a
variety of objections. Reflecting their fears of an
anti-Soviet backlash, many executives felt that advertising
was unacceptable because it would give their firms too much
visibility. Another criticism was that a major advertising

campaign would be highly expensive, and would only be
possible if interested U.S. companies combined their
resources. U.S. firms, it was pointed out, would have to
justify such costs in terms of the current and projected
contribution of Soviet business to corporate income. It
was felt, however, that at best most U.S. companies
regarded the U.S.S.R. as only a moderately important growth
market. Thus, strictly on economic grounds, prospects for
mobilizing a large-scale U.S. corporate public relations
effort on behalf of Soviet-American trade/detente were
viewed as dim. Finally, a pervasive sentiment among SAEs
was that, even if a massive advertising campaign could be
mounted, it would likely be ineffective. Paid advertising,
they believed, just does not have sufficient emotional
appeal, and emotion, not logical reasoning, was seen as
dominating national policy debates on U.S.-Soviet
issues[14].

As one might infer from findings presented earlier,
the preceding views on advertising were often intermixed
with comments having strong overtones of political
alienation, cynicism, and something akin to fatalism. Many
businessmen seemingly felt that, with respect to
U.S.-Soviet issues, any political action undertaken by U.S.
business would inevitably be futile.[15] Relevant here, of
course, is that executives typically held Washington

policy-makers in low esteem, regarding them as the willing
tools of those seeking to undermine Soviet-American trade
and detente.  Also, many executives tended to magnify the
organizational capabilities of opposition forces.  In this
connection, it was generally thought that U.S. Jewish
groups had established an efficient and well-oiled
Congressional lobbying machine which U.S. companies could
not hope to match.  Thus, early repeal of the Jackson-Vanik
Amendment was widely considered to be impossible.[16]
Lastly, some SAEs, particularly those from high-technology
companies, said they had tried in the past to promote
numerous modifications in U.S. export control policies
toward the U.S.S.R.  To their chagrin, most of their advice
had been ignored by the federal government.  Consequently,
these businessmen indicated that they no longer held out
much hope for making an impact on U.S. policies toward the
Soviet Union.[17]  (Reflecting these opinions, Table 34
shows that 48.1% of 1976 survey respondents concurred that
the Executive Branch of the U.S. Government has tended to
ignore the advice of the business community when forming
export control policy.)

In view of their reluctance to engage in highly
visible political activity, SAEs were asked if they had
acted to establish any low-key contacts with national or
local news media, in order to promote more accurate

reporting of "the facts" of U.S.-Soviet trade. The
interviewer suggested, for example, that it would be a
relatively simple matter for U.S. businessmen to let
reporters know of their successes in negotiating with the
Soviets, thereby correcting the public's impression that
American companies usually come out second best when
bargaining with the U.S.S.R. Reacting to these thoughts,
almost all SAEs indicated that their firms had not sought
to open up any lines of communication with the media. In
fact, most executives seemed afraid of dealing directly
with the news media. A primary reason for this attitude
apparently was the fear that any company statements might
be misrepresented by reporters, either intentionally or
unintentionally. As recounted earlier, SAEs for the most
part did not think that the record of the U.S. news media
on U.S.-Soviet issues had been one to inspire trust. Also,
certain executives simply did not regard it as advisable to
attract unnecessary attention to their firms' Soviet
business activities, again because of a possible adverse
reaction from various quarters. Finally, commenting on the
suggestion that U.S. firms should tell the media the true
story about the profitability of Soviet-American trade,
SAEs responded that it would be stupid for them to call
attention to their successes, since Soviet foreign trade
organizations would undoubtedly take note of such

statements and try to cut down profit margins in future negotiations.[18]

## Summary, Conclusions, and Theoretical Implications
### Synopsis

Supplementing findings presented earlier, survey and interview data presented in this chapter vividly document SAEs' deep-seated dissatisfaction with the U.S. Government's handling of Soviet trade matters during the early to mid-1970s. On the whole, the governmental environment for Soviet-American commerce was variously characterized as inconsistent, erratic, and obstructionist. Although businessmen were aware of the U.S. Government's officially stated policy supporting U.S.-Soviet trade, there was a widespread perception that federal policy-makers had failed to follow through on and operationalize their positive public posture. Citing a glaring conflict between symbolic and substantive policy signals coming out of Washington, the majority of executives indicated their displeasure with recently imposed U.S. Government restrictions on Eximbank loans to the U.S.S.R., the absence of clear guidelines governing the transfer of technology between American companies and the Soviet Union, and the continued refusal to grant Most-Favored-Nation tariff status to the U.S.S.R. despite a written U.S. pledge to do so. The behavior of the federal government, it was felt, had caused the Soviets to direct substantial business away from U.S. firms and towards foreign business competitors. In particular, the removal of Eximbank from the U.S.-Soviet trade picture was seen as reducing the financial competitiveness of American business and as deterring U.S. companies from developing bids on Soviet contracts. Additionally, contradictory and increasingly adverse federal policies toward trade with the U.S.S.R. were described as having caused much uncertainty in business circles as to whether the U.S. Government in fact regarded Soviet-American commerce as being in the national interest. This growing uncertainty, by generating concern for political risks to the firm, evidently caused many businessmen to adopt a more cautious stance towards Soviet business opportunities.

The emerging tendency of SAEs to regard the Soviet market with a more careful eye was clearly reinforced by businessmen's anxieties over the perceived gradual re-emergence of an historical and indigenous anti-Soviet sentiment among the American people. Negative trends in the public mood, it was thought, might well engender further federal restrictions on Soviet trade. Also, adverse tendencies in public opinion were viewed as increasing the possibility that U.S. companies doing

business with the U.S.S.R. might become political targets
of the press, ethnic/religious groups, labor unions, and
consumers. Most importantly, however, there was a
widespread and growing fear that one's Soviet business
activities might come under attack from corporate
stockholders and directors. Businessmen also perceived
themselves as becoming less able to ward off such
assaults. Given negative trends in federal trade policy
toward the U.S.S.R., it was regarded as increasingly
untenable to defend corporate activities with the Soviets
by pointing to empty U.S. Government rhetoric supporting
the continued development of U.S.-U.S.S.R. commerce.

While the anti-Soviet public groundswell was viewed as
having a certain momentum of its own, many SAEs were
extremely distraught over perceived attempts by U.S. Jewish
groups to fan the flames of discontent. It was argued that
national Jewish organizations, by popularizing the plight
of Soviet Jews and political dissidents, had caused both
the public and the U.S. Government to lose sight of broader
and longer term considerations of the national interest in
U.S. relations with the U.S.S.R. Fundamentally, SAEs were
greatly troubled by the perception that a single special
interest group had been able to exercise disproportionate
influence on the formulation of the nation's foreign policy.

The national mass media were also indicted for fueling the U.S. public's anti-Soviet passions, and for being all too eager to lend support to U.S. Jewish groups and other interests desiring restrictions on Soviet-American trade. It was generally and strongly believed that news reports on U.S.-Soviet economic and political matters had usually been sensationalist, biased, and inaccurate. The media, it was charged, had ignored the political and economic benefits of U.S.-Soviet trade/detente, had promoted the myth that trade with the U.S.S.R. is a "one-way street" that operates to the Soviets' advantage, had fostered the idea that U.S. firms are "giving away" vast quantities of valuable American knowhow to the Soviets, and had given the American people the inaccurate notion that U.S. companies inevitably come out second best in business negotiations with the U.S.S.R.

Notwithstanding their criticism of the media and U.S. Jewish groups, many executives acknowledged that the Soviets had generously provided anti-Soviet U.S. interest groups with ammunition to use in domestic political debates on U.S.-U.S.S.R. policy issues. Apart from the Soviets' repressive treatment of Jews and political dissidents, anti-Soviet U.S. political forces were viewed as having benefited from the adverse impact on public opinion of the "great grain robbery" of 1972-1973, the Soviets' role in supplying Arab nations with arms prior to the Arab-Israeli war of 1973, and the Soviets' material support of North Vietnamese troops and the ensuing collapse of South Vietnam in 1975. Also, because of the U.S. public's tendency to infer guilt by association, the U.S.S.R.'s image was seen as having been hurt by the growing political power in 1975-1976 of the Portuguese, French, and Italian communist parties.

In commenting on the influence of Jewish groups, the news media, and public opinion on the formulation of U.S. Government trade policies toward the U.S.S.R., SAEs' complaints against the federal government were clearly tinged by a deep personal resentment of Washington policy-makers, which repeatedly found expression in remarks having powerful overtones of political cynicism and alienation. Executives typically agonized that U.S. policies toward the Soviet Union were increasingly being made on the basis of emotionalism rather than being governed by a clear, logical, and consistent concept of the long-term national interest. The federal government, SAEs contended, had responded shamelessly and irrationally to domestic political pressures brought to bear by U.S. interest groups seeking restrictions on Soviet-American commerce. The nation's officials, especially Senators and Congressmen, were often stereotyped as spineless, lacking character, and incapable of independent thought on U.S.-Soviet issues.

Interestingly, SAEs' sweeping condemnation of the U.S. Government was nevertheless characterized by a certain degree of ambivalence. A number of specific federal institutions, notably the Commerce Department and other Executive branch agencies, were regarded favorably despite deep-seated anti-Washington feelings.

Despite their worry and frustration over trends in the U.S. political atmosphere and U.S. Government policy, SAEs on the whole had no clear concept of a political role for individual companies or the U.S. business community in national debates on U.S.-Soviet economic and political issues. In this connection, SAEs were not strong proponents of lobbying and public relations efforts by the U.S. business community on behalf of U.S.-Soviet trade and detente. The reasons underlying these findings are not entirely clear but appear to be many: A few executives simply did not conceive of their firms as active participants in the U.S. political system; i.e., the idea that their companies should or could help shape national policy on U.S.-Soviet trade seemed totally alien to certain businessmen. A much larger group of executives did perceive a role for American business in the U.S. political process, but they saw this role as being carefully

circumscribed, tended to view political activity as a
necessary evil, and regarded U.S.S.R. business as being of
insufficient importance to overcome their intrinsic
reluctance to get involved in political debates on
U.S.-Soviet issues. The majority of SAEs, however, were
seemingly torn between a desire to promote U.S.-Soviet
trade/detente, and a conflicting "subject" mentality; i.e.,
the feeling that in view of the fundamental national
security questions involved, it would somehow be improper
or immoral for business to influence U.S. Government
decisions on basic policies toward the U.S.S.R. Such SAEs
were also inhibited by the fear that visible pro-trade
political activity by American firms or business trade
associations would greatly increase the chances for an
anti-Soviet backlash against U.S. companies by the news
media, ethnic/religious groups, consumers, and
stockholders. In a similar vein, there was great
reluctance to take a political lead because, in the event
of a collapse in superpower relations, U.S. companies would
be left out on a political limb and would be exposed to
fire from all sides. SAEs also lamented the absence of an
effective political vehicle for expressing corporate views
on U.S.-Soviet issues. Traditional business lobbies and
trade associations were characterized as hesitant to get
involved in U.S.-Soviet matters due to the heterogeneous

nature of their corporate constituencies, their desire to
avoid narrow and controversial issues which might offend
some members, and the influence of conservative anti-
Soviet, anti-communist elements within many of these
organizations. Also, it was generally felt that a national
advertising campaign on behalf of trade/detente would be
too expensive, lack the emotional appeal needed to be
effective, and would again raise the prospect of
retaliation by labor unions, stockholders, Jewish groups,
etc. Likewise, most SAEs seemed afraid to deal directly
with the news media for fear of being misrepresented by
reporters and of attracting unnecessary attention to their
firms' Soviet business activities. Finally, there was a
widespread perception that any pro-trade, pro-detente
political action undertaken by U.S. business would
inevitably be futile given Washington's historically
unresponsive attitude toward business advice and the strong
emotional influence of anti-Soviet U.S. interest groups on
pliable federal legislators and bureaucrats.

## Linkage Scenarios

As suggested by the preceding synopsis, survey and
interview data presented in this chapter give substantial
cause to question the validity of Linkage Scenario 2, which
was postulated in Chapter II. To reiterate, Scenario 2
hypothesized that the U.S.S.R. might be able to stimulate

U.S. companies to engage in political activities on behalf
of trade/detente by diverting Soviet purchases of equipment
to foreign competitors of American business:

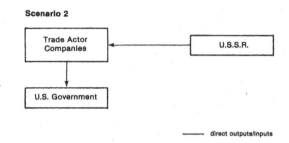

**Scenario 2**

While the preceding sequence of events would seem to
have a certain logical appeal, research results outlined
above strongly indicate that any Soviet efforts to foster a
united, vigorous, pro-detente U.S. corporate lobby in the
United States would likely be frustrated by businessmen's
apparently deeply ingrained resistance to political
involvement in controversial U.S.-Soviet issues. Indeed,
in view of executives' previously described political
inhibitions, there is reason to doubt that, even given a
favorable climate of public opinion, the U.S. business
community would ever become an energetic and consistent
political force working for closer Soviet-American economic
and political relations. To the contrary, gathered data
suggest that any inclination of U.S. businessmen to lend
political support to trade/detente can easily be destroyed

by a variety of influences. This proposition is central to
the following linkage scenarios, which synthesize a wide
range of findings presented in this chapter.

First of all, outlined below is Linkage Scenario 14,
which incorporates certain elements of Scenarios 8, 9, 11A,
and 12 (see Chapters IV and V):

**Scenario 14**

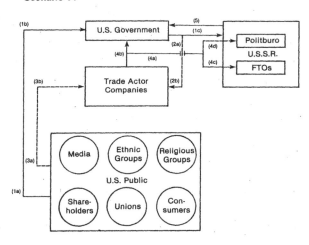

———— direct outputs/inputs
– – – – indirect outputs/inputs

In Scenario 14, growing anti-Soviet sentiment among
the American people--especially among ethnic and religious
groups (e.g., American Jewish organizations)--triggers
direct internal outputs in the form of political lobbying
which results in direct internal inputs in the form of
restrictive federal policies on trade with the U.S.S.R.

(1a-b). Of course, these changes in U.S. Government policy also constitute direct polity outputs designed to influence Soviet behavior and/or to prevent Soviet acquisition of U.S. technology (1c). At the same time, however, modifications in federal policies on Soviet trade generate indirect internal outputs which give rise to indirect internal inputs in trade actor companies (2a-b). As a result of this micro-linkage, Soviet Area Executives perceive inconsistencies in federal commercial policies toward the U.S.S.R., sense an overall downward trend in the governmental policy environment, and assign responsibility for both aforementioned developments to anti-Soviet U.S. political interests. It follows that SAEs become increasingly unsure as to whether the U.S. Government in fact considers Soviet-American trade to be in the national interest, as well as more and more uncertain of the likely impact of federal policy on future business transactions with the Soviets.

The worsening U.S. political climate affects Soviet Area Executives in yet another way. Specifically, anti-Soviet political activity by various U.S. interests, together with generally adverse trends in public opinion, produce indirect internal outputs which yield indirect internal inputs in various firms (3a-b). This micro-linkage is manifested in terms of SAEs' heightened sensitivity to possible criticism of their companies'

Soviet business activities by corporate shareholders and directors, the news media, labor unions, consumers, and religious and ethnic groups. Such political retaliation need not actually take place; rather, the growing <u>potential</u> for a political backlash is sufficient to alter executives' thinking. Relevant here is that, given the success of anti-Soviet interests in engendering restrictive U.S. policies on trade with the U.S.S.R., SAEs regard it as increasingly untenable to point to pro-detente, pro-trade U.S. Government rhetoric in defending one's Soviet business activities. Consequently, SAEs' increasing uneasiness about trends in the U.S. Government's Soviet policies and their growing anxiety over a possible domestic political backlash against their companies tend to reinforce one another in a synergistic manner. As a result, at the urging of their SAEs, numerous trade actor firms ultimately decide to slow the expansion of their commercial relationships with the U.S.S.R., cut back Soviet business efforts, or otherwise adopt a more cautious stance towards opportunities presented by the Soviet market (4a). Likewise, given their decreased interest in Soviet business and their growing desire to keep out of the public eye, trade actor firms also reduce, terminate, or otherwise refrain from pro-detente, pro-trade political activities aimed at the U.S. Government (4b).

It follows that diminished U.S. corporate political support for U.S.-Soviet trade/detente constitutes direct internal outputs which generate direct internal inputs in the U.S. Government. To be specific, because the U.S. business community is a principal U.S. political constituency for Soviet-American commerce, American business' reduced inclination to exercise its political muscle gives an added advantage to those U.S. political elements seeking a stronger U.S. Government stand on U.S.-U.S.S.R. economic and political issues. Thus, the growing political timidity of U.S. firms tends to reinforce the very trends in federal policies towards the U.S.S.R. to which U.S. businessmen object.

In a somewhat different vein, decisions by trade actor companies to adopt a more cautious stance towards the Soviet market constitute direct polity outputs which trigger direct environmental inputs in Soviet foreign trade organizations (e.g., frustration at the inability to conclude desired business deals) (4c). At the same time, however, retrenchment by U.S. companies generates indirect environmental inputs among Soviet political authorities, who begin to doubt the business reliability of American firms (4d). Next, these indirect environmental inputs mix with direct environmental inputs stimulated by the U.S. Government's increasingly tough stand on various

U.S.-Soviet economic and political issues. Soviet leaders
subsequently become increasingly doubtful that the U.S.S.R.
will obtain the major gains from trade with the U.S. that
had originally been hoped for. Consequently, seeing itself
as having a reduced vested interest in following the path
of moderation in its relations with the United States, the
U.S.S.R. begins to adopt less compromising positions on a
host of unresolved issues between Moscow and Washington (5).

Several propositions germane to present and future
U.S.-Soviet relations can be derived from the preceding
hypothetical chain of events. First, Scenario 14, together
with supporting survey and interview data, suggests that
domestic U.S. political forces, over which neither
superpower has direct control, can nevertheless disrupt the
continuity of U.S.-Soviet trade by influencing the decision
calculus of American companies. In addition, one can
postulate that, other things being equal, any major
deterioration in the U.S. public's perceptions of the
U.S.S.R. will tend to reduce any on-going pro-trade,
pro-detente political activity by U.S. business at the very
time that such activity could be especially helpful in
promoting the stability of U.S. economic and political
policies toward the Soviet Union. Stated from a slightly
different perspective, the more vociferous that opponents
of U.S.-Soviet trade/detente are in articulating their

views to the American public and the federal establishment,
the less likely such forces are to encounter effective
political opposition from the U.S. business community. A
corollary to the preceding statements is that any major
negative shift in U.S. public attitudes towards the Soviet
Union will, given the absence of countervailing political
pressure by American business, likely result in an
increasing tendency by the U.S. Government to regard trade
relations with the U.S.S.R. as an instrument of foreign
policy rather than as a central concern of foreign policy.

The behavioral sequence described by Scenario 14 takes
on added theoretical meaning when subsumed in three more
expansive and closely related scenarios which are discussed
in succession below.

In Scenario 15A, the Soviet Union begins by providing
military equipment to anti-Israeli Arab nations and/or by
granting aid to a Third World revolutionary movement (1a).
These direct polity outputs at the same time constitute
indirect polity outputs which generate indirect
environmental inputs throughout the U.S. political system
(1b-e). Specifically, the U.S.S.R.'s actions stimulate
nascent anti-Soviet feelings within the U.S. public,
adversely affect U.S. Government attitudes toward the
Soviet Union, and trigger fears among U.S. businessmen that
worsening U.S.-Soviet political relations might adversely

**Scenario 15A**

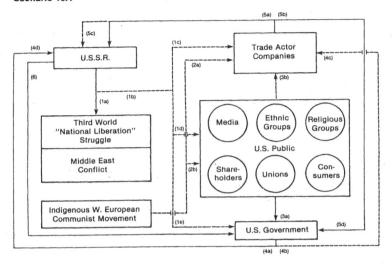

affect the conduct of business with the U.S.S.R. (e.g.,

renewed U.S. export controls, Soviet diversion of contracts

away from U.S. suppliers). Simultaneously, businessmen's

and the public's reactions to the aforementioned Soviet

activities are intensified by other international events

which are not directly related to Soviet behavior, but

which nevertheless cast the U.S.S.R. in a bad light via

guilt by association (e.g., political gains by an

indigenous West European communist party) (2a-b).

Subsequently, the indirect environmental inputs

resulting from Soviet foreign policy activities and the

indirect environmental inputs stemming from random
international developments combine to fuel the chain of
events described in Scenario 14 above. The growing
influence of anti-Soviet lobbying activity (direct internal
input 3a) merges with the U.S. Government's increasingly
negative disposition towards the U.S.S.R. (indirect
environmental input 1e) to produce restrictive federal
policies on Soviet trade (direct polity output 4a and
indirect internal output 4b). In view of the renewed
negativism of U.S. Government policies toward the U.S.S.R.
(indirect internal input 4c), rising apprehension that a
worsening East-West political climate might spill over into
the commercial sphere (indirect environmental inputs 1c and
2a), and growing fear of an anti-Soviet political backlash
against companies involved with the U.S.S.R. (indirect
internal input 3b), trade actor companies decide to adopt a
more cautious stance towards the Soviet market (direct
polity output 5a) and scale down any on-going or planned
pro-trade, pro-detente U.S. political activities (direct
internal output 5b). Once again, the reduced inclination
of U.S. companies to give political support to trade/
detente tends to reinforce the very trends in U.S. policy
to which U.S. executives object (direct internal input 5d).

Next, the growing reluctance of U.S. firms to get
involved in Soviet contracts (indirect environmental input

5c) and the U.S. Government's increasingly tough stand on various U.S.-Soviet economic and political issues (direct environmental input 4d) cause Soviet leaders to revise downward their expectations of gains from Soviet-American trade. Subsequently, viewing itself as having a reduced vested interest in restraint, the Soviet Union begins to take less compromising stands on contentious Soviet-American issues and generally pursues a more adventurous foreign policy (direct polity output 6).

It should be readily apparent that despite some important differences, Scenario 15A is fundamentally an elaboration and composite of Scenarios 8 and 9 (see Chapter IV). Like these earlier scenarios, Scenario 15A, along with relevant research findings presented in this chapter, supports the proposition that periods of U.S.-Soviet tension will tend to reduce the level of any on-going pro-trade, pro-detente political activity by U.S. business at the very time that such activity could be especially helpful in promoting the stability of U.S. commercial policies toward the U.S.S.R. and in moderating U.S. Government political responses to perceived Soviet provocations. Scenario 15A also reaffirms the thesis that international political developments over which neither superpower has direct control (e.g., West European political trends) can nevertheless disturb the continuity

of U.S.-Soviet trade relations by altering the decision
calculus of U.S. firms. Once again, a corollary to the
preceding propositions would seem to be that any
deterioration in the East-West political environment will,
given the lack of effective political opposition from U.S.
business, result in an increasing propensity by federal
policy-makers to view trade relations with the U.S.S.R. as
a tool of U.S. foreign policy rather than as a central
concern of foreign policy.

**Scenario 15B**

Scenario 15B differs from 15A in that the U.S.
political sequences outlined in Scenario 14 are not fueled
by Soviet foreign policy actions nor by a random

international political development. Instead, 15B is
triggered by events within the U.S.S.R. itself.
Specifically, the Soviet government initiates direct
internal outputs which take the form of repressive measures
aimed at certain segments of the Soviet population (Jews,
political dissidents, artists, etc.) Such actions,
however, also constitute indirect polity outputs which
generate unanticipated and widespread indirect
environmental inputs throughout the U.S. political system.
As in Scenario 15A, these environmental inputs tend to
foster anti-Soviet sentiments among the American people,
engender an unfavorable U.S. Government disposition towards
the U.S.S.R., and generate apprehensions among U.S.
executives that worsening U.S.-Soviet political relations
might adversely affect the conduct of business with the
U.S.S.R. For the sake of avoiding repetition, suffice it
to say that the ensuing sequence of events within the U.S.
political system, and between the U.S. political system and
the Soviet political system, is essentially identical to
that described in the above discussion of 15A.

It merits attention that Scenario 15B both complements
and corroborates Scenario 4 (see Chapter II). From a
theoretical standpoint the primary significance of 15B is
that it graphically illustrates how the Soviet Government,
in pursuing political objectives confined to the sovereign

borders of the U.S.S.R., may inadvertently undermine the
achievement of its own economic and political goals
vis-a-vis the United States. Viewed from a slightly
different perspective one can advance the proposition that,
given the dynamics of U.S. corporate decision-making and
the American political process, the inherently repressive
nature of the Soviet political system may in itself be
sufficient to impede the development of robust and enduring
U.S.-Soviet economic ties, to stifle the U.S. business
community from lending active political support to the
cause of trade/detente, and to destabilize overall
political relations between the superpowers.

**Scenario 15C**

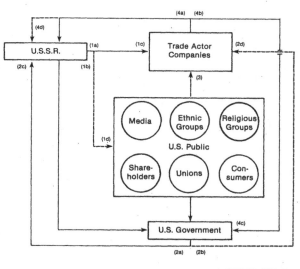

Scenario 15c complements Scenario 11B and Scenario 13B
(see Chapter V) and provides yet another example of how the
Soviet Union might undercut its own foreign policy objectives with respect to the United States. Like 11B and 13B,
15C begins with direct polity outputs by Soviet foreign
trade organizations aimed at U.S. trade actor companies
(1a). Specifically, Soviet officials seek to obtain maximum
contract concessions by living up to their reputation as
unusually difficult business negotiators (e.g., as in the
case of 1972-1973 grain purchases from the U.S.). Soviet
FTOs play off potential sellers against one another, adopt
inflexible bargaining positions, and generally employ frustrating and time-consuming business tactics. The Soviet
strategy may or may not be successful in extracting concessions from American firms, although Soviet behavior inevitably triggers direct environmental inputs in the form of
U.S. corporate dissatisfaction with the U.S.S.R.'s business
habits (1c). At the same time, the Soviets' opportunistic
business activities yield indirect polity outputs which
produce indirect environmental inputs among the American
people (1b and d): The Soviets' image as wily and opportunistic business negotiators stimulates charges by various
segments of the U.S. public that trade with the U.S.S.R. is
a "one-way street" that does not benefit the U.S., and gives
rise to demands that the U.S. Government adopt a less

compromising stand on outstanding Soviet-American issues.
As in Scenarios 14-15B, the growing public resentment of
the Soviet Union ultimately results in tougher U.S. Government positions on economic and political questions dividing
the superpowers (direct polity output 2a, indirect internal
output 2b). Subsequently, businessmen's increasing unhappiness with negative trends in federal trade policy towards
the U.S.S.R. (indirect internal input 2d), their growing
fear of an anti-Soviet political backlash against their
companies (indirect internal input 3), and frustration with
Soviet business tactics (direct environmental input 1c)
combine to cause trade actor companies to scale down their
Soviet business efforts and reduce or refrain from domestic
political activities on behalf of trade/detente (direct
polity output 4a, direct internal output 4b). Again, the
U.S. business community's diminished inclination to engage
in pro-trade, pro-detente political activities tends to
reinforce the very U.S. Government policy trends to which
U.S. executives object (direct internal input 4c). Finally,
as in the scenarios discussed above, U.S. companies' growing
reluctance to get involved in Soviet business (indirect
environmental input 4d), coupled with the U.S. Government's
increasing intransigence on a host of issues (direct
environmental input 2c), eventually results in a more
assertive Soviet foreign policy posture towards the U.S.

In sum, Scenario 15C, like Scenarios 11B and 13B, is indicative of how Soviet business procedures, which are carefully designed to shave Western profit margins and obtain contract concessions, might have various unforeseen effects contrary to the U.S.S.R.'s overall interests in its relations with the United States. One can hypothesize that stubborn and ingrained Soviet commercial practices can act as an additional obstacle to a vigorous U.S.-U.S.S.R. economic relationship, help to destroy businessmen's incentives to exercise their political muscle on behalf of Soviet-American trade and detente, and generally complicate U.S.-Soviet conflict management. Conversely, Scenario 15C reaffirms the proposition first advanced in Chapter V that, other things being equal, a more relaxed Soviet business style could go a long way toward placing U.S.-U.S.S.R. commercial relations on a more even keel.

At this juncture it should be self-evident that Scenarios 14-15C, together with derivative propositions and supporting research findings, suggest some additional possible explanations for the failure of the U.S. business community during the 1970s to act as a forceful political constituency for closer U.S.-Soviet relations, for the stagnation in non-agricultural U.S.-Soviet trade from 1976 to the present, for the U.S.S.R.'s increasingly opportunistic foreign policy since 1975, and for the U.S.

Government's increasingly contentious attitude from 1976
onward with respect to a wide range of outstanding
Soviet-American issues. Furthermore, the linkages proposed
above, like the scenarios postulated in previous chapters,
give further cause to question whether it will ever be
possible to establish a dynamic, stable, and broad-based
U.S.-Soviet commercial relationship as the foundation of a
superpower detente. Contrary to an underlying assumption
of the "spill-over" hypothesis, there would seem to be
ample reason to doubt that international trading
relationships, because they are founded on reciprocal
economic benefit, have an inherent stability not easily
disrupted by international political events. Indeed, as
suggested by Scenario 14, U.S.-U.S.S.R. trade may
indefinitely be at the mercy of volatile domestic U.S.
political forces beyond the control of any governmental
authority. Yet another basic precept of the spill-over
hypothesis would also appear to be vulnerable: A robust
Soviet-American trade relationship, even if one could be
created, might easily fail to have any appreciable
moderating influence on the U.S. Government's foreign
policy approach toward the U.S.S.R. Given businessmen's
ingrained political timidity on U.S.-U.S.S.R. issues, it is
questionable whether the U.S. business community will ever
be willing to mount the strong and consistent political

pressure necessary to make federal policy-makers responsive
to U.S. commercial interests in managing relations with the
Soviets. Instead, with most of corporate America likely to
remain on the U.S. political sidelines and given the strong
anti-Soviet sentiments which pervade U.S. society, the U.S.
Government may invariably be inclined to view trade with
the U.S.S.R. as a convenient instrument of U.S. policy
rather than as a key component of policy around which other
considerations revolve. Stated differently, it can be
hypothesized that the development of any future economic
interdependencies between the United States and the Soviet
Union will automatically tend to be regarded by U.S.
political authorities as new opportunities for exerting
leverage on the U.S.S.R. rather than as added incentives
for mitigating conflict in non-commercial areas.
Conversely, one can advance the proposition, first stated
in Chapter V, that U.S.-Soviet trade may be more effective
in fostering international political restraint among Soviet
leaders than among their U.S. counterparts due in large
measure to the relatively greater insulation of the
U.S.S.R.'s foreign policy process from capricious domestic
political influences.

## Miscellaneous Theoretical Considerations

The preceding scenarios and associated research
results, when viewed in the context of findings presented

in previous chapters, permit the inference of a series of
wide-ranging theoretical statements. Once again, it must
be emphasized that the following propositions and
hypotheses are meant to be heuristic, not definitive, and
require further investigation by other analysts:

1.   Generally speaking, American companies will
individually and collectively tend to refrain from
overt political involvement in any controversial issue
which is not central to their immediate economic
well-being. Phrased somewhat differently, the more
controversial a political question and the less
important it is to near-term corporate survival, the
lower the probability that firms will actively lend
political support to the position which they favor in
principle.

2.   A variation on (1) is that the more controversial
an issue is, the greater the likelihood that the
commercial and political behavior of U.S. companies
with respect to that issue will tend to be responsive
to corporate perceptions of the prevailing balance of
domestic political forces rather than reflective of the
political preferences of the firms themselves.

3.   It follows from the preceding propositions that, as
a general rule, the political activity of U.S.
companies will tend to gravitate toward "mainstream"
U.S. political issues, such as, for example, the proper
role of government regulation in a free enterprise
economy.

4.   The more controversial that an issue is, the
smaller the likelihood that any company or group of
companies will be able to utilize broad-based business
lobbies (e.g., the U.S. Chamber of Commerce, the
National Association of Manufacturers) as vehicles for
effective political expression. Viewed in the opposite
perspective, the ability of broad-based U.S. business
lobbies to formulate and articulate a coherent
political position will tend to vary inversely with the
degree of public controversy surrounding the issue in
question.

In addition to the four preceding hypotheses, there seems ample reason to suggest that U.S. businessmen's reluctance to get politically involved in U.S.-Soviet issues may stem in part from a general reluctance to get involved in fundamental foreign policy questions. On the whole, U.S. businessmen may have an innate tendency to see it as the responsibility of the U.S. Government, not U.S. business, to determine what the national interest is and, subsequently, to provide policy guidance to American companies. Hence, as far as foreign policy is concerned, many businessmen may be strongly influenced by a "subject" mentality which inhibits political action on behalf of a policy position which they may favor in principle. This hypothesis can be expressed in terms of several specific propositions:

5. Other things being equal, the political activity of U.S. companies will tend to be confined to domestic U.S. political questions.

6. A corollary to (5) is that any U.S. corporate participation in the formulation of U.S. foreign policies, to the extent that this occurs, will tend to focus on narrow practical questions of immediate importance to corporate well-being rather than on basic questions of principle.

7. Propositions (5) and (6) not only apply to the political behavior of individual companies or groups of companies, but also to business lobbies and trade associations (under the assumption that such organizations generally reflect the overall political desires of their corporate memberships).

It merits attention that the findings of several other analysts tend to corroborate or otherwise support several of the above propositions and hypotheses. Likewise, the work of these analysts also gives additional credibility to certain survey and interview data as well as relevant linkage scenarios discussed previously.

For instance, relevant to proposition (5) above, Bauer, Dexter and Pool concluded the following in their pioneering 1963 study of businessmen's attitudes and beliefs vis-a-vis foreign trade policy:

> Foreign trade policy was indeed a matter of which most businessmen were aware, about which most were in some measure concerned, but on which only a relatively few would exert major effort and exhibit major interest. . . .
> . . . foreign trade policy was only one among many issues with which American businessmen were concerned and . . . for most it was an item of relatively low priority.[19]

Similarly, in their landmark 1975 study of the foreign policy perspectives of senior U.S. executives, Russett and Hanson came to the following conclusions:

> . . . our material, especially that obtained in the survey and interviews, indicates that foreign policy is generally not terribly important to most businessmen, whether they be hawks or doves. In this they probably are like most other Americans of this era, . . .
> To apply the term 'isolationist' to the businessmen we have studied here would be an overstatement and a distortion, . . . Although they are not particularly hawkish or likely to press for hawkish policies, neither are they especially dovish or likely to fight hard for dovish policies. A certain insularity is

perceptible.  The business of American business is business, and perhaps domestic politics. (Italics mine.)[20]

Also, consistent with the finding that SAEs seemingly had ethical inhibitions against exercising corporate political muscle on behalf of a preferred trade policy position, Bauer, Dexter and Pool found that:

> Rationally or irrationally, rightly or wrongly, foreign competition is seen as a specific problem, to which for years the letter to Congress has been the appropriate remedy, whereas the extension of export markets is seen as a matter of broad national policy in which every citizen's voice is as relevant as any other's.  (Italics mine.)[21]

Relevant to the finding that many SAEs regarded the U.S.S.R. as a marginal low priority growth market, and consistent with propositions (1) and (6) which suggest that an "immediate" threat to corporate well-being is an important pre-condition for corporate political action, Bauer and his colleagues found the following:

> The automobile industry recognized its involvement in the overall economy and the dependence of the economy on trade, but its interest was not sufficiently immediate to warrant vigorous, all-out action [on the tariff/protectionism issue].  (Italics mine.)
>
> The . . . forces inhibiting the auto companies from action must be considered in conjunction with the low priority which they gave this [the tariff/protectionism] issue.  (Italics mine.)
>
> . . . . . . . . . . . . . . . . . . . . . . . .
>
> Businessmen do not often take the same kind of political action to force a particular commodity into a particular foreign market as they do to keep out one that is injuring their established position.[22]

Additionally, Bauer also obtained evidence supportive
of propositions (4) and (7) and which is in accord with the
finding that many SAEs viewed traditional business lobbies
as a poor means through which to make known their opinions
on Soviet-American trade/detente. Commenting on the
ability of trade associations to express a position on
foreign trade issues, Bauer observed that:

> . . . when the minority feels strongly on the
> issue, restraint is imposed on the majority. In
> this common situation, multipurpose organizations
> duck the controversial issues. . . .
> The problem becomes especially crucial in such
> catchall, multipurpose organizations as the Chamber
> of Commerce and the National Association of Manu-
> facturers. Since such organizations are supposed
> to represent a wide range of interests in a wide
> range of businesses, special efforts are taken to
> avoid generating any avoidable internal conflict.
> Cautious procedures are employed for reaching a
> policy position, and spokesmen are confined to
> stating that position without elaboration, for
> fear that the most cautious elaboration may pro-
> duce dissension. . . . Executives of trade asso-
> ciations expressed concern over the danger of
> prejudicing their organizations' strength by
> attempting to take stands on issues on which
> unanimity was absent.[23]

Other data collected by Bauer and his colleagues lend additional support to propositions (1)-(3) and likewise
corroborate previously described survey and interview
results which suggest a high degree of business anxiety
concerning potential political criticism from customers,
community groups, the news media, etc.:

> . . . concern over their public visibility and
> fear of being accused of throwing their weight

> around was expressed by representatives of all the
> large automobile companies, . . .
>      Such sensitivity to external reaction stems
> from a mixture of motives:  fear of public and
> particularly government action, fear of retali-
> ation from business associates, . . . Among the
> largest firms, fear of economic retaliation is
> minimal, but concern over government retaliation
> or public reaction is very high, . . .
> . . . . . . . . . . . . . . . . . . . . . . . .
>      The curse of bigness is most significant where
> the company fears adverse public reaction, which
> may result in further governmental regulation or
> in prosecution.[24]

Supplementing Bauer, Norton Long, in his 1960 investigation

of the role of corporations in American society, similarly

found evidence of business sensitivity to criticism by

local community groups.  Indeed, Long found that executives

and their companies frequently see themselves as being in

an exposed political position and as constantly defending

against irrational attacks from various local interests.

Fundamentally, Long concluded that basic changes have taken

place since 1930 in the structure of ownership and

management in American industry, and that these changes

have resulted in the progressive alienation of companies

from their local communities and fostered a high degree of

political insecurity among businessmen:

>      How oddly the voice of C. Wright Mills' Power
> Elite . . . sounds in . . . querulous appeal(s)
> for affection and understanding from the local
> natives who, in company eyes, seem ready to kill,
> or at least drive away, the goose that lays the
> golden eggs. . . .
>      Company attitude and local attitudes are
> startlingly like that of a Middle East or South
> American oil company and the native inhabitants in

the throes of colonial nationalism and the threats
of withdrawal and shutdown on the one hand and
expropriation on the other. It is interesting to
note that in both cases the company is reduced to
the threat of emigration.[25]

At this juncture it is appropriate to note that the

above findings of Bauer, Russett and Hanson, and Long,

together with research data on Soviet Area Executives

presented in this chapter, are further indicative of the

amorphous and indeterminate nature of the concept of

economic self-interest. Once again, as first suggested in

Chapter IV, it would appear that economic self-interest

must be defined in much broader terms than simply profit

and must incorporate concerns such as the "security of the

firm." In this connection, it is abundantly clear that

when assessing possible dangers to their companies,

businessmen assign a prominent role to external political

factors as well as economic factors. Indeed, potential

political dangers may often be the pre-eminent

consideration in executives' decision calculus. In any

case, the variables which enter into businessmen's

evaluations of their self-interest are likely to vary from

situation to situation, thereby making it difficult if not

impossible to develop a consistent operational definition

of economic self-interest for purposes of comparative

political research.

As noted in Chapter IV, the complex and vague
character of economic self-interest is at odds with various
contemporary economic influence theories, which typically
equate economic self-interest with corporate greed and
profit maximization.  Additionally, however, it merits
emphasis that the portrait of senior American businessmen
sketched in this chapter is starkly different from that
which would be predicted by Domhoff, Marx, Mills and
others.  Rather than a politically omnipotent "power
elite," empirical data on SAEs depict a population of
businessmen who can variously be described as politically
insecure, naive, and frustrated.  Far from viewing the U.S.
Government and the U.S. political system as servile to the
corporate will, many businessmen seemingly saw themselves
and their companies as helpless subjects of the political
system.  Moreover, in common with large numbers of
Americans, many businessmen held the nation's policy-makers
(and especially the U.S. Congress) in low esteem, were
deeply troubled by what they perceived as the failure of
elected officials to act in the nation's best interests,
and generally harbored a strong anti-Washington bias.
Similarly, not unlike the proverbial man-in-the-street,
many businessmen displayed a singular lack of information
on and a limited understanding of American political
processes and institutions.  In sum, information gathered

in the course of this research effort leads one to propose that, instead of constituting an autonomous and purposeful power elite in American society, senior U.S. businessmen and their companies are strongly conditioned in their political outlook and behavior by the prevailing content of U.S. political culture.

FOOTNOTES

[1]One executive's remarks about U.S. policy, both
with respect to the U.S.S.R. in particular and vis-a-vis
the rest of the world in general, were especially
colorful.  For instance, commenting on the Jackson-Vanik
Amendment, this businessman grumbled:

> "If we are going to mix trade with politics, we
> should stop trading with 90% of the world.  We are going
> to end up with all the virtues and our overseas
> competitors are going to end up with all of the
> business."

This same executive went on to allege that:  "When it comes
to providing government credits to facilitate exports, the
United States is the laughing stock of the world."  Another
businessman, although displeased with the U.S. Government's
handling of Soviet trade policy, stated his criticism of
federal policy-makers in a less dramatic manner:  "America
is one of the few countries which uses economic leverage in
international politics, and this presents tremendous
problems for business planning."

[2]The following comment by one executive is typical
of the statements made by SAEs who were interviewed:
"Neither Congress nor the Executive branch has shown one
smidgen of leadership since Harry Truman."

[3]For example, one businessman indicated a somewhat
positive attitude toward the Executive branch when he
remarked that:  "These days business usually gets quicker
action from the Executive branch rather than the
Legislative branch on most issues."  On the other hand,
SAEs' ambivalent stance toward the various executive
departments is evident in the following disparaging
comments of two other businessmen:

> "The Washington bureaucracy is full of abstract
> pin-stripers who badly need some education on issues
> like technology-transfer and licensing."

> "If the Administration really tried to repeal the
> Jackson-Vanik Amendment, they could do it.  But I don't
> think they have the guts to try."

[4]Concerning the Commerce Department's performance on
U.S.-Soviet trade matters, the following opinions were
expressed by five executives interviewed:

"The Commerce Department has been very helpful to our business with Eastern Europe in general and with the U.S.S.R. in particular. We've found that the statistics, publications, and other information provided by the Bureau of East-West Trade are extremely useful."

"The morale in the Export Administration Office is incredibly low. Those guys are constantly getting squeezed by political pressure from all sides, especially from Congress, and the Office's budget is constantly underfunded. It's no wonder that the agency is staffed by cautious buck-passers."

"Since Commerce [i.e., the Export Administration Office] is so timid in presenting the exporter's case in interagency committees, U.S. companies should be able to send their own representatives to argue their case in these deliberations."

"The Export Administration Office is constantly being [taken advantage of] by the Department of Defense. But a big part of the problem is that the guys in the Commerce Department aren't aggressive enough. They just refer export control cases to interagency committees and don't really push the business point of view."

"The Department of Commerce should assume a more aggressive posture in combating stupid rules made by other agencies."

[5]Personal interviews on the subject of the U.S. Congress yielded a host of fascinating commentaries. What follows is a small sample of the most interesting statements, which resulted from discussions with six businessmen:

"When Congress passed the Jackson-Vanik Amendment they put their hands to their eyes."

"Congress is just forcing American jobs overseas by passing restrictive Soviet trade laws."

"We've written a number of letters to our senators and congressmen about U.S.-Soviet trade, and they have been responsive in the sense that they always answer our inquiries. The problem is that they never take a stand on any of the issues."

"Congress will only adopt U.S. business positions when it knows there will be no political penalty for doing so. In my opinion our Congress is a total loss. Its members only seem interested in playing political games and in riding the waves of popular emotion. The national interest doesn't seem to be important to those turkeys."

"When it comes to international business, Congress is made up of a bunch of deadheads."

"There is no empathy at all between U.S. business and the Congress."

[6]The following remarks, which were gathered in discussions with five executives, are typical of the anxieties that were detected in numerous personal interviews:

"It's best to keep any business with the Russians quiet because such trade is now an emotional issue."

"A lot of firms have shied away from publicity because they're afraid of bad reactions from the community. In our case, we managed to keep things quiet until 1974."

"Business must currently keep a low profile because of public opinion. The public associates all trade with the wheat deal. The public feels we got screwed."

"So far, no ethnic or religious groups have jumped on our backs, but we've kept our Russian connection as quiet as possible without being sneaky about it."

"Quite a few businessmen, including myself, are more wary about doing business with the Soviets because of the diminishing popularity of detente here in the U.S. Many of us are worried that our regular customers might regard our Russian activities as un-American and that they might take their business elsewhere. You have to understand that businessmen are basically very short-sighted and practical, which means we are much more likely to be affected by domestic public opinion than by the merits of political policies pursued by other nations. It's only logical that the growing anti-Russian mood in this country should cause U.S. companies to run scared from the Soviet market."

[7]With regard to the 1972-1973 grain deals, the following remarks by two executives were typical of those interviewed:

"There's been bad publicity surrounding the wheat deals. The public's impression is that if they [the Soviets] did it to us on grain, they can screw us elsewhere."

"The public has tended to associate all U.S.-Soviet trade with the [1972-1973] grain deals which have been perceived as a 'ripoff.'"

[8]Several quotations will serve to illustrate the character of businessmen's observations on the changing U.S. political climate. For instance, note the following comments made by a Midwestern machinery manufacturer:

"In a lot of ways, the Soviets have themselves to blame for their increasingly bad public image in the United States. Angola certainly hasn't helped their cause. Also, many people can't understand why we're trading with the Russians in the aftermath of the collapse of Saigon. All this publicity about communists in Portugal, France and Italy has also upset people. They see the Russians fooling around in Africa and Asia and they figure that the Soviets must also be responsible for what's now going on in Europe."

A second executive representing a high-technology capital equipment firm expressed the ensuing opinions:

"I am increasingly pessimistic about the prospects for increasing trade with the Russians over the near term. Besides the logistical hassles of doing business with those guys, public opinion in this country is turning against trade with the Russians. Business has to be sensitive to that. I see U.S.-Soviet trade leveling off, or, at best, growing only very slowly in the years immediately ahead.
"Two things have really hurt the Soviets in this country: The first is the constant publicity that U.S. companies are 'giving away' technology to the U.S.S.R. The other problem has been the wheat deals. This has really hit the consumer; the man in the street simply can't understand what's going on and resents the Soviets."

[9]For example, one executive made the following statement during the course of a personal interview:

"When Congress passed the Jackson-Vanik Amendment, the Soviets felt that the United States had slapped them in the face. They saw this legislation as a deliberate insult and as gross interference in their country's internal affairs. Personally, I agree with them."

[10]On the question of encouraging the liberalization of Soviet society, discussions with five SAEs yielded a series of succinct comments which is illustrative of the opinions held by most executives interviewed:

"Trade means communication between people, which may contribute to a mellowing of the Soviet system."

"Trade will result in new communication between the Soviet Union and the West. This is almost certain to stimulate the Soviet people's material aspirations and remind them of all the promises which the regime has made but has failed to keep."

"Trade is the only feasible way to promote face-to-face contacts between average Americans and average Russians. American business can by-pass Soviet politicians to establish direct communications with the Soviet people. Over the long run, such ties can help to stimulate changes in the Soviet system. We always talk politics with the technical people that the Soviets send to our plant for training. Inevitably, they are the ones who bring up political issues, not us."

"The people-to-people communication brought about through trade will enhance liberal forces in the Soviet system and will help stimulate consumer demand. Both developments will make Soviet society less rigid and perhaps make the U.S.S.R. a less belligerent country."

"It might take a long time, but I really believe that East-West trade is going to open up Soviet society and generate tremendous popular pressure on Soviet leaders for a better way of life."

[11]The ensuing quotations of five executives interviewed are indicative of the plaintive tone which ran through SAEs' commentaries on the U.S. mass media:

"There has been a continuous decline in journalistic quality since Korea. The primary mission of the news media these days is not to report facts objectively, but to destroy anything worthwhile in an insatiable quest for profit. On Soviet trade and political issues, _Time_ and _Newsweek_ have been running amok and have sensationalized the bad aspects of everything."

"Americans have long had a bad image of Russians: that the Russians aren't honest, and the idea that they're cheaters. They're not cheating us but the media help perpetuate the thing."

"Nowhere do you read about the advantages of Soviet-American trade."

"Most Americans don't see the big picture, partly because of the news media which have presented a false picture of things. For example, the coverage of the wheat deal. The news media always sensationalize the bad side of things."

"The media inherently tend to sensationalize 'bad' news while ignoring 'good' news. This is not intentional bias but simply the way they operate on any issue."

[12]For example, when asked why American businessmen had not been more active in promoting their views on Soviet trade among the U.S. public, one executive responded by saying, "Why should they?" In a similar vein, another businessman philosophized as follows:

"Congress would be more responsive to U.S. business' views if we regularly brought our concerns to its attention. A big problem is that businessmen tend to sit back, gripe among themselves, and wait for something to happen."

Likewise, a Cleveland executive related that:

"It's very possible that [Congressman] Vanik hasn't been responsive to the business point of view on Soviet trade because we in the Cleveland business community have neglected to approach him on the subject. I doubt that any companies around here have really tried to push Vanik on this matter."

Finally, another businessman admitted:

"American business hasn't communicated to the press that many jobs have been created from Soviet-American trade. The press doesn't report the number of jobs created because business doesn't tell them. Our own company has kept a low profile in the media."

[13]With regard to the political effectiveness of U.S. business on Soviet trade issues, the following observations of six executives interviewed are particularly interesting:

"Businessmen don't care to change the impression of the public. They don't see that as their job. Even if they wanted to, through what media could they?"

"The traditional ways in which business has made its views known to government have lost their effectiveness, and the opponents of business--particularly the labor unions--have become more effective. Things have developed this way because business lobbies only represent jobs, whereas the unions can actually deliver votes. Another problem is that union leaders don't usually take rational positions on controversial issues like Soviet trade. Instead they always take the position they think will be the most popular."

"Trade associations have not been very effective in Washington on U.S.-Soviet trade issues. One reason is that business lobbies have been preoccupied with product liability legislation. Another reason is that, in general, most U.S. companies just haven't considered the U.S.S.R. to be a prime growth market; right now the Middle East and Africa are seen as much better marketing bets."

"Our national trade association is a very heterogeneous outfit, and this usually results in watered down positions on policy issues that we're interested in. Naturally, this is a big disadvantage when it comes to trying to influence the course of events in Washington."

"Congress responds to those who can mobilize votes, and business just doesn't have the ability to do this. U.S. business lobbies are fragmented and disorganized, whereas the labor lobby is unified and effective."

"The last thing that our trade association wants to bother with at the moment is a political hot potato like Soviet trade. Our Washington lobby already has its hands full fighting OSHA [Occupational Safety and Health Administration] rules and regulations, which are of primary importance to us."

[14]The ensuing commentaries, based on interviews with five executives, are representative of businessmen's general reactions to the suggestion that they advertise their views on Soviet trade:

"Advertising to promote Soviet trade is a bad idea. Business must remain non-political on such issues, because as soon as you start being political, you risk losing half of your customers."

"Paid advertising [by our company] wouldn't be politically astute. We would get all kinds of trouble from various groups in the community."

"Paid advertising by our company would do more harm than good because we would probably get flak from our shareholders."

"Facts won't sell, this is an emotional thing. It would be hard for American companies to mount an [advertising] campaign with an emotional appeal."

"Paid advertising just doesn't have the effect of raw news."

[15]This attitude is graphically illustrated in the following comment by a Midwestern executive:

"Nobody wants to believe what we say anyway. The politicians get more publicity than business--and they use emotional appeals. You can't argue against that kind of thing with facts."

[16]As one businessman lamented during an interview: ". . . now that the Amendment is law it's going to be almost impossible to repeal, because there doesn't seem to be any way that one can oppose it on moral or philosophical grounds."

[17]Reflecting on his adverse experiences with the federal government regarding his attempts to influence export control policy, a senior official of a high-technology California company had this to say: "Dealing with those idiots in Washington makes me sick to my stomach. It's distasteful."

[18]The following comments by three executives
interviewed will serve to illustrate businessmen's overall
reluctance to call public attention to the profitability of
Soviet trade:

"If we went around advertising how much money we
have made, you can bet your last nickel that the Soviets
would try to use it against us. The next time we would
negotiate with them they would say, 'If you are making
so much money, then cut your price.'"

"Only losers talk about their deals--winners don't
talk!"

"We can't run around telling everyone about our
business!"

[19]Bauer, Pool, and Dexter, American Business and
Public Policy, pp. 125, 319.

[20]Russett and Hanson, Interest and Ideology, p. 266.

[21]Bauer, Pool, and Dexter, American Business and
Public Policy, p. 222.

[22]Ibid., pp. 222, 260.

[23]Ibid., p. 333.

[24]Ibid., p. 259.

[25]Norton E. Long, "The Corporation, Its Satellites,
and the Local Community," in The Corporation and American
Society ed. Edward S. Mason (Cambridge, Mass.: Harvard
University Press, 1960), p. 215.

# CHAPTER VII

## A DIMENSIONAL ANALYSIS OF EXECUTIVES' ATTITUDES

At this juncture it would appear that most of the
originally stated goals of this research effort have been
met:  Chapters IV and V provide a comprehensive inventory
of SAEs' views on key U.S.-Soviet issues during 1975-1976,
whereas Chapter VI examines in detail businessmen's
perceptions of the then-existing U.S. political environment
for commercial relations with the U.S.S.R.  As noted at
appropriate points in the text, various arguments and
points of information communicated by SAEs continue to have
substantive relevance for on-going policy debates of
specific Soviet-American political and economic questions
(e.g., technology transfer).  Most importantly, however, it
has been demonstrated that survey and interview findings,
when placed in the context of the International Trade
Politics Model, have wide-ranging theoretical implications
for the present and future conduct of U.S.-Soviet relations.

The next step, then, is to present the results of R
and Q-factor analyses of both the 1975 and 1976 surveys.
This will help clarify patterns in the data which have
already been discussed, facilitate identification of

additional less-obvious underlying dimensions, and set the
stage for a concluding theoretical synopsis and some
closing remarks.

## Survey 1:  R-Factor Analysis

As was outlined in Chapter III, repeated R-factor
analyses of the 1975 survey were conducted in order to
detect meaningful clusters of inter-correlated attitudes.
This was accomplished through application of the
PAI/Varimax technique, which yielded a terminal solution of
3 factors comprised of 12 variables.  Table 35 displays the
resulting Varimax-rotated factor matrix.[1]

### Factor 1

Viewed in the context of the extremely homogeneous
pro-trade and pro-detente opinion distribution of Survey 1,
it should not be surprising that all 3 attitude patterns
delineated in Table 35 are indicative of unwavering
executive support in 1975 for improved U.S.-Soviet economic
and political relations.  In particular, a considerable
number of variables discussed in earlier chapters load
strongly on Factor 1, which might be termed an "approval"
dimension.  Specifically, Factor 1 outlines an attitude
complex consisting of the following tendencies:  (1) to
view increased U.S.-Soviet trade as advantageous for the
U.S. economy ($r = .72$), (2) to view the expansion of

TABLE 35

VARIMAX-ROTATED R-FACTOR MATRIX: 1975 SURVEY*

| Variable Name | Variable Label** | Factor 1 | Factor 2 | Factor 3 |
|---|---|---|---|---|
| VAR002 | Soviet trade will benefit U.S. economy. | (.72) | .34 | .12 |
| VAR004. | Trade with Soviets will contribute to peace. | (.71) | .21 | (.40) |
| FEAR | Trade will not set up U.S.S.R. as a competitor of U.S. business. | (.67) | -.06 | .00 |
| DIPREL | U.S. should improve diplomatic ties with Soviets. | (.58) | .33 | .36 |
| EVOLVE | Trade will hasten Soviet political reform. | (.74) | .09 | -.07 |
| TRADE | U.S. should continue to improve U.S.S.R. trade ties. | (.60) | .43 | .42 |
| VAR001 | Still too many federal restrictions on Soviet trade. | .18 | (.73) | -.17 |
| VAR003 | U.S. trade policies hurting U.S. business' competitiveness. | .21 | (.77) | .16 |
| NEGATE | Inconsistent federal policies hamper U.S. corporate efforts in U.S.S.R. | .01 | (.82) | .21 |
| NOMFN | U.S. should withhold MFN until Soviet emigration improves. | -.27 | -.28 | (-.46) |
| LICENS | Willing to license latest corporate technology to U.S.S.R. | -.09 | -.07 | (.74) |
| SALES | Willing to sell U.S.S.R. products representing up-to-date technology. | .19 | .09 | (.75) |
| | Percent Total Variance | 24.2% | 19.6% | 15.9% |

*Parentheses are used to highlight those factor loadings which give meaning to each dimension.

**In order to display the factor matrix it has been necessary to abbreviate the survey variables. The full text of each of the variables listed can be found in Table 37.

Soviet-American commerce as promoting world peace
(r = .71), (3) to dismiss the possibility that transfers of
U.S. industrial technology to the Soviets might help
transform the U.S.S.R. into an effective international
competitor of American business (r = .67), (4) to advocate
continued U.S. Government efforts to strengthen diplomatic
(i.e., political) ties with the U.S.S.R. (r = .58), (5) to
believe that U.S. trade with the Soviet Union will
contribute to political liberalization in the U.S.S.R. by
helping the Soviet system to evolve in a slow but steadily
positive manner (r = .74), and (6) to advocate continued
U.S. Government efforts to build closer trade ties with the
Soviets (r = .60). It follows, of course, that moderately
high correlations exist between all the aforementioned
variables.

In sum, Factor 1 weaves together all the reasons why
SAEs in 1975 regarded U.S.-Soviet trade/detente as
desirable, and in doing so brings into sharper focus and
expands upon these capitalist executives' rationale,
elaborated in Chapters IV and V, for involving themselves
in business dealings with the United States' principal
communist adversary. Fundamentally, the pattern of high
loadings on Factor 1 clearly corroborates the argument that
the main frame of reference for SAEs' views on U.S.-Soviet
trade/detente was the broad national interests of the

United States, rather than their narrow parochial corporate self-interests. Likewise, Factor 1 is indicative of the fact that during 1975-1976 SAEs generally regarded U.S.-Soviet trade as anything but a "one-way street" that operates in favor of the U.S.S.R. To the contrary, Factor 1 underlines the findings that most executives believed that the United States can secure important economic and political benefits from a commercial relationship with the Soviets, while simultaneously minimizing the potential liabilities of such trade ties.

Factor 2

Complementing Factor 1, and reflecting findings presented in Chapter VI, Factor 2 highlights SAEs' intense aggravation in 1975 with the federal government's policies on trade with the Soviet Union. It follows that Factor 2 is consistent with Linkage Scenario 12 (also outlined in Chapter VI) which suggests that executives' aggravation with the federal government may motivate corporate behavior injurious to overall U.S.-Soviet economic and political relations.

The following attitudes are significantly intercorrelated and load meaningfully on this "frustration" dimension: (1) that the American business community has not been effective enough in bringing about the removal of U.S. Government restrictions on Soviet-American trade

(r = .73), (2) that, because the Soviets can buy most of
what they need in Western Europe and Japan, the U.S.
Government is damaging the competitive position of American
business by its restrictive trade policies toward the
U.S.S.R. (r = .77), and (3) that efforts of American
businessmen to improve U.S.-Soviet commercial relations
have been seriously undercut by inconsistent U.S.
Government trade policies (r = .82).

### Factor 3

Finally, Factor 3 is indicative of SAEs' fundamental
desire in 1975 to engage in Soviet business negotiations.
This "entrepreneurial" pattern is defined primarily by 3
intercorrelated tendencies: (1) to repudiate the idea that
the U.S. Government should withhold Most-Favored-Nation
tariff treatment from the U.S.S.R. until the Soviets relax
their restrictive emigration policies (r = -.46), (2) to be
willing to license one's latest industrial knowhow to the
U.S.S.R. (r = .74), and (3) to desire to sell products to
the Soviets which embody one's latest corporate technology
(r = .75). Additionally, it deserves mention that one
other variable loads meaningfully on this dimension;
namely, the propensity to see U.S.-Soviet trade as
furthering world peace (r = .40). This, of course,
highlights once again executives' tendency to place their

Soviet trade activities in the broad context of U.S. national interests.

### Survey 1:  Q-Factor Analysis

Following the procedures described in Chapter III, data from Survey 1 were also subjected to Q-Factor analysis in an effort to construct typologies of like-minded executives; i.e., whereas R-factor analysis was used to identify clusters of attitudes, Q-factor analysis was employed to identify clusters of people.[2] The result was a terminal solution of 10 factors, 7 of which are seemingly uninterpretable and unimportant (which probably reflects the great homogeneity of the 1975 data). However, Factors 1, 2, and 5 do appear to be meaningful categories, and account for 63% of the executives factored. Factor scores for these factors are shown in Table 36 in order to facilitate description of each typology. It was noted earlier that factor scores generated from a Q-analysis indicate the prominence of various traits in a set of intercorrelated entities, which in this case permits the analyst to delineate a distinctive attitude profile characteristic of executives falling into a given category.[3] Also, as a further aid to interpretation, from time to time reference is made below to frequency distributions on attitudinal variables which were computed for those cases having high loadings on theoretically

TABLE 36

Q-FACTOR SCORE MATRIX: 1975 SURVEY*

| Variable Name | Variable Label** | Factor 1 "Conservatives" | Factor 2 "Opportunists" | Factor 5 "Hard Liners" |
|---|---|---|---|---|
| VAR002 | Soviet trade will benefit U.S. economy. | -0.67 | -0.50 | -0.28 |
| VAR004 | Trade with Soviets will contribute to peace. | -0.54 | (0.71) | (-0.19) |
| FEAR | Trade will not set up U.S.S.R. as a competitor of U.S. business. | (0.59) | (1.06) | (0.06) |
| DIPREL | U.S. should improve diplomatic ties with Soviets. | -0.24 | -0.32 | -1.05 |
| EVOLVE | Trade will hasten Soviet political reform. | -0.61 | (1.80) | (1.83) |
| TRADE | U.S. should continue to improve U.S.S.R. trade ties. | -0.43 | -0.36 | -0.72 |
| VAR001 | Still too many federal restrictions on Soviet trade. | -0.71 | (-0.84) | (-1.62) |
| VAR003 | U.S. trade policies hurting U.S. business' competitiveness. | -0.54 | (-0.87) | -0.33 |

TABLE 36 (continued)

Q-FACTOR SCORE MATRIX: 1975 SURVEY*

| Variable Name | Variable Label** | Factor 1 "Conservatives" | Factor 2 "Opportunists" | Factor 5 "Hard Liners" |
|---|---|---|---|---|
| NEGATE | Inconsistent federal policies hamper U.S. corporate efforts in U.S.S.R. | -0.16 | (-0.44) | -0.01 |
| NOMFN | U.S. should withhold MFN until Soviet emigration improves. | 1.56 | 1.43 | (-1.18) |
| LICENS | Willing to license latest corporate technology to U.S.S.R. | (2.40) | (-1.37) | (1.06) |
| SALES | Willing to sell U.S.S.R. products representing up-to-date technology. | -0.64 | -0.33 | -0.81 |

*Factor scores which trend toward the negative (-) indicate agreement with the respective variables, whereas scores which trend toward the positive indicate disagreement. Parentheses are used to highlight those factor scores which give meaning to each typology. See Chapter 3, pp. 125-126, for additional data on the calculation and interpretation of factor scores.

**In order to display the factor score matrix, it has been necessary to abbreviate the survey variables. The full text of each of the variables listed can be found in Table 37, which provides frequency distributions for the three typologies delineated here.

important factors. These frequency distributions are shown in Table 37. (The varimax-rotated factor matrix itself is only of incidental importance, because the main focus of this study is not individual cases, but rather general patterns and trends. For this reason and because of its size the 100 x 10 factor matrix is not reproduced here.)

## Factor 1

Thirty-six SAEs (i.e., 36% of the 100 executives in the original correlation matrix) loaded strongly on Factor 1, making this the most prominent typology generated by the 1975 Q-analysis. The factor scores for this dimension, when evaluated relative to factor scores on other factors and with respect to the overall opinion distribution on Survey 1, suggest that Factor 1 is comprised of businessmen who favored a very cautious business strategy towards the Soviet Union. Specifically, SAEs belonging to this "Conservative" category can be distinguished by their strong opposition to the transfer of up-to-date U.S. industrial technology to the U.S.S.R. This is highlighted by a factor score of 2.40 for the LICENS variable, signifying that a high proportion of executives who loaded on Factor 1 did not favor licensing their firms' latest technology to the Soviets. Additional evidence is provided

TABLE 37

ATTITUDE PROFILE OF EXECUTIVE TYPOLOGIES: 1975 SURVEY

(Percentaged Vertically)

| | Factor 1 "Conservatives" | Factor 2 "Opportunists" | Factor 5 "Hard Liners" | Entire Sample |
|---|---|---|---|---|
| **Increased trade with the U.S.S.R. will be generally beneficial to the U.S. economy (VAR002).** | | | | |
| Agree | 97.2% | 95.5% | 100% | 86.1% |
| Not sure, depends | 2.8 | 4.5 | 0 | 10.2 |
| Disagree | 0 | 0 | 0 | 3.7 |
| (N) | (36) | (22) | (5) | (108) |
| **Developing stronger trade ties with the U.S.S.R. will contribute significantly to world peace (VAR004).** | | | | |
| Agree | 94.5 | 68.2 | 40.0 | 80.8 |
| Not sure, depends | 5.6 | 27.3 | 40.0 | 11.0 |
| Disagree | 0 | 4.5 | 20.0 | 8.3 |
| (N) | (36) | .(22) | (5) | (109) |

TABLE 37 (continued)

ATTITUDE PROFILE OF EXECUTIVE TYPOLOGIES: 1975 SURVEY
(Percentaged Vertically)

| | Factor 1 "Conservatives" | Factor 2 "Opportunists" | Factor 5 "Hard Liners" | Entire Sample |
|---|---|---|---|---|
| Although post-WWII sales of U.S. technology set up Japan and W. Europe as our competitors in international markets, we really don't have to worry about the same thing happening again in the case of the U.S.S.R. (FEAR). | | | | |
| Agree | 17.7 | 19.0 | 20.0 | 23.4 |
| Not sure, depends | 38.2 | 19.0 | 0 | 26.2 |
| Disagree | 44.1 | 61.9 | 80.0 | 50.5 |
| (N) | (34) | (21) | (5) | (107) |
| The U.S. should continue improving diplomatic relations with the U.S.S.R. (DIPREL). | | | | |
| Agree | 97.2 | 100 | 100 | 94.4 |
| Not sure, depends | 0 | 0 | 0 | 3.7 |
| Disagree | 2.8 | 0 | 0 | 1.8 |
| (N) | (36) | (22) | (4) | (107) |

TABLE 37 (continued)

ATTITUDE PROFILE OF EXECUTIVE TYPOLOGIES: 1975 SURVEY

(Percentaged Vertically)

|  | Factor 1 "Conservatives" | Factor 2 "Opportunists" | Factor 5 "Hard Liners" | Entire Sample |
|---|---|---|---|---|
| The U. S. can help eliminate the worst features of the Soviet political system through closer trade ties, because continuous trade will help the Soviet system evolve in a slow but steadily positive manner (EVOLVE). | | | | |
| Agree | 61.1 | 27.3 | 0 | 53.2 |
| Not sure, depends | 30.6 | 27.3 | 0 | 22.9 |
| Disagree | 8.3 | 45.4 | 100 | 23.9 |
| (N) | (36) | (22) | (5) | (109) |
| At this time, the U. S. Government should try to improve trade relations with the U.S.S.R. (TRADE). | | | | |
| Agree | 100 | 100 | 100 | 93.5 |
| Not sure, depends | 0 | 0 | 0 | 3.7 |
| Disagree | 0 | 0 | 0 | 2.8 |
| (N) | (36) | (22) | (5) | (108) |

TABLE 37 (continued)

ATTITUDE PROFILE OF EXECUTIVE TYPOLOGIES: 1975 SURVEY
(Percentaged Vertically)

| | Factor 1 "Conservatives" | Factor 2 "Opportunists" | Factor 5 "Hard Liners" | Entire Sample |
|---|---|---|---|---|
| The American business community generally has not been effective enough in bringing about relaxation of U.S. Government restrictions on U.S.-Soviet trade (VAR001). | | | | |
| Agree | 80.5 | 90.9 | 25.0 | 69.8 |
| Not sure, depends | 19.4 | 4.5 | 25.0 | 17.9 |
| Disagree | 0 | 4.5 | 50.0 | 12.2 |
| (N) | (36) | (22) | (4) | (106) |
| Our government is damaging the competitive position of American business by its restrictive trade policies toward the U.S.S.R. because the Soviets can buy most of what they need in W. Europe and Japan (VAR003). | | | | |
| Agree | 75.0 | 86.4 | 80.0 | 69.5 |
| Not sure, depends | 19.4 | 9.1 | 0 | 12.0 |
| Disagree | 5.6 | 4.5 | 20.0 | 18.5 |
| (N) | (36) | (22) | (5) | (108) |

TABLE 37 (continued)

ATTITUDE PROFILE OF EXECUTIVE TYPOLOGIES: 1975 SURVEY

(Percentaged Vertically)

| | Factor 1 "Conservatives" | Factor 2 "Opportunists" | Factor 5 "Hard Liners" | Entire Sample |
|---|---|---|---|---|
| Efforts of American businessmen to improve U.S.-Soviet trade have been seriously undercut by inconsistent U.S. Government trade policies toward the U.S.S.R. (NEGATE). | | | | |
| Agree | 77.1 | 86.4 | 60.0 | 72.2 |
| Not sure, depends | 20.0 | 13.6 | 40.0 | 22.2 |
| Disagree | 2.9 | 0 | 0 | 5.6 |
| (N) | (35) | (22) | (5) | (108) |
| The U.S. should continue to withhold Most-Favored-Nation status from the U.S.S.R. under provisions of the Jackson Amendment until the Soviet government relaxes its restrictive emigration policies (NOMFN). | | | | |
| Agree | 0 | 13.6 | 80.0 | 11.0 |
| Not sure, depends | 0 | 0 | 20.0 | 2.8 |
| Disagree | 100 | 86.3 | 0 | 86.2 |
| (N) | (36) | (22) | (5) | (109) |

TABLE 37 (continued)

ATTITUDE PROFILE OF EXECUTIVE TYPOLOGIES: 1975 SURVEY

(Percentaged Vertically)

| | Factor 1 "Conservatives" | Factor 2 "Opportunists" | Factor 5 "Hard Liners" | Entire Sample |
|---|---|---|---|---|
| **Within limits set by export controls, do you personally favor licensing your firm's latest technology to the U.S.S.R. (LICENS)?** | | | | |
| Yes | 0 | 100 | 0 | 55.8 |
| Not sure, depends | 3.6 | 0 | 0 | 1.1 |
| No | 96.4 | 0 | 100 | 43.2 |
| (N) | (28) | (20) | (3) | (95) |
| **Within limits set by export controls, do you personally favor product sales to the U.S.S.R. incorporating your firm's latest technology (SALES)?** | | | | |
| Yes | 93.8 | 100 | 100 | 93.9 |
| Not sure, depends | 0 | 0 | 0 | 0 |
| No | 6.3 | 0 | 0 | 6.1 |
| (N) | (32) | (20) | (4) | (98) |

by frequency distributions, which show that the licensing
of technology was opposed by 96.4% of the 36 SAEs who
correlated strongly on this dimension, compared with 43.2%
for the overall 1975 survey sample.

Apart from their resistance to licensing, however,
executives who loaded on Factor 1 are fairly representative
of most respondents to Survey 1. In particular, it merits
attention that the factor score of .59 for the FEAR variable
does not suggest that these businessmen were unusually
apprehensive about the possibility that U.S. technology
might help set up the U.S.S.R. as an effective international
competitor of American business. As a matter of fact,
whereas 50.5% of the overall 1975 survey sample feared the
prospect of future Soviet competition, the comparable
figure for executives loading on Factor 1 was a somewhat
smaller 43%. It follows, of course, that the attitude
profile on this dimension corroborates survey and interview
findings presented in Chapter V, which indicate that in
1975-1976 sizeable numbers of SAEs opposed licensing
technology to the U.S.S.R. for a variety of reasons
unrelated to the competitor issue (e.g., the inherently
complex nature of licensing contracts, the time-consuming
nature of Soviet business negotiations). Hence, Factor 1
tends to support the proposition (also set forth in Chapter
V) that even under extremely positive U.S.-Soviet political

circumstances a great many American businessmen would still
be reluctant to enter into licensing agreements with the
Soviets. Similarly, Factor 1 is consistent with the
contention that even if most existing national security
controls on U.S. exports to the U.S.S.R. were abolished,
many companies interested in product transactions with the
Soviets would still balk at getting involved in licensing
arrangements.[4]

## Factor 2

Twenty-two businessmen (i.e., 22% of those in the
initial correlation matrix) loaded strongly on Factor 2,
rendering this the second most populous typology
constructed by the Q-factor analysis. A careful assessment
of the factor scores for Factor 2 clearly reveals that this
category is made up of executives who might well be
labelled "Opportunists." Perhaps the strongest contrast
with Factor 1 is that this second dimension is marked by a
factor score of -1.37 for the LICENS variable, which
suggests that most SAEs in this category had a positive
attitude towards the sale of U.S. industrial knowhow to the
U.S.S.R. Indeed, this is confirmed by frequency
distributions, which show that 100% of the SAEs who loaded
on Factor 2 favored licensing their firms' latest
technology to the Soviets; compared with 55.8% for the
overall 1975 survey sample.

Additionally, another major difference between Factor 1 and Factor 2 is that executives comprising the latter were much more fearful that transfers of U.S. technology to the U.S.S.R. might transform the Soviet Union into a future competitor in world markets. This is indicated by a factor score of 1.06 on the FEAR variable, and is reflected in the fact that 61.9% of Factor 2's constituent members expressed anxiety about possible future Soviet competition (again, compared to 50.5% for the entire sample). Thus, Factor 2 brings into sharp focus the paradox outlined in Chapter V; namely, that many SAEs were eager to license technology to the U.S.S.R. despite deep concerns that their actions might come back to haunt them. As recounted earlier, various SAEs felt that if U.S. companies refuse to license technology to the Soviets, the U.S.S.R. will simply buy most of what it needs from alternative suppliers in Western Europe and Japan. It was further noted that executives believed that they could minimize the risks of technology-transfer by confining licenses to proven technology.

It was also reported in Chapter V that many SAEs viewed a stable and positive inter-governmental atmosphere as especially critical for the negotiation of successful licensing agreements. Thus, given their avid desire to license technology to the U.S.S.R., it should not be surprising that those executives who loaded on Factor 2 were considerably more agitated than other SAEs about the then-recent evolution of federal trade policies toward the Soviet Union. This intense dissatisfaction with the U.S. Government's behavior is evidenced by factor scores of -.84 on VAR001, -.87 on VAR003, and -.44 on NEGATE. In less abstract terms, these respective factor scores are reflected in the following opinion distributions: Compared to 69.8% for the overall 1975 sample, 90.9% of Factor 2's constituent members felt that the U.S. business community has not been effective enough in bringing about the relaxation of federal restrictions on U.S.-Soviet trade. Likewise, in contrast with 49.1% for the overall sample, 77.3% of those loading on Factor 2 believed "strongly" that restrictive U.S. Government commercial policies toward the U.S.S.R. have damaged the competitive position of American business. Lastly, 86.4% of those belonging to this typology reported that efforts of U.S. businessmen to improve U.S.-Soviet trade relations have been seriously undercut by inconsistent U.S. Government commercial policies vis-a-vis the U.S.S.R., whereas the comparable figure for the overall 1975 survey sample was 72.2%.

Apart from their acute displeasure with federal trade policies and ardent support for licensing, executives who loaded on Factor 2 can be distinguished by two additional traits, which figured prominently in the decision to label

this group of SAEs "Opportunists." Specifically, although
this category of SAEs strongly supported the continued
development of U.S.-Soviet trade (as indicated by a factor
score of -.36 for the TRADE variable), executives who
correlated strongly with Factor 2 generally were somewhat
more skeptical than other businessmen that the U.S. would
secure certain political benefits from commercial relations
with the U.S.S.R. Reflecting a factor score of .71 for
VAR004, 68.2% of the Opportunists (as opposed to 80.7% for
the overall sample) believed that increased Soviet-American
trade will contribute significantly to world peace.
Similarly, mirroring a factor score of 1.80 for EVOLVE,
only 27.3% of the Opportunists (compared with 53.2% for the
entire sample) felt that closer trade ties with the U.S.S.R.
will help the Soviet political system to evolve in a slow
but steadily positive manner. In sum, then, SAEs who loaded
on Factor 2 seemingly placed heavier emphasis than others
on the economic benefits of U.S.-Soviet trade as part of
their rationale and justification for doing business with
the communist U.S.S.R.

## Factor 5

Factor 5 delineates a small group of 5 SAEs (i.e., 5%
of the 100 businessmen in the initial correlation matrix)
who can be labelled "Hard Liners." This characterization
is based primarily on the finding that those who correlated

with this typology were much more inclined than other
respondents to advocate the overt use of U.S. economic
"leverage" to encourage moderation of Soviet policies on
human rights questions. Reflecting a factor score of -1.18
for the NOMFN item, 80.0% of the Hard Liners (as opposed to
only 11.0% for the overall 1975 sample) argued that the
U.S. Government should continue to withhold Most-Favored-
Nation tariff status from the U.S.S.R. under provisions of
the Jackson-Vanik Amendment until the U.S.S.R. relaxes its
restrictive emigration policies. Apparently, this attitude
was based on the belief that alternative, more subtle U.S.
tactics would be ineffective in modifying Soviet positions
on such issues. In this regard, corresponding to a factor
score of 1.83 for the EVOLVE item, the Hard Liners unanimously repudiated the idea that closer U.S.-Soviet trade
ties will help the Soviet political system to evolve in a
slow but steadily positive manner. (This, of course, is in
striking contrast with the above-noted fact that 53.2% of
the entire 1975 survey sample felt that Soviet- American
commerce would facilitate Soviet political liberalization.)

Also, consistent with their comparatively negative
outlook, the Hard Liners were considerably more uncertain
than most other executives concerning the proposition that
increased Soviet-American trade will contribute to world
peace. Mirroring a factor score of -.19 for VAR004, only

40.0% (i.e., 2 of the 5 executives who loaded on Factor 5)
indicated a belief in the trade-peace hypothesis, whereas
it was noted earlier that the comparable figure for the
overall 1975 sample was an overwhelming 80.7%.

Given the above it should not be surprising that 100%
of the Hard Liners also were opposed to the licensing of
their firms' latest technology to the U.S.S.R. (as is
indicated by a factor score of 1.06 for the LICENS
variable). While their opinion on this question is almost
identical to that expressed by the Conservatives on Factor
1, an important difference between these two typologies
should be noted: Whereas the Conservatives were not unduly
anxious that U.S. industrial technology might transform the
U.S.S.R. into an effective international competitor of U.S.
business, the small group of Hard Liners clearly was very
fearful of such a prospect. In this connection, corresponding to a factor score of .06 on the FEAR item, 80% of
the Hard Liners (as opposed to 43% for those loading on
Factor 1 and 50.5% for the overall survey sample) were
apprehensive about the possibility of future Soviet
competition.

Consistent with the preceding views on technology-
transfer and the Jackson-Vanik Amendment, a factor score of
1.62 was calculated for VAR001. This is a further
indication of the fact that the Hard Liners were much less

disturbed than other respondents about overall federal
policies governing commercial relations with the U.S.S.R.
Compared with 69.8% for the entire sample, only 25% of the
Hard Liners (i.e., just one executive) complained that the
American business community has not been effective enough
in bringing about the relaxation of U.S. Government
restrictions on U.S.-Soviet trade.

Finally, despite the aforementioned departures from
the mainstream of SAEs' thinking, it requires emphasis that
the Hard Liners delineated by Factor 5 were fairly typical
of other respondents in most other respects. Thus, 80%
thought U.S.-Soviet trade would be generally beneficial for
the U.S. economy, 100% felt that the then-recent warm-up in
diplomatic (i.e., political) relations with the U.S.S.R.
had been desirable and should continue, and 100% supported
continued U.S. Government efforts to improve Soviet-
American trade ties.

Although Factor 5 delineates an extremely small
category of executives, this group nevertheless has
substantial theoretical importance. Specifically, it would
seem extremely difficult to account for the Hard Liners'
views on U.S.-Soviet trade/detente by any reasonable
criterion of economic self-interest. Thus Factor 5, like
other findings noted throughout this study, corroborates
the work done by other analysts which casts doubt on the

proposition that economic self-interest is the key
determinant of businessmen's political behavior.

## Survey 2:   R-Factor Analysis

Just as in the case of Survey 1, data collected by the
1976 survey were subjected to R-factor analysis in an
effort to identify underlying attitude dimensions.
However, whereas the 1975 analysis was confined to the
computation of first-order factors, Survey 2 required a
second-order factoring to achieve a parsimonious factor
solution.  As outlined in Chapter III, the PAI/Varimax
technique was used to generate both first-order and
second-order factors.  The resulting rotated factor
matrixes are discussed in succession below.[5]

### First-Order Factors

#### Factor 1

Table 38 displays the Varimax factor solution for the
23 variables from Survey 2 which were found to load
meaningfully on at least one dimension.  Unquestionably,
the most striking feature of this matrix is Factor 1, which
brings into sharp focus the "national welfare" attitude
complex that was noted in both Chapters IV and V.  To be
specific, the following tendencies are interrelated and
correlate significantly with this vector:  (1) to be less
supportive of continued U.S. Government efforts to improve

TABLE 38

VARIMAX-ROTATED FIRST-ORDER R-FACTOR MATRIX: 1976 SURVEY*

| Variable Name | Variable Label** | Factor 1 | Factor 2 | Factor 3 | Factor 4 | Factor 5 | Factor 6 | Factor 7 |
|---|---|---|---|---|---|---|---|---|
| TRADE | U.S. should continue to improve U.S.S.R. trade ties. | (-.39) | (.31) | .18 | .14 | (.49) | .06 | .19 |
| PEACE | Trade with Soviets will contribute to peace. | (-.21) | (.55) | .27 | .12 | (.44) | .04 | .01 |
| HURT 1 | U.S. business outlook on U.S.S.R. trade hurt by Soviet foreign policy. | (.62) | -.18 | .10 | .15 | -.02 | .01 | -.01 |
| HURT 2 | Your company's Soviet business outlook hurt by Soviet foreign policy. | (.76) | -.01 | -.01 | .03 | -.16 | .10 | .04 |
| HURT 3 | U.S. business outlook on U.S.S.R. trade hurt by Euro-communist successes. | (.71) | -.14 | .00 | -.16 | .01 | .03 | -.16 |
| HURT 4 | Your company's Soviet business outlook hurt by Eurocommunist successes. | (.18) | .08 | -.03 | -.08 | -.13 | .11 | -.03 |
| NORML | Trade should not be conditional upon Soviet domestic or international policies. | (-.20) | (.35) | .15 | .29 | (.40) | .14 | .19 |
| FEAR 1 | Trade might set up U.S.S.R. as U.S. business competitor in LDCs. | (.37) | -.05 | -.19 | -.04 | -.11 | (.74) | -.19 |
| FEAR 2 | Trade might set up U.S.S.R. as U.S. business competitor in industrial nations. | (.36) | -.12 | -.16 | -.04 | -.04 | (.73) | -.25 |
| DEFENS | Trade will not lead to more Soviet military spending. | (-.22) | (.74) | .11 | .05 | .00 | -.06 | -.08 |
| NATSEC | Sales of "sensitive" high technology OK if precautions taken. | (-.37) | (.49) | .16 | .21 | .09 | -.18 | .23 |
| TECGAP | Soviets lag behind U.S. in civilian but not military technology. | (.31) | .16 | -.02 | .10 | .10 | (-.54) | -.25 |
| SOVIND | Trade will benefit Soviet civilian economy. | .18 | (.64) | -.09 | .06 | .14 | -.18 | -.11 |
| RELY 1 | U.S.S.R. might rely on U.S. for everyday technological needs. | -.12 | -.02 | (.71) | .00 | .20 | -.09 | .06 |
| RELY 2 | Trade may foster lasting U.S.S.R. technological dependence on West. | .04 | .09 | (.81) | -.12 | .01 | -.13 | .14 |
| PROVEN | Soviets prefer to buy "proven" production technology. | .09 | .09 | (.65) | .03 | .01 | .00 | -.03 |

TABLE 38 (continued)

VARIMAX-ROTATED FIRST-ORDER R-FACTOR MATRIX: 1976 SURVEY*

| Variable Name | Variable Label** | Factor 1 | Factor 2 | Factor 3 | Factor 4 | Factor 5 | Factor 6 | Factor 7 |
|---|---|---|---|---|---|---|---|---|
| NEWTEC | Soviets have on-line technology U.S. could use. | -.12 | .14 | -.03 | (.80) | .14 | -.03 | .09 |
| IDEAS | Soviets have good technical ideas U.S. could develop. | .07 | .07 | -.05 | (.87) | -.01 | -.08 | .01 |
| FORCE | U.S. policies forcing Soviets to foreign suppliers. | -.12 | -.06 | .15 | .05 | (.78) | .03 | -.05 |
| CAPTAL | Eximbank credit restrictions unjustified. | -.09 | .07 | -.08 | .02 | (.70) | -.13 | .37 |
| STABLE | Soviet trade mitigates effects of U.S. business cycle. | .08 | .24 | .03 | -.01 | (.68) | -.30 | -.07 |
| LICENS | Willing to license latest corporate technology to U.S.S.R. | -.01 | -.14 | .01 | .25 | -.01 | -.16 | (.70) |
| SALES | Willing to sell U.S.S.R. products representing up-to-date technology. | -.10 | .23 | .16 | -.11 | .18 | .03 | (.75) |
| | PERCENT TOTAL VARIANCE | 13.1% | 8.7% | 8.2% | 7.5% | 10.2% | 7.2% | 6.8% |

*Parentheses are used to highlight those factor loadings which give meaning to each dimension.

**In order to display the factor matrix, it has been necessary to abbreviate the survey variables. The full text of each of the variables listed can be found in Table 42.

trade relations with the U.S.S.R. (r = -.38), (2) to be somewhat skeptical of the idea that stronger trade ties with the Soviets will contribute to world peace (r = -.21), (3) to feel that then-recent Soviet foreign policy activities (e.g., the Angola affair) had adversely affected the outlook of the entire U.S. business community on doing business with the U.S.S.R. (r = .62), (4) to regard the Soviet market more cautiously as a result of the aforementioned Soviet international behavior (r = .76), (5) to feel that the then-growing power of West European communist parties had adversely affected the willingness of the entire American business community to participate in U.S.-Soviet trade (r = .71), (6) to be more reluctant to pursue Soviet commercial opportunities as a result of concerns over the Eurocommunist movement (r = .81), (7) to be somewhat less resistant to linking federal trade policies toward the U.S.S.R. (e.g., MFN status) to Soviet performance on outstanding world issues and human rights questions (e.g., Angola, Jewish emigration) (r = .20), (8) to fear the prospect that transfers of U.S. technology might help the U.S.S.R. to become an effective business competitor in LDCs (r = .37), (9) to fear possible future Soviet business competition in industrialized countries (r = .36), (10) to believe that economic benefits obtained from trade with the U.S. might encourage Soviet leaders to boost military spending (r = -.22), (11) to feel that sales of "sensitive" high technology to the U.S.S.R. necessarily endanger U.S. national security (r = -.37), and (12) to regard the technological level of the Soviet defense industry as close to that of the U.S. military sector (r = .31).

In sum, the "national welfare" dimension denoted by Factor 1 corroborates a key observation made during personal interviews; namely, that a small group of SAEs perceived then-recent Soviet international activities as inconsistent with a true detente. It will be recalled that certain executives indicated the suspicion that the U.S.S.R. was simply using detente as a smokescreen for expansionist objectives. Consequently, they had begun to doubt the wisdom of their own involvement and the nation's involvement in commercial relations with the Soviets. Besides reflecting such views, Factor 1 makes it abundantly clear that SAEs' budding distrust was manifested on a wide range of U.S.-Soviet issues, not just on a few discrete matters. Thus, Factor 1 further supports the argument (initially made in Chapter IV) that negative perceptions of Soviet international behavior were an important contributing factor to the moderate across-the-board reduction in business support for trade/detente which took place between Survey 1 and Survey 2. Additionally, Factor

1 is consistent with Scenarios 8, 9, 10 (see Chapters IV and V) which suggest that executives' growing distrust of the U.S.S.R. may have resulted in corporate behavior counter-productive to the stability of Soviet-American commercial and political relations.[6]

## Factor 2

Factor 2 is clearly analogous to the "approval" dimension which was extracted from the 1975 survey data. Factor 2, like its counterpart from Survey 1, pulls together various elements from Chapters IV and V and further documents executives' propensity to frame their views on U.S.-Soviet relations in the context of U.S. national interests. Once again, Factor 2 underlines the finding that most executives believed that the United States can secure important economic and political benefits from a commercial relationship with the Soviets, while simultaneously minimizing the potential liabilities of such a relationship. The following views are intercorrelated and load meaningfully on this attitude complex: (1) to be supportive of continued U.S. Government efforts to improve trade relations with the U.S.S.R. ($r = .31$), (2) to believe that stronger trade ties with the Soviets will contribute to world peace ($r = .55$), (3) to disapprove of the linkage of federal trade policies toward the U.S.S.R. to Soviet performance on outstanding world issues and human rights questions ($r = .35$),

(4) to believe that the Soviet civilian economy will benefit significantly from trade with the United States (r = .64), (5) to believe that economic benefits obtained from trade with the U.S. will not encourage Soviet leaders to boost military spending (r = .74), and (6) to feel that sales of sensitive high technology to the U.S.S.R. will not necessarily endanger U.S. national security if precautions are taken by relevant U.S. firms (r = .49).

Factor 3

Factor 3 might best be described as a "dependency" dimension which synthesizes several findings presented in Chapter V. It will be recalled that many SAEs believed there is substantial potential for the gradual development of a lasting Soviet technological reliance on the U.S. and the West.[7] Reflecting this view, Factor 3 is defined by the following interrelated tendencies: (1) to see prospects for a continuous Soviet dependency on U.S. industrial knowhow for meeting practical everyday needs (e.g., spare parts for equipment exported to the U.S.S.R.) (r = .71), (2) to believe that if the Soviets buy advanced Western technology for a period of time and subsequently try to "go it alone," their civilian economy will still find it impossible to keep pace with Western research and development (r = .81), and (3) to argue that the Soviets usually buy "proven" production technology from U.S. firms,

which soon makes it outmoded in terms of advances which
American industry is preparing to put into operation (r =
.65). Hence, Factor 3 brings into better focus the
reasoning behind SAEs' contention, outlined in Chapter V,
that Soviet technological dependence on the U.S. would
provide the U.S.S.R. with a strong vested interest in
political restraint, as well as benefit American industry
via continuous Soviet demand for U.S. products.

Factor 4

Factor 4 delineates yet another aspect of business
opinion that was recounted in Chapter V; i.e., that a
sizeable minority of respondents to Survey 2 believed that
there is a substantial possibility that the U.S. might be
able to obtain useful technology from the U.S.S.R.[8]
Thus, Factor 4 identifies what might be labelled a
"technological benefits" dimension, although it is perhaps
inappropriate to characterize this factor as a "dimension,"
since it is basically comprised of only two variables.
Specifically, the following attitudes are intercorrelated
and load meaningfully on Factor 4: (1) to view Soviet
industry as possessing advanced on-line technology which
could greatly benefit the U.S. economy (r = .80), and (2)
to view Soviet scientists and engineers as having
innovative ideas which U.S. companies could borrow and

develop themselves to their substantial benefit (r = .87).

## Factor 5

Reflecting SAEs' dissatisfaction with federal trade policies toward the U.S.S.R., Factor 5 appears to correspond to the "frustration" dimension which was derived from Survey 1. However, this attitude complex is not as well-defined as it is in the 1975 data. Several key components of Factor 2 (the "approval" dimension) also correlate with Factor 5, rendering the latter something of a hybrid. Nevertheless, Factor 5 can easily be differentiated from Factor 2 by two high loadings that are indicative of businessmen's intense aggravation with the U.S. Government. These are: (1) the view that U.S. tariff policy and restrictions on Eximbank lending to the U.S.S.R. are, for financial reasons, forcing the Soviets away from American suppliers and towards West European/Japanese companies (r = .78), (2) the belief that existing legislative restrictions on Eximbank credit to the U.S.S.R. cannot be justified in terms of future U.S. capital requirements (r = .70).

It follows that those elements from Factor 2 which also correlate with Factor 5 complement the above views. In this connection, the "frustration" dimension incorporated the following additional components: (1) to support continued U.S. Government efforts to improve trade relations with the U.S.S.R. (r = .48), (2) to believe that stronger trade ties with the Soviets will contribute to world peace (r = .44), and (3) to disapprove of linking federal trade policies toward the U.S.S.R. to Soviet performance on outstanding world issues and human rights questions (r = .40). Also, although it does not load on Factor 2, another attitude consistent with the preceding opinions correlates strongly with Factor 5; i.e., that trade with the U.S.S.R.'s planned economy exercises a beneficial stabilizing effect on U.S. industries which are highly sensitive to fluctuations in the business cycle (r = .68).

In sum, Factor 5 delineates a somewhat confusing pattern which draws together a wide range of findings presented in Chapters 4-6. Factor 5's central distinguishing feature, however, is that it highlights SAEs unhappiness in 1976 with the recent evolution of U.S. Government policy on Soviet trade. In particular, Factor 5 underlines businessmen's displeasure with restrictions on Eximbank lending to the U.S.S.R., which were seen as reducing the ability of U.S. firms to develop financially competitive bids on Soviet contracts. It follows that Factor 5, like 1975 R-Factor 2, is consistent with Linkage Scenario 12 (outlined in Chapter VI), which suggests that executives' aggravation with the federal government may

have motivated corporate behavior injurious to overall
U.S.-Soviet economic and political relations[9].

## Factor 6

Factor 6 clearly outlines what may be termed an
"anxiety" dimension that mirrors businessmen's
apprehensions (discussed in Chapter V) that transfers of
U.S. industrial knowhow might help the Soviet Union to
become an effective international competitor of American
business. Three interrelated tendencies comprise this
attitude complex: (1) to feel that the U.S. business
community has reason to fear setting up the U.S.S.R. as a
future commercial competitor in LDCs ($r = .74$), (2) to fear
the possibility of future Soviet business competition in
industrialized countries ($r = .73$), and (3) to view the
Soviet civilian economy as having a substantial capacity
for developing and applying technology to problems of
large-scale commercial production ($r = -.54$). In essence,
then, those SAEs who were apprehensive about the prospect
of transforming the U.S.S.R. into a competitive force in
international markets had a corresponding propensity to
magnify Soviet abilities for absorbing and building upon
imported foreign knowhow.

Note that Factor 6, like 1975 Q-Factor 1, tends to
support the proposition (set forth in Chapter V) that even
under extremely positive U.S.-Soviet political

circumstances a great many American businessmen would still refuse to grant industrial licenses to the Soviets. Also, Factor 6 is consistent with the argument that even if most existing national security controls on U.S. exports to the U.S.S.R. were abolished, many companies would still be inhibited from participation in Soviet licensing arrangements.[10]

Factor 7

Lastly, Factor 7 corresponds to the "entrepreneurial" dimension which was extracted from the 1975 survey data. Again, very little can be said about this pattern, other than that it is indicative of SAEs' general desire in 1976 to participate in commercial transactions with the U.S.S.R. As is clearly evident from Table 38, Factor 7 is defined by two intercorrelated attitudes: (1) to be willing to license one's latest industrial knowhow to the Soviet Union ($r = .70$), and (2) to desire to sell products to the Soviets which embody one's corporate technology ($r = .75$).

## Second-Order Factors

Given the relatively large number of factors displayed in Table 38, further efforts were made to simplify the R-solution to Survey 2. To recapitulate the procedures outlined in Chapter III, factor scores were calculated for each of the 7 R-factors discussed above, thereby enabling these first-order factors to be treated as composite variables. Next, these 7 composite factor-score variables were themselves factored in order to identify second-order factors representing broad attitude complexes present in the data. The final result of this process was three higher-order dimensions, which are displayed in Table 39.

## Factor 1

Second-order Factor 1 delineates what might be labelled a "disruption" dimension. Specifically, the pattern of loadings on this factor shows that first-order Factor 1 (the "national welfare" dimension) is positively correlated with first-order Factor 7 (the "entrepreneurial" dimension), and that both these first-order attitude complexes are inversely correlated with first-order Factor 5 (the "frustration" dimension). In concrete terms, this suggests that those executives who had the strongest direct interest in U.S.-Soviet trade were also among those who had the strongest emerging doubts about the wisdom of such trade from the standpoint of the national interest. These doubts, it would appear, were also associated with reduced opposition to federal policies inhibiting the development of economic relations with the U.S.S.R. (e.g., Jackson-Vanik, curbs on Eximbank lending).

TABLE 39

VARIMAX–ROTATED SECOND-ORDER R-FACTOR MATRIX: 1976 SURVEY*

| Variable Name | Variable Label | Factor 1 "Disruption" | Factor 2 "Anxiety" | Factor 3 "Pro-Detente" |
|---|---|---|---|---|
| FACTOR 1 | National welfare | (.47) | .14 | .24 |
| FACTOR 2 | Approval | .28 | .10 | (.55) |
| FACTOR 3 | Dependency | -.16 | (-.43) | (.50) |
| FACTOR 4 | Technological benefits | -.10 | .03 | (.60) |
| FACTOR 5 | Frustration | (-.58) | .34 | .18 |
| FACTOR 6 | Anxiety | .01 | (.82) | .07 |
| FACTOR 7 | Entrepreneurial perspective | (.61) | .07 | -.05 |
| | PERCENT TOTAL VARIANCE | 11.6% | 14.4% | 14.4% |

*Parentheses are used to highlight those first-order factor loadings which give meaning to each second-order dimension.

Basically, then, negative perceptions of Soviet
international activity during 1975-1976 seemingly had a
disruptive impact on the thought processes of those
businessmen who were otherwise inclined to do business with
the U.S.S.R. Hence, second-order Factor 1, like first-
order Factor 1, is consistent with Linkage Scenarios 8, 9,
and 10 (see Chapters IV and V) which suggest that
executives' growing distrust of the U.S.S.R. may have
resulted in corporate behavior counter-productive to the
stability of Soviet-American commercial and political
relations.[11]

## Factor 2

Second-order Factor 2 appears to be an expanded
version of first-order Factor 6 (the "anxiety" dimension).
In this regard, Factor 6 loads more strongly on
second-order Factor 2 than any other first-order factor (r
= .82) and is inversely correlated with first-order Factor
3 (the "dependency" dimension), which has the second
highest loading on this higher-order pattern (r = -.43).
Thus, those executives who were most fearful that U.S.
technology might set up the U.S.S.R. as an effective
competitor, and who tended to magnify Soviet abilities for
absorbing imported knowhow, likewise had a propensity to
dismiss the possibility that the U.S.S.R. might develop a
lasting technological dependence on the U.S. and the West.

It goes without saying that all these views are reflective of internally consistent reasoning.

## Factor 3

Second-order Factor 3 outlines a "pro-detente" dimension which is comprised of first-order Factor 2 (the "approval" dimension)($r$ = .55), first-order Factor 3 (the "dependency" dimension)($r$ = .50), and first-order Factor 4 (the "technological benefits" dimension)($r$ = .60). It follows that all three of these first-order factors are positively intercorrelated. Hence, those executives who felt that U.S.-Soviet trade will contribute to world peace and will not endanger U.S. national security had a corresponding propensity to believe that U.S. industry might obtain useful technology from the U.S.S.R. while fostering a permanent Soviet dependency on American industrial knowhow.

In sum, second-order Factor 3, by lacing together the reasons underlying SAEs' general support in 1976 for trade/detente, enlarges upon first-order Factor 2 and furnishes a more comprehensive perspective on these capitalist executives' justification and rationale for doing business with the communist U.S.S.R. Basically, the evidence once again suggests that the principal frame of reference for businessmen's views on U.S.-Soviet economic and political relations was the broad national interests of the United States and not the narrow concerns of their individual companies.

## Survey 2:  Q-Factor Analysis

Again, as was done for Survey 1, data collected by Survey 2 were also Q-factor analyzed to develop typologies of like-minded executives.  However, whereas first-order Q-analysis was sufficient to achieve categorization of the 1975 data, second-order Q-factor analysis was required to arrive at a comparable solution for the 1976 data.[12] This was necessitated by the large size of Survey 2's Q-correlation matrix and the SPSS program's limited data-handling capabilities.  Following the procedures described in Chapter III, it was essential to divide the 200 cases in the data matrix into two sub-groups, labelled A and B, and to factor them separately.  As outlined earlier, this resulted in 18 first-order factors (i.e., typologies) for Group A and 19 for Group B.  Next, factor scores for the factors in each sub-group were combined into a single data matrix; i.e., the 37 first-order factors were transformed into 37 composite factor score variables.  The composite variables were then themselves factored to produce 18 higher-order factors representing comprehensive typologies incorporating all 200 cases in the original data matrix.  The resulting varimax-rotated matrix, which shows the intercorrelations among the first-order factors, is exhibited in Table 40.

A careful evaluation of factor scores for these factors revealed that of the 18 typologies generated by the second-order analysis, only factors 5, 7, and 14 are interpretable. However, these three categories account for a total of 124 businessmen and therefore represent a 62.0% majority of the 200 SAEs originally factored. To augment the following discussion of these meaningful dimensions, the factor scores for factors 5, 7, and 14 are shown in Table 41. Additionally, Table 42 displays frequency distributions on attitudinal variables for those cases comprising each interpretable typology.

### Factor 5

As can be seen from Table 40, second-order Factor 5 consists of first-order Factor 1, Group A (FACA01), and first-order Factor 1, Group B (FACB01). A total of 59 businessmen (i.e., 29.5% of the 200 executives in the original correlation matrix) loaded strongly on these two first-order dimensions, thereby making Factor 5 the most populous second-order typology. A thorough examination of relevant factor scores and frequency distributions suggests that the 59 businessmen delineated by Factor 5 can best be characterized as "Advocates" of U.S.-Soviet trade and

TABLE 40

VARIMAX-ROTATED SECOND-ORDER Q-FACTOR MATRIX: 1976 SURVEY*

| Variable Name | Factor 1 | Factor 2 | Factor 3 | Factor 4 | Factor 5 | Factor 6 | Factor 7 | Factor 8 | Factor 9 | Factor 10 | Factor 11 | Factor 12 | Factor 13 | Factor 14 | Factor 15 | Factor 16 | Factor 17 | Factor 18 |
|---|---|---|---|---|---|---|---|---|---|---|---|---|---|---|---|---|---|---|
| FACA01 | -.01 | -.03 | -.02 | -.01 | (.91) | .15 | -.10 | .11 | .05 | .21 | .02 | .02 | .21 | .08 | .02 | .06 | .03 | .07 |
| FACA02 | -.01 | -.09 | -.02 | .23 | .19 | .13 | (.77) | -.22 | .00 | -.06 | -.10 | .04 | -.16 | -.26 | .31 | -.05 | -.06 | -.11 |
| FACA03 | -.25 | -.08 | -.09 | -.25 | -.17 | .11 | .44 | .09 | -.20 | .20 | -.23 | -.22 | .11 | (.52) | .00 | -.10 | -.33 | -.11 |
| FACA04 | .35 | .20 | -.18 | -.16 | -.04 | -.09 | .17 | .32 | -.33 | .01 | -.55 | -.23 | .05 | .22 | -.18 | .11 | -.17 | -.13 |
| FACA05 | .03 | -.11 | .38 | .36 | -.06 | -.10 | -.05 | .25 | -.19 | -.04 | -.39 | .36 | .01 | .28 | .36 | .15 | -.07 | -.22 |
| FACA06 | .38 | -.13 | -.06 | -.34 | -.12 | -.24 | .07 | -.21 | -.54 | .17 | .07 | .16 | -.31 | .30 | -.01 | .03 | -.09 | -.14 |
| FACA07 | .08 | .32 | .13 | .35 | -.02 | .47 | -.02 | .00 | .03 | .02 | .19 | .34 | -.21 | .13 | -.50 | -.09 | -.21 | -.11 |
| FACA08 | .09 | -.11 | .29 | .14 | -.12 | -.51 | .26 | .31 | .04 | -.05 | .06 | .16 | .04 | -.21 | .48 | -.01 | .25 | -.24 |
| FACA09 | .02 | -.06 | -.25 | -.12 | -.06 | .03 | .10 | .40 | -.08 | .36 | -.15 | -.18 | .05 | .02 | .16 | -.64 | -.19 | .05 |
| FACA10 | .12 | -.57 | .05 | .32 | -.07 | -.22 | .00 | -.16 | -.07 | .43 | -.09 | -.34 | -.23 | .08 | -.14 | -.18 | -.16 | -.11 |
| FACA11 | .47 | -.02 | .11 | .19 | -.07 | -.05 | .08 | .06 | .14 | -.07 | .58 | -.19 | .29 | .07 | .23 | .34 | -.25 | -.03 |
| FACA12 | -.54 | -.17 | -.12 | .13 | .02 | -.28 | -.03 | -.20 | .08 | .23 | -.01 | -.06 | .15 | .23 | -.04 | .15 | -.38 | -.31 |
| FACA13 | .12 | -.04 | -.10 | .21 | .10 | -.29 | -.19 | -.09 | .57 | .04 | .08 | .06 | -.49 | .22 | .24 | -.29 | .08 | -.13 |
| FACA14 | .21 | -.16 | -.51 | .24 | -.11 | -.07 | -.05 | -.04 | -.02 | .21 | -.07 | .44 | .47 | -.06 | .02 | -.25 | .01 | -.12 |
| FACA15 | .02 | .63 | -.06 | .30 | -.09 | -.09 | -.05 | .04 | -.18 | .21 | -.04 | -.25 | .09 | -.06 | .08 | .07 | .45 | .07 |
| FACA16 | -.10 | .08 | .30 | -.33 | -.12 | .16 | -.12 | -.04 | .27 | .46 | -.05 | .36 | -.05 | -.42 | .15 | .24 | .00 | -.20 |
| FACA17 | .22 | -.05 | .50 | -.09 | .03 | .06 | -.01 | -.54 | .14 | -.15 | -.17 | -.07 | -.35 | .21 | -.04 | -.25 | -.24 | -.01 |
| FACA18 | .07 | -.05 | -.03 | -.04 | -.01 | -.35 | .15 | -.25 | .16 | -.28 | -.08 | -.05 | -.01 | -.13 | -.22 | .04 | -.28 | .71 |
| FACB01 | -.01 | -.02 | -.01 | .01 | (.97) | -.08 | .09 | -.05 | -.02 | .03 | -.03 | -.01 | -.09 | -.02 | .00 | .00 | -.04 | -.04 |
| FACB02 | .02 | -.02 | -.01 | -.05 | -.07 | -.05 | (.98) | -.05 | -.02 | -.07 | .01 | -.02 | .04 | .07 | -.07 | .00 | .02 | -.06 |
| FACB03 | -.05 | -.03 | -.02 | -.03 | .12 | -.01 | -.01 | .03 | -.02 | .95 | .01 | -.01 | .00 | -.01 | -.03 | -.09 | -.03 | .08 |
| FACB04 | .00 | .04 | -.04 | -.01 | .03 | -.04 | -.08 | .02 | .01 | -.02 | .07 | -.01 | .01 | -.02 | .95 | -.07 | .01 | -.06 |
| FACB05 | -.01 | -.04 | .00 | .00 | .10 | -.03 | -.04 | -.02 | .01 | -.01 | .03 | .01 | .98 | .02 | .02 | .01 | .02 | -.01 |
| FACB06 | .04 | -.06 | .00 | .01 | .06 | .96 | .05 | .00 | -.02 | -.03 | -.03 | .01 | .01 | .00 | .01 | .04 | .02 | -.07 |
| FACB07 | -.02 | -.01 | .00 | -.02 | .02 | .02 | .03 | .00 | -.02 | -.02 | .00 | .99 | .00 | .00 | -.04 | .00 | .00 | -.02 |
| FACB08 | -.02 | .03 | .02 | .98 | .01 | .01 | .04 | .01 | .02 | -.02 | .04 | .01 | .00 | -.02 | -.03 | .00 | .00 | .00 |
| FACB09 | .03 | .03 | .02 | .01 | .04 | .01 | -.05 | .99 | .02 | -.02 | -.05 | .00 | -.02 | .02 | -.02 | -.06 | .02 | -.06 |
| FACB10 | -.01 | .01 | .04 | .00 | .05 | .03 | -.07 | -.02 | -.01 | -.04 | -.02 | -.02 | -.02 | (.97) | -.01 | -.04 | -.03 | -.01 |
| FACB11 | -.01 | .98 | .01 | .00 | -.02 | .03 | .03 | -.03 | .02 | .01 | -.03 | .01 | .01 | .02 | -.02 | .01 | -.01 | -.04 |
| FACB12 | -.01 | -.01 | .02 | -.04 | .02 | .03 | .03 | -.02 | .99 | .01 | .00 | .00 | -.04 | .00 | -.04 | .04 | -.03 | -.01 |
| FACB13 | .07 | -.09 | .81 | .10 | -.08 | -.12 | .00 | .02 | .04 | .16 | -.06 | .06 | -.01 | .04 | .11 | .11 | -.08 | -.04 |
| FACB14 | .02 | .00 | -.04 | -.01 | .00 | .00 | -.01 | .01 | .01 | .02 | .97 | .01 | -.03 | .04 | -.02 | -.01 | -.03 | -.04 |
| FACB15 | -.02 | -.01 | .06 | -.03 | .03 | .04 | .01 | .05 | -.06 | .02 | .05 | .06 | .02 | -.02 | -.02 | .91 | -.03 | .01 |
| FACB16 | .98 | .01 | .02 | .00 | .01 | .01 | -.02 | .01 | -.03 | .01 | .01 | .00 | .00 | -.02 | -.04 | .00 | .00 | .01 |
| FACB17 | .13 | -.10 | -.57 | .12 | -.09 | -.16 | .02 | -.01 | -.08 | .20 | -.15 | .07 | -.01 | .12 | .21 | -.22 | -.09 | -.04 |
| FACB18 | .01 | .01 | .01 | .02 | .00 | -.03 | .02 | -.05 | .01 | .03 | -.03 | -.01 | .01 | .03 | .02 | .02 | .92 | -.11 |
| FACB19 | .01 | .02 | .02 | .04 | .02 | .07 | -.03 | .02 | -.04 | -.02 | .00 | .00 | .02 | .06 | .02 | -.02 | -.01 | .91 |
| PERCENT TOTAL VARIANCE | 5.4% | 5.4% | 5.4% | 5.4% | 5.4% | 5.3% | 5.4% | 5.4% | 5.4% | 5.3% | 5.3% | 5.3% | 5.3% | 5.3% | 5.3% | 4.9% | 4.7% | 4.7% |

*Parentheses are used to highlight those first-order factor loadings which are the principal constituents of the second-order typologies delineated by factors 5, 7, and 14.

TABLE 41

SECOND-ORDER Q-FACTOR SCORE MATRIX: 1976 SURVEY*

| Variable Name | Variable Label** | Factor 5 "Advocates" | Factor 7 "Conservatives" | Factor 14 "Skeptics" |
|---|---|---|---|---|
| TRADE | U.S. should continue to improve Soviet trade ties. | (-.61) | -0.72 | (1.04) |
| PEACE | Trade with Soviets will contribute to peace. | (-0.68) | -0.75 | (0.71) |
| HURT1 | U.S. business outlook on U.S.S.R. trade hurt by Soviet foreign policy. | (1.27) | -0.28 | -(1.33) |
| HURT2 | Your company's Soviet business outlook hurt by Soviet foreign policy. | (1.98) | 0.40 | (0.66) |
| HURT3 | U.S. business outlook on U.S.S.R. trade hurt by Eurocommunist successes. | (1.58) | 0.11 | 0.47 |
| HURT4 | Your company's Soviet business outlook hurt by Eurocommunist successes. | (1.74) | 0.42 | -0.14 |
| NORML | Trade should not be conditional upon Soviet domestic or international policies. | (-0.92) | -0.99 | 1.57 |
| FEAR1 | Trade might set up U.S.S.R. as U.S. business competitor in LDCs. | (0.93) | -0.60 | (-0.42) |
| FEAR2 | Trade might set up U.S.S.R. as U.S. business competitor in industrial nations. | (1.23) | 0.36 | (-0.82) |
| DEFENS | Trade will not lead to more Soviet military spending. | (-1.60) | 0.04 | (-0.64) |
| NATSEC | Sales of "sensitive" high technology OK if precautions taken. | (-1.08) | 0.51 | (0.80) |
| TECGAP | Soviets lag behind U.S. in civilian but not military technology. | -0.15 | -0.68 | (-0.67) |
| SOVIND | Trade will benefit Soviet civilian economy. | (-0.39) | 0.26 | (1.58) |
| RELY1 | U.S.S.R. might rely on U.S. for everyday technological needs. | (-0.60) | -0.82 | -0.41 |

TABLE 41 (continued)

SECOND-ORDER Q-FACTOR SCORE MATRIX:  1976 SURVEY*

| Variable Name | Variable Label** | Factor 5 "Advocates" | Factor 7 "Conservatives" | Factor 14 "Skeptics" |
|---|---|---|---|---|
| RELY2 | Trade may foster lasting U.S.S.R. technological dependence on West. | -0.61 | -0.69 | 0.49 |
| PROVEN | Soviets prefer to buy "proven" production technology. | -0.19 | 0.37 | -1.13 |
| NEWTEC | Soviets have on-line technology U.S. could use. | 0.04 | 1.30 | (1.09) |
| IDEAS | Soviets have good technical ideas U.S. could develop. | -0.41 | 0.04 | (0.49) |
| FORCE | U.S. policies forcing Soviets to foreign suppliers. | (-0.45) | -0.72 | -1.38 |
| CAPTAL | Eximbank credit restrictions unjustified. | (-0.91) | 0.63 | -1.52 |
| STABLE | Soviet trade mitigates effects of U.S. business cycle. | 0.73 | 0.78 | (1.32) |
| LICENS | Willing to license latest corporate technology to U.S.S.R. | (-1.54) | (3.35) | (-0.96) |
| SALES | Willing to sell U.S.S.R. products representing up-to-date technology. | -0.80 | -1.58 | -0.82 |

*Factor scores which trend toward the negative (-) indicate agreement with the respective variables, whereas scores which trend toward the positive indicate disagreement.  Parentheses are used to highlight those factor scores which give meaning to each typology.  See Chapter 3, pp. 125-126, for additional data on the calculation and interpretation of factor scores.

**In order to display the factor score matrix it has been necessary to abbreviate the survey variables.  The full text of each of the variables listed can be found in Table 42, which provides frequency distributions for the three typologies delineated here.

TABLE 42

ATTITUDE PROFILE OF EXECUTIVE TYPOLOGIES: 1976 SURVEY

(Percentaged Vertically)

| | Factor 5 "Advocates" | Factor 7 "Conservatives" | Factor 14 "Skeptics" | Entire Sample |
|---|---|---|---|---|
| At this time, the U.S. Government should try to improve trade relations with the U.S.S.R. (TRADE). | | | | |
| Agree | 93.1% | 90.4% | 63.6% | 81.4% |
| Not sure, depends | 5.2 | 7.7 | 27.3 | 13.1 |
| Disagree | 1.7 | 1.9 | 9.1 | 5.5 |
| (N) | (58) | (52) | (11) | (199) |
| Developing stronger trade ties with the U.S.S.R. will contribute significantly to world peace (PEACE). | | | | |
| Agree | 91.4 | 88.5 | 30.8 | 72.3 |
| Not sure, depends | 8.6 | 5.8 | 15.4 | 15.8 |
| Disagree | 0 | 5.8 | 53.9 | 11.9 |
| (N) | (58) | (52) | (13) | (202) |
| In general, recent Soviet foreign policy (e.g., Angola) has adversely affected the outlook of the U.S. business community toward trade with the U.S.S.R. (HURT 1). | | | | |
| Agree | 31.0 | 55.1 | 83.3 | 56.9 |
| Not sure, depends | 32.8 | 20.4 | 8.3 | 18.8 |
| Disagree | 36.2 | 24.5 | 8.3 | 24.3 |
| (N) | (58) | (49) | (12) | (197) |

TABLE 42 (continued)

ATTITUDE PROFILE OF EXECUTIVE TYPOLOGIES:  1976 SURVEY

(Percentaged Vertically)

| | Factor 5 "Advocates" | Factor 7 "Conservatives" | Factor 14 "Skeptics" | Entire Sample |
|---|---|---|---|---|
| Specifically, recent Soviet foreign policy activities (e.g., Angola) have adversely affected your company's outlook on doing business with the U.S.S.R. (HURT 2). | | | | |
| Agree | 5.3 | 12.2 | 41.7 | 20.3 |
| Not sure, depends | 10.5 | 26.5 | 8.3 | 18.8 |
| Disagree | 84.2 | 61.2 | 50.0 | 61.0 |
| (N) | (57) | (49) | (12) | (192) |
| In general, the increased strength of communist parties in W. Europe has adversely affected the outlook of the U.S. business community toward trade with the U.S.S.R. (HURT 3). | | | | |
| Agree | 9.1 | 20.4 | 41.7 | 25.4 |
| Not sure, depends | 21.8 | 24.5 | 33.3 | 22.8 |
| Disagree | 69.1 | 55.1 | 25.0 | 51.8 |
| (N) | (55) | (49) | (12) | (189) |

TABLE 42 (continued)

ATTITUDE PROFILE OF EXECUTIVE TYPOLOGIES: 1976 SURVEY
(Percentaged Vertically)

|  | Factor 5 "Advocates" | Factor 7 "Conservatives" | Factor 14 "Skeptics" | Entire Sample |
|---|---|---|---|---|
| The increased strength of communist parties in W. Europe has adversely affected your company's outlook toward trade with the Soviets (HURT 4). | | | | |
| Agree | 0 | 10.0 | 16.7 | 13.6 |
| Not sure, depends | 7.1 | 18.0 | 8.3 | 14.1 |
| Disagree | 92.8 | 72.0 | 75.0 | 72.3 |
| (N) | (56) | (50) | (12) | (191) |
| Trade is a normal condition which should exist between two nations having diplomatic relations, and should not be conditional upon negotiable differences on world issues nor on either country's domestic political policies (NORML). | | | | |
| Agree | 87.9 | 84.3 | 25.0 | 70.7 |
| Not sure, depends | 6.9 | 5.9 | 8.3 | 11.6 |
| Disagree | 5.2 | 9.8 | 66.6 | 17.7 |
| (N) | (58) | (51) | (12) | (198) |

TABLE 42 (continued)

ATTITUDE PROFILE OF EXECUTIVE TYPOLOGIES: 1976 SURVEY

(Percentaged Vertically)

| | Factor 5 "Advocates" | Factor 7 "Conservatives" | Factor 14 "Skeptics" | Entire Sample |
|---|---|---|---|---|
| The U.S. business community has reason to fear setting up the U.S.S.R. as a future competitor in international markets in the lesser developed countries as a result of sales of American industrial knowhow to the Soviet Union (FEAR 1). | | | | |
| Agree | 19.3 | 42.0 | 58.3 | 40.8 |
| Not sure, depends | 22.8 | 20.0 | 16.7 | 17.9 |
| Disagree | 57.9 | 38.0 | 25.0 | 41.4 |
| (N) | (57) | (50) | (12) | (196) |
| The U.S. business community has reason to fear setting up the U.S.S.R. as a future competitor in international markets in the industrialized countries as a result of sales of American industrial knowhow to the Soviet Union (FEAR 2). | | | | |
| Agree | 10.7 | 35.3 | 50.0 | 31.1 |
| Not sure, depends | 7.1 | 9.8 | 25.0 | 9.7 |
| Disagree | 82.1 | 54.9 | 25.0 | 59.2 |
| (N) | (56) | (51) | (12) | (196) |

TABLE 42 (continued)

ATTITUDE PROFILE OF EXECUTIVE TYPOLOGIES: 1976 SURVEY
(Percentaged Vertically)

| | Factor 5 "Advocates" | Factor 7 "Conservatives" | Factor 14 "Skeptics" | Entire Sample |
|---|---|---|---|---|
| **If U.S.-U.S.S.R. trade were to help the Soviet civilian economy, this would not encourage Soviet leaders to increase allocations to the defense sector (DEFENS).** | | | | |
| Agree | 45.5 | 37.5 | 0 | 30.9 |
| Not sure, depends | 40.0 | 45.8 | 15.4 | 37.1 |
| Disagree | 14.5 | 16.7 | 84.6 | 31.9 |
| (N) | (55) | (48) | (13) | (194) |
| **The sale of "sensitive" high technology to the U.S.S.R. (computers, programmed machine tools, etc.) will not necessarily endanger our national security if precautions are taken by U.S. firms involved (NATSEC).** | | | | |
| Agree | 78.6 | 60.4 | 15.4 | 53.3 |
| Not sure, depends | 12.5 | 16.7 | 15.4 | 14.7 |
| Disagree | 8.9 | 22.9 | 69.3 | 32.0 |
| (N) | (56) | (48) | (13) | (197) |

TABLE 42 (continued)

ATTITUDE PROFILE OF EXECUTIVE TYPOLOGIES: 1976 SURVEY

(Percentaged Vertically)

|  | Factor 5 "Advocates" | Factor 7 "Conservatives" | Factor 14 "Skeptics" | Entire Sample |
|---|---|---|---|---|
| In terms of a "technology gap," the Soviet Union does not lag far behind the U.S. in the area of defense production; their main difficulty is the development and application of technology in the civilian sector with reference to problems of large-scale commercial production (TECGAP). |  |  |  |  |
| Agree | 80.7 | 91.8 | 90.9 | 85.1 |
| Not sure, depends | 12.3 | 4.1 | 0 | 7.7 |
| Disagree | 7.0 | 4.0 | 9.1 | 7.2 |
| (N) | (57) | (49) | (11) | (194) |
| U.S.-U.S.S.R. trade will have a significant beneficial impact on the Soviet civilian economy (SOVIND). |  |  |  |  |
| Agree | 81.0 | 72.5 | 23.1 | 69.2 |
| Not sure, depends | 12.1 | 15.7 | 15.4 | 16.7 |
| Disagree | 6.9 | 11.8 | 61.6 | 14.1 |
| (N) | (58) | (51) | (13) | (198) |

TABLE 42 (continued)

ATTITUDE PROFILE OF EXECUTIVE TYPOLOGIES: 1976 SURVEY
(Percentaged Vertically)

| | Factor 5 "Advocates" | Factor 7 "Conservatives" | Factor 14 "Skeptics" | Entire Sample |
|---|---|---|---|---|
| Prospects exist for continuous Soviet dependence on U.S. industrial knowhow in meeting practical everyday needs such as spare parts for equipment exported to the U.S.S.R. (RELY 1). | | | | |
| Agree | 85.7 | 78.4 | 75.0 | 72.4 |
| Not sure, depends | 10.7 | 13.7 | 8.3 | 12.8 |
| Disagree | 3.6 | 7.9 | 16.6 | 14.8 |
| (N) | (56) | (51) | (12) | (196) |
| If the Soviets buy advanced Western industrial technology for a period of time and then try to go it alone, they will find it impossible in their civilian economy to keep up with Western research and development (RELY 2). | | | | |
| Agree | 71.9 | 70.6 | 75.0 | 65.6 |
| Not sure, depends | 10.5 | 15.7 | 8.3 | 13.1 |
| Disagree | 17.5 | 13.8 | 16.6 | 21.3 |
| (N) | (57) | (51) | (12) | (198) |

TABLE 42 (continued)

ATTITUDE PROFILE OF EXECUTIVE TYPOLOGIES: 1976 SURVEY
(Percentaged Vertically)

| | Factor 5 "Advocates" | Factor 7 "Conservatives" | Factor 14 "Skeptics" | Entire Sample |
|---|---|---|---|---|
| **The Soviets usually buy "proven" production technology from American vendors, which soon makes it outmoded in terms of the advances we are preparing to put on line (PROVEN).** | | | | |
| Agree | 70.2 | 64.7 | 75.0 | 64.4 |
| Not sure, depends | 21.1 | 15.7 | 8.3 | 16.5 |
| Disagree | 8.8 | 19.6 | 16.7 | 19.0 |
| (N) | (57) | (51) | (12) | (194) |
| **Soviet industry possesses advanced technology already on-line which, if acquired by American firms, could greatly benefit the U.S. economy (NEWTEC).** | | | | |
| Agree | 34.5 | 22.0 | 0 | 24.5 |
| Not sure, depends | 31.0 | 28.0 | 8.3 | 25.0 |
| Disagree | 34.5 | 50.0 | 91.7 | 50.5 |
| (N) | (58) | (50) | (12) | (196) |

515

TABLE 42 (continued)

ATTITUDE PROFILE OF EXECUTIVE TYPOLOGIES: 1976 SURVEY
(Percentaged Vertically)

|  | Factor 5 "Advocates" | Factor 7 "Conservatives" | Factor 14 "Skeptics" | Entire Sample |
|---|---|---|---|---|
| Soviet scientists & industrial engineers have some innovative ideas—as yet undeveloped—which we could borrow and develop here with substantial benefits for U.S. industry (IDEAS). |  |  |  |  |
| Agree | 57.1 | 43.8 | 27.3 | 49.7 |
| Not sure, depends | 26.8 | 37.5 | 0 | 25.9 |
| Disagree | 16.1 | 18.8 | 72.8 | 24.4 |
| (N) | (56) | (48) | (11) | (193) |
| Current U.S. tariff policy toward the U.S.S.R. and restrictions on Eximbank credit are, for financial reasons, forcing the Soviets to move away from American suppliers and back toward the W. Europeans and Japanese whose governments offer the U.S.S.R. better terms of trade (FORCE). |  |  |  |  |
| Agree | 93.1 | 85.7 | 92.3 | 87.1 |
| Not sure, depends | 6.9 | 12.2 | 7.7 | 8.2 |
| Disagree | 0 | 2.0 | 0 | 4.6 |
| (N) | (58) | (49) | (13) | (194) |

## TABLE 42 (continued)

### ATTITUDE PROFILE OF EXECUTIVE TYPOLOGIES: 1976 SURVEY
(Percentaged Vertically)

| | Factor 5 "Advocates" | Factor 7 "Conservatives" | Factor 14 "Skeptics" | Entire Sample |
|---|---|---|---|---|
| **The present restrictions on Eximbank credit to the U.S.S.R. contained in the 1975 Trade Act are not justifiable in terms of future U.S. capital needs (CAPTAL).** | | | | |
| Agree | 88.7 | 55.3 | 83.3 | 66.3 |
| Not sure, depends | 9.4 | 25.5 | 8.3 | 18.8 |
| Disagree | 1.9 | 19.2 | 8.3 | 14.9 |
| (N) | (53) | (47) | (12) | (181) |
| **Trade with the U.S.S.R.'s planned economy has had a beneficial stabilizing effect on industries which are highly sensitive to fluctuations in the business cycle (STABLE).** | | | | |
| Agree | 47.3 | 45.1 | 15.4 | 43.5 |
| Not sure, depends | 25.5 | 25.5 | 23.1 | 23.6 |
| Disagree | 27.2 | 29.4 | 61.6 | 33.0 |
| (N) | (55) | (51) | (13) | (191) |

TABLE 42 (continued)

ATTITUDE PROFILE OF EXECUTIVE TYPOLOGIES: 1976 SURVEY

(Percentaged Vertically)

| | Factor 5 "Advocates" | Factor 7 "Conservatives" | Factor 14 "Skeptics" | Entire Sample |
|---|---|---|---|---|
| **Within limits set by export controls, do you personally favor <u>licensing</u> your firm's latest technology to the U.S.S.R. (LICENS)?** | | | | |
| Yes | 86.3 | 0 | 30.8 | 44.0 |
| Not sure, depends | 0 | 0 | 0 | 1.6 |
| No | 13.7 | 100 | 69.2 | 54.3 |
| (N) | (51) | (49) | (13) | (184) |
| **Within limits set by export controls, do you personally favor <u>product</u> sales to the U.S.S.R. incorporating your firm's latest technology (SALES)?** | | | | |
| Yes | 100 | 100 | 100 | 89.6 |
| Not sure, depends | 0 | 0 | 0 | 2.2 |
| No | 0 | 0 | 0 | 8.2 |
| (N) | (51) | (48) | (13) | (182) |

detente. In other words, Factor 5 denotes those SAEs who in 1976 were most supportive of closer economic and political relations with the U.S.S.R. Thus, Factor 5 is seemingly analogous to the "pro-detente" dimension which was generated by the second-order R-analysis of Survey 2.

By way of illustration, an extremely strong belief in the positive character of Soviet-American trade is indicated by factor scores of -.61 for the TRADE variable, -.68 for PEACE, and -.60 for RELY1. In concrete terms, these respective factor scores translate into the following opinion distributions: Compared to 81.4% for the overall survey sample, 93.1% of the Advocates supported continued U.S. Government efforts to develop closer trade relations with the Soviet Union. Similarly, in contrast with 72.3% for the entire sample, 91.4% of those comprising Factor 5 believed that closer trade ties with the U.S.S.R. will contribute significantly to world peace. Lastly, compared with 72.4% for the overall sample, 85.7% of the executives belonging to this typology felt that U.S.-Soviet trade might result in long-term Soviet technological dependence on U.S. industrial knowhow for meeting practical everyday needs (e.g., spare parts for machinery exported to the U.S.S.R.).

Given their enthusiasm for Soviet-American trade and detente, it should not be surprising that SAEs delineated by Factor 5 had a corresponding tendency to minimize the economic and national security risks connected with the expansion of U.S.-U.S.S.R. commercial relations. For instance, reflecting a strong factor score of -1.60 for the DEFENS item, only 14.5% of the Advocates (as opposed to 31.9% for the entire survey sample) thought that economic benefits obtained from trade with the U.S. might encourage Soviet leaders to boost military spending. Instead, as suggested by a factor score of -.39 for the SOVIND item, 81.0% of the Advocates (compared with 69.2% for the overall sample) believed that the Soviet civilian economy and, hence, Soviet consumers would be the primary beneficiaries of the U.S.S.R.'s commercial contacts with the United States. Consistent with these views and reflecting a factor score of -1.08 on NATSEC, 78.6% of those comprising Factor 5 (as opposed to 53.3% for the entire sample) felt that sales of "sensitive" high technology to the Soviet Union will not necessarily endanger U.S. national security. Similarly, the Advocates on the whole dismissed the possibility that transfers of U.S. industrial knowhow might help the Soviet Union to become an effective international competitor of American business. As indicated by a factor score of .93 for the FEAR1 item, only 19.3% of those belonging to this typology felt that the U.S. business community has reason to fear setting up the

U.S.S.R. as a future commercial competitor in LDCs, whereas the comparable figure for the entire sample was 40.8%. Likewise, reflecting a factor score of 1.23 for FEAR2, a mere 10.7% of the Advocates feared the prospect of future Soviet business competition in industrialized countries, compared to a much larger 31.1% for the overall survey sample.

In light of such views, it is to be expected that those businessmen denoted by Factor 5 also evinced a strong positive orientation toward the licensing of knowhow to the U.S.S.R. Indeed, this is a major distinguishing feature of this typology: Whereas 44% of all respondents to Survey 2 favored licensing their latest corporate technology to the Soviets, this was true for an overwhelming 86.3% of the Advocates (as indicated by a factor score of -1.54 on the LICENS item).

It follows from the preceding opinions that the Advocates were considerably more disturbed than other executives about U.S. Government policies inhibiting the development of U.S. commercial relations with the Soviets. Hence, mirroring a factor score of -.92 for NORML, 82.9% of Factor 5's constituent members (compared with 70.7% for the overall sample) opposed linking federal trade policies toward the U.S.S.R. (e.g., MFN tariff status) to Soviet performance on outstanding world issues and human rights

questions (e.g., Angola, Jewish emigration). Reflecting a
factor score of -.91 for CAPTAL, 88.7% of the Advocates (as
opposed to 66.3% for the entire sample) also felt that the
U.S. Government's legislative restrictions on Eximbank
credit to the Soviets cannot be justified in terms of
future U.S. capital requirements. Additionally, in
contrast with 87.1% for the overall sample, 93.1% of the
Advocates believed that U.S. tariff policy and restrictions
on Eximbank lending to the U.S.S.R. are, for financial
reasons, forcing the Soviets away from American suppliers
and towards West European/Japanese companies (a view
indicated by a factor score of -.45 for FORCE). In fact,
72.4% of the Advocates held this conviction "strongly,"
whereas the same was true of a comparatively smaller 58.2%
of all 1976 respondents.

Finally, to complete this internally consistent train
of thought, Advocates were much more apt than other SAEs to
disavow any negative impact of then-recent Soviet
international behavior on U.S. corporate attitudes toward
trade with the U.S.S.R.: As highlighted by a factor score
of 1.27 for HURT1, only 31.0% of the executives comprising
Factor 5 (compared to 56.9% for the overall sample)
reported that recent Soviet foreign policy activities
(e.g., the Angola affair) had adversely affected the
outlook of the entire U.S. business community on doing

business with the Soviets.  Likewise, reflecting a factor score of 1.98 for HURT2, only 5.3% of the Advocates (as opposed to 20.3% for the entire sample) indicated that recent Soviet foreign policy activities had caused their own companies to adopt a more cautious stance towards the Soviet market.  In addition, only 9.1% of the Advocates (compared to 25.4% for the overall sample) felt that the then-growing power of West European communist parties had adversely affected the willingness of the entire American business community to participate in U.S.-Soviet trade (as indicated by a factor score of 1.58 on HURT3).  Consequently whereas 13.6% of all respondents said that the increasing influence of the Eurocommunists had made their companies more reluctant to pursue Soviet commercial opportunities, none of the Advocates acknowledged any such effect (as suggested by a factor score of 1.74 for HURT4).

To sum up, Factor 5 crystallizes numerous findings presented in Chapters IV-VI to provide a more comprehensive perspective on SAEs' support for trade/detente as well as a more complete understanding of their eagerness to do business with the United States' principal international adversary.  Hence, second-order Q-Factor 5 is in certain respects similar to second-order R-Factor 3 (the "pro-detente" dimension), which was described earlier in this chapter. Both the aforementioned dimensions, as well as several other factors that have been discussed so far, reaffirm the proposition that businessmen tended to formulate their views on U.S.-Soviet economic and political relations in the context of overall U.S. national interests. Additionally, second-order Q-Factor 5 once again underlines the observation that businessmen generally rejected the notion of U.S.-Soviet trade as a "one-way street" benefiting the U.S.S.R. Instead, second-order Q-Factor 5 further highlights the fact that most executives believed that the United States can obtain important political and economic benefits from a commercial relationship with the U.S.S.R., while simultaneously minimizing the potential liabilities of such trade ties.

## Factor 7

Second-order Factor 7 is principally defined by first-order Factor 2, Group A (FACA02), and first-order Factor 2, Group B (FACB02). A total of 52 executives (i.e., 26.0% of the 200 businessmen in the original correlation matrix) loaded strongly on these two first-order factors, thereby making Factor 7 the second most populous higher-order typology. A careful evaluation of the factor scores and frequency distributions for Factor 7 indicates that this dimension is roughly equivalent to Factor 1 of the 1975 Q-analysis. Like its counterpart from

Survey 1, Factor 7 delineates a group of "Conservatives"
who advocated a cautious business strategy towards the
Soviet Union. Once again, these Conservatives can be
differentiated from other executives primarily by their
intense opposition to the transfer of up-to-date U.S.
industrial technology to the U.S.S.R. Reflecting an
extremely high factor score of 3.35 on the LICENS item,
100% of the executives comprising Factor 7 (compared to
54.3% for the overall 1976 sample) were against licensing
their firms' latest knowhow to the Soviets.

However, apart from their opposition to licensing, the
businessmen delineated by Factor 7 are fairly typical of
most respondents to Survey 2 (just as the 1975
Conservatives are generally representative of most
respondents to Survey 1). Again, importance must be
attached to the fact that those belonging to this typology
were not unusually anxious about the possibility that U.S.
technology might help set up the U.S.S.R. as an effective
international competitor of American business. Indeed,
responses of the Conservatives on the competitor issue are
virtually identical to those for the overall 1976 survey
sample. Hence, Factor 7, like its 1975 counterpart,
further supports the survey and interview data outlined in
Chapter V, which suggest that in 1975-1976 numerous
executives opposed licensing technology to the Soviet Union

for a host of reasons not associated with the fear of possible future Soviet competition (e.g., perceptions of political risk, the inherent complexity of licensing agreements, and frustration with Soviet negotiating tactics).[13]

Finally, it merits attention that Factor 7 lends additional credibility to the thesis (outlined in Chapter V) that even under highly favorable U.S.-Soviet political conditions many American businessmen would still refrain from licensing their technology to the U.S.S.R. Likewise, Factor 7 supports the proposition that even if most existing national security controls on U.S. exports to the Soviet Union were eliminated, many firms interested in product transactions with the U.S.S.R. would nevertheless hesitate to involve themselves in licensing agreements.[14]

## Factor 14

Second-order Factor 14 is principally defined by first-order Factor 3, Group A (FACA03), and first-order Factor 10, Group B (FACB10). A total of 13 businessmen (i.e., 6.5% of the executives in the original correlation matrix) loaded strongly on these two first-order factors, thereby making Factor 14 the least populous of the interpretable second-order typologies. A thorough review of factor scores and frequency distributions for Factor 14 reveals that this dimension is the antithesis of

second-order Q-Factor 5. Whereas Factor 5 denotes those
SAEs who were enthusiastic "Advocates" of closer economic
and political relations with the U.S.S.R., Factor 14
delineates a small group of "Skeptics" who were much less
supportive of Soviet-American trade and detente. As will
be shown below, Factor 14 is clearly the Q-equivalent of
the "national welfare" dimension outlined by Factor 1 of
the 1976 first-order R-factor analysis. Like its R
counterpart, Q-Factor 14 underscores the impact of
then-recent Soviet international activities on SAEs'
orientations on a wide range of U.S.-Soviet issues.

A central distinguishing characteristic of Factor 14
is that the Skeptics reacted much more strongly than other
executives to reports of Soviet interventionist behavior in
Angola, the Horn of Africa, etc. Reflecting a factor score
of -1.33 for HURT1, 83.3% of those comprising this typology
(compared to 56.9% for the overall survey sample) reported
that recent Soviet foreign policy activities had adversely
affected the outlook of the entire U.S. business community
on doing business with the Soviets. Similarly, mirroring a
factor score of .66 for HURT2, 41.7% of the Skeptics (as
opposed to 20.3% for the entire sample) indicated that
Soviet foreign policy activities had caused their own
companies to adopt a more cautious stance towards the
Soviet market.

Consequently, the Skeptics were more doubtful than other businessmen that U.S.-Soviet trade/detente would yield economic and political benefits to the United States. This is suggested by factor scores of .71 for PEACE, 1.32 for STABLE, 1.09 for NEWTEC, and .49 for IDEAS. As is evident from Table 42, these respective factor scores are indicative of the following opinion distributions: In contrast with 72.3% of the entire 1976 survey sample, only 30.8% of those comprising Factor 14 believed that closer trade ties with the U.S.S.R. will contribute significantly to world peace. Also, compared to 43.5% for the overall sample, a mere 15.4% of the Skeptics (i.e., only 2 executives) thought that trade with the Soviet Union's planned economy will have a beneficial stabilizing effect on U.S. industries which are highly sensitive to fluctuations in the business cycle. In addition, whereas 24.5% of the entire sample felt that U.S. industry might acquire useful on-line advanced technology from the U.S.S.R., this possibility was unanimously dismissed by Factor 14's constituent members. Similarly, only 27.3% of the Skeptics, compared to 49.7% for all respondents, characterized Soviet scientists and engineers as having innovative ideas which U.S. companies might acquire and develop.

Complementing their disparagement of the benefits of U.S.-Soviet commerce, the Skeptics had a corresponding propensity to magnify the national security risks posed by trade with the U.S.S.R. For instance, reflecting a factor score of 1.58 for SOVIND, only 23.1% of those belonging to this typology (as opposed to a large majority of 69.2% for the overall sample) thought that the Soviet civilian economy and Soviet consumers would be important beneficiaries of the U.S.S.R.'s commercial contacts with the United States. Rather, most of the Skeptics apparently believed that a principal Soviet goal in expanding trade with the West is to enhance the U.S.S.R.'s defense capabilities via purchases of foreign technology and manufacturing capacity. Hence, as indicated by a factor score of -.64 for DEFENS, a striking 84.6% of the Skeptics (compared to only 31.9% for the entire survey sample) held the view that economic benefits obtained from trade with the U.S. might encourage Soviet leaders to boost military spending. In addition, as suggested by a factor score of .80 for NATSEC, 69.3% of those comprising Factor 14 (as opposed to a meager 32.0% for the overall sample) felt that sales of "sensitive" high technology to the Soviet Union will necessarily endanger U.S. national security. Evidently, the Skeptics had great respect for the technological capabilities of the Soviet military establishment, and did not wish to see the U.S. compromise its slim technical lead in the defense area. Consistent with this interpretation and reflecting a factor score of -.67 for TECGAP, 72.7% of the Skeptics, compared to 45.4% of all survey respondents, felt "strongly" that the technological level of the U.S.S.R.'s military sector does not lag far behind that of the U.S.

Given the above concerns for the national welfare, it should not be surprising that the Skeptics also tended to amplify the economic risks associated with the transfer of U.S. industrial knowhow to the Soviet Union: As indicated by a factor score of -.42 for FEAR1, a 58.3% majority of those in this typology believed that the U.S. business community has reason to fear setting up the U.S.S.R. as a future commercial competitor in the LDCs, whereas the comparable figure for the overall survey sample was 40.8%. Also, corresponding to a factor score of -.82 for FEAR2, 50.2% of the Skeptics feared the prospect of future Soviet business competition in industrialized countries, in contrast with 31.1% for the entire sample.

It follows from all the preceding that the Skeptics were less enthusiastic than other executives about U.S. Government efforts to improve economic relations with the U.S.S.R. Whereas 81.4% of the overall survey sample thought that federal authorities should endeavor to build

closer trade ties with the Soviets, this was true of a
comparatively smaller majority of 63.6% of the Skeptics
(reflecting a factor score of 1.04 on TRADE). Also, 27.3%
of the Skeptics were "not sure" whether they supported U.S.
Government efforts to boost Soviet-American commerce,
whereas only 13.1% of all survey respondents expressed such
uncertainty.

It is noteworthy that the Skeptics' anxieties about
U.S.-Soviet trade/detente were primarily manifested in
terms of increased opposition to the transfer of U.S.
industrial knowhow to the Soviet Union. Although they were
still willing in principle to engage in high-technology
product transactions with the Soviets, 69.2% of those
comprising Factor 14 (compared to 54.3% for the overall
sample) opposed licensing their latest corporate technology
to the U.S.S.R. This, of course, is consistent with
findings presented in Chapter V, which suggest that SAEs'
growing perceptions of Soviet international "adventurism"
had a disproportionately adverse impact on businessmen's
willingness to license knowhow as opposed to their
willingness to sell technology in the form of products.

In sum, Q-Factor 14, like first-order R-Factor 1 (the
"national welfare" dimension), brings into sharp focus a
central discovery of personal interviews; i.e., that
certain executives displayed a nascent distrust of the

Soviets and had a corresponding tendency to question the
wisdom of trade with the U.S.S.R. from the standpoint of
the U.S. national interest. Likewise, Q-Factor 14 further
supports the proposition (advanced in both Chapters IV and
V) that emerging suspicions of the U.S.S.R.'s basic motives
vis-a-vis the United States seemingly caused some
businessmen to reformulate their conceptions of their
corporate self-interests in Soviet trade. This is
manifested in terms of the Skeptics' heightened opposition
to technology licensing and their amplified fears of
setting up the U.S.S.R. as a future U.S. business
competitor. Finally, Q-Factor 14 lends additional
credibility to Linkage Scenarios 8, 9, and 10 (see Chapters
IV and V) which postulate that executives' growing
perceptions of Soviet "adventurism" and their resulting
distrust of the U.S.S.R. may have resulted in corporate
behavior counter-productive to the stability of
Soviet-American commercial and political relations.[15]

FOOTNOTES

[1]For a thorough explanation of the techniques employed in the R-factor analysis of the 1975 survey data, see above, pp. 107-109.

[2]A detailed description of the procedures used to Q-factor analyze the 1975 survey data can be found above, pp. 110-115.

[3]For information on the calculation and interpretation of factor scores, see Chapter III, footnote 6, pp. 125-126.

[4]A comprehensive presentation of survey findings on the issues of licensing and technology-transfer can be found above, pp. 257-280.

[5]See pp. 107-109 above for a complete accounting of the methods employed to R-factor analyze the 1976 survey data.

[6]For further discussion of executives' "national welfare" response to international developments during 1975-1976 see Chapter IV, pp. 182-184. Details regarding Linkage Scenarios 8 and 9 can be found in Chapter IV, pp. 197-203. Linkage Scenario 10 is elaborated in Chapter V, pp. 328-330.

[7]For data on businessmen's views on the dependency issue, see above, pp. 300-304.

[8]SAEs' opinions on the prospects for obtaining technology from the Soviet Union can be found on pp. 304-308.

[9]See pp. 335-338 for an outline of Linkage Scenario 12.

[10]An inventory of survey findings on technology transfer and licensing questions can be found above, pp. 257-280.

[11]Data regarding Linkage Scenarios 8 and 9 can be found in Chapter IV, pp. 197-203. Linkage Scenario 10 is elaborated in Chapter V, pp. 328-330.

[12]For a comprehensive explanation of the methods used to extract second-order Q-factors from the 1976 survey data, see Chapter III, pp. 115-120.

[13]For these views, see pp. 266-268.

[14]See pp. 331-332 for further discussion of these hypotheses.

[15]For details concerning Linkage Scenarios 8 and 9, see pp. 197-203. Further information on Scenario 10 is presented on pp. 328-330.

CHAPTER VIII

FINAL CONCLUSIONS

Having presented the findings of the R and Q factor
analyses, all research data and the interpretations
attached to these data have now been reported. Thus, it
remains to summarize briefly the most salient propositions/
hypotheses derived throughout the course of this
wide-ranging study, as well as to set forth some concluding
theoretical and substantive remarks.

## Summary of Central Propositions/Hypotheses

(1) It will be extremely difficult ever to establish an
enduring, vigorous, and broad-based Soviet-American
trading relationship as the cornerstone of a superpower
detente. Contrary to an underlying assumption of the
"spill-over" hypothesis, there would seem to be ample
reason to doubt that U.S.-Soviet trade, even when
founded on reciprocal economic benefit, has an inherent
stability not easily disrupted by political events.
Domestic U.S. political forces beyond the purview of any
governmental authority (e.g., trends in U.S. public
opinion) may easily disturb the continuity of U.S.-
Soviet trade by influencing the business decision-making
calculus of American companies. To a lesser degree the
same can be said of international political events over
which neither superpower has direct control (e.g., West
European political trends). Similarly, to the extent'
that the Soviet Union pursues interventionist foreign
policies, this may inadvertently albeit seriously undercut any Soviet efforts to build lasting commercial
contacts with U.S. firms. Under the aforementioned
adverse circumstances, negative corporate reactions are
apt to stem from one or more of the following factors:
fears of a possible domestic political backlash against

534

U.S. firms engaged in Soviet business, perceptions
that Soviet business entails unusual "political risks"
(e.g., uncertainties connected with U.S. export
controls), perceptions of the U.S.S.R. as a marginal
and secondary growth market, and nascent doubts about
whether Soviet trade is in U.S. national interests.

(2) U.S. businessmen seemingly have a deeply ingrained
resistance to political involvement in controversial
U.S.-Soviet issues.  Therefore, even given a favorable
climate of public opinion, it is doubtful that the
U.S. business community will ever become an energetic
and consistent political force working for closer
Soviet-American economic and political relations.  A
corollary to the preceding is that any future Soviet
effort to foster a united, vigorous pro-detente,
pro-trade U.S. corporate lobby in the United States
will likely be frustrated by businessmen's innate
reluctance to embroil themselves in national debates
on U.S.-Soviet policy questions.

(3) It follows from (1) and (2) above that any
increase in U.S.-Soviet tension and/or decline in U.S.
public support for U.S.-Soviet trade/detente will tend
to reduce any on-going pro-trade, pro-detente
political activity by U.S. business at the very time
that such activity could be especially helpful in
promoting the stability of U.S. commercial policies
toward the U.S.S.R. and in moderating U.S. Government
political responses to perceived Soviet threats.

(4) In light of the Soviets' time-consuming
negotiating habits and the U.S.S.R.'s reputation as an
expensive place in which to do business, many
businessmen clearly viewed the Soviet Union as a
residual growth market; i.e., the U.S.S.R. was seen as
a customer to be courted during bad economic times but
relegated to secondary importance during good times.
Consequently, assuming a direct connection between
immediate corporate well-being and the likelihood of
corporate political action, it follows that the U.S.
business community's political support for Soviet
trade, to the extent this occurs, will tend to vary
inversely with the availability of traditional
domestic and international markets for U.S. products.
Viewed differently, even if a domestic political
environment conducive to Soviet-American trade could
one day be established, this fragile political climate
could well be difficult to maintain for long, because
fluctuating U.S. and world business conditions, by

reducing corporate incentives to engage in pro-trade, pro-detente political action, might help to destabilize the underlying balance of political forces in the United States.

(5) Since U.S. business would seem to be the primary U.S. political constituency for Soviet trade and given the low probability that this constituency will ever be willing to act as a forceful political counterweight to pervasive anti-Soviet sentiments in American society, it is questionable whether federal policy-makers can ever be made responsive to U.S. commercial interests in managing relations with the U.S.S.R. Thus, a robust Soviet-American trade relationship, even if one could be created, might easily fail to have any appreciable moderating influence on the U.S. Government's foreign policy approach toward the U.S.S.R. Instead, the U.S. Government may invariably be inclined to view trade with the U.S.S.R. as a convenient tool of U.S. policy rather than as a key component of policy around which other considerations revolve. Hence, the development of any future economic interdependencies between the United States and the Soviet Union likely will automatically tend to be regarded by U.S. political authorities as new opportunities for exerting leverage on the U.S.S.R. rather than as added incentives for mitigating conflict in non-commercial areas. Conversely, U.S.-Soviet trade may be more effective in fostering international political restraint among Soviet leaders than among their U.S. counterparts; due in large measure to the relatively greater insulation of the U.S.S.R.'s foreign policy process from capricious domestic political influences.

(6) Any U.S. Government efforts to fine-tune Soviet-American trade in accordance with broad U.S. policy objectives may be doomed to ineffectiveness. This is because repeated shifts in U.S. trade policies toward the U.S.S.R. will tend to foster increasing U.S. business fears of future policy reversals, thereby generating growing hesitancy to invest heavily in the Soviet market in response to any warmup in superpower relations. Stated otherwise, U.S.-Soviet trade may be calibrated downward rather easily, but it may be much more difficult to calibrate trade in an upward direction. Hence, any attempt by the U.S. Government to calibrate its Soviet trade policies with respect to Soviet political behavior may have unforeseen side effects injurious to long-term prospects for improved Soviet-American economic and political relations.

(7) Unlike straightforward product sales, licensing transactions involving transfers of industrial knowhow to the U.S.S.R. require the maintenance of mutual trust between U.S. and Soviet business partners for an extended period. Since mutual trust is an intrinsically fragile commodity, it follows that U.S. corporate fears and anxieties resulting from any deterioration in the East-West political environment [see (1) above] will tend to have a substantially greater impact on U.S. companies' willingness to grant industrial licenses to the Soviets than on their willingness to conclude transactions consisting primarily of equipment. More specifically, the undermining of U.S. businessmen's trust in the U.S.S.R. will tend to be manifested in terms of nascent U.S. business suspicions that the Soviets might misuse licensed American technology to the detriment of U.S. national and corporate interests (e.g., diversion of imported technology to military applications, employing American technology to compete with U.S. companies for world markets). Since licensing is one of the most efficient forms of technology-transfer, it follows that any negative impact of political factors on the willingness of U.S. companies to issue licenses to the U.S.S.R. will prove particularly damaging to any Soviet efforts to acquire and effectively utilize American corporate technology.

(8) Even under extremely positive U.S.-Soviet political circumstances a great many American businessmen would still be inhibited from licensing knowhow to the Soviets. Indeed, even if most existing national security controls on U.S. exports to the U.S.S.R. were abolished, it is probable that many U.S. companies interested in entering into product transactions with the Soviets would still balk at getting involved in licensing arrangements. The likelihood of such self-restraint stems in large measure from numerous executives' fundamental disapproval of licensing--not just with respect to the U.S.S.R. but as a matter of general principle--because of the unusually complicated and long-term nature of licensing contracts, major difficulties in pricing licenses to insure a fair return, and deep-seated fears that transfers of industrial knowhow may one day transform one's customers into viable competitors. Even among those businessmen not irreconcilably opposed to licensing, there would still likely be substantial reluctance to pursue license negotiations because of the Soviets' reputation as difficult business negotiators and

executives' perceptions that this would magnify the
knotty problems normally connected with any license.

(9) It follows from proposition (8) as well as (4) that
inflexible and time-consuming Soviet business
negotiating tactics, which are designed to shave
Western profit margins and secure other contract
concessions, may result instead in various unforeseen
side-effects contrary to the U.S.S.R.'s overall
interests in its relations with the United States.
Specifically, it can be stated that stubborn and
ingrained Soviet commercial practices can act as an
additional obstacle to a vigorous U.S.-U.S.S.R.
economic relationship, help to destroy businessmen's
incentive to exercise their political muscle on behalf
of Soviet-American trade and detente, and generally
complicate U.S.-Soviet conflict management.

## Directions for Future Research

As suggested by the preceding hypotheses/propositions

(as well as those of lesser consequence scattered

throughout the preceding chapters) this research effort has

yielded multi-faceted results of fundamental theoretical

and substantive importance. For example, it has been

established that certain "obvious" linkage processes (i.e.,

those which postulate the U.S. business community as a

strong political advocate of Soviet trade) may at best have

only limited validity. Conversely, survey and interview

findings are suggestive of numerous other scenarios, which,

from an historical standpoint, seemingly have substantial

explanatory potential. As has been noted at appropriate

points throughout the text, those scenarios and derivative

propositions which are supported by gathered empirical data

may collectively provide new insights into the gradual

demise of U.S.-Soviet detente which occurred throughout the
latter half of the 1970s.  Additionally, although the
scenarios and propositions are based on information
collected during 1975-1976, they nevertheless have a
timeless quality and are clearly of great relevance to the
present and future conduct of Soviet-American relations.
To the extent that these research findings and theoretical
statements receive attention in Washington and Moscow, they
may help to educate policy-makers to some potential
consequences of their actions of which they might otherwise
be unaware.  Given honorable intentions on the part of both
superpowers, a better understanding of the past might one
day help to facilitate a future U.S.-Soviet accommodation
as well as to place any trade between the two nations on a
firmer foundation.  In particular, it should be
self-evident that the results of this study have major
import for the Reagan Administration's on-going efforts to
develop and administer coherent, well-founded political and
commercial policies vis-a-vis the Soviet Union.  Once
again, as in past administrations, the issues of economic
"leverage," technology-transfer, the relationship of
East-West trade to Soviet military capabilities, etc., are
all being debated vigorously.

It remains, however, that the scenarios and
propositions postulated in this study are not definitive,

but are merely tentative theoretical statements which require further testing. Thus, while these hypotheses may provide food for thought and may be factored into debates on policy, they are in themselves an insufficient basis on which to found policy. Additional investigation into questions raised in the course of this research is necessary. Indeed, this would seem imperative given the negative implications of many of the hypotheses for the continuing evolution of U.S.-Soviet relations. Further study is also needed to determine with greater precision the extent to which findings and theoretical statements presented here can be inferred beyond the Soviet-American case.

For instance, it has been shown that the dynamics of U.S. corporate decision-making give considerable cause to doubt the efficacy of the "spill-over" hypothesis with respect to U.S.-U.S.S.R. relations. What is uncertain, however, is the degree to which similar U.S. corporate factors might serve to undermine the spill-over hypothesis generally; e.g., as applied to the developing U.S. political relationship with the People's Republic of China.

Also, it has repeatedly been noted that businessmen apparently formulated their views on U.S.-Soviet trade/detente in the context of broad U.S. national interests, not their parochial corporate interests. Does this finding simply reflect the unique national security aspects of U.S.-U.S.S.R. relations, or is it generally true of U.S. businessmen's views on most foreign policy matters? Despite some work by other researchers which tends to support the latter conclusion, additional investigation into this question would seem warranted. Likewise, survey and interview results provide tantalizing indications that shifts in executives' perceptions of the national interest in U.S.-Soviet economic/political relations led to shifts in some individuals' perceptions of corporate self-interest. To say the least, this is a provocative suggestion which merits further attention by other analysts.

Additionally, the Soviet-American case suggests that economic self-interest cannot simply be equated with the pursuit of profit but must also incorporate concepts such as the "security of the firm." In this connection it was noted that, when assessing potential dangers to the firm, businessmen evidently assign substantial weight to domestic and international political factors. It was subsequently argued that since the political (as well as economic) variables which enter into businessmen's evaluations of their firms' self-interests are likely to vary from company to company as well as from situation to situation, it may well be impossible to operationalize corporate "self-interest" consistently for purposes of political analysis. These propositions concerning the nature of corporate self-interest obviously demand further scrutiny, for they clearly have important and wide-ranging implications for the conduct of future empirical research into the political behavior of U.S. companies.

Yet another fertile area for additional investigation is the extent to which businessmen through their companies are apt to translate their moral support for a political position into concrete political action on behalf of that position. Relevant here, of course, is the finding that although many executives strongly supported Soviet-American trade/detente as matters of principle, these same executives were highly averse to taking practical political measures consistent with their policy preferences. Numerous political and economic environmental factors, as well as certain ideological biases which appear basic to the political culture of U.S. business, clearly constrained businessmen from taking a political lead in national policy debates on U.S.-U.S.S.R. economic and political issues. As suggested in a series of specific propositions advanced in Chapter VI, it could be that such influences may generally inhibit U.S. business from exercising its political muscle on a host of domestic and international issues. Once again, pioneering work by a number of other analysts tends to corroborate the preceding hypothesis, but much more research remains to be done.

On a related subject, one of the most fascinating findings of this study is the extent to which senior U.S. businessmen tended to exhibit aspects of U.S. political culture often ascribed to the proverbial man-in-the-street. To reiterate an observation made in Chapter VI, American executives who participated in this research effort contrasted sharply with the image of a politically omnipotent "power elite" as presented by Mills and others. Rather, the empirical findings of surveys and interviews depict a population which can variously be described as politically insecure, naive, disinterested, frustrated, cynical, and alienated. Indeed, for reasons which are totally unclear, some businessmen seemingly had a better understanding of the subtleties of Soviet-American relations and of the Soviet political system than they did of the U.S. political system. Once again, although these observations pertain specifically to the Soviet-American case, they have broad implications that merit further study by political scientists.

In conclusion, this comprehensive and innovative analysis has charted a number of important new directions for political research both with regard to the dynamics of Soviet-American relations and as concerns the overall

relationship of U.S. corporate actors to domestic and
international political processes. Likewise, considerable
evidence has been produced indicating that U.S.
businessmen's political thinking and motivations may
generally be much more complex than has been assumed by
many political scientists. Perhaps most important,
however, is that this ambitious effort has demonstrated
unequivocally that large-scale empirical research on the
U.S. business community can yield meaningful results
despite the presence of formidable methodological
obstacles. Thus, it is hoped that this study will serve as
a stimulus to other analysts who might otherwise be
deterred from scientific investigations of corporate
political actors.

BIBLIOGRAPHY

I.  Background Material

A.  Political

"Americans Endorse Detente."  Current Opinion, March 1976,
        pp. 28-29.

"America's Hopes for Future."  Current Opinion, February
        1973, p. 4.

"Approve of Kissinger."  Current Opinion, September 1976,
        p. 98.

Armitage, John A.  "The Political Climate and U.S.-Soviet
        Trade."  Columbia Journal of World Business 8
        (December 1973):  42-46.

"At European Summit, Russia Will Achieve a Major Goal."
        U.S. News & World Report, July 28, 1975, pp. 17-18.

Ball, George W.  "Capitulation at Helsinki."  Newsweek,
        August 4, 1975, p. 13.

Ball, George W., ed. Global Companies:  The Political
        Economy of World Business.  Englewood Cliffs, N.J.:
        Prentice-Hall, 1975.

Barbash,Fred.  "U.S. Export Licenses Are Linked to Soviet
        Cooperation."  Washington Post, 26 June 1978, p. 45.

"Battle Over Weaponry:  B-1, AWACS, Cruise Missile, . . ."
        Congressional Quarterly:  Weekly Report, March 27,
        1976, pp. 4-5.

"Behind U.S. Threats to Cuba."  U.S. News & World Report,
        April 5, 1976, pp. 21-22.

Behrman, Jack N.; Boddewyn, J. J.; and Kapoor, Ashok.
        International Business-Government Communications.
        Lexington, Mass.: D.C. Heath, 1975.

Benjamin, Milton R. "A Russian Scorecard." _Newsweek_,
     August 11, 1975, pp. 35-36.

Benjamin, Milton R., and Clark, Evert. "Message from
     Moscow." _Newsweek_, June 27, 1977, pp. 14-16.

Bergsen, Abram; Goldman, Marshall; and Holzman, Franklyn.
     "Trends and Prospects in U.S.-U.S.S.R. Economic
     Relations." Cambridge, Mass.: Russian Research
     Center, Harvard University, 1974. (Mimeographed.)

"Big Push for Detente: Is U.S. Moving Too Fast?" _U.S.
     News & World Report_, July 28, 1975, pp. 12-13.

Buchan, David. "Carter Stops Computer Sale to Russians."
     _Financial Times_ (London), 19 July 1978, p. 1.

Buchan, David. "New Rebuff for Russia but Schlesinger to
     Visit China." _Financial Times_ (London), 26 July
     1978, p. 4.

Burnham, James. "Bulletins from the Detente Front."
     _National Review_, July 20, 1973, p. 779.

Butler, David; Coleman, Fred; and Whitmore, J. "To Catch a
     Foreigner." _Newsweek_, July 3, 1978, p. 42.

Butler, David; Coleman, Fred; and Sullivan, Scott.
     "Moscow's Zigzags." _Newsweek_, July 10, 1978,
     p. 40.

Butler, David; DeFrank, Thomas M.; Clift, Eleanor; and
     Sullivan, Scott. "Zbig on the Rise." _Newsweek_,
     June 12, 1978, pp. 28-29.

"Campaign Fodder." _Time_, September 18, 1972, pp. 19-20.

Campbell, Robert W., and Marer, Paul, eds. _East-West Trade
     and Technology Transfer: An Agenda of Research
     Needs_. Bloomington, Ind.: Indiana University
     Press, 1974.

"Carter May Counter Soviet Actions." _Journal of Commerce_ 18
     July 1978, p. 10.

Casey, William R. "Soviet Union Should Receive Most Favored
     Nation Status." _Journal of Commerce_, 12 July 1978,
     p. 4.

"The Chevrolet Summit of Modest Hopes." _Time_, July 8, 1974, pp. 9-12.

"CIA Estimates of Soviet Defense Expenditures." _Congressional Quarterly: Weekly Report_, March 27, 1976, p. 7.

Cocks, Paul; Daniels, Robert V.; and Heer, Nancy W., eds. _The Dynamics of Soviet Politics_. Cambridge, Mass.: Harvard University Press, 1977.

Coleman, Fred. "Crawford's Complaint." _Newsweek_, July 17, 1978, p. 24.

Committee for Economic Development. _A New Trade Policy Toward Communist Countries_. New York: Committee for Economic Development, 1972.

"Congressmen Urging Soviet Trial Protest." _Journal of Commerce_, 12 July 1978, p. 9.

"Congress Weighs Risks, Benefits of Detente." _Congressional Quarterly: Weekly Report_, September 14, 1974, pp. 17-21.

Cousins, Norman. "Brief Encounter with A. Solzhenitsyn." _Saturday Review_, August 23, 1975, pp. 4-6.

"Criticism of Defense Budget Declines Amid Perceptions of Growing Soviet Military Power." _Gallup Opinion Index_, Report 129, April 1976, pp. 19-21.

"Dead Wrong to Trust Russia." _U.S. News & World Report_, March 15, 1976, pp. 29-32. (Interview with Donald H. Rumsfeld, Secretary of Defense.)

"Dealing with the Russians." _Newsweek_, July 24, 1972, pp. 57-58.

De Borchgrave, Arnaud. "Russia's Trade Coup." _Newsweek_, July 26, 1976, pp. 52-53.

"Defense, Foreign Policy Poll." _Congressional Quarterly: Weekly Report_, October 9, 1976, p. 3.

Deming, Angus; Sullivan, Scott; DeFrank, Thomas M.; and Coleman, Fred. "A Challenge to Carter." _Newsweek_, July 17, 1978, pp. 22-24.

Deming, Angus; Sullivan, Scott; DeFrank, Thomas M.;
and Coleman, Fred. "A New Cold War?" Newsweek,
June 12, 1978, pp. 26-27, 29-30, 36-37.

Deming, Angus; Sullivan, Scott; Clift, Eleanor; DeFrank,
Thomas M.; and Coleman, Fred. "Show of Strength."
Newsweek, July 3, 1978, pp. 20-21.

Deming, Angus; Sullivan, Scott; Clift, Eleanor; and Coleman,
Fred. "Strong Words for Moscow." Newsweek, June
19, 1978, pp. 41, 43-44.

Deming, Angus; Sullivan, Scott; and Coleman, Fred. "The
Push for Human Rights." Newsweek, June 20, 1977,
pp. 46-48, 53-54.

Deming, Angus; Joyce, Thomas; Friendly, Alfred, Jr.; and
DeFrank, Thomas M. "Tough Talk on Detente."
Newsweek, September 1, 1975, pp. 14-15.

"Detente 'Da,' Fewer Conflicts 'Nyet,'" U.S. News & World
Report, January 5, 1976, p. 25.

"Detente: End of Illusions." Newsweek, February 25, 1974,
pp. 41-43.

"Detente: H. K. v. J. S." Time, November 17, 1975, p. 20.

"Detente Hearings." Congressional Quarterly: Weekly
Report, August 31, 1974, p. 3.

"Detente: Loaded in Russia's Favor?" U.S. News & World
Report, December 8, 1975, pp. 21-22. (Interviews
with Sens. Henry M. Jackson and Charles Mathias, Jr.)

"Detente: Now the Questions." Newsweek, September 30,
1974, pp. 39-40.

"Detente Spawns Supporters, Skeptics." Congressional
Quarterly: Weekly Report, September 14, 1974, p. 18.

"Development of Minnesotans' Views on U.S.-Russia Relations." Current Opinion, February 1974, p. 22.

"Dissidents--They Won't Lie Down." The Economist (London),
July 22, 1978, pp. 40, 43.

"Domestic Issues Top Concerns." Current Opinion, September
1976, p. 92.

Downey, Arthur T. "East-West Trade: Where Are We Now and Where Will We Be?" Address before the Thirteenth Annual Meeting of the Licensing Executives Society, Palm Beach, Florida, October 10, 1977. Washington, D.C.: Sutherland, Asbill and Brennan, Attorneys at Law, 1977. (Mimeographed.)

Draper, Theodore. "Appeasement & Detente." Commentary, February 1976, pp. 27-38.

"East-West Accord--How Europeans Size It Up." U.S. News & World Report, July 28, 1975, p. 18.

Evans, Rowland, and Novak, Robert. "Confusing Signals on Trade with Russia." Washington Post, 16 August 1974, p. A15.

"Ex-Im Loses Credit on Capitol Hill." Business Week, September 21, 1974, pp. 34-35.

"Fantastic Market Over There." U.S. News & World Report, July 28, 1975, p. 22. (Interview with Donald M. Kendall, Chairman of Pepsico.)

"Farewell to Adam Smith." Forbes, December 2, 1972, pp. 25-26.

Flieger, Howard. "By Any Other Name . . ." U.S. News & World Report, April 5, 1976, p. 92.

Flieger, Howard. "Moscow's One-Way Road." U.S. News & World Report, May 19, 1975, p. 80.

"Ford Given Negative Ratings on Foreign Policy." Current Opinion, April 1976, p. 34.

"Full Text of Trade Act of 1974 Signed by President Ford." U.S. Export Weekly (Special Supplement), January 7, 1975.

Gardner, Judy. "Kissinger Retains Primary Role in Foreign Policy." Congressional Quarterly: Weekly Report, November 8, 1975, p. 7.

Garrett, Stephen A. "Eastern European Ethnic Groups and American Foreign Policy." Political Science Quarterly 93 (Summer 1978): 301-323.

Gillette, Philip S. "Recent Trends in Soviet Trade." Current History 67 (October 1974): 169-172, 180.

Goff, Kristin. "Carter Erred on Computer, Sperry Says." Washington Post, 26 July 1978, pp. D6, D9.

Gordon, Al. "U.S. Chamber: It Speaks Through Members." Congressional Quarterly: Weekly Report, November 15, 1975, pp. 1-7.

Gravel, Mike. "Solzhenitsyn and Detente." The Progressive, October 1975, pp. 6-7.

Greenfield, Meg. "Henry vs. Henry." Newsweek, November 11, 1974, p. 46.

Greider, William. "U.S. Should Help Russia Alleviate Its Oil Crisis." Washington Post, 13 August 1978, p. C8.

Griffith, Thomas. "Must Business Fight the Press?" Fortune, June 1974, pp. 202-206, 208, 212, 214.

Gwertzman, Bernard. "Soviet Trade Aide Sees Carter Today." New York Times, 11 November 1977, p. A8.

Hammer, Armand. "Improved Relations Through Trade." Journal of the U.S.-U.S.S.R. Trade and Economic Council 2 (January-February 1976): 15.

"Happiness Under Red Stars." Time, July 8, 1974, p. 11.

"Harriman: A Veteran's View." Time, July 1, 1974, p. 22.

Harris, Louis. "The Harris Survey." Press release of May 22. Washington, D.C. 1978. (Mimeographed).

"Henry Kissinger--Well Known and Quite Favorably Known." Gallup Opinion Index, Report 95, May 1973, p. 26.

Hewett, Edward A. "The Economics of East European Technology Imports from the West." Paper presented at the Annual Meeting of the American Economics Association, San Francisco, December 1974. (Mimeographed.)

Hoagland, James. "A Carefully Primed Soviet Bear Trap." Washington Post, 20 August 1978, pp. A1, A14.

Holzman, Franklyn D. International Trade Under Communism-- Politics and Economics. New York: Basic Books, 1976.

Holzman, Franklyn D., and Legvold, Robert. "The Economics and Politics of East-West Relations." In World Politics and International Economics, pp. 275-320. Edited by C. Fred Bergsten and Lawrence B. Krause. Washington, D.C.: Brookings Institution, 1975.

"How Far Can Russia Push?" U.S. News & World Report, January 5, 1976, pp. 24-26.

"How We Will Do Business With Russia." U.S. News & World Report, July 31, 1972, pp. 27-29.

"'I Don't Think We Have Reached a Detente . . .'" Forbes, July 15, 1974, pp. 16-17. (Interview with Melvin Laird.)

"In Russia, Too--Detente's Bad Week." U.S. News & World Report, April 5, 1976, p. 22.

"It's Russia's Turn to Give." U.S. News & World Report, August 11, 1975, pp. 11-12, 14.

"Jewish Emigration." Congressional Quarterly: Weekly Report, December 7, 1974, p. 2.

"Jimmy Carter on the U.S. Economy and Business." Fortune, May 1976, pp. 184-185, 290, 292, 295-296.

Kaiser, Robert G. "Tough Choices on U.S.-Soviet Trade Await Carter's Return." Washington Post, 16 July 1978, p. A14.

Kaplan, Morton A. "Kissinger & Foreign Policy." Commentary, February 1974, pp. 11, 14-15.

Kendall, Donald M. "Present and Future Prospects for East-West Trade--A View from Donald Kendall." In The International Essays for Business Decision Makers, pp. 1-7. Edited by Mark B. Winchester. Dallas: SMU School of Business, 1976.

Kennan, George F. "Is Detente Worth Saving?" Saturday Review, March 6, 1976, pp. 12-17.

"Kissinger Contempt Citation." Congressional Quarterly: Weekly Report, November 15, 1975, p. 10.

"Kissinger, Golda Meir Win 'Most Admired' Derbies Again." Gallup Opinion Index, Report 115, January 1975, pp. 26-27.

Kissinger, Henry A. "The Future of Business and the International Environment." Address before the Future of Business Project, Center for Strategic and International Studies, Georgetown University, June 28, 1977. Washington, D.C. 1977. (Mimeographed.)

"Kissinger's Mission to Moscow--New Obstacles to Detente." U.S. News & World Report, April 8, 1974, pp. 23-24.

"Kissinger's Rating Down:  But He Has Vote of Confidence." Gallup Opinion Index, Report 127, February 1976, pp. 16-17.

"Kissinger Tops List of Men Americans Admire the Most." Gallup Opinion Index, Report 103, January 1974, pp. 16-17.

Korbonski, Andrej. "Detente, East-West Trade, and the Future of Economic Integration in Eastern Europe." Paper presented at the National Meeting of the American Association for the Advancement of Slavic Studies. Atlanta, Ga., October 1976. (Mimeographed.)

Kraft, Joseph. "The Russian People Are a Proud People." Washington Post, 11 July 1978, p. A11.

Kraft, Joseph. "The Russian Perspective on Dissidents." Washington Post, 18 July 1978, p. A11.

Laird, Melvin. "Let's Not Fool Ourselves About U.S.-Soviet Detente." Reader's Digest, February 1974, pp. 57-60.

Lawrence, Richard. "Joint U.S.-Soviet Ventures in Energy Field Pushed." Journal of Commerce, 16 December 1977, pp. 3, 19.

Marder, Murray. "'Sobered' Superpowers Looking Ahead." Washington Post, 13 August 1978, pp. A1, A4.

Mathews, Tom; Clift, Eleanor; and DeFrank, Thomas M. "Zeroing in on Zbig." Newsweek, January 30, 1978, pp. 49-50.

Maxfield, David M. "Disputes over New Weapons Imperil Arms Pact." Congressional Quarterly:  Weekly Report, November 29, 1975, pp. 1-6.

Maxfield, David M. "Pro-Detente Move in Senate Collapses." Congressional Quarterly:  Weekly Report, March 27, 1976, p. 9.

McCormick, Brooks. "IH's Involvement in Soviet Trade."
    Journal of the U.S.-U.S.S.R. Trade and Economic
    Council 3 (October-November 1977): 18.

"Meeting the Isolationist Challenge." Fortune, June 1975,
    pp. 79-80.

Meier, Gerald M. Problems of Trade Policy. Oxford: Oxford
    University Press, 1973.

Nagorski, Zygmunt, Jr. The Psychology of East-West Trade:
    Illusions and Opportunities. New York: Mason &
    Lipscomb, 1974.

National Foreign Trade Council. Policy Declaration of the
    National Foreign Trade Council, Inc. New York:
    National Foreign Trade Council, Inc., 1975.

"New Legislation Will Affect Trade with Socialist Nations."
    Commerce Today, January 20, 1975, pp. 23-27.

"Nixon Rating Near Low Despite Mid-East Tour." Gallup
    Opinion Index, Report 109, July 1974, pp. 1-5.

"Nixon's Job Rating Holds, at 31 Per Cent Positive."
    Current Opinion, July 1974, p. 74.

Noonan, Norma C. "Soviet Foreign Trade as an Indicator of
    Trends in Soviet Foreign Policy." Paper presented
    at the National Meeting of the American Association
    for the Advancement of Slavic Studies. St. Louis,
    October 1976.

"Opponents Move to Block Further Angola Aid." Congressional
    Quarterly: Weekly Report, December 20, 1975,
    pp. 8-10.

O'Reilly, A. Koffmann. "Sperry Sale to Soviets Is Defended."
    Journal of Commerce, 26 July 1978, p. 1.

"Policy Toward Moscow." Congressional Quarterly: Weekly
    Report, March 20, 1976, p. 2.

"Portugal: A Test of Whether Moscow Will Keep Hands Off."
    U.S. News & World Report, July 28, 1975, p. 21.

Prettyman, E. Barrett, Jr. "An Arrest in Moscow: What's at
    Stake for U.S. Business." Washington Post, 9 August
    1978, p. A23.

"Prospects for World Peace Dubious During Coming Year."
    Gallup Opinion Index, Report 104, February 1974, pp.
    6-10.

"Public Gives Kissinger a Vote of Confidence; Congress Rating
    Also Up." Gallup Opinion Index, Report 120, June
    1975, pp. 24-27.

"Public Makes 1976 Predictions: Increased Power for Rivals,
    Higher Unemployment at Home." Gallup Opinion Index,
    Report 126, January 1976, pp. 21-26.

"Public Rejects Income Surtax, Would Cut Defense Budget and
    Impose Wage/Price Regulations." Gallup Opinion
    Index, Report 113, November 1974, pp. 1-10.

"Public Still Backs Kissinger, Would Object to His Ouster
    Before Administration's End." Gallup Opinion Index,
    Report 131, June 1976, pp. 27-29.

Ray, Jack H.  Personal letter from the president of Tennessee
    Gas Transmission Co., Tenneco, Inc., to Dr. Samuel
    P. Huntington, Coordinator of Security Planning,
    National Security Council, July 6, 1978.

"Reagan's Views on Defense and Detente." Congressional
    Quarterly: Weekly Report, November 8, 1975, p. 5.

Reichley, A. James.  "A Foreign Policy for the Era of
    Interdependence." Fortune, April 1975, pp.
    152-160.

Reston, James.  "Detente--Soviet Style." Reader's Digest,
    November 1975, pp. 171-172.

"Rules Ease on Trade with Russia." Business Week, June 12,
    1971, p. 94.

"Russia--Suddenly a 'Silent Partner' in Detente." U.S. News
    & World Report, April 14, 1975, p. 33.

Samuelson, Robert J.  "The Wheels of Trade Could Use Some
    Oil." National Journal, August 10, 1977, pp.
    1566-1571.

Schlesinger, James R.  "A Testing Time for America."
    Fortune, February 1976, pp. 74-77, 147-149, 153.

"Scoop Jackson: Meanwhile, Back at Peking . . ." Time,
    July 8, 1974, pp. 12-13.

Seligman, Daniel. "Communism's Crisis of Authority." _Fortune_, February 1976, pp. 92-95, 168-170, 172.

Seligman, Daniel. "Communist Ideology and Soviet Power." _Fortune_, January 1976, pp. 112-116, 188, 190, 192.

Seligman, Daniel. "Communists in Democratic Clothing." _Fortune_ March 1976, pp. 116-119, 188, 190, 192-193.

"Senate Committee Debates Soviet Trade Concessions." _Congressional Quarterly: Weekly Report_, March 9, 1974, p. 12.

Smith, Donald; Gordon, Al.; and Ehrenhalt, Alan. "Questions Raised on Defense, Bush, Politics." _Congressional Quarterly: Weekly Report_, November 8, 1975, pp. 1-4, 6.

Smith, Hedrick. "The Russians Mean Business . . . About Business." _Atlantic_, December 1974, pp. 41-48.

Solzhenitsyn, Aleksandr. _Detente: Prospects for Democracy and Dictatorship_. New Brunswick, N.J.: Transaction Books, 1976.

Solzhenitsyn, Alexandr. "No More Concessions." _Reader's Digest_, October 1975, pp. 73-78.

Solzhenitsyn, Aleksandr. _Warning to the West_. New York: Farrar, Straus & Giroux, 1976.

Solzhenitsyn, Alexandr. "Words of Warning to America." _U.S. News & World Report_, July 14, 1975, pp. 44-50.

"Soviet Statement: U.S. Course 'Fraught with Serious Danger.'" _Washington Post_, 18 June 1978, p. A17.

Steele, Richard; Sullivan, Scott; Norman, Lloyd H.; and Coleman, Fred. "Mission to Moscow." _Newsweek_, April 4, 1977, pp. 20-22.

Steele, Richard; Coleman, Fred; Sullivan, Scott; and DeFrank, Thomas M. "Testing Carter." _Newsweek_, April 11, 1977, pp. 26-30.

Steele, Richard; Clift, Eleanor; DeFrank, Thomas M.; and Sullivan, Scott. "The Limits of Morality." _Newsweek_, March 7, 1977, pp. 14-15.

Steele, Richard. "What Price Detente?" Newsweek, July 28, 1975, pp. 14-15.

Stern, Laurence, and Barbash, Fred. "Carter Orders Trade Reprisal Against Soviets." Washington Post, 19 July, 1978, pp. A1, A22.

"A Sudden Frost in the Thaw." Newsweek, January 27, 1975, pp. 33-34.

"Summit's Deadly Stakes." Time, July 1, 1974, p. 25.

Szulc, Tad. "U.S. Has Little Leverage on Soviet Actions." Washington Post, 16 July, 1978, pp. B1, B3.

Tennessee Gas Transmission Co. "Update to March 31, 1978, Paper on the Carter Administration's Policy on U.S.-Soviet Trade Relations." Internal company memorandum, June 22, 1978.

Tennessee Gas Transmission Co. "U.S.-U.S.S.R. Trade and the North Star Project." Company position paper, July 6, 1978.

"The Economic Story Behind the Nixon-Brezhnev Detente." Forbes, September 1, 1972, pp. 22-23.

"The Kremlin Cracks Down." Newsweek, May 16, 1977, pp. 69-70.

"The Third Summit: A Time of Testing." Time, July 1, 1974, pp. 20-22, 26, 30-32.

Towell, Pat. "Defense Outlook: New Support in Congress." Congressional Quarterly: Weekly Report, March 27, 1976, pp. 1-3, 5-6, 8.

Towell, Pat. "Detente: Still an Issue in Both Parties." Congressional Quarterly: Weekly Report, March 20, 1976, p. 13.

Towell, Pat, and Maxfield, David M. "94th Congress Backed Ford's Defense Policy." Congressional Quarterly: Weekly Report, October 2, 1976, pp. 1-4.

"Trade: A Key Link." Newsweek, May 29, 1972, p. 41.

"Trade Reform." Congressional Quarterly: Weekly Report, April 20, 1974, p. 5.

United Nations. Economic Commission for Europe. <u>Economic Bulletin for Europe</u> (E.74.II.E.4), 1974.

United Nations. Economic and Social Council, 57th Session. <u>The Impact of Multinational Corporations on the Development Process and on International Relations: Report of the Secretary-General</u> (E/5500), June 14, 1974.

"U.S. Commitments Should Remain Unchanged in Post-Vietnam Era." <u>Gallup Opinion Index</u>, Report 121, July 1975, p. 14.

U.S. Congress. Commission on Security and Cooperation in Europe. <u>Hearings Before the Commission on Security and Cooperation in Europe on Basket II--Helsinki Final Act: East-West Economic Relations</u>, 95th Cong., 1st sess., 1977.

U.S. Congress. Commission on Security and Cooperation in Europe. <u>Implementation of the Final Act of the Conference on Security and Cooperation in Europe: Findings and Recommendations Two Years after Helsinki. Report Transmitted to the Committee on International Relations, U.S. House of Representatives</u>. 95th Cong., 1st sess., 1977.

U.S. Congress. General Accounting Office. <u>The Government's Role in East-West Trade--Problems and Issues</u>. GAO Report No. ID-76-13A, February 1976.

U.S. Congress. House. Committee on Banking, Currency and Finance. <u>Hearings before the Subcommittee on International Trade, Investment and Monetary Policy</u>, 94th Cong., 1st sess., 1975.

U.S. Congress. House. Committee on Foreign Affairs. <u>Detente. Hearings before the Subcommittee on Europe</u>, 93d Cong., 2d sess., 1974.

U.S. Congress. House. Committee on Foreign Affairs. <u>East-West Trade. Hearings before the Subcommittee on Europe</u>, 90th Cong., 2d sess., 1968.

U.S. Congress. House. Committee on Foreign Affairs. <u>Recent Developments in East-West Relations. Hearings before the Subcommittee on Europe</u>, 89th Cong., 2d sess., 1966.

U.S. Congress. House. Committee on Foreign Affairs. U.S.-
Soviet Commercial Relations: The Interplay of
Economics, Technology Transfer, and Diplomacy, by
John P. Hardt and George D. Holliday. 93d Cong.,
1st sess., 1973.

U.S. Congress. House. Committee on Foreign Relations.
Detente: Prospects for Increased Trade with Warsaw
Pact Countries. Report of a Special Study Mission
to the Soviet Union and Eastern Europe, August 22 to
September 8, 1974. 93d Cong., 2d sess., 1974.

U.S. Congress. House. Committee on Science and Astronau-
tics. The Technology Balance. U.S.-U.S.S.R.
Advanced Technology Transfer. Hearings before the
Subcommittee on International Cooperation in Science
and Space, 93d Cong., 1st & 2d sess., 1973.

U.S. Congress. House. Committee on Science and Technology.
Background Material on U.S.-U.S.S.R. Cooperative
Agreements in Science and Technology. H. Doc.
613360, 94th Cong., 1st sess., 1975.

U.S. Congress. Joint Economic Committee. A Foreign Economic
Policy for the 1970s. Hearings before the
Subcommittee on Foreign Economic Policy, Part 6,
East-West Economic Relations, 91st Cong., 2d sess.,
1970.

U.S. Congress. Joint Economic Committee. East European
Economies Post-Helsinki. Joint Committee Print,
95th Cong., 1st sess., 1977. Washington, D.C.:
Government Printing Office, 1977.

U.S. Congress. Joint Economic Committee. Soviet Economy in
a New Perspective. Joint Committee Print, 94th
Cong., 2d sess., 1976. Washington, D.C.:
Government Printing Office, 1976.

U.S. Congress. Library of Congress. Congressional Research
Service. "A Reassessment of U.S. Export Licensing
in East-West Commercial Relations." Statement by
John P. Hardt, Senior Specialist in Soviet
Economics, submitted to the House International
Affairs Committee, March 11, 1976. Washington, D.C.
1976. (Mimeographed.)

U.S. Congress. Library of Congress. Congressional Research
     Service. "East-West Commercial Relations:
     Assessment and Prospects." Statement of John P.
     Hardt, Senior Specialist in Soviet Economics,
     submitted to the Senate Commerce Committee, February
     4, 1976. Washington, D.C. 1976. (Mimeographed.)

U.S. Congress. Library of Congress. Congressional Research
     Service. "Rapporteur's Report on East-West
     Commercial Relations Workshop," by Ronda A.
     Bresnick. Washington, D.C. 1978. (Mimeographed.)

U.S. Congress. Library of Congress. Congressional Research
     Service. Statement of John P. Hardt, Senior
     Specialist in Soviet Economics, before the Senate
     Commerce Committee, February 4, 1976. Washington,
     D.C. 1976. (Mimeographed.)

U.S. Congress. Library of Congress. Congressional Research
     Service. "Technology Transfer and Change in the
     Soviet Economic System," by John P. Hardt and George
     D. Holliday. Washington, D.C. 1975. (Mimeographed.)

U.S. Congress. Library of Congress. Congressional Research
     Service. "Testimony to and Answers to Questions
     from the Commission on Security and Cooperation in
     Europe," by John P. Hardt. Washington, D.C.,
     January 1977. (Mimeographed.)

U.S. Congress. Senate. Commission on the Operation of the
     Senate. Major U.S. Foreign and Defense Policy
     Issues: A Compilation of Papers. S. Doc. 83-330,
     95th Cong., 1st sess., 1977.

U.S. Congress. Senate. Committee on Commerce. Export
     Expansion Act of 1971. Hearings before the
     Subcommittee on Foreign Commerce and Tourism of the
     Committee on Commerce on S. 2754, 92d Cong., 2d
     sess., 1972.

U.S. Congress. Senate. Committee on Finance. Analysis of
     the Trade Agreements Program and the Trade Reform
     Act of 1973. Staff Papers Provided by the U.S.
     Tariff Commission for the Committee on Finance.
     93d Cong., 2d session, 1974.

U.S. Congress. Senate. Committee on Finance. Background
Materials Relating to United States-Romanian Trade
and the Extension of the President's Authority to
Waive Section 402 of the Trade Act of 1974. 94th
Cong., 2d sess., 1976.

U.S. Congress. Senate. Committee on Finance. Digest of
Testimony Received on H.R. 10710: The Trade Reform
Act of 1973. 93d Cong., 2d sess., 1974.

U.S. Congress. Senate. Committee on Finance. Summary and
Analysis of H.R. 10710--The Trade Reform Act of
1973. 93d Cong., 2d sess., 1974.

U.S. Congress. Senate. Committee on Finance. Summary of
the Trade Reform Act of 1974 as Ordered Reported by
the Committee on Finance. 93d Cong., 2d sess.,
1974.

U.S. Congress. Senate. Committee on Finance. The Trade
Act of 1973. Hearings before the Committee on
Finance on H.R. 10710, 93d Cong., 2d sess., 1974.

U.S. Congress. Senate. Committee on Foreign Relations.
Detente: Hearings before the Committee on Foreign
Relations, 93d Cong., 2d sess., 1974.

U.S. Congress. Senate. Committee on Foreign Relations.
Report of a Conference between Members of the U S.
Senate and Delegates to the Supreme Soviet of the
Soviet Union. Moscow and Leningrad, June 29-July 5,
1975. 94th Cong., 1st sess., 1975.

U.S. Department of Commerce. Bureau of East-West Trade.
Address by Arthur Downey, Deputy Assistant Secretary
of Commerce for East-West Trade, at the Arden House,
November 1, 1976. Washington, D.C. 1976.
(Mimeographed.)

U.S. Department of Commerce. Bureau of East-West Trade.
Office of East-West Policy and Planning. "A Summary
of U.S. Laws Applying to Imports of Communist
Products." Washington, D.C. 1978. (Mimeographed.)

U.S. Department of Commerce. Bureau of East-West Trade.
Office of East-West Policy and Planning.
"Preliminary Assessment of Raymond Vernon's and
Marshall Goldman's 'U.S. Policies in the Sale of
Technology to the USSR,'" by Thomas A. Wolf.
Washington, D.C. 1974. (Mimeographed.)

U.S. Department of Commerce. Bureau of East-West Trade.
Office of East-West Policy and Planning. "Principal
Statutes Specifically Impacting on East-West
Trade." Washington, D.C. 1978. (Mimeographed.)

U.S. Department of Commerce. Bureau of East-West Trade.
Office of East-West Policy and Planning. Statement
by W. Averell Harriman before the Subcommittee on
Future Foreign Policy Research and Development of
the House Committee on International Relations, July
15, 1975. Washington, D.C. 1975. (Mimeographed.)

U.S. Department of Commerce. Bureau of East-West Trade.
Office of East-West Policy and Planning. Statement
by W. Averell Harriman before the Select Committee
to Study Governmental Operations with Respect to
Intelligence Activities, January 20, 1976.
Washington, D.C. 1976. (Mimeographed.)

U.S. Department of Commerce. Bureau of East-West Trade.
Office of East-West Policy and Planning. "Update of
Legislative Activity," by John P. Young.
Washington, D.C. 1978. (Mimeographed.)

U.S. Department of Commerce. Bureau of East-West Trade.
Office of East-West Trade Development.
American-Soviet Trade:  A Joint Seminar on the
Organizational and Legal Aspects, Moscow 1975.
Washington, D.C. 1976.

U.S. Department of Commerce. Bureau of East-West Trade.
"Soviet Trade Agreements with Developed Western
Countries." Washington, D.C. 1975. (Mimeographed.)

U.S. Department of Commerce. Bureau of East-West Trade.
Statement of Steven Lazarus, Deputy Assistant
Secretary of Commerce for East-West Trade, before
the Subcommittee on Foreign Agricultural Policy of
the Senate Committee on Agriculture and Forestry,
July 11, 1973.  Washington, D.C. 1973.
(Mimeographed.)

U.S. Department of Commerce. Bureau of East-West Trade. "The
Framework of East-West Economic Relations," by
Gerald Feldman, Judith Robinson, and Paulette
Wolfson.  Washington, D.C. 1973.  (Mimeographed.)

U.S. Department of Commerce. Bureau of East-West Trade. "The U.S. Government and Department of Commerce Role in Promoting Imports from Socialist Countries." Washington, D.C. 1974. (Mimeographed.)

U.S. Department of Commerce. Bureau of East-West Trade. "U.S. Antitrust Laws and East-West Trade," by Donald Businger and Thomas Hoya. Washington, D.C. 1975. (Mimeographed.)

U.S. Department of Commerce. Bureau of East-West Trade. "What Is Government's Proper Role in East-West Trade?" Address by Arthur T. Downey, Deputy Assistant Secretary for East-West Trade before the Arden House Conference on U.S.-Soviet Trade, April 2, 1977. Washington, D.C. 1977. (Mimeographed.)

U.S. Department of Commerce. Bureau of International Commerce. Remarks by Edward L. Allen, Deputy Assistant Secretary of Commerce for International Economic Research and Analysis, prepared for delivery to the International Trade Center of New England, Sheraton Plaza Hotel, Boston, Massachusetts, September 13, 1972. Washington, D.C. 1972. (Mimeographed.)

U.S. Department of Commerce. Domestic and International Business Administration. "Comments of the Domestic and International Business Administration on the Final GAO Report Entitled, 'The Government's Role in East-West Trade--Problems and Issues.'" Washington, D.C. 1976. (Mimeographed.)

U.S. Department of Commerce. New York District Export Council. Policy Statement of the Committee for the Promotion of East-West Trade. New York, 1975.

U.S. Department of Commerce. Office of Public Affairs. Address by Secretary of Commerce Juanita M. Kreps prepared for delivery to the Board of Directors of the U.S.-U.S.S.R. Trade and Economic Council, Los Angeles, November 15, 1977. (Mimeographed.)

U.S. Department of Commerce. Office of Public Affairs. Text of press conference by Peter G. Peterson, Secretary of Commerce, U.S. Embassy-Moscow, August 1, 1972. Washington, D.C. 1972. (Mimeographed.)

U.S. Department of Commerce. Statement of the Honorable
    Elliot L. Richardson, Secretary of Commerce, before
    the Commission on Security and Cooperation in
    Europe, January 14, 1977. Washington, D.C. 1977.
    (Mimeographed.)

U.S. Department of Commerce. The United States Role in East-
    West Trade: Problems and Prospects, by Rogers
    Morton, Secretary of Commerce. Washington, D.C.:
    Government Printing Office, August 1975.

U.S. Department of Commerce. U.S.-Soviet Commercial
    Relationships in a New Era, by Peter G. Peterson,
    Secretary of Commerce. Washington, D.C.:
    Government Printing Office, August 1972.

U.S. Department of State. Cooperation in the Field of
    Energy. Agreement between the United States of
    America and the Union of Soviet Socialist
    Republics. Treaties and Other International Acts
    Series 7899 (1973).

U.S. Department of State. Department of State Bulletin 70
    (June 3, 1974). "U.S.-Soviet Detente: Perceptions
    and Purposes," statement by Arthur A. Hartman,
    Assistant Secretary for European Affairs, pp.
    597-602.

U.S. Department of State. Department of State Bulletin 71
    (October 14, 1974). "Detente with the Soviet
    Union: The Reality of Competition and the
    Imperative of Cooperation," statement by Secretary
    Kissinger, pp. 505-519.

U.S. Department of State. Department of State Bulletin 72
    (February 3, 1975). "Secretary Kissinger's News
    Conference of January 14," pp. 139-143.

U.S. Department of State. Department of State Bulletin 74
    (February 23, 1976). "Questions and Answers
    Following the Secretary's Address at San Francisco,"
    pp. 212-220.

U.S. Department of State. Department of State Bulletin 74
    (February 23, 1976). "The Permanent Challenge of
    Peace: U.S. Policy toward the Soviet Union,"
    address by Secretary Kissinger, pp. 201-211.

U.S. Department of State. Department of State Bulletin 74
    (April 19, 1976). "The Triangular Relationship of
    the United States, the U.S.S.R., and the People's
    Republic of China," statement by Winston Lord,
    Director, Policy Planning Staff, pp. 514-518.

U.S. Department of State. Department of State Bulletin 74
    (May 3, 1976). "U.S.-Soviet Relations in the
    Nuclear Age," address by Helmut Sonnenfeldt,
    Counselor of the Department, pp. 576-583.

U.S. Department of State. Department of State Bulletin 76
    (February 7, 1977). "Secretary Kissinger
    Interviewed for the New York Times," pp. 102-107.

U.S. Department of State. Department of State Bulletin 76
    (May 23, 1977). "Human Rights and Foreign Policy,"
    address by Secretary Vance, pp. 505-508.

U.S. Department of State. Department of State Bulletin 76
    (June 13, 1977). "A Foreign Policy Based on
    America's Essential Character," address by President
    Carter, pp. 621-625.

U.S. Department of State. Department of State Bulletin 77
    (November 21, 1977). "Secretary Vance Interviewed
    for U.S. News and World Report," pp. 732-738.

U.S. Department of State. Economic, Industrial, and
    Technical Cooperation: Agreement between the United
    States of America and the Union of Soviet Socialist
    Republics. Treaties and Other International Acts
    Series 7910 (1974).

U.S. Department of State. Office of Media Services.
    "America's Permanent Interests." Address by
    Secretary of State Henry A. Kissinger before the
    Boston World Affairs Council, March 11, 1976.
    (Mimeographed.)

U.S. Department of State. Office of Media Services.
    "Conference on Security and Cooperation in Europe:
    Final Act." Copy of the English-language version
    taken from a bound volume containing the text of the
    Final Act in the six official languages of the
    Helsinki Conference. Washington, D.C. 1975.
    (Mimeographed.)

U.S. Department of State. Office of Media Services. "The Cohesion of the Industrial Democracies: The Precondition for Global Progress." Address by Secretary of State Henry A. Kissinger before the Organization for Economic Cooperation and Development, Paris, France, June 21, 1976. Washington, D.C. 1976. (Mimeographed.)

U.S. Department of State. Office of Media Services. "U.S.-Soviet Relations." Speech by President Carter to the Southern Legislative Conference. Press release of July 21, 1977. (Mimeographed.)

U.S. Export-Import Bank. Statement of William J. Casey, President and Chairman, Export-Import Bank of the United States, before the Senate Commerce Committee, December 11, 1975. Washington, D.C. 1975. (Mimeographed.)

U.S. President. Office of the Special Representative for Trade Negotiations. "Summary of Major Provisions of the Trade Act of 1974." Washington, D.C. 1975. (Mimeographed.)

U.S. President. Office of the White House Press Secretary. Remarks of the President at Wake Forest University. Press release of March 17, 1978. Washington, D.C. 1978. (Mimeographed.)

U.S. President. Office of the White House Press Secretary. Text of the President's address to the 1978 Graduating Class of the U.S. Naval Academy. Press release of June 6, 1978. Washington, D.C. 1978. (Mimeographed.)

U.S. President. Office of the White House Press Secretary. "U.S. Government Documents on Soviet-American Grain and Oil Negotiations." Washington, D.C. 1976. (Mimeographed.)

U.S. President. President's Export Council. "Policy Statement of the President's Export Council on East-West Trade." Washington, D.C. 1976. (Mimeographed.)

"U.S. Industry, Government Officials, Soviet Spokesman Call for Trade Continuity." Commerce Today, March 3, 1975, p. 20.

"U.S. Opinion on Russia." Fortune, September 1945,
     pp. 233-234, 236, 238, 240, 243.

"U.S., Soviets Forming Joint Commercial Unit," Commerce
     Today, December 13, 1971, pp. 35-37.

"U.S.-Soviet Ventures Blocked by Policies of U.S., Kreps
     Says." Wall Street Journal, 16 December 1977, p. 10.

"U.S. Trade Position Lags in Principal World Markets, Gains
     in Smaller Nations." Commerce Today, October 28,
     1974, pp. 23-24.

"Using Trade to Influence Russia." Business Week, July 24,
     1978, p. 181.

Verity, William. "Toward Trade Normalization." Journal of
     the U.S.-U.S.S.R. Trade and Economic Council 5
     (January-February 1979): 14.

"Vigilance Is the Price of Detente." Time, July 1, 1974,
     p. 26.

Wallace, James N. "The Kremlin: Nixon Will Be Welcome in
     June." U.S. News & World Report, April 8, 1974,
     p. 24.

Walsh, John. "Soviet-U.S. Science Agreements: Press
     Presides over Reappraisal." Science, June 3, 1977,
     pp. 1064-1066.

Wasowski, Stanislaw, ed. East-West Trade and the Technology
     Gap: A Political and Economic Appraisal. New
     York: Praeger, 1970.

Ways, Max. "Business Needs a Different Political Stance."
     Fortune, September 1975, pp. 96-99.

"We Are Determined to Resist Expansionism." U.S. News &
     World Report, March 15, 1976, pp. 24-28. (Interview
     with Dr. Henry Kissinger, Secretary of State.)

"The West Gives Everything Away." U.S. News & World Report,
     March 15, 1976, p. 23. (Excerpts from an interview
     with Alexander Solzhenitsyn on BBC television.)

Whipple, Christopher, and Sullivan, Scott. "Human Rights:
     Carter Backs Off." Newsweek, October 10, 1977, pp.
     48-49.

"Why Detente Is in Trouble." Fortune, April 1976, pp. 81-82.

Wiggins, Philip H. "Computer-Sale Bar Irks Sperry." New York Times, 26 July 1978, pp. Dl-D7.

Willey, Fay, and Coleman, Fred. "A Charge of Treason." Newsweek, June 13, 1977, pp. 42, 47.

Willey, Fay; Coleman, Fred; and Sullivan, Scott. "Detente: Damage Control." Newsweek, June 26, 1978, p. 37.

Willey, Fay; Sullivan, Scott; and Coleman, Fred. "Detente: The New Morality." Newsweek, February 14, 1977, pp. 36-37, 39.

Willey, Fay; Sullivan, Scott; Hubbard, Henry W.; and Coleman, Fred. "Human Rights--The Soviet Side." Newsweek, February 21, 1977, p. 30.

Wolf, Thomas A. "East-West Tradeoffs." International Institute of Management. Berlin, 1976. (Mimeographed.)

Wolf, Thomas A. "New Elements in U.S.-East-West Trade Policy." International Institute of Management. Berlin, 1974. (Mimeographed.)

Wolf, Thomas A. U.S. East-West Trade Policy. Lexington, Mass.: Lexington Books, 1973.

"Words Are Not Enough." Economist (London), July 22, 1978, pp. 9-10.

"World Peace Attainable, Most Believe." Current Opinion, January 1974, pp. 19-20.

"A Yellow Light on the Road to Detente." Time, April 8, 1974, pp. 23-24.

568

B.  Economic/Business

"All About That Soviet Wheat Deal."  U.S. News & World
    Report, October 9, 1972, pp. 28-30.

"Another Rum Deal with Russia."  Nation, December 9, 1973,
    pp. 558-559.

"Area Report on '74 Trade Shows Many Gains, Offset by Oil
    Deficit."  Commerce Today, March 17, 1975, pp. 10-12.

"Armand Hammer:  On Trade with Russia."  Business Week, July
    13, 1974, pp. 64-66.  (Interview with Armand Hammer,
    Chairman of Occidental Petroleum Corp.)

Basche, James R., Jr.  Evolving Corporate Policy and
    Organization for East-West Trade.  New York: The
    Conference Board, Inc., 1974.

Benedict, Roger.  "Russia Negotiating to Sell Siberian
    Gas to Tenneco, Texas Eastern, Halliburton."  Wall
    Street Journal, 15 June 1972, p. 42.

"The Big Breakthrough in East-West Trade."  Business Week,
    June 19, 1971, pp. 84-88.

Boardman, Christopher.  "Large LNG Import Looms."  Journal of
    Commerce, 4 January 1978, pp. 1, 29, 32.

Boretsky, Michael.  "Soviet Technology:  Current Level and
    Prospective Progress Relative to the United States."
    Paper presented at the Annual Meeting of the American
    Institute of Aeronautics and Astronautics, Sheraton
    Park Hotel, Washington, D.C., February 26, 1975.
    Washington, D.C. 1975.  (Mimeographed.)

Bradley, Gene E.  "East-West Trade."  Columbia Journal of
    World Business 8 (December 1973):  39-41.

Brainard, Lawrence J.  "Criteria for Financing East-West
    Trade."  Paper presented at the National Meeting of
    the American Association for the Advancement of
    Slavic Studies.  Banff, Canada, September 1974.

Brainard, Lawrence J.  "Eastern Europe's Indebtedness:
    Policy Choices for East and West."  Paper presented
    at an international workshop on "Monetary and
    Financial Problems in East-West Trade," Budapest,
    Hungary, October 16-20, 1977.  New York:  Bankers
    Trust Co., 1977.  (Mimeographed.)

Brement, Marshall. "Organizing Ourselves to Deal with the Soviets." Rand Corporation. Santa Monica, Cal., September 1977. (Mimeographed.)

"Bridging the East-West Credit Gap." Business Week, October 28, 1972, p. 30.

"Bundles for Russia." Time, December 4, 1972, p. 46.

Business International S.A. Corporate Strategy, Planning, Organization and Personnel Practices for Eastern Europe. Geneva: Business International S.A., 1971.

Business International S.A. Doing Business with the USSR. Geneva: Business International S.A., 1971.

"Can Exporters Keep DISC Alive?" Business Week, August 25, 1975, pp. 33-34.

"Can Semiconductors Keep It Up?" Business Week, August 3, 1974, p. 22.

"Cargill Claims Loss on Russian Wheat Sale of Almost Cent a Bushel, Rebutting Critics." Wall Street Journal, 3 November 1972, p. 4.

Casey, Samuel B. "Pullman and World Trade in Perspective." American Review of East-West Trade 10 (May 1979): 40.

Clawson, Robert W. "How to Introduce Your Products to the Soviet Buyer." Today's Manager, September 1975, pp. 8-12.

Conference Board. East West Trade: The Lessons from Experience. New York: The Conference Board, 1971.

"Continental Grain Got Soviet Wheat Order 3 Days Before the U.S.-Russia Grain Accord." Wall Street Journal, 20 September 1972, p. 2.

"Cooking Big Deals with Russia." Business Week, December 4, 1971, pp. 28-29.

"David Karr's Soviet Connection." Business Week, May 19, 1975, pp. 142, 144.

De Pauw, John W. "Soviet-American Trade: A Case Study of U.S.-Soviet Commercial Negotiations." Paper presented at the Annual Meeting of the Southern Conference on Slavic Studies. Birmingham, Ala., October 1977. (Mimeographed.)

"Detailed List of Oil Exploration Equipment Needing
       Validated License Being Prepared." U.S. Export
       Weekly, July 25, 1978, pp. AA1-AA2.

"Dictating Product Safety." Business Week, May 18, 1974,
       pp. 56-58, 60, 62.

Dufey, Gunter. "Financing East-West Business." Columbia
       Journal of World Business 9 (Spring 1974): 37-41.

"East-West Trade Boomerang?" Forbes, September 1, 1974,
       p. 64. (Interview with Cyrus Eaton, Jr., President
       of Tower International Corp.)

"East-West Trade Bureau Seeks Workable Contacts Between Two
       Systems." Commerce Today, January 8, 1973, pp. 4-6.

Elliott, James F. "Estimates of Export Sales to Eastern
       Europe and the U.S.S.R. by U.S. Subsidiaries Located
       in Western Europe." Journal of International
       Business Studies 8 (Fall/Winter 1977): 63-68.

"El Paso Natural, Occidental Petroleum Sign With Russians to
       Import Gas Over 25 Years." Wall Street Journal, 11
       June 1973, p. 7.

"Export-Import Bank." Congressional Quarterly: Weekly
       Report, August 31, 1974, pp. 18-19.

"Export-Import Bank." Congressional Quarterly: Weekly
       Report, October 12, 1974, p. 12.

"Farewell to Adam Smith." Forbes, December 1, 1972,
       pp. 25-26.

Feinschreiber, Robert. "The U.S. Tax Law Provides Two
       Export Incentives." Columbia Journal of World
       Business 10 (Summer 1975): 46-49.

"Fresh Help for Trade Talks." Business Week, August 24,
       1974, pp. 14-15.

"Funds for Ex-Im." Business Week, October 12, 1974, p. 35.

"Getting Down to Business with Russia." Industry Week, July
       24, 1972, pp. 32-33.

Giffen, James Henry. "Developing Market Programs for the
       U.S.S.R." Columbia Journal of World Business 8
       (December 1973): 61-68.

Giffen, James H. The Legal and Practical Aspects of Trade with the Soviet Union. New York: Praeger, 1971.

"A Global List of Casualties." Business Week. October 26, 1974, pp. 34-35.

Goldman, Marshall I. Detente and Dollars. New York: Basic Books, 1975.

"Gould Credits Technology for Its Soviet Success." Journal of the U.S.-U.S.S.R. Trade and Economic Council 2 (July-August 1976): 17.

"The Grain Drain." Newsweek, September 18, 1972, pp. 77-78.

"The Great Grain Robbery." America, October 14, 1972, p. 279.

Green, Donald W., and Levine, Herbert S. "Implications of Technology Transfers for the USSR." Paper presented at the Annual Meeting of the Eastern Economic Association. Bloomsburg, Pa., April 1976. (Mimeographed.)

Hackett, J.E. "Soviet Management in Action (Inaction)." Paper presented to a seminar at the Center for Russian and East European Studies, University of Birmingham, January 30, 1973. (Mimeographed.)

Hambleton, George B. E. "Company Presence in the U.S.S.R." Columbia Journal of World Business 8 (December 1973): 78-82.

Hammer, Armand. "It's a Deal: A Personal History of Trade with the Soviet Union." American Review of East-West Trade 10 (May 1979): 34.

Hanson, Philip. USSR: Foreign Trade Implications of the 1976-80 Plan. London: The Economist Intelligence Unit Ltd., 1976.

Hayden, Eric W. Technology Transfer to East Europe: U.S. Corporate Experience. New York: Praeger, 1976.

"He Bets High Stakes on Siberian LNG." Business Week, June 24, 1972, p. 110.

Hewett, Edward A. "On Differences in the Foreign Trade Behavior of Centrally Planned and Market Economies." Paper presented at the Conference on Integration in Eastern Europe and East-West Trade, Indiana University, October 28-31, 1976. Bloomington, Ind., 1976. (Mimeographed.)

House, Karen E. "Energy Agency Clears Plans for Importation of Indonesian LNG." Wall Street Journal, 3 January 1978, pp. 3, 8.

Huhs, John I. "Developing Trade with the Soviet Union." Columbia Journal of World Business 8 (Fall 1973): 116-130.

International Trade Advisory Group, Inc. "Twenty-Five Soviet Market Problems." Kent, Ohio, 1973. (Mimeographed.)

"Kama Truck Project Gets Rolling." Business Week, August 14, 1971, p. 32.

Kaser, Michael. "Soviet Trade Turns to Europe." Foreign Policy, Summer 1975, pp. 123-135.

Kosnik, Joseph T. Natural Gas Imports from the Soviet Union. Financing the North Star Joint Venture Project. New York: Praeger, 1975.

Lewis, Vivian. "The Big Prickly Problem of Lending to the Soviet Bloc." Financier, May 1977, pp. 19-21, 24.

Link, Mary. "Grain Export Policy: No Easy Solutions." Congressional Quarterly: Weekly Report, September 20, 1975, pp. 1-4.

"Mack Quits Red Deal." Automotive Industries, October 1, 1971, p. 18.

"Major Trade Bill Reported in Senate, 17-0." Congressional Quarterly: Weekly Report, December 7, 1973, pp. 1-4.

Marer, Paul. Soviet and East European Foreign Trade, 1946-1969. Bloomington, Ind.: Indiana University Press, 1972.

"Massive Grain Sales to Soviet Union in 1972 Spurred Search for New U.S. Export Policy." Congressional Quarterly: Weekly Report, September 20, 1975, pp. 2-3.

Melloan, George. "Going into Partnership with Ivan." Wall Street Journal, 29 March 1973, p. 14.

Meyer, Herbert E. "A Plant that Could Change the Shape of Soviet Industry." Fortune, November 1974, pp. 150-157, 229-230, 232.

Meyer, Herbert E. "Why that Soviet Buying Spree Won't Last." Fortune, January 1975, pp. 94-97, 132, 136, 138.

Meyer, Herbert E. "Why the Russians Are Shopping the U.S." Fortune, February 1973, pp. 66-72, 148.

Milosh, E. J. "Imaginative Marketing in Eastern Europe." Columbia Journal of World Business 8 (December 1973): 69-72.

Morgan, John P. "The Financial Aspects of East-West Trade." Columbia Journal of World Business 8 (December 1973): 51-56.

"MT Builders Eye $5 billion Soviet Market." Iron Age, November 9, 1972, p. 58.

National Association of Manufacturers. Proceedings of the U.S.-Soviet Trade Conference. Washington, D.C. 1973.

National Association of Manufacturers. U.S.-Soviet Trade Conference. "Participant Planning Workbook." Washington, D.C., February 1973. (Mimeographed.)

"New Trade Act Aims at Fair Access to Markets, Industry Safeguards." Commerce Today, January 6, 1975, pp. 5-8.

"Nixon Uses Credit to Push Soviet Trade." Business Week, June 1, 1974, p. 24.

"Not All Is Going Well in Russia." U.S. News & World Report, September 9, 1974, pp. 56-57.

Occidental LNG Corporation. American-Siberian Natural Gas Co. "Yakutia LNG Project." Internal company document, November 1977. (Mimeographed.)

Occidental LNG Corporation. American-Siberian Natural Gas Co. "Yakutia LNG Project: Preliminary Project Analysis Summary." Internal company document, November 1977. (Mimeographed.)

"Occidental Petroleum—USSR Contract." Chemical Week, July 26, 1978, p. 12.

O'Conner, John. "PepsiCo Gets Bottling Pact with Soviets." Advertising Age, November 20, 1972, p. 116.

Organization for Economic Cooperation and Development. "Annotations to Agenda Item 2, 18th Special Session of the Executive Committee." Paris, 1976. (Mimeographed.)

Organization for Economic Cooperation and Development. Statistics of Foreign Trade (Series A), July 1976, pp. 8-9.

Organization for Economic Cooperation and Development. Working Party of the Trade Committee. "East—West Trade: Trends in East—West Trade." Paris, 1977. (Mimeographed.)

"Oxy, Soviets Sign 5-Year Business Deal." Oil and Gas Journal, July 24, 1972, pp. 14-15.

"The Pepski Generation." Time, November 27, 1977, pp. 74-75.

"Picking Up Where Mack Left Off." Business Week, September 25, 1971, pp. 42-43.

Pisar, Samuel. Coexistence and Commerce: Guidelines for Transactions Between East and West. New York: McGraw-Hill Book Company, 1970.

Quigley, John. The Soviet Foreign Trade Monopoly: Institutions and Laws. Columbus: Ohio State University Press, 1974.

"Reopening Moscow's Credit Line." Business Week, August 4, 1975, p. 81.

Rushing, Francis W., and Lieberman, Anne R. "U.S.-U.S.S.R. Trade and Soviet Technology Requirements." Association for Comparative Economic Studies Bulletin 18 (Fall 1976): 61-79.

Russell, Jeremy. "CIA Too Gloomy over Russian Oil Prospects." Times (London), 27 July 1977, p. 23.

"Russia, Seeking Top Quality, Pays a Premium Price for American Made Equipment." Wall Street Journal, 7 May 1973, p. 6.

."A Russian Made Fiat Gives Fiat Competition." Business
     Week, June 9, 1975, p. 38.

"The Russians Are Coming." Forbes, October 15, 1974,
     p. 50-51.

"Russia's Car Challenge." Business Week, June 16, 1975,
     p. 30.

Rosefielde, Steven. "The Changing Pattern of Soviet
     Trade." Current History 69 (October 1975): 133-136,
     147-148.

Rosefieldé, Steven. Soviet International Trade in
     Heckscher-Ohlin Perspective. Lexington, Mass.:
     Lexington Books, 1973.

Sauer, Walter C. "Eximbank Credits Back East-West Trade."
     Columbia Journal of World Business 8 (December
     1973): 57-60.

Schukin, George S. "The Soviet Position on Trade with the
     United States." Columbia Journal of World Business
     8 (December 1973): 47-50.

"Semiconductors Take a Sudden Plunge." Business Week,
     November 16, 1974, pp. 64-65.

"Siberian Resources Slip from Japan's Grasp." Business
     Week, July 28, 1975, p. 32.

Smith, Glen A. Soviet Foreign Trade: Organization,
     Operations, and Policy, 1918-1971. New York:
     Praeger, 1973.

"Some Russian Deals Start to Unravel." Business Week,
     February 3, 1975, pp. 22, 24.

"The Soviet Bloc Opens the Door." Business Week, July 6,
     1974, pp. 194, 196.

"Soviet Grain Deal May Raise the Curtain." Business
     Week, July 15, 1972, p. 23.

"Soviet Offices Sought by First National City and Chase
     Manhattan." Wall Street Journal, 1 November 1972,
     p. 40.

"Soviet Stability Is Costly: Trade Keyed to Financing."
     Commerce Today, March 17, 1975, pp. 27-28.

"Soviet Trade: Pro and Con." Congressional Quarterly: Weekly Report, September 14, 1974, p. 20.

"Soviet Union: Small U.S. Suppliers Line Up a Big Deal." Business Week, July 1, 1972, p. 29.

"Soviet Union: The Export Drive in Consumer Goods." Business Week, October 27, 1975, p. 38.

"Soviet Union: Grabbing a Big Share of the Shipping Trade." Business Week, January 12, 1976, p. 46.

"Soviet Union: A Slower Timetable for Completing Kamaz." Business Week, October 19, 1974, pp. 56, 60.

"Soviet Union: Why the Russians Are Paying Cash." Business Week, November 30, 1974, pp. 40, 44.

"Soviet Union: Why U.S. Trade Is Winding Down." Business Week, June 2, 1975, p. 34.

Starr, Robert, ed. East-West Business Transactions. New York: Praeger, 1974.

Stowell, Christopher E. Soviet Industrial Import Priorities with Marketing Considerations for Exporting to the USSR. New York: Praeger, 1975.

"A Sudden Slowing in Trade with Russia." Business Week, January 27, 1975, pp. 48-49.

"Sweden: How a Little Company Won a Big Soviet Job." Business Week, October 6, 1975.

"Thaw in U.S-Soviet Trade?" U.S. News and World Report, November 15, 1971, p. 39.

"There's Plenty of Green in the Big Red Market." Chemical Week, August 2, 1972, pp. 12-13.

Theriot, Lawrence H. "Financing American Exports in East-West Trade." In The International Essays for Business Decision Makers, pp. 108-114. Edited by Mark B. Winchester. Dallas: SMU School of Business, 1976.

"To Russia with Profit--U.S. Tools." Iron Age, June 17, 1971, pp. 39-41.

"Trade Negotiations at Last." Business Week, October 26, 1974, p. 48.

"Trade with Russia." Business Week, May 25, 1974, p. 84.

"Trade with Russia Stays on Course." Business Week, January 20, 1975, pp. 24-25.

"Trade with Socialist Nations Maintains Favorable Balance." Commerce Today, August 4, 1975, pp. 23-27.

"Trade with the Soviet Bloc Takes Off." Business Week, August 5, 1972, p. 16.

"Trading with Russia Gets Down to Hardware." Business Week, June 12, 1971, p. 95.

Turpin, William N. Soviet Foreign Trade. Lexington, Mass.: Lexington Books, 1977.

United Nations. Economic Commission for Europe, Committee on the Development of Trade, 3d Seminar on East-West Trade Promotion, 13-15 May 1975, Licensing and Leasing. (TRADE/INF.2 1976).

U.S. Central Intelligence Agency. National Foreign Assessment Center. Organization and Management in the Soviet Economy: The Ceaseless Search for Panaceas. Research Paper (ER 77-10769), December 1977. [Available from Document Expediting (DOCEX) Project, Exchange and Gift Division, Library of Congress.]

U.S. Central Intelligence Agency. Office of Economic Research. "A Discussion Paper on Soviet Petroleum Production Prepared for the Advisory Committee on East-West Trade, U.S. Department of Commerce." Washington, D.C. 1977. (Mimeographed.)

U.S. Central Intelligence Agency. Office of Economic Research. Prospects for Soviet Oil Production. Research Paper (ER 77-10270), April 1977. [Available from Document Expediting (DOCEX) Project, Exchange and Gift Division, Library of Congress.]

U.S. Central Intelligence Agency. Office of Economic
     Research. Prospects for Soviet Oil Production: A
     Supplemental Analysis. Research Paper (ER
     77-10425), July 1977. [Available from Document
     Expediting (DOCEX) Project, Exchange and Gift
     Division, Library of Congress.]

U.S. Central Intelligence Agency. Office of Economic
     Research. Recent Developments in Soviet Hard
     Currency Trade. Research Aid (ER 76-10015), January
     1976. [Available from Document Expediting (DOCEX)
     Project, Exchange and Gift Division, Library of
     Congress.]

U.S. Central Intelligence Agency. Office of Economic
     Research. "Role of U.S. Subsidiaries in East-West
     Trade." Washington, D.C. 1974. (Mimeographed.)

U.S. Central Intelligence Agency. Office of Economic
     Research. Soviet Economic Problems and Prospects.
     Research Paper (ER 77-10436U), July 1977. [Available
     from Document Expediting (DOCEX) Project, Exchange
     and Gift Division, Library of Congress.]

U.S. Central Intelligence Agency. Office of Economic
     Research. The International Energy Situation to
     1985. Research Paper (ER 77-10240U), April 1977.
     [Available from Document Expediting (DOCEX) Project,
     Exchange and Gift Division, Library of Congress.]

U.S. Central Intelligence Agency. Office of Economic
     Research. USSR: Long-Range Prospects for Hard
     Currency Trade. Research Aid (A[ER]75-61), January
     1975. [Available from Document Expediting (DOCEX)
     Project, Exchange and Gift Division, Library of
     Congress.]

U.S. Congress. General Accounting Office. Exporters'
     Profits on Sales of U.S. Wheat to Russia. GAO
     Report No. B-176943, February 1974.

U.S. Congress. House. Committee on International
     Relations. First Semiannual Report by the President
     to the Commission on Security and Cooperation in
     Europe. S. Doc. 80-008, 94th Cong., 2d sess., 1976.

U.S. Congress. House. Committee on Ways and Means. <u>First Quarterly Report to the Congress and the East-West Foreign Trade Board on Trade between the United States and the Nonmarket Economy Countries. Submitted to the Congress by the International Trade Commission, March 31, 1975.</u> H. Doc. 50-703 0, 94th Cong., 1st sess., 1975.

U.S. Congress. House. <u>East-West Foreign Trade Board Fourth Quarterly Report 1975.</u> H. Doc. 94-430, 94th Cong., 2d sess., 1976.

U.S. Congress. Joint Economic Committee. <u>Soviet Economic Outlook. Hearings before the Joint Economic Committee</u>, 93d Cong., 1st sess., 1973.

U.S. Congress. Joint Economic Committee. <u>Economic Developments in Countries of Eastern Europe. A Compendium of Papers Submitted to the Subcommittee on Foreign Economic Policy.</u> Joint Committee Print, 91st Cong., 2d sess., 1970. Washington, D.C.: Government Printing Office, 1970.

U.S. Congress. Joint Economic Committee. <u>Soviet Economic Problems and Prospects.</u> Joint Committee Print, 95th Cong., 1st sess., 1977. Washington, D.C.: Government Printing Office, 1977.

U.S. Congress. Joint Economic Committee. <u>Soviet Economic Prospects for the Seventies. A Compendium of Papers Submitted to the Joint Economic Committee.</u> Joint Committee Print, 93d Cong., 1st sess., 1973. Washington, D.C.: Government Printing Office, 1973.

U.S. Congress. Library of Congress. Congressional Research Service. "East-West Financing by Export-Import Bank and National Interest Criteria," by John P. Hardt and George D. Holliday. Washington, D.C. 1975. (Mimeographed.)

U.S. Congress. Library of Congress. Congressional Research Service. "East-West Trade and Commercial Relations During 1977," by Ronda Bresnick. Washington, D.C. 1977. (Mimeographed.)

U.S. Congress. Library of Congress. Congressional Research Service. "Soviet Oil and Gas in the Global Perspective," by John P. Hardt and Ronda A. Bresnick. Washington, D.C. 1977. (Mimeographed.)

U.S. Congress. Library of Congress. Congressional Research
Service. "Western Technology and Economic
Performance in the Eastern Countries," by John P.
Hardt and George D. Holliday. Washington, D.C.
1976. (Mimeographed.)

U.S. Congress. Senate. Committee on Energy and Natural
Resources. Project Interdependence. U.S. and World
Energy Outlook Through 1990. 95th Cong., 1st sess.,
1977.

U.S. Congress. Senate. Committee on Foreign Relations.
Western Investment in Communist Economies, by John
P. Hardt and George D. Holliday. 93d Cong., 2d
sess., 1974.

U.S. Department of Agriculture. Economic Research Service.
Foreign Demand and Competition Division. Prospects
for Agricultural Trade with the USSR. Washington,
D.C. 1974. (ERS-Foreign 356.)

U.S. Department of Commerce. Bureau of East-West Trade.
East-West Trade Financing: An Introductory Guide,
by Suzanne F. Porter. Washington, D.C.: Government
Printing Office, 1976.

U.S. Department of Commerce. Bureau of East-West Trade.
Export Administration Report: First Quarter 1975;
11th Report on U.S. Export Controls to the President
and the Congress. Washington, D.C.: Government
Printing Office, 1975.

U.S. Department of Commerce. Bureau of East-West Trade.
Office of East-West Policy and Planning. "Communist
Country Hard Currency Debt in Perspective," by
Lawrence H. Theriot. Washington, D.C. 1978.
(Mimeographed.)

U.S. Department of Commerce. Bureau of East-West Trade.
Office of East-West Policy and Planning. "Communist
Exports to the West in Import Sensitive Sectors," by
Karen Taylor and Deborah Lamb. Washington, D.C.
1978. (Mimeographed.)

U.S. Department of Commerce. Bureau of East-West Trade.
Office of East-West Policy and Planning. "Current
Soviet Indebtedness and the Future Availability of
Credits from Western Europe and Japan." Washington,
D.C. 1976. (Mimeographed.)

U.S. Department of Commerce. Bureau of East-West Trade.
Office of East-West Policy and Planning. "East-West
Consortium Banks--A Source for Expanded U.S.
Lending?," by Lawrence H. Theriot. Washington, D.C.
1978. (Mimeographed.)

U.S. Department of Commerce. Bureau of East-West Trade.
Office of East-West Policy and Planning.
"Industrial Cooperation Agreements: Soviet
Experience and Practice," by Maureen R. Smith.
Washington, D.C. 1976. (Mimeographed.)

U.S. Department of Commerce. Bureau of East-West Trade.
Office of East-West Policy and Planning. "Legal
Lending Limits and the Theoretical Capacity of the
U.S. Commercial Banking System for Financing
East-West Trade," by William F. Kolarik, Jr.
Washington, D.C. 1978. (Mimeographed.)

U.S. Department of Commerce. Bureau of East-West Trade.
Office of East-West Policy and Planning. "Potential
1980 and 1985 Hard Currency Debt of the USSR and
Eastern Europe Under Selected Hypotheses," by Allen
J. Lenz. Washington, D.C. 1978. (Mimeographed.)

U.S. Department of Commerce. Bureau of East-West Trade.
Office of East-West Policy and Planning. "Potential
U.S. Governmental Sources for Financing East-West
Trade," by Lawrence H. Theriot. Washington, D.C.
1976. (Mimeographed.)

U.S. Department of Commerce. Bureau of East-West Trade.
Office of East-West Policy and Planning.
"Quantification of Export Sales to Eastern Europe
and the U.S.S.R. by West European Based U.S.
Majority-Owned Subsidiaries," by James S. Elliott.
Washington, D.C. 1977. (Mimeographed.)

U.S. Department of Commerce. Bureau of East-West Trade.
Office of East-West Policy and Planning. "Quanti-
fication of Western Exports of High Technology
Products to the Communist Countries," by John P.
Young. Washington, D.C. 1978. (Mimeographed.)

U.S. Department of Commerce. Bureau of East-West Trade.
Office of East-West Policy and Planning. Selected
Trade and Economic Data of the Centrally Planned
Economies. Washington, D.C. 1976.

U.S. Department of Commerce. Bureau of East-West Trade. Office of East-West Policy and Planning. Selected Trade and Economic Data of the Centrally Planned Economies. Washington, D.C. 1977.

U.S. Department of Commerce. Bureau of East-West Trade. Office of East-West Policy and Planning. "Soviet and East European Export Performance to the Industrialized West: An Update Incorporating 1976 Data," by Hedija H. Kravalis. Washington, D.C. 1978. (Mimeographed.)

U.S. Department of Commerce. Bureau of East-West Trade. Office of East-West Policy and Planning. "Statistical Abstract of East-West Trade Finance," by William F. Kolarik, Jr. Washington, D.C. 1978. (Mimeographed.)

U.S. Department of Commerce. Bureau of East-West Trade. Office of East-West Policy and Planning. "The Potential for a Reversal in the East-West Trade Balance," by Allen J. Lenz. Washington, D.C. 1976. (Mimeographed.)

U.S. Department of Commerce. Bureau of East-West Trade. Office of East-West Policy and Planning. "The Potential Role of Eximbank Credits in Financing U.S.-Soviet Trade," by Allen J. Lenz and Lawrence H. Theriot. Washington, D.C. 1978. (Mimeographed.)

U.S. Department of Commerce. Bureau of East-West Trade. Office of East-West Policy and Planning. "The U.S. Perspective on East-West Industrial Cooperation." Washington, D.C. 1976. (Mimeographed.)

U.S. Department of Commerce. Bureau of East-West Trade. Office of East-West Policy and Planning. U.S. Trade Status with Socialist Countries. Washington, D.C., May 26, 1976.

U.S. Department of Commerce. Bureau of East-West Trade. Office of East-West Policy and Planning. U.S. Trade Status with Socialist Countries. Washington, D.C., July 20, 1978.

U.S. Department of Commerce. Bureau of East-West Trade. Office of East-West Policy and Planning. U.S. Trade with the Communist Countries by Seven Digit Commodity Code for 1977. Washington, D.C. 1978.

U.S. Department of Commerce. Bureau of East-West Trade.
Office of East-West Policy and Planning. "U.S.-
U.S.S.R. Trade Trends Through First Quarter, 1977."
Washington, D.C. 1977. (Mimeographed.)

U.S. Department of Commerce. Bureau of East-West Trade.
Office of East-West Policy and Planning. "U.S.-
U.S.S.R. Trade Trends, 1977." Washington, D.C.
1978. (Mimeographed.)

U.S. Department of Commerce. Bureau of East-West Trade.
Office of East-West Trade Analysis. "Trading
Apparatus of a Non-Market," by Allen J. Lenz. Paper
presented at the Houston World Trade Conference,
April 18, 1975. Washington, D.C. 1975.
(Mimeographed.)

U.S. Department of Commerce. Bureau of East-West Trade.
Office of East-West Trade Analysis. "U.S. Import
Dependency on Socialist Countries for Metallic
Minerals Through 1980," by Donald Businger.
Washington, D.C. 1976. (Mimeographed.)

U.S. Department of Commerce. Bureau of East-West Trade.
Polymerization Processes and Related Production
Equipment: A Market Assessment for the U.S.S.R.
Washington, D.C., June 1974.

U.S. Department of Commerce. Bureau of East-West Trade.
Trade Development Assistance Division. "U.S.
Companies with Science and Technology Cooperation
Agreements with the Soviet State Committee for
Science and Technology." Washington, D.C., 1976.
(Mimeographed.)

U.S. Department of Commerce. Bureau of East-West Trade.
U.S.S.R. Affairs Division. "Recent Soviet
Performance Growth Rates." Washington, D.C. 1976.
(Mimeographed.)

U.S. Department of Commerce. Bureau of East-West Trade.
U.S.S.R. Affairs Division. U.S.-Soviet Commercial
Agreements 1972. Washington, D.C. 1973.

U.S. Department of Commerce. Bureau of International
Commerce. Metalworking and Finishing Equipment:
Union of Soviet Socialist Republics. Country Market
Survey (CMS 74-045), October 1974. Washington, D.C.
1974.

U.S. Department of Commerce. Domestic and International
    Business Administration. Basic Data on the Economy
    of the Union of Soviet Socialist Republics.
    Overseas Business Report (OBR 74-25), July 1974.
    Washington, D.C. 1974.

U.S. Department of Commerce. Domestic and International
    Business Administration. An Introduction to the
    Bureau of East-West Trade. Washington, D.C. 1974.

U.S. Department of Labor. Bureau of International Labor
    Affairs. Office of Foreign Economic Research.
    Discussion Papers on International Trade, Foreign
    Investment and Employment, by Jack Baranson.
    Washington, D.C. 1976.

U.S. Department of Labor. Bureau of International Labor
    Affairs. Office of Foreign Economic Research.
    "Technology Transfer: Effects on U.S.
    Competitiveness and Employment," by Jack Baranson.
    Washington, D.C. 1976. (Mimeographed.)

U.S. Department of State. Bureau of Intelligence and
    Research. Office of External Research. "Soviet
    Economic Relations with Eastern Europe and Their
    Impact on East-West and U.S.-USSR Trade," by Paul
    Marer. Washington, D.C. 1975. (Mimeographed.)

U.S. International Trade Commission. Eleventh Report on
    Trade between the United States and the Nonmarket
    Economy Countries. ITC Publication 836, September
    1977. Washington, D.C. 1977.

U.S. International Trade Commission. Special Report to the
    Congress and the East-West Foreign Trade Board on
    the Probable Impact on U.S. Trade of Granting
    Most-Favored-Nation Treatment to the U.S.S.R. ITC
    Publication 812, April 1977. Washington, D.C. 1977.

U.S. President. International Economic Report of the
    President. Washington, D.C.: Government Printing
    Office, 1976.

U.S. President. International Economic Report of the
    President. Washington, D.C.: Government Printing
    Office, 1977.

"The U.S. Trade Lag with Eastern Europe." Business Week,
    February 23, 1976, pp. 44, 49, 51.

"U.S. Trade Rose Steeply in 1974; Oil Price Increase Led to Deficit." Commerce Today, February 17, 1975, pp. 7-9.

"U.S. Trade Share Performance Remains Strong in about Half of World's Leading Markets." Commerce Today, February 3, 1975, pp. 23-24.

U.S.-U.S.S.R. Trade and Economic Council. Finance Committee. "Report of the Meeting of the Finance Committee." New York, 1975. (Mimeographed.)

U.S.-U.S.S.R. Trade and Economic Council. "Financing U.S.-Soviet Trade: 1980." New York, 1974. (Mimeographed.)

U.S.-U.S.S.R. Trade and Economic Council. "President's Report to the Council," by Harold B. Scott. New York, 1977. (Mimeographed.)

"The Warmup in Russian Trade." Business Week, May 6, 1972, pp. 68-72.

"Was Mack Sold Down the Kama River?" Iron Age, November 4, 1971, p. 49.

Ways, Max. "Business Faces Growing Pressures to Behave Better." Fortune, May 1974, pp. 193-195, 310, 314, 316, 319-326.

"What Business Thinks." Fortune, October 1969, pp. 139-140, 196.

"What It's Like To Do Business with the Russians." Fortune, May 1972, pp. 166-169.

"Who Knifed Mack Out of the Kama Plant?" Iron Age, September 23, 1971, p. 47.

"Will U.S. Let Mack Hack It in USSR?" Iron Age, August 5, 1971, p. 41.

Winter, David. "Protecting East-West Trade Contracts and Operations." Columbia Journal of World Business 8 (December 1973): 73-77.

Wolf, Thomas A. "Industry Problems in East-West Trade." Columbus: Ohio State University, Department of Economics, 1975. (Mimeographed.)

Wolf, Thomas A. "On the Adjustment of Centrally Planned
    Economies to External Economic Disturbances." Paper
    presented at the National Meeting of the American
    Association for the Advancement of Slavic Studies.
    Washington, D.C., October 1977. (Mimeographed.)

"World Economy: The Order Books Begin to Empty." <u>Business
    Week</u>, August 24, 1974, pp. 30-31.

II.  Policy-Related Studies

Aberbach, Joel S.  "Alienation and Political Behavior."
    American Political Science Review 63 (March 1969):
    86-99.

Almond, Gabriel A., and Verba, Sidney.  The Civic Culture:
    Political Attitudes and Democracy in Five Nations.
    Princeton:  Princeton University Press, 1963.

Atlantic Council Committee on East-West Trade.  East-West
    Trade:  Managing Encounter and Accommodation.
    Boulder, Colorado:  Westview Press, 1977.

Bauer, Raymond A.; Pool, Ithiel DeSola; and Dexter, Lewis
    Anthony.  American Business and Public Policy.  2nd
    edition.  Chicago:  Aldine-Atherton, 1972.

Bell, Coral.  The Diplomacy of Detente:  The Kissinger Era.
    New York:  St. Martin's Press, 1977.

Berg, Norman.  "Strategic Planning in Conglomerate
    Companies."  Harvard Business Review 43 (May-June
    1965):  79-92.

Birnbaum, Karl E.  "Human Rights and East-West Relations."
    Foreign Affairs 55 (July 1977):  783-799.

Blough, Roy.  "U.S. Trade Policy:  Past Successes, Future
    Problems."  Columbia Journal of World Business 8
    (Fall 1973):  7-19.

Boddewyn, Jean, and Cracco, Etienne, F.  "The Political
    Game in World Business."  Columbia Journal of World
    Business 7 (January-February 1972):  45-56.

Bray, Charles W.  "The Media and Foreign Policy."  Foreign
    Policy, Fall 1974, pp. 109-125.

"The Breakdown of U.S. Innovation."  Business Week,
    February 16, 1976, pp. 56-60, 65-68.

Brooks, Harvey.  "What's Happening to the U.S. Lead in
    Technology?"  Harvard Business Review 50 (May-June
    1972):  110-118.

Brookstone, Jeffrey M.  The Multinational Businessman and
    Foreign Policy.  Entrepreneurial Politics in East-
    West Trade and Investment.  New York:  Praeger, 1976.

Brown, Alan A.; Marer, Paul; and Neuberger, Egon. "Prospects for U.S.-East European Trade." American Economic Review 64 (May 1974): 300-306.

Brown, Seyom. "A Cooling-Off Period for U.S.-Soviet Relations." Foreign Policy, Fall 1977, pp. 3-21.

Campbell, John C. "Soviet-American Relations: Detente and Dispute." Current History 69 (October 1975): 113-116, 146-147, 149-151.

Cooper, Richard N. "Economic Interdependence and Foreign Policy in the Seventies." World Politics 24 (January 1972): 159-181.

Cooper, Richard N. "Trade Policy Is Foreign Policy." Foreign Policy, Winter 1972-1973, pp. 18-36.

DeMartino, Eduardo, and Searle, Bruce A. "Operating on a Global Basis . . . Today and Tomorrow." Columbia Journal of World Business 7 (September-October 1972): 51-61.

Dent, Frederick B. "U.S. Foreign Trade: The Challenge of the 1970s." Columbia Journal of World Business 8 (Fall 1973): 26-29.

Diebold, William J. "U.S. Trade Policy: The New Political Dimensions." Foreign Affairs 52 (April 1974): 472-496.

Dixon, John W. "Technology Transfer--An Essential Export Resource." In The International Essays for Business Decision Makers, pp. 123-127. Edited by Mark B. Winchester. Dallas: SMU School of Business, 1976.

Draper, Theodore, ed. Defending America: Toward a New Role in the Post-Detente World. New York: Basic Books, 1977.

Drucker, Peter F. "Multinationals and Developing Countries: Myths and Realities." Foreign Affairs 53 (October 1974): 121-134.

East-West Trade Council. Proceedings of a Symposium on National Policy Trends in East-West Trade, October 5, 1972. Washington, D.C. 1976. (Mimeographed.)

Finifter, Ada W. "Dimensions of Political Alienation."
American Political Science Review 64 (June 1970):
389-410.

Finley, David D. "Detente and Soviet-American Trade: An
Approach to a Political Balance Sheet." Paper
presented at the Central Slavic Conference. St.
Louis, November 1974. (Mimeographed.)

Fitzpatrick, Peter B. "Soviet-American Trade, 1972-1974: A
Summary." Virginia Journal of International Law 15
(Fall 1974): 39-71.

Friesen, Connie M. The Political Economy of East-West Trade.
New York: Praeger, 1976.

Gat, Charles. "The Forgotten Region." Foreign Policy,
Summer 1975, pp. 135-145.

Gift, Richard E. "Trading in a Threat System: The U.S.-
Soviet Case." Journal of Conflict Resolution 13
(December 1969): 418-437.

Gillette, Philip S. "The Interaction of Trade and Political
Detente in Soviet-American Relations." Paper
presented at the Central Slavic Conference. St.
Louis, November 1974. (Mimeographed.)

Goldmark, Francis M. "Strategy: Worldwide Long-Range
Market Analysis." Columbia Journal of World
Business 9 (Winter 1974): 50-53.

Greenman, W. Frank; Brockett, W. Don; Brown, Malcolm C.;
Dunn, Thomas C.; Shearer, Daniel D.; Levine, Herbert
S.; Earle, M. Mark, Jr.; and Lieberman, Anne R.
Impact on U.S. Foreign Trade and Investment from
Commercial Transfers of Advanced Technology to the
Soviet Union and Eastern Europe. Task 3: Product
Impact Studies. Menlo Park, Cal.: Stanford
Research Institute, 1975.

Grossman, Gregory. "Prospects and Policy for U.S.-Soviet
Trade." American Economic Review 64 (May 1974):
289-298.

Hammer, Darrell P. USSR: The Politics of Oligarchy.
Hinsdale, Ill.: Dryden, 1974.

Harriman, W. Averell. America and Russia in a Changing World: A Half Century of Personal Observation. New York: Doubleday, 1971.

Hayden, Eric W., and Nau, Henry R. "East-West Technology Transfer: Theoretical Models and Practical Experiences." Columbia Journal of World Business 10 (Fall 1975): 70-82.

Hazen, W. William. "U.S. Foreign Trade in the Seventies." Columbia Journal of World Business 6 (September-October 1971): 47-60.

Hewett, Edward A. "The Economics of East European Technology Imports from the West." American Economic Review 65 (May 1975): 377-382.

Hofer, Charles W. "Research on Strategic Planning: A Survey of Past Studies and Suggestions for Future Efforts." Journal of Economics and Business 28 (Spring-Summer 1976): 261-286.

Hosoya, Chihiro; Owen, Henry; and Shonfield, Andrew. Collaboration with Communist Countries in Managing Global Problems: An Examination of the Options. New York: The Trilateral Commission, 1977.

Hough, Jerry F., ed. The Soviet Union and Social Science Theory. Cambridge, Harvard University Press, 1977.

Hough, Jerry F. "The Bureaucratic Model and the Nature of the Soviet System." Journal of Comparative Administration 5 (August 1973): 134-167.

House, James S., and Mason, William M. "Political Alienation in America, 1952-1968." American Sociological Review 40 (April 1975): 123-147.

Johnson, D. Gale. "Soviet Agriculture and United States-Soviet Relations." Current History 73 (October 1977): 118-122, 133-134.

Josephs, Ray. "A Global Approach to Public Relations." Columbia Journal of World Business 8 (Fall 1973): 93-97.

Kaikati, Jack G. "The Reincarnation of Barter Trade as a Marketing Tool." Journal of Marketing 40 (April 1976): 17-24.

Kanet, Roger E., and Bahry, Donna. "Soviet Policy in East Europe." Current History 69 (October 1975): 126-128, 154.

Kearns, Henry. "Credit: A Key to Export Sales." Columbia Journal of World Business 6 (March-April 1971): 31-38.

Kennedy, Edward M. "Beyond Detente." Foreign Policy, Fall 1974, pp. 3-29.

Keohane, Robert O. "Not 'Innocents Abroad': American Multinational Corporations and the United States Government." Comparative Politics 8 (January 1976): 307-320.

Kiser, John W., III. "Technology Is Not a One-Way Street." Foreign Policy, Summer 1976, pp. 131-148.

Kissinger, Henry A. American Foreign Policy. 3d edition. New York: Norton, 1977.

Klingbert, Frank L. "The Historical Alternation of Moods in American Foreign Policy." World Politics 4 (January 1952): 239-273.

Kolarik, William F., Jr., and Clawson, Robert W. "The Businessmen: Soviet and American Trade Actors." Paper presented at the Central Slavic Conference, University of Missouri, 1974. St. Louis, November 1974. (Mimeographed.)

Kolodziej, Edward A. "Foreign Policy and the Politics of Interdependence: The Nixon Presidency." Polity 9 (Winter 1976): 121-157.

Korbel, Josef. "Changes in Eastern Europe and New Opportunities for American Policy." World Politics 18 (July 1966): 749-757.

Lambeth, Benjamin S. "The Evolving Soviet Strategic Threat." Current History 69 (October 1975): 121-125, 152-153.

Lange, Irene, and Elliott, James F. "U.S. Role in East-West Trade: An Appraisal." Journal of International Business Studies 8 (Fall/Winter 1977): 5-16.

. Leff, Nathaniel H. "International Sourcing Strategy." Columbia Journal of World Business 9 (Fall 1974): 71-79.

Leonhard, Wolfgang. "The Domestic Politics of the New
        Soviet Foreign Policy." Foreign Affairs 52 (October
        1973): 59-74.

Lerner, Daniel. "French Business Leaders Look to EDC: A
        Preliminary Report." Public Opinion Quarterly 20
        (Spring 1956): 212-221.

Levine, Herbert S.; Earle, M. Mark, Jr.; Movit, Charles H.;
        and Lieberman, Anne R. Transfer of U.S. Technology
        to the Soviet Union: Impact on U.S. Commercial
        Interests. Menlo Park, Ca.: Stanford Research
        Institute, 1976.

Levine, Herbert S.; Zuehlke, Arthur A.; Movit, Charles H.;
        Cole, James E.; Rushing, Francis W.; Earle, M. Mark,
        Jr.; and Foster, Richard B. Study of the Political
        and Military Utility of U.S.-U.S.S.R. Economic
        Relations. Menlo Park, Ca.: Stanford Research
        Institute, 1976.

Lieberman, Anne R., and Rushing, Francis W. The Role of
        U.S.-Soviet Trade in Soviet Growth Strategy for the
        Seventies. Menlo Park, Ca.: Stanford Research
        Institute, 1976.

Louis, Arthur M. "What Business Thinks." Fortune,
        September 1969, pp. 93-96, 208.

Matthias, Willard C., ed. Common Sense in U.S.-Soviet Trade.
        Washington, D. C.: American Committee on East-West
        Accord, 1979.

McLellan, David, and Woodhouse, Charles T. "The Business
        Elite and Foreign Policy." Western Political
        Quarterly 13 (March 1960): 172-190.

Mansfield, Edwin. "International Technology Transfer:
        Forms, Resource Requirements, and Policies."
        American Economic Review 65 (May 1975): 372-376.

Marantz, Paul. "Internal Politics and Soviet Foreign Policy:
        A Case Study." Western Political Quarterly 28
        (March 1975): 130-146.

Marcy, Carl, ed. Common Sense in U.S.-Soviet Relations.
        Washington, D.C.: American Committee on East-West
        Accord, 1978.

Marer, Paul, ed. U.S. Financing of East-West Trade: The Political Economy of Government Credits and the National Interest. Bloomington, Ind.: International Development Research Center, Indiana University, 1975.

Martin, Andrew. The Politics of Economic Policy in the United States: A Tentative View from a Comparative Perspective. Beverly Hills, Cal: Sage Professional Papers in Comparative Politics 01-040, 1973.

Miller, Arthur H. "Political Issues and Trust in Government 1964-1970." American Political Science Review 68 (September 1974): 951-972.

Mondale, Walter F. "Beyond Detente: Toward International Economic Security." Foreign Affairs 53 (October 1974): 1-23.

Morganthau, Hans J. "Changes and Chances in American-Soviet Relations." Foreign Affairs 49 (April 1971): 429-441.

Mueller, Robert K. "Venture Vogue: Boneyard or Bonanza?" Columbia Journal of World Business 8 (Spring 1973): 78-82.

Neal, Fred W. "Are We Headed Toward a Cool War?" Report to the American Committee on East-West Accord. Washington, D.C., September 1977. (Mimeographed.)

Newman, William H. "Is Management Exportable?" Columbia Journal of World Business 5 (January/February 1970): 7-18.

Nitze, Paul H. "Assuring Strategic Stability in an Era of Detente." Foreign Affairs 54 (January 1976): 207-232.

Nutter, G. Warren. Kissinger's Grand Design. Washington, D.C.: American Enterprise Institute, 1976.

Nye, Joseph S., Jr. "Multinational Corporations in World Politics." Foreign Affairs 53 (October 1974): 153-175.

Odom, William E. "Who Controls Whom in Moscow." Foreign Affairs 19 (Summer 1975): 109-123.

Olsen, Marvin E. "Alienation and Political Opinions."
Public Opinion Quarterly 29 (Summer 1965): 200-212.

Parenti, Michael. The Anti-Communist Impulse. New York:
Random House, 1969.

Pierce, John C., and Rose, Douglas H. "Nonattitudes and
American Public Opinion: The Examination of a
Thesis." American Political Science Review 68 (June
1974): 626-649.

Portes, Richard. "East Europe's Debt to the West:
Interdependence is a Two-Way Street." Foreign
Affairs 55 (July 1977): 751-782.

Ramsey, James A. "East-West Business Cooperation: The
The Twain Meets." Columbia Journal of World
Business 5 (July-August 1970): 17-20.

Rhodes, John B. "U.S. New Business Activities Abroad."
Columbia Journal of World Business 9 (Summer 1974):
99-105.

Richman, Barry M. "Ideology and Management: Communism and
Compromise." Columbia Journal of World Business 6
(May-June 1971): 45-58.

Richman, Barry M. "Ideology and Management: The Soviet
Evolution." Columbia Journal of World Business 6
(March-April 1971): 62-72.

Robock, Stefan H. "Political Risk: Identification and
Assessment." Columbia Journal of World Business 6
(July-August 1971): 6-20.

Rosecrance, Richard. "Detente or Entente?" Foreign Affairs
53 (April 1975): 464-481.

Rosefielde, Steven. "Factor Proportions and Economic
Rationality in Soviet International Trade 1955-1968."
American Economic Review 64 (September 1974):
670-681.

Rosenfield, Stephen S. "Pluralism and Policy." Foreign
Affairs 52 (January 1974): 263-272.

Rubinstein, Alvin Z. "Soviet-American Relations." Current
History 71 (October 1976): 101-104, 136-137.

Russett, Bruce M., and Hanson, Elizabeth C. Interest and Ideology: The Foreign Policy Beliefs of American Businessmen. San Francisco: W. H. Freeman, 1975.

Seider, Maynard S. "American Big Business Ideology: A Content Analysis of Executive Speeches." American Sociological Review 39 (December 1974): 802-815.

Shulman, Marshall D. "On Learning to Live with Authoritarian Regimes." Foreign Affairs 55 (January 1977): 326-338.

Shulman, Marshall D. "Toward a Western Philosophy of Coexistence." Foreign Affairs 51 (October 1973): 221-236.

Sonnenfeldt, Helmut. "Russia, America and Detente." Foreign Affairs 56 (January 1978): 275-294.

Sorensen, Theodore C. "Most-Favored-Nation and Less Favorite Nations." Foreign Affairs 52 (January 1974): 273-286.

Stern, Paula. Water's Edge: Domestic Politics and the Making of American Foreign Policy. Westport, Conn.: Greenwood Press, 1979.

Sutton, Francis X.; Harris, Seymour E.; Kaysen, Carl; and Tobin, James. The American Business Creed. Cambridge, Mass.: Harvard University Press, 1956.

Ulam, Adam B. "Detente Under Soviet Eyes." Foreign Policy, Fall 1976, pp. 145-159.

U.S. Congress. General Accounting Office. A Progress Report on United States-Soviet Union Cooperative Programs. GAO Report No. ID-75-18, January 1975.

U.S. Congress. Library of Congress. Congressional Research Service. Discussion Materials for "Issues in East-West Commercial Relations," workshop held at the Whittall Pavilion, Library of Congress, April 5, 1978. (Mimeographed.)

U.S. Congress. Library of Congress. Congressional Research Service. "Soviet Commercial Relations and Political Change," by John P. Hardt. Washington, D.C. 1974. (Mimeographed.)

U.S. Congress. Senate. Committee on Commerce. American Role in East-West Trade. S. Doc. 78-600, 95th Cong., 1st sess., 1977.

U.S. Congress. Senate. Committee on Commerce. American Role in East-West Trade: Prospects, Problems, and Issues, 1976-80. Hearings before the Committee on Commerce, 94th Cong., 1st and 2d sess., 1975 and 1976.

U.S. Department of Commerce. Bureau of East-West Trade. Office of East-West Policy and Planning. Advisory Committee on East-West Trade. "Policy Implications of Expanded U.S.-Soviet Economic Relations." Washington, D.C. 1977. (Mimeographed.)

U.S. Department of Commerce. Bureau of East-West Trade. Office of East-West Policy and Planning. Advisory Committee on East-West Trade. "Summary Minutes and Transcript of Proceedings, September 25, 1974." Washington, D.C. 1974. (Mimeographed.)

U.S. Department of Commerce. Bureau of East-West Trade. Office of East-West Policy and Planning. Advisory Committee on East-West Trade. "Summary Minutes and Transcript of Proceedings, December 10, 1974." Washington, D.C. 1974. (Mimeographed.)

U.S. Department of Commerce. Bureau of East-West Trade. Office of East-West Policy and Planning. Advisory Committee on East-West Trade. "Summary Minutes and Transcript of Proceedings, March 14, 1975." Washington, D.C. 1975. (Mimeographed.)

U.S. Department of Commerce. Bureau of East-West Trade. Office of East-West Policy and Planning. Advisory Committee on East-West Trade. "Summary Minutes and Transcript of Proceedings, June 11, 1975." Washington, D.C. 1975. (Mimeographed.)

U.S. Department of Commerce. Bureau of East-West Trade. Office of East-West Policy and Planning. Advisory Committee on East-West Trade. "Summary Minutes and Transcript of Proceedings, September 24, 1975." Washington, D.C. 1975. (Mimeographed.)

U.S. Department of Commerce. Bureau of East-West Trade.
Office of East-West Policy and Planning. Advisory
Committee on East-West Trade. "Summary Minutes and
Transcript of Proceedings, December 10, 1975."
Washington, D.C. 1975. (Mimeographed.)

U.S. Department of Commerce. Bureau of East-West Trade.
Office of East-West Policy and Planning. Advisory
Committee on East-West Trade. "Summary Minutes and
Transcript of Proceedings, March 10, 1976."
Washington, D.C. 1976. (Mimeographed.)

U.S. Department of Commerce. Bureau of East-West Trade.
Office of East-West Policy and Planning. Advisory
Committee on East-West Trade. "Summary Minutes and
Transcript of Proceedings, May 26, 1976."
Washington, D.C. 1976. (Mimeographed.)

U.S. Department of Commerce. Bureau of East-West Trade.
Office of East-West Policy and Planning. Advisory
Committee on East-West Trade. "Summary Minutes and
Transcript of Proceedings, September 16, 1976."
Washington, D.C. 1976. (Mimeographed.)

U.S. Department of Commerce. Bureau of East-West Trade.
Office of East-West Policy and Planning. Advisory
Committee on East-West Trade. "Summary Minutes and
Transcript of Proceedings, December 8, 1976."
Washington, D.C. 1976. (Mimeographed.)

U.S. Department of Commerce. Bureau of East-West Trade.
Office of East-West Policy and Planning. Advisory
Committee on East-West Trade. "Summary Minutes and
Transcript of Proceedings, March 30, 1977."
Washington, D.C. 1977. (Mimeographed.)

U.S. Department of Commerce. Bureau of East-West Trade.
Office of East-West Policy and Planning. Advisory
Committee on East-West Trade. "Summary Minutes and
Transcript of Proceedings, June 29, 1977."
Washington, D.C. 1977. (Mimeographed.)

U.S. Department of Commerce. Bureau of East-West Trade.
Office of East-West Policy and Planning. Advisory
Committee on East-West Trade. "Summary Minutes and
Transcript of Proceedings, December 14, 1977."
Washington, D.C. 1977. (Mimeographed.)

U.S. Department of Commerce. Bureau of East-West Trade.
     Office of East-West Policy and Planning. Advisory
     Committee on East-West Trade. "Summary Minutes and
     Transcript of Proceedings, March 29, 1978."
     Washington, D.C. 1978. (Mimeographed.)

U.S. Department of Commerce. Bureau of East-West Trade.
     Office of East-West Policy and Planning. Advisory
     Committee on East-West Trade. "Summary Minutes and
     Transcript of Proceedings, June 6, 1978."
     Washington, D.C. 1978. (Mimeographed.)

U.S. Department of Commerce. Bureau of East-West Trade.
     Office of East-West Policy and Planning. Antitrust
     in East-West Trade. An Excerpt from the March 10,
     1976 Meeting of the Advisory Committee on East-West
     Trade. Washington, D.C. 1976.

U.S. Department of Commerce. Bureau of East-West Trade.
     Office of East-West Policy and Planning. "East-West
     Trade Credit Policy: A Comparative Analysis," by
     Thomas A. Wolf. Washington, D.C. 1978.
     (Mimeographed.)

U.S. Department of Commerce. Bureau of East-West Trade.
     Office of East-West Policy and Planning. "East-West
     Trade in 1987: Toward a U.S. Strategy."
     Washington, D.C. 1977. (Mimeographed.)

U.S. Department of Commerce. Bureau of East-West Trade.
     Office of East-West Policy and Planning. "LNG Gas
     Projects--Neglected Keystone of a U.S.-Soviet
     Economic Interdependence," by Allen J. Lenz and
     Paige Bryan. Washington, D.C. 1978. (Mimeographed.)

U.S. Department of Commerce. Bureau of East-West Trade.
     Office of East-West Policy and Planning. "Major
     East-West Trade Issues." Washington, D.C. 1978.
     (Mimeographed.)

U.S. Department of Commerce. Bureau of East-West Trade.
     Office of East-West Policy and Planning. "Public
     Opinion and Special Interest Group Influences on
     East-West Trade Policy," by Allen J. Lenz.
     Washington, D.C. 1978. (Mimeographed.)

U.S. Department of Commerce. Bureau of East-West Trade.
Office of East-West Policy and Planning. "Report on
East-West Technology Transfer Research and Policy
Developments, First Quarter 1978." Washington, D.C.
1978. (Mimeographed.)

U.S. Department of Commerce. Bureau of East-West Trade.
Office of East-West Policy and Planning. "Update of
Legislative Activity," by Laurence Lasoff.
Washington, D.C., March 1977. (Mimeographed.)

U.S. Department of Commerce. Bureau of East-West Trade.
Office of East-West Policy and Planning. "Update of
Legislative Activity," by Margaret E. Kalvar and
Laurence Lasoff. Washington, D.C., June 1977.
(Mimeographed.)

U.S. Department of Commerce. Bureau of East-West Trade.
Office of East-West Policy and Planning. "U.S.
Policies in the Sale of Technology to the USSR," by
Raymond Vernon and Marshall I. Goldman. Washington,
D.C. 1974. (Mimeographed.)

U.S. Department of Commerce. Bureau of East-West Trade.
Office of East-West Policy and Planning. U.S.-
U.S.S.R. Trade and the Whipsaw Controversy. An
Excerpt from the March 30, 1977 Meeting of the
Advisory Committee on East-West Trade, William F.
Kolarik, Jr., ed. Washington, D.C. 1977.

U.S. Department of Commerce. National Technical Information
Service. Proceedings of the East-West Technological
Trade Symposium. November 19, 1975, Betsy Ancker
Johnson and William C. Holt, eds. NTIS Report No.
CTAB-76-2 (1976).

U.S. Department of Defense. National Defense University.
Proceedings of the National Security Affairs
Conference, July 12-14, 1976. Washington, D.C.:
National Defense University, 1976.

U.S. Department of Defense. Office of the Director of
Defense Research and Engineering. An Analysis of
Export Control of U.S. Technology--A DOD
Perspective. A Report of the Defense Science Board
Task Force on Export of U.S. Technology.
Washington, D.C. 1976.

U.S. Department of State. Bureau of Intelligence and
     Research. Office of External Research. Report on
     the Potential for Technology Transfer from the
     Soviet Union to the United States, by John W. Kiser,
     III. Contract 1722-620217, July 1977.

U.S. Department of State. Bureau of Intelligence and
     Research. Office of External Research. "The
     Distribution of Gains from Trade between the U.S.
     and the Soviet Union," by Thomas A. Wolf.
     Washington, D.C. 1977. (Mimeographed.)

U.S. Military Academy. Department of Social Sciences.
     "Integrating National Security and Trade Policy: The
     United States and the Soviet Union." Discussion
     agenda and readings for the 1978 Senior Conference,
     June 15-17. West Point, N.Y. 1978. (Mimeographed.)

Vernon, Raymond. "Apparatchiks and Entrepreneurs: U.S.-
     Soviet Economic Relations." Foreign Affairs 52
     (January 1974): 249-262.

Weeks, Albert L. The Troubled Detente. New York: New
     York University Press, 1977.

Wilczynski, Josef. The Economics and Politics of East-West
     Trade. New York: Praeger, 1969.

Yanov, Aleksandr. Detente after Brezhnev: The Domestic
     Roots of Soviet Foreign Policy. Berkeley:
     Institute of International Studies, University of
     California, 1977.

Yergin, Daniel. "Politics and Soviet-American Trade: The
     Three Questions." Foreign Affairs 55 (April 1977):
     517-538.

Yergin, Daniel H. "Strategies of Linkage in Soviet-American
     Relations." Paper presented at the Annual Meeting
     of the American Political Science Association.
     Chicago, September 1976. (Mimeographed.)

Zurawicki, Leon. "The Cooperation of the Socialist State
     with the MNCs." Columbia Journal of World Business
     10 (Spring 1975): 109-115.

III. Organizing Frameworks/Approaches

Alderson, Wroe. Marketing Behavior and Executive Action: A
     Functionalist Approach to Marketing Theory.
     Homewood, Ill.: Richard D. Irwin, Inc., 1957.

Anderson, Charles W. "Political Design and the
     Representation of Interests." Comparative Political
     Studies 10 (April 1977): 127-152.

Bakke, E. Wight. The Fusion Process. New Haven: Yale
     University, Labor and Management Center, 1953.

Barnard, Chester I. The Functions of the Executive.
     Cambridge, Mass.: Harvard University Press, 1962.

Bay, Christian. "Politics and Pseudopolitics: A Critical
     Evaluation of Some Behavioral Literature." American
     Political Science Review 59 (March 1965): 39-51.

Benjamin, Roger W. "Strategy Versus Methodology in
     Comparative Research." Comparative Political
     Studies 9 (January 1977): 475-484.

Cochran, Clarke E. "The Politics of Interest: Philosophy
     and the Limitations of the Science of Politics."
     American Journal of Political Science 17 (November
     1973): 745-766.

Crockett, Norman L., ed. The Power Elite in America.
     Lexington, Mass.: D.C. Heath & Co., 1970.

Cropsey, Joseph. "On the Relation of Political Science and
     Economics." American Political Science Review 54
     (March 1960): 3-14.

Cyert, Richard M., and March, James G. A Behavioral Theory
     of the Firm. Englewood Cliffs, N.J.: Prentice-
     Hall, 1963.

Domhoff, G. William. Who Rules America? Englewood Cliffs,
     N. J.: Prentice-Hall, 1967.

Dougherty, James E., and Pfaltzgraff, Robert L., Jr., eds.
     Contending Theories of International Relations.
     Philadelphia, Pa.: Lippincott, 1971.

Easton, David. "An Approach to the Analysis of Political
     Systems." World Politics 9 (April 1957): 383-400.

Epstein, Edwin M. The Corporation in American Politics. Englewood Cliffs, N. J.: Prentice-Hall, 1969.

Glueck, W. F. Business Policy: Strategy Formation and Executive Action. New York: McGraw-Hill, 1976.

Graham, George, Jr., and Carey, George W., eds. The Post-Behavioral Era: Perspectives on Political Science. New York: David McKay Co., 1972.

Gunnell, John G. "Deduction, Explanation, and Social Scientific Inquiry." American Political Science Review 63 (December 1969): 1233-1246.

Haner, F. T. "Balancing International Risk and Profit." Planning Review 6 (March 1978): 9-12.

Hirschman, Albert O. "The Search for Paradigms as a Hindrance to Understanding." World Politics 22 (January 1970): 329-343.

Holsti, Ole R. "The Belief System and National Images: A Case Study." Journal of Conflict Resolution 6 (September 1962): 244-252.

Holt, Robert T., and Turner, John E., eds. The Methodology of Comparative Research. New York: Free Press, 1970.

Hoole, Francis W., and Zinnes, Dina A. Quantitative International Politics: An Appraisal. New York: Praeger, 1976.

Horowitz, David, ed. Corporations and the Cold War. New York: Monthly Review Press, 1969.

Jacoby, Neil H. "The Multinational Corporation." Center 3 (May-June 1970): 37-55.

Kegley, Charles W., Jr. A General Empirical Typology of Foreign Policy Behavior. Beverly Hills, Cal.: Sage Professional Papers in International Studies 02-014, 1973.

Keohane, Robert O., and Nye, Joseph S., Jr. "International Economics and International Politics: A Framework for Analysis." In World Politics and International Economics, pp. 3-36. Edited by C. Fred Bergsten and Lawrence B. Krause. Washington, D.C.: Brookings Institution, 1975.

Key, V. O., Jr. Public Opinion and American Democracy.
    New York: Alfred A. Knopf Co., 1961.

Likert, Rensis. New Patterns of Management. New York:
    McGraw-Hill, 1961.

Knorr, Klaus, and Rosenau, James N., eds. Contending
    Approaches to International Politics. Princeton,
    N.J.: Princeton University Press, 1969.

Labovitz, Sanford, and Hagedorn, Robert. Introduction
    to Social Research. New York: McGraw-Hill, 1971.

Lijphardt, Arend. "The Comparable-Cases Strategy in
    Comparative Research." Comparative Political
    Studies 8 (July 1975): 158-177.

Long, Norton E. "The Corporation, Its Satellites, and the
    Local Community." In The Corporation and American
    Society. Edited by Edward S. Mason. Cambridge,
    Mass.: Harvard University Press, 1960.

McGowan, Patrick J., and Shapiro, Howard B. The
    Comparative Study of Foreign Policy: A Survey of
    Scientific Findings. Beverly Hills, Cal.: Sage
    Publications, 1973.

Mack, Andrew. "Numbers Are Not Enough: A Critique of
    Internal/External Conflict Behaviour Research."
    Comparative Politics 7 (July 1975): 597-618.

Mayer, Lawrence C. Comparative Political Inquiry: A
    Methodological Survey. Homewood, Ill.: Dorsey
    Press, 1972.

Mills, C. Wright. The Power Elite. New York: Oxford
    University Press, 1956.

Morgan, Patrick M. Theories and Approaches to International
    Politics: What Are We to Think? San Ramon, Ca.:
    Consensus Publishers, 1972.

Mullins, Nicholas C. "Theory Construction from Available
    Materials: A System for Organizing and Presenting
    Propositions." American Journal of Sociology 80
    (July 1974): 1-15.

Padelford, Norman J.; Lincoln, George A.; and Olvey, Lee D.
    The Dynamics of International Politics. New York:
    Macmillan, 1976.

Parry, Geraint. *Political Elites*. New York: Praeger, 1969.

Pfaltzgraff, Robert L., Jr., ed. *Politics and the International System*. 2nd edition. New York: J. B. Lippincott Co., 1972.

Phillips, Warren W. "Where Have All the Theories Gone?" *World Politics* 26 (January 1974): 155-188.

Presthus, Robert. *Elites in the Policy Process*. New York: Cambridge University Press, 1974.

Putnam, Robert D. "The Political Attitudes of Senior Civil Servants in Western Europe." *Revista Italiana di Scienza Politica* 3 (April 1973): 145-186.

Przeworski, Adam, and Teune, Henry. *The Logic of Comparative Social Inquiry*. New York: John Wiley & Sons, 1970.

Rogers, Kenn. *Managers--Personality and Performance*. London: Associated Book Publishers, 1967.

Rosenau, James N. *National Leadership and Foreign Policy: A Case Study in the Mobilization of Public Support*. Princeton: Princeton University Press, 1963.

Rosenau, James N. *The Scientific Study of Foreign Policy*. New York: Free Press, 1971.

Rosenau, James N., ed. *Linkage Politics*. New York: Free Press, 1969.

Russett, Bruce M. "The Young Science of International Politics." *World Politics* 22 (October 1969): 87-94.

Rustow, Dankwart A. "The Study of Elites: Who's Who, When and How." *World Politics* 18 (July 1966): 690-717.

Salamon, Lester M., and Siegfried, John J. "Economic Power and Political Influence: The Impact of Industry Structure on Public Policy." *American Political Science Review* 71 (September 1977): 1026-1043.

Seligman, Lester G. "Political Elites Reconsidered: Process, Consequences and Values." *Comparative Politics* 6 (January 1974): 299-314.

Simon, Herbert H. *Administrative Behavior*. 2nd edition. New York: Macmillan, 1957.

Teune, Henry. "Comparative Research, Experimental Design, and the Comparative Method." Comparative Political Studies 8 (July 1975): 195-199.

Trice, Robert H. "Foreign Policy Interest Groups, Mass Public Opinion, and the Arab-Israeli Dispute." Western Political Quarterly 31 (June 1978): 239-252.

Vital, David. "On Approaches to the Study of International Relations: Or, Back to Machiavelli." World Politics 19 (July 1967): 551-562.

Walker, Jack L. "A Critique of the Elitist Theory of Democracy." American Political Science Review 60 (June 1966): 285-295.

Warwick, Donald P., and Osherson, Samuel, eds. Comparative Research Methods. Englewood Cliffs, N.J.: Prentice-Hall, 1973.

Whiting, Allen S. "The Scholar and the Policymaker." World Politics 24 (Spring 1972): 229-247.

Wilkenfeld, Jonathan, ed. Conflict Behavior and Linkage Politics. New York: David McKay Co., 1973.

Young, Oran R. "The Perils of Odysseus: On Constructing Theories of International Relations." World Politics 24 (Spring 1972): 179-203.

IV. Research Methodology/Techniques

Acock, Alan C., and De Flear, Melvin L. "A Configurational Approach to Contingent Constituency in the Attitude Behavior Relationship." American Sociological Review 37 (December 1972): 714-726.

Alker, Hayward R., Jr. "The Long Road to International Relations Theory: Problems of Statistical Nonadditivity." World Politics 18 (July 1966): 623-655.

Anderson, Charles W. "Comparative Policy Analysis: The Design of Measures." Comparative Politics 4 (October 1971): 117-131.

Andriole, Stephen J.; Wilkenfeld, Jonathan; and Hopple, Gerald W. "A Framework for the Comparative Analysis of Foreign Policy Behavior." International Studies Quarterly 19 (June 1975): 160-198.

Atkin, Charles K., and Chaffee, Steven H. "Instrumental Response Strategies in Opinion Interviews." Public Opinion Quarterly 36 (Spring 1972): 69-79.

Bachrack, Stanley D., and Scable, Harry M. "Mail Questionnaire Efficiency: Controlled Reduction of Nonresponse." Public Opinion Quarterly 31 (Summer 1967): 265-270.

Barrett, James P., and Goldsmith, Leland. "When is 'n' Sufficiently Large?" The American Statistician 30 (May 1976): 67-70.

Bartlett, M. S. "A Further Note on Tests of Significance in Factor Analysis." British Journal of Psychology Statistical Section 4 (March 1951): 1-2.

Bartlett, M. S. "Tests of Significance in Factor Analysis." British Journal of Psychology Statistical Section 3 (June 1950): 77-85.

Bauer, R. K., and Meissner, Frank. "Structures of Mail Questionnaires: Test of Alternatives." Public Opinion Quarterly 27 (Summer 1963): 307-311.

Blalock, H. M., Jr., ed. Measurement in the Social Sciences: Theories and Strategies. Chicago: Aldine, 1974.

Blumberg, Herbert H.; Fuller, Carolyn; and Hare, A. Paul.
    "Response Rates in Postal Surveys." Public Opinion
    Quarterly 38 (Spring 1974): 113-123.

Boek, Walter E., and Lade, James H.  "A Test of the
    Usefulness of the Post-Card Technique in a Mail
    Questionnaire Study." Public Opinion Quarterly 27
    (Summer 1963): 303-306.

Bohmstedt, George W.  "A Quick Method for Determining the
    Reliability and Validity of Multiple-Item Scales."
    American Sociological Review 34 (August 1969):
    542-548.

Brannon, Robert.; Cyphers, Gary; Hesse, Sharlene; Hesselbart,
    Susan; Keane, Robert; Schuman, Howard; Viccaro,
    Thomas; and Wright, Diana.  "Attitude and Action:  A
    Field Experiment Joined to a General Population
    Survey." American Sociological Review 38 (October
    1973): 625-636.

Bridge, R. Gary; Reeder, Leo G.; Kanouse, David; Kinder,
    Donald R.; Nagy, Vivian Tong; and Judd, Charles M.
    "Interviewing Changes Attitudes--Sometimes." Public
    Opinion Quarterly 41 (Spring 1977): 56-64.

Broedling, Laurie A.  "On More Reliably Employing the Concept
    of 'Reliability.'" Public Opinion Quarterly 38
    (Fall 1974): 372-378.

Brown, Morton L.  "Use of Postcard Query in Mail Surveys."
    Public Opinion Quarterly 29 (Summer 1965): 635-637.

Brown, Steven R.  "Perspective, Transfiguration, and
    Equivalence in Communication Theory:  Review and
    Commentary." In Communication Yearbook 3, pp.
    51-64. Edited by Dan Nimmo. New Brunswick, N. J.:
    Transaction Books, 1979.

Carpenter, Edwin H.  "Personalizing Mail Surveys:  A
    Replication and Reassessment." Public Opinion
    Quarterly 38 (Winter 1974-1975):  614-620.

Cattell, Raymond B.  "Extracting the Correct Number of
    Factors in Factor Analysis." Educational and
    Psychological Measurement 18 (Winter 1958):  791-838.

Cattell, Raymond B. "Higher Order Factor Structures and Reticular-vs.-Hierarchical Formulae for Their Interpretation." In Studies in Psychology, pp. 223-265. Edited by Charlotte Banks and P. L. Broadhurst. New York: Barnes and Noble, 1966.

Costner, Herbert L. "Theory, Deduction, and Rules of Correspondence." American Journal of Sociology 75 (September 1969): 245-263.

Crespi, Irving. "Attitude Measurement, Theory, and Prediction." Public Opinion Quarterly 41 (Fall 1977): 285-294.

Crespi, Irving. "What Kinds of Attitude Measures Are Predictive of Behavior?" Public Opinion Quarterly 35 (Fall 1971): 327-334.

Daily, John H. "Underlying Patterns of Legislative Voting Behavior: The Case of the 105th Ohio House of Representatives." Master's thesis, Kent State University, 1968.

Dillman, Don A.; Carpenter, Edwin H.; Christenson, James A.; and Brooks, Ralph M. "Increasing Mail Questionnaire Response: A Four State Comparison." American Sociological Review 39 (October 1974): 744-756.

Ferber, Robert. "Item Nonresponse in a Consumer Survey." Public Opinion Quarterly 30 (Fall 1966): 399-415.

Filion, F. L. "Estimating Bias Due to Nonresponse in Mail Surveys." Public Opinion Quarterly 39 (Winter 1975-1976): 482-492.

Forbes, Hugh Donald, and Tufts, Edward R. "A Note of Caution in Causal Modelling." American Political Science Review 62 (December 1968): 1258-1264.

Francis, Joe D., and Busch, Lawrence. "What We Know About 'I Don't Knows.'" Public Opinion Quarterly 39 (Summer 1975): 207-218.

Fruchter, Benjamin, and Jennings, Earl. "Factor Analysis." In Computer Applications in the Behavioral Sciences, pp. 243-249. Edited by Harold Borko. Englewood Cliffs, N. J.: Prentice-Hall, 1966.

Fruchter, Benjamin. Introduction to Factor Analysis. Princeton, N. J.: Van Nostrand, 1954.

Fuller, Carol H. "Weighting to Adjust for Survey Nonresponse." Public Opinion Quarterly 38 (Summer 1974): 239-246.

Goodman, Leo A. "A General Model for the Analysis of Surveys." American Journal of Sociology 77 (May 1972): 1035-1086.

Goudy, Willis J. "Nonresponse Effects on Relationships Between Variables." Public Opinion Quarterly 40 (Fall 1976): 260-369.

Graham, George J., Jr. Methodological Foundations for Political Analysis. Waltham, Mass.: Xerox College Publishing, 1971.

Gross, Steven J., and Niman, C. Michael. "Attitude-Behavior Consistency: A Review." Public Opinion Quarterly 39 (Fall 1975): 358-368.

Gullahorn, Jeanne E. and John T. "An Investigation of the Effects of Three Factors on Response to Mail Questionnaires." Public Opinion Quarterly 27 (Summer 1963): 294-296.

Guttman, Louis. "Some Necessary Conditions for Common Factor Analysis." Psychometrika 19 (June 1954): 154-155.

Hammond, John L. "Two Sources of Error in Ecological Correlations." American Sociological Review 38 (December 1973): 764-777.

Harman, Harry J. Modern Factor Analysis. Chicago: University of Chicago Press, 1967.

Henrysson, Sten. "The Significance of Factor Loadings: Lawley's Test Examined by Artificial Samples." British Journal of Psychology Statistical Section 3 (November 1950): 159-165.

Hudson, Michael L. "Data Problems in Quantitative Comparative Analysis." Comparative Politics 5 (July 1973): 611-629.

Hull, C. Hadlai, and Nie, Norman H., eds. SPSS Update: New Procedures and Facilities for Releases 7 and 8. New York: McGraw-Hill, 1979.

Humphreys, Lloyd G., and Ilgen, Daniel R. "Note on a Criterion for the Number of Common Factors." Educational and Psychological Measurement 29 (Autumn 1969): 571-578.

Humphreys, Lloyd G. "Number of Cases and Number of Factors: An Example Where N is Very Large." Educational and Psychological Measurement 24 (Fall 1964): 457-466.

Janda, Kenneth. Data Processing: Applications to Political Research. 2nd edition. Evanston, Ill.: Northwestern University Press, 1969.

Kaiser, Henry F. "Image Analysis." In Problems in Measuring Change, pp. 156-166. Edited by C. W. Harris. Madison: University of Wisconsin Press, 1963.

Kaiser, Henry F. "The Application of Computers to Factor Analysis." Educational and Psychological Measurement 20 (Spring 1960): 141-151.

Kalleberg, Arthur L. "The Logic of Comparison: A Methodological Note on the Comparative Study of Political Systems." World Politics 19 (October 1966): 69-82.

Kerlinger, Frederick N. Foundations of Behavioral Research. New York: Holt, Rinehart, and Winston, 1964.

Kim, Jae-On. "Multivariate Analysis of Ordinal Variables." American Journal of Sociology 81 (September 1975): 261-297.

Klemmack, David L.; Legette, Thomas A.; and Mayer, Lawrence S. "Non-Random Exogenous Variables in Path Analysis." American Sociological Review 38 (December 1973): 778-784.

Lehnen, Robert G. "Assessing Reliability in Sample Surveys." Public Opinion Quarterly 35 (Winter 1971-1972): 578-592.

Lieberson, Stanley. "Measuring Population Diversity." American Sociological Review 34 (December 1969): 850-862.

Linsky, Arnold S. "Stimulating Responses to Mailed
    Questionnaires: A Review." Public Opinion
    Quarterly 39 (Spring 1975): 82-101.

Liska, Allen E. "Emergent Issues in the Attitude Behavior
    Consistency Controversy." American Sociological
    Review 39 (April 1974): 261-272.

Luttbeg, Norman R., and Zeigler, Harmon. "Attitude Consensus
    and Conflict in an Interest Group: An Assessment of
    Cohesion." American Political Science Review 60
    (September 1966): 655-666.

McClosky, Herbert. Political Inquiry: The Nature and Uses
    of Survey Research. New York: Macmillan, 1969.

McDonagh, Edward C., and Rosenblum, A. Leon. "A Comparison
    of Mailed Questionnaires and Subsequent Structured
    Interviews." Public Opinion Quarterly 29 (Spring
    1965): 131-136.

Mandell, Lewis. "When to Weight: Determining Nonresponse
    Bias in Survey Data." Public Opinion Quarterly 38
    (Summer 1974): 247-252.

Mayer, Charles S., and Pratt, Robert W., Jr. "A Note on
    Nonresponse in a Mail Survey." Public Opinion
    Quarterly 30 (Winter 1966): 637-646.

Nichols, Robert C., and Meyer, Mary Alice. "Timing Postcard
    Follow-Ups in Mail-Questionnaire Surveys." Public
    Opinion Quarterly 30 (Summer 1966): 306-307.

Nie, Norman H.; Hull, C. Hadlai; Jenkins, Jean G.;
    Steinbrenner, Karin; and Bent, Dale H. SPSS:
    Statistical Package for the Social Sciences. 2nd
    ed. New York: McGraw-Hill, 1975.

Parsons, Robert J., and Medford, Thomas S. "The Effect of
    Advance Notice in Mail Surveys of Homogeneous
    Groups." Public Opinion Quarterly 36 (Summer
    1972): 258-262.

Plog, Stanley C. "Explanations for a High Return Rate on a
    Mail Questionnaire." Public Opinion Quarterly 27
    (Summer 1965): 297-298.

Putnam, Robert D. "Political Attitudes and the Local
    Community." American Political Science Review 60
    (September 1966): 640-654.

Rao, C. Radhakrishna. "Estimation and Tests of Significance in Factor Analysis." Psychometrika 20 (June 1955): 93-111.

Roeher, G. Allan. "Effective Techniques in Increasing Response to Mailed Questionnaires." Public Opinion Quarterly 27 (Summer 1963): 299-302.

Rogers, Theresa F. "Interviews by Telephone and in Person: Quality of Responses and Field Performance." Public Opinion Quarterly 40 (Spring 1976): 51-65.

Rosenau, James N. "Meticulousness as a Factor in the Response to Mail Questionnaires." Public Opinion Quarterly 28 (Summer 1964): 312-314.

Rummel, R. J. Applied Factor Analysis. Evanston, Ill.: Northwestern University Press, 1970.

Rummel, R. J. "Understanding Factor Analysis." Journal of Conflict Resolution 11 (December 1967): 444-479.

Savage, Robert L. "Policy Traditions in the American States." Paper presented at the 1979 meeting of the Southwestern Political Science Association. Fort Worth, Tex., March 28-31, 1979.

Schuman, Howard. "Attitudes vs. Action 'Versus' Attitudes vs. Attitudes." Public Opinion Quarterly 36 (Fall 1972): 347-354.

Shively, W. Phillips. "'Ecological' Inference: The Use of Aggregate Data to Study Individuals." American Political Science Review 63 (December 1969): 1183-1196.

Sieber, Sam D. "The Integration of Fieldwork and Survey Methods." American Journal of Sociology 78 (May 1973): 1335-1359.

Stevens, Robert E. "Does Precoding Mail Questionnaires Affect Response Rates?" Public Opinion Quarterly 38 (Winter 1974-1975): 621-622.

Stinchcombe, Arthur L. "A Heuristic Procedure for Interpreting Factor Analyses." American Sociological Review 36 (December 1971): 1080-1084.

Suchman, Edward A. "An Analysis of 'Bias' in Survey
    Research." Public Opinion Quarterly 26 (Spring
    1962): 102-111.

Thurstone, Louis L. Multiple-Factor Analysis. Chicago:
    University of Chicago Press, 1947.

Tittle, Charles R., and Hill, Richard J. "The Accuracy of
    Self-Reported Data and Prediction of Political
    Activity." Public Opinion Quarterly 31 (Spring
    1967): 103-106.

Tufte, Edward R. "Improving Data Analysis in Political
    Science." World Politics 21 (July 1969): 641-654.

U.S. Department of Defense. Army Air Forces Aviation
    Psychology Program. Printed Classification Tests,
    by J. P. Guilford and J. I. Lacey. Research Report
    No. 5. Washington, D. C.: Government Printing
    Office, 1947.

Warner, Lyle G., and DeFleur, Melvin L. "Attitude as an
    Interactional Concept: Social Constraint and Social
    Distance as Intervening Variables Between Attitudes
    and Action." American Sociological Review 34 (April
    1969): 153-169.

Weinstein, Alan G. "Predicting Behavior from Attitudes."
    Public Opinion Quarterly 36 (Fall 1972): 355-360.

Wiseman, Frederick. "Methodological Bias in Public Opinion
    Surveys." Public Opinion Quarterly 36 (Spring 1972):
    105-108.

For Product Safety Concerns and Information please contact our EU
representative GPSR@taylorandfrancis.com Taylor & Francis Verlag GmbH,
Kaufingerstraße 24, 80331 München, Germany

Printed and bound by CPI Group (UK) Ltd, Croydon, CR0 4YY
08/05/2025
01864480-0001